MW01089726

WITHDRAWN

Textiles

Beverly Gordon

Textiles
The Whole Story

USES · MEANINGS · SIGNIFICANCE

With 380 illustrations, 318 in color

Thames & Hudson

BALDWIN PUBLIC LIBRARY

{page 1} *Detail of a needle lace edging, Europe, c. 1870–90.*

{page 2} *Detail of* Subways of Paris, *furnishing fabric designed by Elsa Schiaparelli, 1936.*

{below} *Parka made of sea-mammal intestine, sewn with sinew and cotton cord, Inupiat or Yup'ik Inuit, Western Arctic, 1919.*

For everyone everywhere who has fallen under the textile spell

Copyright © 2011 Beverly Gordon

Designed by Karolina Prymaka

All Rights Reserved. No part of this publication may be reproduced or transmitted in any form or by any means, electronic or mechanical, including photocopy, recording or any other information storage and retrieval system, without prior permission in writing from the publisher.

First published in 2011 in hardcover in the United States of America by Thames & Hudson Inc., 500 Fifth Avenue, New York, New York 10110

thamesandhudsonusa.com

Library of Congress Catalog Card Number 2011922631

ISBN 978-0-500-51566-2

Printed and bound in China by C&C Offset Printing Co. Ltd

Contents

Preface
Why textiles matter

A decade ago, I came upon a feature entitled "Air Conditioned Clothes" in a widely distributed Sunday newspaper supplement aimed at teenagers. Models wearing crudely cut, frayed garments were shown under a headline stating, "turn stuff you've got into trendy...summer styles." Girls were told to cut out most of a T-shirt to transform it into a "hipster halter," and to "slice and ice" a pair of jeans by removing the waistband and dipping the frayed top into undiluted bleach. Boys were advised to cut off the sleeves and tails of a shirt and the bottom of a pair of pants.[1]

When I asked students in a fashion history class what they could learn about contemporary clothing norms from this feature, they thought about gender roles, silhouettes, seasonal styles, and individuality. What remained invisible to them, however, was how cheap and expendable cloth must be in a society where young people are casually instructed to bleach and cut up their garments and throw away the parts they aren't interested in. Even when I pointed out how they take cloth for granted, most students remained unimpressed. It wasn't until we had studied the high value of fabric in previous eras—the fact that clothing was passed on in wills, for example, or used in political power plays between rival rulers—that the point began to hit home.

Living as we do in a post-industrialized world, fabric has become ubiquitous and inexpensive. Most of us are very distant from its production, and the magic of cloth-making has thus for the most part become invisible; few who have not witnessed the laborious processes and multiple steps that go into making even the simplest cloth realize what treasures they may be wearing or holding in their hands. Furthermore, while textile-making formerly took place both in (often prestigious) workshop or commercial contexts as well as within the home, the visibility of the former decreased considerably after the Industrial Revolution. Textiles became, at least in the Western mind, increasingly seen as something domestic and feminine, and textile-making as a primarily frivolous pastime pursued by women who were confined to the home. It was either identified as women's work, or, especially in the 20th century, as a kind of "non-work;" an old-fashioned activity that we might grow out of or leave behind when we move on to "real" work such as medicine or the law. Another way of understanding this is to say that when we no longer have to make our own textiles because they are manufactured affordably in faraway factories, textile-making takes on something of a hobby status. The varied historical meanings and significance of textiles faded from view, and they were generally left out of the broader historical narrative. By the modern age, they were treated in the West as part of the "background"—the realm of daily, repetitive, and cyclical work that was, at least until quite recently, not taken very seriously. Schoolchildren were not taught about cloth, but about the great deeds of the "foreground"—the battles, political activities, and alliances—that were usually conducted by men. (Ironically, textiles were a part of that foreground arena too, but those stories were underplayed or even forgotten.)[2]

I do not mean to underestimate the importance of textile-making as a hobby. There are millions of people who choose to sew, knit, quilt, and otherwise work with cloth today, and I know they may well be among the most enthusiastic readers of this book. Most of them take up these activities because they are creative pastimes that provide a sense of aesthetic satisfaction and perhaps a link with others in their community. However, even the most avid craftspeople of today typically think of textiles primarily in terms of their expressive function or their potential for income generation. Few know about the roles cloth plays worldwide in myth or symbolic ritual, or the way it has been used to further political and social power. Few think about all the ways in which textiles impact their own daily lives. In sum, most people are unaware of the wide reach of this subject because they have never had the opportunity to think about the topic holistically. They do not realize the rich and textured stories cloth can tell. I am writing this book because I want others to see why this subject really *does* matter. My intention is to shine new light on the taken-for-granted but fascinating subject of the roles and meanings that textiles hold in cultures throughout the world. I hope to make it undeniably evident that to be human is to be involved with cloth.

Paris Bordone, Portrait of a Woman from the Fugger Family, *oil on canvas, c. 1540.*

I come to this topic with far more than intellectual or academic interest. While I explore a wealth of ideas in the book and synthesize information from many disciplines and literatures, my relationship with textiles also extends deeply into emotional, physical, and spiritual realms. I hope to communicate about these dimensions as well. Some of my fondest childhood memories relate to the sensual pleasures of cloth. I spent many hours making clothes for my dolls out of the neckerchiefs that were fairly ubiquitous in the 1950s. These small silk squares came in a wide variety of colors and patterns. They weren't expensive—I think we got them at Woolworth's —but they were wonderful to handle. They felt soft and smooth, and draped beautifully. I enjoyed folding and pleating the silk and tying it around the figures. I wasn't really concerned with style; this was simply cloth play. I also have a poignant memory of the first time I was allowed to go clothes shopping on my own, when I came home with a sensuous red velvet dress. Again I remember the fabric rather than the shape of the garment—I can still see its saturated hue, the way the nap rippled when it was touched, and the way it caught the light. Also imprinted in my memory are visits to the American Museum of Natural History in New York, where I saw African and Native American artifacts made from raffia and other texturally exciting fibers. They made such a strong impression that, even now, I can almost feel the material between my fingers.

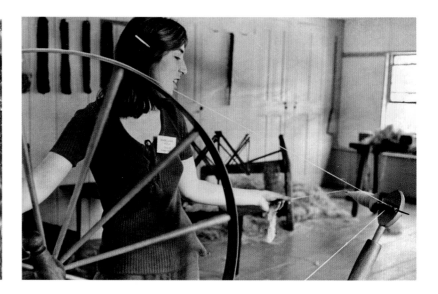

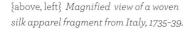

{above, left} *Magnified view of a woven silk apparel fragment from Italy, 1735–39.*

{above, right} *Beverly Gordon spinning at Hancock Shaker Village, Pittsfield, Massachusetts, c. 1974.*

I have strong body memories too from the later years when I began to create textiles—the meditative feeling of moving back and forth at the "great" or "walking" wheel, spinning wool, or the sensation in my back when sitting at the loom, pushing my feet on the pedals and bending over the yarns. My hands remember the smooth patina of the equipment. I can easily call up the smells of wet wool, fresh silk, fermenting indigo, or flowers cooking on the stove to yield a yellow dye, and the physical pleasure of winding a beautifully sequenced warp. That was both a visual and a tactile experience. I loved watching the colors emerge, as well as the sensation of literally bouncing my fingers on the threads as they grew taut. Kinetic memories also come from the intimate encounters I have had with the textiles I have studied over the years: pushing down the resilient fibers of an Oriental pile carpet or the bumpy beads of a heavily dimensioned Iroquois pincushion or Yoruba scabbard, dealing with the sensual overload of a Victorian crazy quilt or a Baroque tapestry. I have been entranced by close-up views of finely worked textiles that bear witness to patient workmanship and skillful play with color.

Emotional and spiritual associations are equally salient. I learned to weave in high school from a Dutch woman I admired deeply who had been active in the Resistance movement during World War II. She was gentle and modest, a quiet heroine who was appreciative and conversant with a world of art and beauty. She opened me up to the joy of thread and pattern and the sheer enchantment of seeing cloth come to life, and I still associate that magic with the goodness she embodied. Years later, when I returned to weaving, I was living in a communal household. I traveled to a local "Y" to take classes, but was saving money for a loom of my own. I set up a box labeled "Loom Fund" in the living room, and my housemates frequently dropped in small donations. I treasured the "investment" they made in me, and when I had finally amassed enough to make that all-important purchase, I felt their support like an invisible hand behind my back. Weaving was intimately associated with a network of generous friends.

Soon after, I was given the opportunity of teaching and demonstrating weaving at historic Shaker sites near Pittsfield, Massachusetts. I loved working with the old equipment. All of it was plain and sturdy, but graceful, and everything was made to fit just perfectly with the body and the hand. I felt the energy of the people who had used those tools in that very space, and learned a great deal from them. It was inevitable in a Shaker setting, where I would frequently repeat Mother Ann's adage, "Put your hands to work and your hearts to God," that Shaker philosophy would become part of my own work. I took on their high standards, hearing the Shakers' admonitions to make sure that everything was done well, or right—if there was an error in the weaving, it had to be taken out and started again. As I learned more about the work they had done, I became more patient, more willing to work precisely and at a leisurely pace, and more able to move into a reverent state. When at one point I set about reproducing a sample of "poplar cloth," a unique Shaker fabric primarily used to cover small sewing boxes, I experienced a particularly deep sense of connection. This cloth was made with thin strips of shaved poplar wood (logs were stripped of bark while frozen, cut into sheets that were hand-shaved and then cut into narrow strips), and I found a stash that had been prepared decades before.[3]

The first step involved softening the strips in water to make them pliable, and I was immediately struck by the pleasant aroma the damp wood exuded. Working with the delicate wefts was completely absorbing, for there was a right and wrong side to each strip, and each had to lay perfectly flat, aligned precisely so no sharp edges would cut into the warp threads. As I gave myself over to the exacting task, I felt connected to the people who had come up with this laborious process and experienced the same kind of

{below} *Iroquois (probably Caughnawaga) "whimsey" (beaded needlecase), Montreal, Canada, c. 1900.*

{bottom} *This rich and exquisitely worked textile is believed to be a late 19th-century coffin cover. Its origins are unknown.*

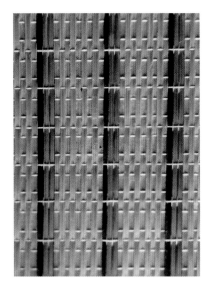

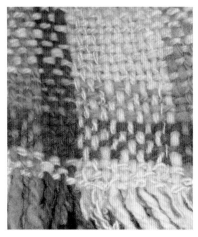

{top} *Detail of Shaker poplar cloth fabric,* c. *1910.*

{above} *Detail of a shawl made by the author from handspun wool dyed with natural dyestuffs, 1970s.*

quiet intensity while engaged with it, connected to the materials, and even connected to the poplar trees that had supplied them. Poplar cloth may be an unusual fabric, but the depth of this kind of cloth-making experience is not. One of the reasons that textiles "matter" is that they may bring those who deal with them into states of absorption and communion.

Many of my experiences with cloth have been journeys of intellectual discovery. For example, I was able to visit some of the last textile mills in New England when they were closing down in the early 1970s. The experience of standing among literally acres of industrial spinning and weaving equipment helped me understand the scope of the early textile industry, and led me further into labor history. Learning about the workings of the machinery also gave me an abiding respect for human ingenuity and invention. At about the same time, I studied spinning and dyeing. Experimenting with natural dye recipes necessitated a review of basic chemistry, and the process of seeking native dye plants brought me deeper into gardening and an understanding of seasonal rhythms and the local ecology. I learned to look more closely at the landscape, scanning for potential sources of color. While I have lived in the Midwest for over thirty years, it is the New England landscape I came to know so closely in that period that is most deeply imprinted on my mind. Learning to spin also contributed to my knowledge of plants, and I became more attuned to wool- and fur-bearing animals, learning to see sheep, goats, and even dogs and rabbits with a new understanding.

The fiber art movement burgeoned in the 1970s, and it was a time when many artists, especially women, were beginning to look with new appreciation and respect at textile traditions from around the world. The first books that attempted to investigate worldwide textile history were published at this time. There was a simultaneous explosion of publications that dealt with topics such as the history of hooked rugs, dyeing in Africa, and cardweaving in Egypt[4]—topics that were formerly arcane or known only to a few intrepid travelers, but were suddenly available to us all. Everything I learned in this heady period led me to something else and opened up new areas of investigation. Working on my book *Feltmaking: Traditions, Techniques and Contemporary Explorations* led me to learn about the cultures of Central Asia and the archaeological finds in the Scythian tombs in the Ural Mountains. It brought me to visit a factory that produced Stetson-type cowboy hats, and to connect with individuals who had studied shepherds' protective garments in Turkey and Hungary. In turn, felt-making led me to the related subject of cloth finishing. I found obscure recordings of women singing at "waulking" bees on the Hebridean islands (see chapter 3); I prowled through fields of fuller's teasel to learn about the plant; I scanned the Bible to find verses about "fuller's earth." (This kind of open-ended investigation is much more common—and simple—with the advent of the worldwide web, but decades ago, such explorations were still unusual and quite exhilarating.) I conducted controlled experiments with acrylic coatings.

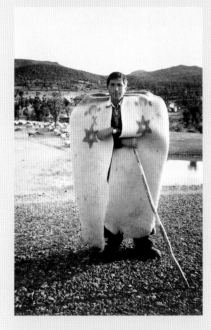

{top} *Ben Shahn's untitled painting depicting a textile mill was made in the 1930s as part of the U.S. Public Works Administration's commissioning of artworks for public buildings.*

{above, left} *A shepherd from western Anatolia wearing a kepenek (an age-old protective felt cloak).*

{above, right} *Felt hats on display in a shop in Istanbul, Turkey, 2009.*

Long after earning a Ph.D. with a specialization in textile history and teaching these topics to generations of university students, I am still awestruck by the most fundamental textile phenomena. The silkworm, for example, will always remain a wonderful mystery. I still love to unravel the fiber end of a cocoon—the fiber the worm has extruded from its body— and contemplate how the creature wrapped it around and around for up to half a mile (nearly a kilometer). I have recently encountered an intriguing silk felt fabric made by the Miao (Hmong) people of China by forcing silkworms to build their cocoons on a flat plane—it produces sheets of matted silk rather than round cocoons[5]—and I love to touch the paper-like fabric. Fascinating as this phenomenon is, I am no less delighted by contemplating the "ordinary" felting process I discovered decades ago, in which loose wool is laid out on a mat and then subjected to moisture and heavy pressure. These few steps can result in a non-woven fabric that is solid and warm enough to cover a house and provide protection in the coldest climate.

Over the course of my career, I have investigated many different kinds of textiles: Native American baskets and beadwork, sentimental 1930s samplers, Victorian fancywork, Guatemalan and Chinese costume, the work of individual fiber artists. I have been privileged to have had inspiring mentors, and to have worked side by side with many of the most talented and dedicated people in the textile field. I have also been able to work closely with several textile collections and develop a range of classes concerned with textile appreciation. My students have taught me a great deal, for they continually ask questions that lead to new avenues of investigation. I bring this accumulated wealth of ideas, information, and inspiration to this volume. If I can communicate even a fraction of my enthusiasm and passion for this subject to others, I will have succeeded in passing on the gifts that were given to me.

A note on terminology and scope is in order here. I use the words "cloth," "textile," and "fabric" more or less interchangeably in this book, both because they do largely function as synonyms in English, and because the different terms allow me to craft less repetitive sentences and livelier prose. I also take an inclusive approach to "textiles," including the fiber (string, thread, cord, etc.) with which cloth is made, as well as finished fabrics. Nor do I limit my discussion to soft, pliable cloth, but include baskets, which are made with the same fibrous linear elements and interlace techniques; they demand similar skills and decisions on the part of their makers, and serve many of the same functions. In short, they can be considered "hard" textiles. I also consider skins as cloth, at least when they are treated as fabric, and are sewn and stitched.

I am not primarily concerned here with dress, or with fashion, although as my own stories of early cloth memories indicate, the topics are never completely separable. Clothes are made from textiles, and many of the important textile traditions are made to be displayed on the body. Thus, I do at times talk about garments, but I do not focus on style, silhouette,

View of completed, unbroken silk cocoons.

or the fashion system. These topics are very well covered elsewhere; there is a vast and growing body of literature on clothing and adornment. I remain focused on the textiles—the cloth—or their component parts.

This book is not the first to address the vital importance of textiles, but I believe it is the first to do so with such a broad scope and holistic approach. Discussion is not limited to one aspect of textiles, to one technique or style, one period in history, or one area of the world. I build on the work of many thoughtful researchers who have come before me. Elizabeth Barber discussed the importance of cloth in the development of civilization in *Women's Work: The First 20,000 Years – Women, Cloth and Society in Early Times* (1994), for example, and anthropologists Annette Weiner and Jane Schneider edited a remarkable volume, *Cloth and Human Experience* (1989), which essentially argued that to study cloth was a way to study society.[6]

These studies were by design more narrowly focused. Barber was not concerned with more recent periods or the full range of textile meanings.

Center detail of a Miao embroidered silk felt hanging, or dance apron, China, probably late 20th century.

Some of the garments worn by the Umatilla girl seen in this 1910 photograph are made from materials that are not always thought of as "textiles," although they are treated that way in this book. Her hat is essentially a corn husk basket, ornamented with wool, and her dress is made of sewn buckskin ornamented with beads. The Umatilla live in northeastern Oregon.

Weiner and Schneider considered cloth in social, political, and economic life, but less so its importance on individual or spiritual levels. More recently, in 2002, Colin Gale and Jasbir Kauer tried to map out the general importance of cloth in *The Textile Book*.[7]

They too are interested in textiles and human life, but they approach the field primarily from the perspective of textile design and the textile industry. Their examples are less global in scope, and are also not concerned with individual stories or spiritual contexts.

Others have focused more specifically on topics such as gender roles (women as cloth-makers), textiles in trade, or the textiles of specific cultures. Exciting work is also being done on the new technological advancements in textiles. My purpose is to bring this rich material together, using the particulars that I and others have written about to construct a comprehensive overview. My discussion not only bridges past and present and extends across the globe, but also integrates the fields of art, science, history, and anthropology. I consider both the exceptional (the magnificent textiles made for pre-Columbian rulers, African kings, or Chinese emperors) and the everyday ("homely" textiles such as gauze bandages, apron ties, and salt bags).

Lest this overview seem too grandiose, I readily admit I could *never* include every aspect of this vast subject. While I've tried to make my points by drawing on diverse examples, I have unquestionably left out a great deal. Readers may think of many other relevant stories or details that they consider important. There may well be even more compelling stories than the ones I have chosen to make any given point—certainly there is no dearth of examples about oppressive conditions in the textile industry, for example, and there are thousands of other artists whose work I might have chosen to include as examples of creative expression. I learn new things about textiles all the time, and were I to write the book at a later date, I would no doubt be struck by new information and provide many different cases in point. If there are readers who feel frustrated that the textiles they are personally passionate about are not included, I can easily empathize. In a sense, however, readers' disappointment might be a sign of success; it would indicate that I have indeed helped people think about even more ways that textiles matter. I hope the discussion will continue to expand in new directions, and I welcome feedback and further ideas.

Experience has shown me that the overarching concepts and organizational strategies I use in this book will stay with readers far longer than the specific details I recount. I have presented this material to diverse audiences for a number of years, and many individuals have told me how much the ideas have affected them. Students have repeatedly confirmed that the frameworks I offer allow them to make sense of a vast body of information. I am pleased to present these same ideas and frameworks to a broader audience, and hope they will provide a similar avenue of understanding and appreciation. Again, my goal is to encourage as many people as I can to see the importance of this topic to our human story. Textiles are part of the fiber of our lives, and they matter deeply.

I would like to share one final story that conveys something of my background and motivations for writing this book. In the mid-1970s, when I was beginning to study textiles in earnest, I was also studying meditation and learning about some of the esoteric traditions of the world. I came upon a concept that caught my imagination completely; though the expression seems trite, it did almost take my breath away. In Hindu philosophy, a textile serves as the primary metaphor about the human condition. Hindus maintain that we are all cloaked in a web of illusion, unable to see the essential wholeness of creation or our fundamental unity with God. Because we live under—or inside—this "veil of Maya," we experience ourselves as separate beings. The veil prevents us from seeing the spiritual planes that lie beyond it. Caught by its materiality, we remain in the incarnate, dense, physical realm, knowing reality only as that which we see, touch, and feel through our senses. Everything we think we "know"—the world of forms and names, the world of individuality—is Maya. Paradoxically, the veil has been created specifically so that we can come to *know* we are in illusion; the very purpose of human life is to break free of the veil to experience unity with the divine. A parallel image was used by the ancient Egyptians. They spoke of the seven stoles of Isis, the great mother who created a "garment of matter."[8]

Captivated by this textile metaphor for the human condition, I dreamed of making a literal veil of Maya as a room-sized art installation. I envisioned people walking into a space filled with a shimmering, gauzy white textile, which would essentially ensnare them. Light would shine through and they could push the threads aside, but it would be all-encompassing. I wanted it to be stunningly beautiful, like the Earth itself; I pictured making it in hundreds of different yarns and threads, some of which were beaded or shot with silver, and using a range of techniques including weaving, crochet, and netting. The veil would be so visually interesting that visitors would get lost in its details; they would literally experience, as a kind of epiphany, the web of illusion in which we are caught. Unfortunately, my vision was stronger than my technical prowess. I couldn't resolve the logistical problems or find the way to make this vision really come to life. I feel, however, that through this book I am in some ways revisiting my long-ago dream. While I am not making a literal textile, I am fashioning a kind of textile "installation," filled with the same kind of complexity and variety. Like the veil of Maya, my book is concerned with the highly engaging practical, earthly plane we all live in, as well as the mythic, transcendent planes we sometimes fleetingly glimpse. I hope this volume will shimmer for my readers, and lead them to discoveries and understandings that will stay with them, deep in their beings.

The very fabric
of existence

Textiles in human consciousness

Take your needle, my child, and work at your pattern; it will come out a rose by and by. Life is like that—one stitch at a time taken patiently and the pattern will come out all right like the embroidery.

Oliver Wendell Holmes, *The Guardian Angel*, 1867

{preceding page} *Crocheted model of hyperbolic space by Daina Taimina, 2006.*

Textiles are a central part of human consciousness. We can all see this, for example, in the constant references to cloth and thread that not only appear in archetypal mythic stories, but serve as metaphors for important core cultural ideas throughout the world. We have long used textile ideas to describe ourselves, our societies, and even our place in the universe. The very qualities of textiles, such as their ability to absorb, enfold and contain, expand, and tie together, make them important symbols; they have strong associations and stand for many of our organizing concepts. They seem to have a "living" presence, in part due to their malleability and the fact that they can, seemingly magically, become larger. Cloth-making (starting with spinning) is seen as a generative activity; it is equated to making life. Cloth is universally also significant in every ritual that is part of the mortal human journey, from birth to death. This chapter focuses on the centrality of textiles in human consciousness and outlines the roles they play in that journey. It also introduces the organizing framework that guides the subsequent chapters, considering textiles in relation to each of our "needs" or realms of activity.

Language and imagery

The English language is full of expressions that indicate how central textiles are in our collective consciousness; we often visualize our reality in textile terms. The expressions and metaphors refer to textile elements (fibers, filaments, cords, strings, or threads), to textile processes, and to finished cloth. Sometimes the metaphors are biological—fiber terms, in particular, are used to express the essential stuff of which we are made. We have long had metaphoric expressions such as "life cord," "life hanging by a thread," "moral fiber," and the "fiber of our being." Since the original thread in many cultures was sinew (animal muscle fiber), this primal correspondence makes perfect sense. Now, our metaphors extend into realms of sophisticated science. We routinely describe DNA—our very genetic codes and the

{below, left} *Amadu Karta inserting the shuttle in his weaving, Bamako, Mali, 1985.*

{below, right} *Laying out warp in a Yao village, China, c. 2000.*

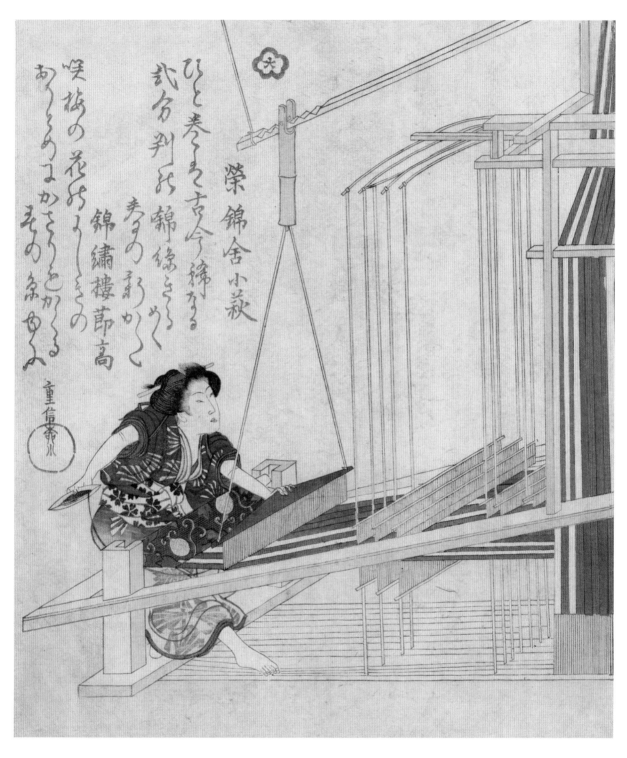

Hataori, *print by Shigenobu Yanagawa,*
Japan, 1825–32.

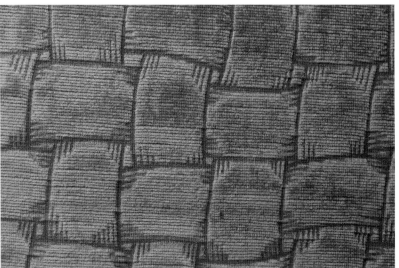

{above, left} *Nineteenth-century engraving of a woman using a hand spindle and distaff.*

{above, right} *Detail of velveteen furnishing fabric which imitates a classic over-and-under (tabby) weave pattern, 1960–80.*

building blocks of life—as strands that twist or ply around one another. Even the birth of the universe is seen as a vibrating filament of energy, as theoretical physicists speak of "string theory," which relates to the smallest known bit of matter coming into existence. (If we could magnify a sub-atomic particle billions of times, it would look like a pulsating loop of violin string.) The structure of space is likened to a textile as well. Physicist Lee Smolin noted, "space may be 'woven' from a network of loops...just like a piece of cloth is 'woven' from a network of threads."

Mathematician Daina Taimina recently devised a literal textile to demonstrate the concept of hyperbolic space. Her crocheted hyperbolic planes can expand infinitely in all directions. The number of stitches can be increased on each row, thus building a structure with no apparent limits or end. Taimina's models, which are on display in the American Mathematical Collection in the Smithsonian Institution, Washington, D.C.,[1] bring to mind other nets with no end: the veil of Maya, discussed in the Preface, and the internet, an infinitely expanding virtual connective web.

The web of illusion is not the only esoteric concept symbolically explained in textile terms. A number of Sanskrit words relate to both textiles and the spiritual path. *Sutra*, for example, can be simply translated as "text or scripture," although it refers specifically to the sacred texts that Hindus or Buddhists memorize about religious precepts. The term comes from sut or "thread," and the concept of stringing together. *Tantra* is variously translated as "weave," "woven together," or "continuity." Its root is *tant*, the word used for a stretched warp; the term can also be understood as "to stretch beyond." Tantrism is a particular Indian yogic tradition that focuses on the resolution of polar opposites, often interpreted as the union of male and female principles. It seeks realization of spiritual truths by means of personal, bodily experience; like the veil of Maya, it is grounded in the earthly plane. *Yantra*, which can be literally translated as "loom," is a two-dimensional symbolic representation of the aspects of divinity, with

an interlocking matrix of figures and patterns, which is used in yogic practice as a meditation tool.[2]

Parul Begum weaving a cane mat in Madhya Chandpur, Feni, Bangladesh, 1995.

Western philosophers also draw on textile imagery. In his 1962 book, *The Joyous Cosmology*, Alan Watts used the image of a woven textile to describe the interplay between the physical plane and the world of consciousness. The warp, according to Watts, is made up of the sensate world, including sound, touch, taste, and smell. The weft that moves in and out of this is the "dimension of meaning," and includes moral and aesthetic values, logic, and personal uniqueness.[3] Most of us are also familiar with a Biblical textile metaphor that reminds us of the impermanent nature of all things human. In Ecclesiastes 3:1–7 we learn "To every thing there is a season, and a time to every purpose under Heaven," including "A time to rend, and a time to sew" (i.e., during the course of our lives, we will both make fabric and tear it apart). One of the very earliest verses in the Bible also implies that to be human is to be involved with cloth. Immediately after they "fell" into a mortal (human) state, according to Genesis 3:7, Adam and Eve started sewing—they joined fig leaves together and made aprons to cover their nakedness.

Some textile expressions imply or allude to the magic of creation: when we draw out a thread or make a solid fabric from mere wisps of fiber, we are seemingly making something out of nothing. We speak of "spinning a yarn" when we draw out words and put them together to tell a tale, and we "put a spin on" ideas or events, shaping them as we would like them to be. People who dabble in magic "weave" spells. Other phrases that reference the idea of interlaced fiber address the idea of human and planetary interconnection. We are "interwoven," and speak of the "web of life," the "social fabric," or the "fabric of human relationships." Our lives are "entwined" or "inextricably bound" with one another. In addition, there are many more prosaic textile metaphors that help us describe daily activities or relationships. "Shuttling back and forth," for example, is a phrase that literally describes the weaving process.

A 19th-century flax hackle.

SOME COLLOQUIAL EXPRESSIONS WITH TEXTILE ORIGINS

Cast a pall over Enshroud in negative or "cloudy" energy. A "pall" is a cloth draped over a coffin (the root is the Latin word *pallium*, or cloak; men in ancient Rome were covered by their *pallia* at their funerals).

Cut from the same cloth Have the same essential characteristics. The expression comes from the time when cloth was cut to order.

Distaff side The woman's (mother's) side of a family. A distaff is an implement that holds fibers during the spinning process. Because spinning was so identified with women, the term came to stand for woman's work or domain, and by extension, the female branch of a family.

Dyed-in-the-wool Thoroughgoing or complete; deeply ingrained; out-and-out. Wool that was dyed before it was spun or woven was most evenly and thoroughly colored.

Fair to middling Usually used to express quality (medium), although the term is also used to express a state of mind. The expression originated in 19th-century cotton mills. "Fair to middling" cotton was good, but not the best.

Get down to brass tacks Be precise or specific. The expression comes from tacks that were used to measure cloth on the counter of a dry goods store.

Get one's hackles up (raise one's hackles) Implies one is on the offensive, with sharp barbs standing upright. The image comes from the hackle (also called heckle, hatchel), a large comb with iron teeth used to straighten and align flax fiber before spinning.

Heirloom An object or property that is passed down to one's heirs. The expression indicates how valuable looms once were, since such equipment was worth bequeathing to the next generation.

Put on sackcloth and ashes Implies one is repentant, enough to put on the roughest fabric as a sign of humility and an admission of responsibility or guilt.

Roll out the red carpet To welcome with great hospitality or ceremony, make someone feel special, or treat them as if they are a celebrity. The phrase comes from a practice known in the ancient Mediterranean world. Red dyestuffs were labor-intensive to produce and large red textiles were thus very expensive. Placing such a textile under someone's feet—literally having a person walk on it when it was so valuable—showed just how important the person was.

Shoddy Poor quality. Originally, shoddy was a manufactured cloth made from unraveled and rewoven old fibers; it did not hold up well.

Sleazy Corrupt, distasteful, cheap. Comes from Silesia cloth, a poor quality linen fabric made in Silesia (now in Poland).

To be bonded To be held or secured. Bond was a Middle English variation on the word "band."

To be on tenterhooks To be in a state of uncomfortable suspense. Tenterhooks were used to stretch and block cloth after it was woven. The related word "tent" refers to a stretched cloth shelter.

To cotton to To be attracted to; comes from the electrically charged cotton dust or lint in the air in weaving mills.

To make the bed To neaten or arrange the bed linens in a pleasing fashion. Originally referred literally to constructing (sewing) the mattress and bed linens.

To needle To (metaphorically) poke at or prick someone, as one pricks a cloth when sewing.

To tie up loose ends To complete all details of a given task. Comes from sailing ships; the ends of the ropes used in a ship's rigging had to be tightly bound so they would not fray.

Whole cloth The phrase is now sometimes used in the U.S. to mean something "completely fabricated," but it originally referred descriptively to uncut fabric and had a more positive connotation. Before the Industrial Revolution, few people had ready access to brand new cloth that had not been joined together from smaller pieces. "Whole cloth" referred to a cloth that was the full size, as manufactured, and it implied prestige and high quality. The later implication may have come from deceptive advertising of 19th-century tailors, whose "whole cloth" was in fact not whole at all but made from different pieces.

The potency of textile metaphors

One of the reasons that there are so many expressions relating to textiles is that textiles are multivalent: they have many different qualities and characteristics, each of which lends itself to metaphor and associations. To help my readers fully appreciate this, I have separated out the five major qualities below and examined them one at a time. These characteristics—the idea of thread as a pathway; how thread and cloth symbolize connection, wholeness, and strength; how textiles symbolize birth and growth; how cloth serves as a wrapper, container, or framer; and the "living" qualities of cloth—also underlie many of the ritual and social situations in which cloth interfaces with human life, and thus reappear in examples and stories throughout the book.

Theseus in the Labyrinth, *a tile design by Edward Burne-Jones, 1862.*

The first and perhaps most obvious arena for metaphor is the idea of thread as a pathway—a line to follow. There are mythological references to such pathways, the most familiar coming from ancient Greece. Ariadne, daughter of the King of Crete, fell in love with Theseus, an Athenian who had been sent to Crete to be ritually sacrificed to the monstrous Minotaur. The Minotaur lived in an underground maze called the Labyrinth, a place from which no human had ever emerged alive. Determined to help her lover escape, Ariadne gave Theseus two tools—a sword and a ball of thread. As he went into the Labyrinth, Theseus tied one end of the thread to the entrance, and let it unwind behind him as he went deeper inside. After he killed the monster with the sword, he was able to find his way out of the maze and the dark cave by physically following the thread. Some theorists claim the Minotaur symbolizes our lower or more unconscious, ignorant, selves. Ariadne's ball of thread stands for the guidance coming from our soul and our higher intuition to overcome the beast of ignorance and selfishness. Symbolically, the thread links all states of being to one another, and ultimately, to the source (we must always follow the thread back to its beginning). In "The Spindle, the Shuttle, and the Needle," a fairy-tale collected by the Brothers Grimm, a prince follows the thread from a magic spindle to find his bride. The thread metaphor is also found in ancient India: the sutra, or thread, according to the *Upanishads* (Hindu scriptures), "links this world to the other world and to all beings."[4]

The threads we follow can also be stories, as the "spinning a yarn" expression implies. Historian Helen Bradley Foster, who wrote about slave clothing in the antebellum American south, used textile metaphors throughout her book. She claimed to be "warping a folk history," that is, threading a loom with the strands that would later be joined together to tell the tale.[5] These days we also follow "threads" in online conversations, as our discussions weave in and out of each other.

The central story we are all involved with, of course, is the story of our human lives. "The threads of time" is an expression that links textile strands and the linear, mortal path. We talk about life "hanging by a thread," which similarly reminds us of our fragility and the preciousness of our time on Earth. (We were literally connected to our mother through a cord, which had

to be cut for us to enter this world and breathe on our own.) The threads of time metaphor extends even further, as textiles are often associated with fate. The very word "cloth" possibly has roots in the name of Clotho, one of the three Moirae, the goddesses in Greek mythology who controlled human life. (Clotho was technically the spinner, who spun the Thread of Life.) Linguists tell us that when we use the English phrase "life span" we are using a word that is a variation on "to spin." Even when someone puts a spin on information, they are controlling fate much like Clotho.[6]

The second set of textile metaphors are those in which thread and cloth symbolize connection, wholeness, and strength. If threads serve as connectors that literally and figuratively tie things or people to one another, then intertwined filaments are particularly potent images, as they are strong and durable. We ply many cords together to make rope or cable, for example, which we can trust to hold our body weight. We weave individual threads into a coherent piece of cloth. Images of entwinement— the idea that we are all threads, entangled together—symbolize the idea that the whole is much more than the sum of its parts. Sometimes the imagery comes from making cloth, as in weaving, and other times it comes from the practice of joining or fitting many separate bits of cloth together, as in pieced quilts or other patchwork.

A new textile, like a new life, is clean and fresh, and unused cloth often functions as a symbol of purity as well as wholeness. Unsoiled fabric represents promise and possibility. In contrast, worn cloth represents the end of wholeness and, like a worn-out life, has little future. Fiber terms are thus also used to describe deterioration or coming apart—things are frayed, ripped, tattered, or shredded. A phrase commonly used at funerals is "a rip in the fabric of human relationship."[7] The ultimate fragility of cloth— it is subject to degenerative processes such as illness and decay—is another reason it is tied to mortality and the passage of time.

Similarly, and perhaps paradoxically, textile metaphor and imagery sometimes connote the absence of wholeness, or a sense of apartness. Thread or linear elements can markedly separate, as when a crime scene is marked off by police tape. When we bind too tightly together, the binding is a kind of entrapment—we may be "caught in a bind," or find ourselves in a "double bind." (Spider webs, made of the lightest of filaments, are the deadliest traps.) We can also be caught in the tight cords of a straightjacket, or in sexual bondage. A different type of being tied down is the religious Jewish man's practice of winding *tefillin* (cords) around his arms during daily prayers. The cords serve as a bodily reminder of the worshipper's covenant with God; he wraps them as a "sign upon his arm" that he must turn his heart to his religious duty. They connect him with God and in that sense make him whole, but also mark him off and bind him in a promise.

The third quality of textiles that makes them potent metaphors is that they may symbolize birth and growth. I have introduced the idea that textiles are symbolically linked to generation, or the creation of life, and this topic is explored in much greater detail below. Here, I simply note that, by

{opposite} Cheerful pieced ralli quilts are made in the northwestern India/Sindh, Pakistan area. They are multipurpose textiles that may be used as covers for sleeping cots, or as carrying cloths, saddle covers, cradles, or canopies.

{below} Detail of a "pinwheel" style log cabin quilt, 1880–1900, North America.

{bottom} Ron Ullmann learning to tie teffilin on his arm, "binding" him in daily prayer, Temple Gates Synagogue, Bayside, Queens, New York, 2008.

Unidentified woman coiling a raffia basket in Sierra Leone, 1973–74.

extension, textiles and textile-making often serve as symbols of expansion and growth. Basketmaker Julia Parker used this metaphor when she noted, "My life is like my basket. We all begin as a little tiny circle, [and over time] we grow into a [complete container]."[8] The circle to which she was referring is the tight roll of fiber that one starts coiling and then building upon; each row is added to the last. All cloth-making involves incremental growth. When you knit or weave, you build up a structure row by row; when you make a quilt, you build it stitch by stitch.

Because textiles can be continuously added to—made larger like Taimina's model of space, or layered or piled on top of one another—they suggest expansive possibilities. Stacks of bedding and other textiles once decorated homes in Eastern Europe and Central Asia, not only because they were functional, but also because they alluded to abundance. In cultures throughout the world, people cover their bodies with many layers or large pieces of fabric in order to feel and appear larger—to take up more literal and psychic space.

The fourth aspect of cloth is its frequent use as a wrapper, container, or framer. All of us know that cloth enfolds and holds—we remember cuddling under blankets on cold nights, or wrapping up in a towel when emerging from a bath. Enfolding cloth can provide reassurance and protection. "Swaddling" clothes and other tight wrappings keep babies calm and comforted, and cushioning fabric is wrapped around fine china when it is being transported from place to place. Wrapping occurs in other contexts too: the ancient Egyptians and Peruvians wrapped mummies to help preserve them for the afterlife; we wrap pipes with insulation to keep them from freezing, and wrap teapots and even eggs in cloth "cozies."

We also wear "wraps" that drape over our shoulders or envelop our bodies and keep us warm. There are enveloping atmospheric conditions or emotions that we liken to enveloping textiles—we may be "clothed in darkness," or "cloaked in fear." Cloth can provide a visual block or barrier;

{opposite, below, left} *Yoruba (of Nigeria) Egungun Society masquerade costumes are worn by members of the society not only to hide the dancer's identity, but also to add to their spiritual presence. They include hundreds of overlapping lappets of rich (often imported) cloth.*

{opposite, below, right} *Stacked woolen textiles in a Peruvian market, 2007.*

{below} *Singer Mary Garden dressed for an operatic role, c. 1909.*

{right} *French street festival, St. Denis, outside Paris, France, 1983.*

{top left} *Women in wrapped garments,*
Timbuktu, Mali, 1995.

{top right} *Dyak baby in a suspended*
cloth cradle, Borneo.

{above} *English patchwork tea cozy,*
late 18th century.

{right} *Family posing playfully behind*
a curtain in Wisconsin, U.S., c. 1900.

it can block off unwanted light, as in a World War II blackout curtain, or a 19th-century photographer hiding his camera under a dark tent of fabric. It can provide privacy, as in a voting booth, and completely envelop or "cover up," what someone may wish to hide, such as a deformity or imperfection, a too-alluring body part, or a particularized identity.

Partially wrapped or draped cloth can be an effective framing device. Stage and window draperies help frame their respective views and make them more dramatic. Dramatic moments may also take place when cloth is pulled aside, revealing the person, object, or unexpected scene that lay behind it.

Cloth containers are flexible and reusable. They can hold almost anything, from babies to food, sand, books, and even entire buildings. They also "contain" power—amuletic objects, in some cases, or relics from powerful people of the past. Saints' relics from medieval Europe—tiny slivers of bone, or more commonly, small objects that the saints had come in contact with—were invariably kept in cloth, both because they were considered too powerful to be touched with the naked hand, and because the textile helped keep their power intact.

Even bits of ribbon or string may "contain" reminders. The image of the string tied around the finger that serves as a mnemonic device is strong enough in public consciousness that it is sometimes used as a graphic icon for memory.

Rembrandt Harmenszoon van Rijn, The Holy Family with a Curtain, *oil on canvas, 1646.*

THE WORLD HANGS BY A THREAD

Cloth is literally our second skin, our first home out of the womb, sculpting
to our bodies, building comfort from a net of crossed threads. Each day we
ask the cloth to comfort us...the cushion of our seat, the softness for the wall,
the flannel for the next child... Cloth is receptive, fills the contours, listens
to the need, finds its strength in flexibility... Cloth belongs to the body.

Debra Frasier, 1985

The fifth property of cloth is that it has
"living" qualities. Cloth absorbs. It takes
in physical substances—bodily fluids such
as saliva, sweat, and blood, and gaseous
substances from the air, such as odor and
smoke. It absorbs sound. Universally, it is
also felt to take in and absorb more invisible
energies. We are all familiar with the idea that someone's clothing comes
to hold their essence; clothes are often spoken of, in fact, as a kind of "second
skin" that seems to hold the living substance of the wearer. Essayist Peter
Stallybrass reflected on the presence he felt in the clothes left behind by
his deceased partner, Allon White. Stallybrass explained that it was as if the
garments were still inhabited. When he put on White's jacket, he felt that
"Allon wore [him]. He was there in the wrinkles of the elbows...he was there
in the stains at the bottom...he was there in the smell." Stallybrass could not

bring himself to throw them out. "The magic of cloth," he mused, "is that it receives us: receives our smells, our sweat, our shape even."[9]

There are many examples of the ways in which textiles seem to take on someone's essence and come to stand for that individual. We all know of situations like the one Stallybrass describes, when letting go of someone's garments seems akin to getting rid of the person. I was at a child's funeral where the body was covered with the boy's beloved quilt; for a while, he was still "alive" in that piece of cloth. I also remember hearing what happened to an anthropologist who bought a beautifully woven garment from a Mayan woman in Guatemala in the 1940s. This was the weaver's own blouse, and it had become an extension of her being. Before she would release it, she conducted a kind of deconsecration ritual to ensure that her energy would not be taken away with the garment. Similarly, even tiny pieces of medieval saints' garments—fibers that had been close to their bodies—were felt to have absorbed the energy of the holy ones, so they became holy in themselves (they often comprised the very relics that were themselves wrapped in protective cloth). In pre-Columbian Peru, Andean warriors believed they could harm or kill an enemy if they could get his clothes and hang them in effigy. The Inka also routinely sacrificed textiles, similarly treating them as symbolic people.[10]

Clothing can also seem to hold the energy of a particular quality or status. We refer to ministers as "men of the cloth," not just because their outfits are distinct, but because those garments seem to contain the energy of their religious office. William Elliott tells the story of Jagir Singh, a Nepalese holy man who encountered a pilgrim when he was wearing street clothes rather than robes. The seeker was so taken aback by the lack of "holy" garments that he decided to return the next day, when Singh would be in appropriate costume. While the story comments on the illusion of appearances, it also alludes to the way the robes themselves embody the energy of the spiritual teacher. Individuals operating in the secular realm

{opposite top left} *Unidentified woman carrying a feed sack on her straw hat, Indonesia.*

{opposite bottom, left} *Detail of a Qing dynasty dragon robe, China, c. 1900, showing the masterful way in which the woven fabric has been shaded with paint.*

{opposite right} *Sand bags holding back the River Ouse, York, England, 2000.*

{below} *Detail of a Turkish towel showing the embroidered end and the central looped pile area, c. 1900. When Pietro della Valle visited Turkey in the 1620s he was impressed by the absorbency of their "truly marvelous" towels. This kind of looped surface structure was not used at that time in Europe, but it was eventually adopted by commercial towel manufacturers.*

{bottom} *Laundry day in Burano, Italy, 2005.*

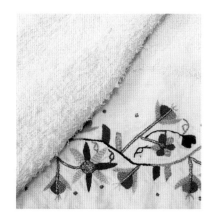

The Start of the Hunt, *part of the* Hunt of the Unicorn *tapestries, 1495–1505.*

also take on new mantles or robes of office, and, when they are "clothed" in new identities, the cloth itself often becomes associated with the transformation.[11]

The personified quality of cloth is acknowledged in different cultures. Some cloth-starching practices, for example, are spoken of in terms of nourishment. In Guatemala, Mayan weavers size or stiffen their warp threads by "feeding" them a maize gruel. In India, women take thickened water that comes from boiling rice and brush it onto their saris in order to give them proper body. They speak about the process as a way of keeping the cloth "alive."[12]

In fact, cloth is not a static material; it does have a living quality. The reality of this became dramatically apparent to individuals involved with the conservation of the magnificent *Hunt of the Unicorn* tapestries in the collection of New York's Metropolitan Museum of Art. Woven in a northern

European guild workshop about 1500 CE, these were made as a set of seven (or possibly more) self-contained but contiguous narrative textiles, each about 12 by 12 feet (3.6 x 3.6 meters). Needless to say, the restoration of these large pieces was a complicated and demanding undertaking. As part of the process, the conservators needed detailed, quality images that would document literally every square inch of the tapestry fabric. They took a great many high resolution digital photographs—enough to fill over 200 compact disks. The idea was that the images would function as "tiles" that could later be pieced together, like a jigsaw puzzle. However, when the conservators tried to compile the photos, the images wouldn't fit together properly. Richard Preston, who described the process in the *New Yorker* in 2005, explained, "It was as if [the] tapestry had not been the same object from one moment to the next as it was being photographed." The textiles had been hanging in a horizontal position for centuries, but when laid flat for cleaning and photography:

> The warp threads relaxed. The tapestries began to breathe, expanding, contracting, shifting. It was as if, when the conservators removed the backing, the tapestries had woken up. The threads twisted and rotated restlessly. Tiny changes in temperature and humidity in the room had caused the tapestry to shrink or expand from hour to hour, from minute to minute. The gold- and silver-wrapped threads changed shape at different speeds and in different ways from the wool and silk threads.[13]

Cloth's living quality is thus related to its flexible, mobile nature. Fabric flutters and waves; it moves in even a slight breeze. Fluttering textiles literally look alive—they constantly change form, position, and direction, and they fill with air and become more expansive. One of the reasons flags can be such potent symbols is that they move with the wind. When a nation is represented by a waving flag, that nation is symbolically alive and active; it is a dynamic presence.

Helen Klebesadel's watercolor, Handmade I, *2005, captures the animated quality of fluttering curtains.*

As will be discussed at length in chapter 6, cloth is also believed to have the potential of taking on "higher" energies and thus assisting in spiritual transformation. The widespread use of prayer flags in the Himalayan region is due to the belief that they carry prayers into the etheric realm. Flying streamers or wide-skirted garments that move with the wind are also widely used in rituals where individuals enter into a different state of consciousness. They literalize the metaphor of moving energy, both symbolizing and helping to induce a trance state.

Fiber's flexibility allows it to take on a range of different forms and shapes (flexibility is even true for seemingly stiff baskets; a basket must be made when the fibers are fresh, damp, and pliable, and at that stage they can be molded into diverse forms). Fiber and cloth can be manipulated in myriad ways: folded, pleated, gathered, twisted, and knotted, fluffed, cut into, pulled taut, or draped loosely. Fabric can be made stiff or soft, transparent or solid, and can take on an almost limitless number of different surface characteristics. All of this applies to the fashioning of a textile, of course, but many of these qualities apply even after a cloth is finished: we can still drape or fold a finished cloth, crush it between our fingers, or move it so that it may catch the light in a different way. Cloth has such strong sensual appeal precisely because of this flexibility and aliveness; cloth seems animate, interactive, and responsive.

If cloth is "alive," it is vulnerable. There is an assumption in many cultures that cloth may be in danger of being taken over by negative energy. In Morocco, for example, it is believed that unfinished weavings must be protected from envy and the evil eye.[14] Even without purposeful interference, cloth is still fragile material, subject to deterioration from the elements, insects, and sharp objects. Fabrics thus are always in need of care and protection. Robyn Maxwell tells us that because the well-being of Indonesian society hung on the quality and quantity of textiles available for ritual purposes, the culture also ritualized cloth preservation. Fabrics were kept

Detail of an Egyptian shawl with Assyut silverwork where small strips of silver are worked around the threads of a net foundation. Shawls like this were very popular with tourists in the 1920s.

{above, left} *Translucent lace curtain in La Pedrera apartment building, designed by architect Antoni Gaudí, Barcelona, Spain, 2007.*

{above, right} *Issey Miyake's "Pleats Please" line fully exploited the interesting effects that can be created with the use of pleats. This 2008 dress, dubbed "Madame T," is essentially a rectangle, with a slit, that can be tied in different ways. It can also function as a blouse.*

{left} *Felted balls and beaded fringe at the bottom of a long hair-tie ornament from northwestern India. The balls are highly textural, and the ties swing with every step.*

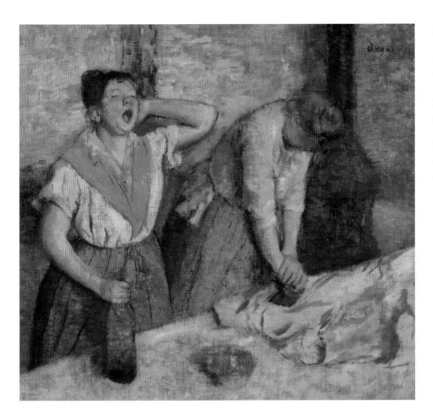

{opposite, above} *Detail of Utagawa Toyokuni's woodcut* Kawa de no sentaku *(Washing Clothes in the River), which was made between 1818 and 1830.*

{opposite, below} *Laundry drying at the washing ghats, Mumbai, India.*

{left} *Edgar Degas*, Les Repasseuses (The Laundresses), *oil on canvas, c. 1884–86 (detail).*

in dark chests made with aromatic woods and coated with insect-repelling substances. People cleansed, blessed, and paraded the cloths through the community on an annual basis, assuring that they were routinely aired and repositioned.[15]

Whatever culture we come from, and even if we take cloth for granted, it, like a being, still makes demands on us. We must clean it regularly, press it, and make sure it has just the right amount of air, light, and moisture. In pre-industrial cultures, cleaning cloth was an onerous and physically demanding task. In her book, *Never Done: A History of American Housework*, Susan Strasser explains that laundry was the single chore that 19th-century housewives hated most:

> Without running water, gas, or electricity, even the most simplified laundry process consumed staggering amounts of time and labor. One wash...used about fifty gallons of water—or four hundred pounds— which had to be moved from pump or well or faucet to stove and tub, in buckets and wash boilers that might weigh as much as forty or fifty pounds. Rubbing, wringing and lifting water-laden clothes and linens... wearied women's arms and wrists and exposed them to caustic substances. They lugged [the laundry outside to dry and later] ironed [it] by heating several irons on the stove and alternating them as they cooled.[16]

There are many places in the world, of course, where laundry is still done without the help of running water, electricity or machines.

Betsy Ross stitching the first American flag, 1908. This print by F. A. Schneider is based on a painting by Gustav Liebscher.

Making cloth, making life

The idea that cloth-making is seen as a generative or life-giving activity shows up in many of the world's creation stories, myths, and fairy-tales. Typically, the immortals (usually goddesses) involved in creating life are portrayed as spinners and weavers. These deities are often also associated with the sun and/or moon or other cosmic elements (and by extension, the weather), and with life-giving fire, agriculture, and healing. The spinning and weaving tools they use may function to create the Earth or heavens, to help hold them up (serving as a kind of *axis mundi*), or to tie them together. The Norse goddess Frigg was understood to be spinning the sky; in Scandinavia, in fact, the constellation many know as "Orion's Belt" is called "Frigg's distaff." Plato had a similar vision of the great goddess Ananke ("Necessity") spinning the universe (the sun, moon, and planets were her spindle whorls). The Navajo (Diné) hold that Spider Woman instructed the women how to weave on a loom that her husband, Spider Man, told them how to make. Its cross poles were made of sky, and its structure was supported with cords of earth. The warp sticks were made of sun rays, the heddles of rock crystal and sheet lightning. The batten, or beater, was made from the halo of the sun.[17]

The ancient Egyptians used similar imagery. The roots of their words for "weaving" and "being" were the same: *nnt*. Not surprisingly, they characterized Isis (who had strong associations with motherhood and fertility and was, at least in later periods, considered a fertility goddess) as a weaver, and portrayed her with a red sash or string around her hips. According to some scholars, women circled their own hips and wore red strings when they danced to praise her. This image has proved resonant with contemporary goddess followers, who feel that the red thread references fertility and symbolically represents the moment when intention becomes physical—the transition point from nothing to something. Poet Normandi Ellis penned a prayer based loosely on a very famous example of the Egyptian *Book of the Dead*, the Papyrus of Ani: "At the ends of the universe is a blood red cord that ties life to death, man to woman, will to destiny. Let [it]...bind in me the ends of life and dream." A related tradition that is still popular today takes place in Bethlehem, at Rachel's tomb. Women seeking to become pregnant or to deliver a baby safely tie red cords around the tomb, and sometimes subsequently wear a bit of the string on their wrists. Rachel, the Old Testament matriarch, is associated with fertility and is sometimes even referred to as "Mother."[18]

In the Middle Ages, the Virgin Mary was often portrayed as a cloth-maker—a spinner, primarily, but occasionally a weaver. In many medieval illustrations, Mary was shown spinning at the very moment when she was approached by the Archangel Gabriel. A distaff or basket of wool appeared by her side. Mary was holding the thread of life, and was sometimes even pictured spinning it out from her body.[19]

Cloth-making magic can seem alchemical, for through it an ordinary and often not highly valued substance can be transformed—"reborn"—into another, "higher" state. This is the source of the central conceit in the Rumpelstiltskin fairy-tale, in which the heroine is asked to spin straw into gold. The primal associations between making thread and/or making life are also implicit in that story, for the dwarf demands her first-born child as his ultimate price for completing the transformation. Many European folk tales posit women as spinners and weavers; in fact, "good" women are usually portrayed as those who are the most skilled and industrious cloth-makers. A good spinner was the embodiment of a good housewife, precisely because she was able to create life (comparatively little attention was paid in these folk tales to other housewifely tasks such as cooking and cleaning). Ironically, spinning was considered so potentially powerful that uncontrolled spinners could be seen as dangerous. In many medieval texts and illustrations, aggressive women who disobeyed their husbands were portrayed as charging forward, with long distaffs functioning as lances or spears. Spinning could also serve as a reminder of original sin.[20]

A different kind of myth about birth and textile creation—a myth relating to the birth of the U.S.—was discussed in the *New York Times* several years ago. According to legend,

{below, right} *Andy Tsihnahjinnie*, Spider Woman and the Twins, *1971.*

A GREAT WEAVING

In his book about the Amazon rain forest, *One River*, Wade Davis describes how the Kogi people understand their place in the cosmos as part of a great weaving.

[As they] pass over the earth, they [weave] a sacred cloak over the Great Mother, each journey like a thread...[Even] a person's thoughts are like threads. The act of spinning is the act of thinking. The cloth they weave and the clothes they wear become their thoughts. [Everything they do is conceived of as a fabric, and] everything begins and ends with the loom.

{left} *The close association between spinning and fertility is an underlying message in this romanticized image of a gypsy woman creating thread on a hand spindle, while her baby rests in her lap. It was taken "by the wayside" near Orsava, Hungary (officially now Orsova, Romania) in 1913 and sold as a stereograph by the Keystone View Company.*

the original American flag was made on July 4, 1776, when a small committee of revolutionaries, including General George Washington, visited seamstress Betsy Ross in her home in Philadelphia to discuss the need for a new flag for the aspiring nation. She immediately complied by designing the banner with the five-pointed star and the red-and-white stripes, and sewing the first prototype. Realizing that this story was completely "fabricated," historian Michael Frisch looked for its deeper meanings. He compared Ross to the Virgin Mary, who, blessed by the father (Washington), gave birth to the iconic cloth. "The flag itself was not quite powerful enough to shape the symbol," Frisch explained. "It was the coming together of the flag with the woman that gives it its unique power."[21]

The Ladakh people of the Himalayas liken their weaving warps to a mother, and the wefts to the child conceived within her womb. As the weaving proceeds, the child grows along with the fabric. By association, Ladakhi spinning and weaving tools also function as metaphors for birth, fertility, and reproduction. The loom beater too is known as the "mother," while other loom parts are the "children."[22] Among the Maya, textiles, like babies, are said to be "birthed." Mayan women weave on a backstrap (hip tension) loom, one end of which is typically tied to a tree or upright post. The cord that attaches the weaving to this "mother" tree is known as the "umbilical cord." When a woman weaves in this position, her work is not only generative, but also reproduces the cycle of life, helping to keep cosmic forces in balance. Similar ideas are prevalent among the Wixárika (Huichol) people of northern Mexico, who also use a backstrap loom. They too see the supportive tree as a kind of *axis mundi*, and the weaver as a physical representation of earthly connection to the cosmos.[23]

Textile equipment sometimes also plays a symbolic part in women's rituals among the native people of the Americas. The Maya used looms to help women with menstrual problems, for example, and among the Navajo, loom battens and other weaving tools have a role in female coming-of-age ceremonies. Even today, when a girl is initiated into womanhood, she is "shaped" as an adult (literally, patted down with the tools) by her elders.[24]

A variety of mythic and folk figures embody this association of cloth with time, mortality, and fate. In addition to Clotho the spinner, the ancient Greek "Fates" included Lachesis, who measured the thread, and Atropos, who cut it off when the allotted lifespan was completed. The Norns were a triad of parallel deities in Norse myth. In Lithuania, there were seven goddesses to share the work (they wove fabric as well). The fairy-tale heroine, Sleeping Beauty, who effectively went to sleep—moved out of mortal time—when she pricked her finger on a sharp spindle, was probably based in turn on an older Germanic tale about Frau Holde. There, too, a spindle served as a link between the earthly and magical realms, and through it young girls were able to contact the goddess. Among the Wixárika, it was the loom that helped individuals escape from their ordinary limitations of time and space.[25]

A Mayan woman weaving on a backstrap loom in Guatemala, 2009.

A THREAD IN THE HANDS OF FATE

As I at my wheel sit spinning
I think of my maiden state,
For I am, at my life's beginning,
A thread in the hands of Fate.

W.S. Gilbert

{above} Penelope at her Loom, *as envisioned
in a 15th-century tapestry. The illustrated
fragment is from* The Story of Penelope, France
or the Franco-Flemish territories, 1480–83.

{right} *Sioux moccasins with red quillwork
ornamentation, 19th century.*

Goddess or mythological figure	Culture(s) of origin	Attributed qualities
Amaterasu (Amateratsu)	Japan (Shinto)	Shinto Sun goddess who "rules" sericulture (cultivation of silkworms), weaving, and agriculture. She weaves garments for the gods.
Anansi (Ananse) (Spider or Spider Man)	West Africa (e.g., Asante people)	Played a role in creation and brought humans wisdom, fire, and even water and food from heaven during a drought. He is a beloved trickster figure. The Asante believe he taught men to weave, and some of his other qualities parallel female spider deities.
Ariadne	Ancient Crete	Fertility goddess (in Greek myth, her divine nature is sometimes underplayed) who is also a weaver.
Athena	Ancient Greece	The goddess of wisdom, war, arts and industry (including weaving), justice and skill. (Jealous that her acolyte, Arachne, was a better weaver, she turned her into a spider.)
Biliku	Adamanese islands, Bay of Bengal	A Spider Woman goddess who made the sun, moon, and Earth and, in some versions, humans. She invented the things that are now made and used by women, such as baskets and nets.
Frigg (In Germany, Freyja is another manifestation of Frigg, concerned with magic)	Norse	Odin's wife, the goddess of love and fertility. She is the patron of marriage and motherhood, and is a spinner. She also knows the fate of men. (In Scandinavia the "Orion's Belt" constellation is named "Frigg's distaff.")
Holda (Holle)	Germany	The goddess of birth and protector of unborn children who has control of the weather. She is the patron of spinners.
Indra	India (Vedic/Hindu, with Buddhist origins)	The great god Indra resides in an infinite net (web) that stretches in all directions. There is a jewel at each junction, which reflects each of the others and the whole. Indra's web thus stands as a metaphor for the interconnectedness and oneness of the universe and everything within it.
Isis	Dynastic Egypt	Goddess known as life-giver, protector, provider, healer, and teacher. She brings light, rules over the Earth and the harvest, and teaches women spinning, weaving, and agricultural skills.
Ixchel (also called Chacel and the "World-Weaver")	Maya people, Mexico and Guatemala	Creator goddess associated with the Earth and moon. She is the patroness of pregnant women and associated with healing. She invented the art of weaving. She is often portrayed with spindles and spindle whorls.
Maya	Hindu	Deity representing the feminine principle. Creator of the veil of illusion—makes the mortal world entrancing.
Moirae (Fates)	Ancient Greece	Three female deities (Clotho, Lachesis, and Atropos) whose spinning and weaving determine the fates of humans.
Nit (Neith)	Pre-Dynastic Egypt	The most ancient one, goddess of weaving, war, and wisdom. Nit is identifiable by her emblems, which sometimes include a weaving shuttle.
Norns	Norse	Three female deities roughly equivalent to the Greek Moirae or Fates, whose spinning and weaving determine the fates of humans and gods alike.
Penelope (heroine of Homer's epic, *The Odyssey*)	Ancient Greece	Not immortal, but mythically was able to "stop time" as she unwove her threads every night, waiting for the return of her husband, Odysseus.
Saule	Baltic peoples	Sun goddess who spins as she traverses the heavens.
Si Boru Deak Parujar	Toba Batak people, Indonesia	Creator of the Earth and human beings; first weaver. She retreats to her lunar home to spin, thus creating the phases of the moon.
Spider Woman (Spider Grandmother also called Thought Woman or Creation Thinker)	Native American cultures, including the Pueblo (Hopi, Tewa, Kiwa, etc.), Navajo, Cherokee	Goddess who creates from "the great galactic center;" every living being is linked in her web. As variously told, she created the world by thinking or dreaming it; by connecting the four corners of the Earth by her silver spider strands; or by bringing the sun to the heavens for the Great Spirit. She also created people, brought them fire, and taught them to weave and be creative. She is a protector as well.
Takutsi Nakawe	Wixárika (Huichol) people, Mexico	Great-grandmother of growth and germination. Created the world and makes it turn with her spindle.
Virgin Mary	Europe/Middle East	In Europe, from approximately the 8th to the 13th centuries, Mary was sometimes portrayed as spinning at the moment of the Annunciation.

{left} The Norns, *an engraving by L.B. Hansen from Fredrik Sander's 1893 edition of* The Poetic Edda.

{below} *The glyph embroidered on this pan-Mayan style* huipil, *from Santiago Atitlán, Guatemala, probably depicts the goddess Ixchel, 1999.*

{below} *An embroidery depicting* The Three Fates, *Megisti Island (Castellorizo), Greece, 1936.*

Other heroines were able to stop time by *undoing* the textiles they were making. In Homer's epic, *The Odyssey*, Penelope was trying to hold off her many suitors, hoping that her husband Odysseus would return even though he had been away for many years. She promised to marry one of the suitors when she finished the weaving she was working on, but secretly took out the rows she had completed each night so she never made substantial progress. A similar story is told by the Lakota people. In a hidden cave, an old woman sits making a decorative strip for a buffalo robe, working in the traditional manner by embroidering with porcupine quills. Her faithful dog, Shunka Sapa, pulls out the quills whenever her back is turned, so she never gets very far; her quillwork remains forever unfinished. The people say that if the woman ever completed her work, the world would come to an end at the very moment she put in the last quill. (Sometimes the onus is placed on the dog; the world as we know it will end when he gets so old that he has no teeth and can't pull out quills any more.)[27]

Textile-making is often also conceptually related to maintaining order. In ancient China, the term for untangling and reeling silk, *zhi*, was by extension used to refer to any form of bringing or restoring order, including governing the state and healing the sick body. The term for the warp thread, *jing*, was also used to refer to regularity in structure, including the lines of kinship that unfolded over generations. In Ladakh, the activity of women's weaving was believed to be necessary for the maintenance of a greater order, both in the everyday world and in terms of long-term continuity.[28]

Textiles and our mortal journey

Since textiles are metaphorically equated with life and mythically linked to time, we can easily understand why they hold important meaning at every point in life's mortal journey. This may begin even before birth. In Sumatra, for example, a Batak woman is presented with a "soul cloth" during the seventh month of pregnancy, which is believed to extend protective power to the fetus. The Javanese sometimes tie a thread around a mother during pregnancy, and when the child is due the father will cut it off, symbolically allowing the baby to emerge.[29] In every culture, babies are quickly wiped down and wrapped up in cloth—surrounded by fabric—when they come into the world, immediately establishing an intimate relationship with textiles. Cloth is then part of all subsequent rites of passage when there is a literal or metaphoric change of state or being. Examples of this phenomenon are given throughout the book, but a brief survey of the way this works is in order here, to give a flavor of its universality.

In the West, it is primarily a practical matter that babies are "received" in soft blankets and diapered as soon as they are born. In some cultures, however, receiving cloths hold symbolic resonance or protective power. Wixárika babies are wrapped in fresh cotton fabric, which is considered synonymous with the materialization of a living, breathing infant. (The Wixárika associate unwoven cotton with clouds, and believe that human souls first appear in cloud form.) For Ottoman Turks of aristocratic rank,

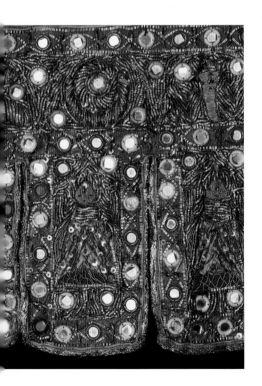

Detail of an embroidered toran hung in a house doorway during childbirth, Jaipur, India, 1950-70. The mirrors and zardozi (gold thread) work make this a very celebratory textile.

This photograph of an African-American child in a christening dress was exhibited at the Paris Exposition Universelle in 1900. It is from the W. E. B. Du Bois Global Resource Collection of photograph albums of African-Americans.

wrapping cloths held different meanings. Newborns were immediately draped in costly robes of honor, representing their new lives as leaders.[30]

In rituals that welcome children into the community soon after birth, ceremonial cloth is often used to reinforce the idea of cultural continuity. Christians dress babies in elaborate christening or baptism gowns, which may be passed down in families for generations. At the circumcision ceremony for an Ottoman prince, costly gold and silver fabrics were spread on the ground and ceremonially trampled by the hooves of his father's horse; the ritual marked the idea that the infant would one day take the place of the father. Eastern European Jews in the early part of the last century used fabric in a different kind of circumcision practice recounted by Julius Lester. A baby's mother would save the cloth used at her son's circumcision ritual and, on his first birthday, she would bring it to the synagogue and tie it to the Torah scroll, symbolically connecting him with the holy word. The same cloth later came to represent the boy's passage through childhood. It would go back into storage until his thirteenth year, and then, when he came of age, would once again be tied to the scroll when he recited its verses on the day of his Bar Mitzvah.[31]

People of many cultures also used a single cloth repeatedly at subsequent rites of passage. In Slovakia and some of the nearby Czech communities, the same shawl a woman used at her wedding functioned as a "pulling cloth" at the birth of her child, and was then used as a screening device for the bed where she had to remain for over a month. It was temporarily removed to wrap the baby when he or she was carried to the church for baptism. Among the Toba Batak in Indonesia, the same ceremonial mantle announced a boy's birth and was later used at his wedding. In the indigenous Bali Mula community, striped cloths that symbolized the human life cycle first honored babies at three months of age, and then were taken out at every life-transition ceremony for that individual.[32]

New fibers or textiles were also incorporated into initiation, coming-of-age, or graduation rituals. Sometimes it was a ritual thread that tied the initiate to his new state. This was the case among Brahmin Hindu boys, who had threads tied around their waists to indicate they were coming of age religiously and were thus tied to the community. At other times individuals were given new garments to mark their new life status. In ancient Rome, upper-class boys put on the *toga virilis* for the first time. In Morocco, Ait Kabbash Amazigh girls begin to wear a sequined embroidered veil at puberty. Jewish boys (and more recently in some congregations, girls) traditionally receive a prayer shawl at their Bar (or Bat) Mitzvah.[33] Graduates wear special gowns in much this same spirit, and ritually move tassels on their mortarboard hats from one side to another when the ceremony is complete.

Some graduation traditions are relatively local. Until the 1950s, girls in the New York City school system had to sew dresses for their eighth grade graduations, and New York women who reminisced about their lives often spoke of them as part of their coming of age. In Portugal, college students carry bouquet-like bunches of ribbons painted with congratulatory wishes at their graduation ceremonies. The events themselves culminate with the burning of the ribbons on wooden poles, signifying the end of student life.[34]

Textiles and textile-related tools played parts in the rituals surrounding marriage negotiations. European men, for example, used to adorn textile tools for their sweethearts. Tradition has it that in Norway, a would-be groom would carve an elaborate mangle board (for ironing linen) for the woman he hoped to marry. He would hang it on the door of her house, and if she accepted his proposal, she would bring it inside. If it remained on the door, it meant the offer was refused. Bobbins and distaffs were also decorated as betrothal gifts. Some were inscribed with loving sentiments; others were painted with wedding scenes. In 2010, a website promoting tourism to the Italian province of Calabria suggested that tourists buy a decorated distaff as an appropriate souvenir, since these were once such common engagement gifts that they now held "symbolic value."

{above} *The end of a 19th-century decorative cushion from Aceh, Indonesia. Cushions and other textiles are piled up on ceremonial pavilions during life-transition rituals in Aceh.*

{opposite} *Graduation imagery on a "Dutch wax" print manufactured by Vlisco Company and marketed in West Africa.*

{top} *An 18th-century Muslim* rumal *embroidery depicting a wedding ceremony in Chamba, India. (Note the central canopy.) Such cloths are typically given as gifts, sometimes at the wedding itself.*

{above, left} *Married woman's cap, Slovakia, c. 1870–1930.*

{above, right} *An image of a bride carried to her wedding on a horse is featured in this detail of a Baluchi (Pakistan) "presentation"-style pile carpet, 20th century.*

{right} *Uygur woman's embroidered wedding boots, Xingjing, China, 1900–60.*

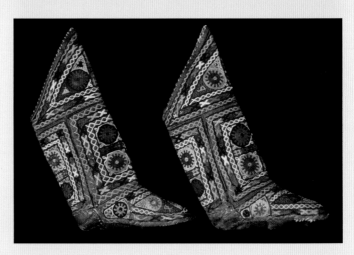

A hand spindle similarly functioned as a marriage license for a Kogi girl of the South American Amazon.[35]

Among the Akha people of Burma (Myanmar), the mark of commitment was a thread. A prospective bridegroom might come to a village with fresh clothing for his intended bride, and if she decided she was ready to continue the relationship, she gave him a bouquet of flowers tied with cotton string. Long after the flowers died, it remained as a literal reminder of the couple's bond. Among the Kirghiz of China, the day of the engagement would be marked by a ritual in which the man's family would deliver a horse with a fluff of cotton tied to it. The woman's family would tie the cotton, thereby indicating they were willing to give her in marriage.[36]

Trousseaux or dowry textiles had meaning before, during, and after a wedding. Dowry traditions were particularly strong in Central and Eastern Europe and in the Ottoman Empire. In the pre-modern period in Turkey (and to some extent even today), girls would begin working on their trousseau (çeyiz) from when they were very young. Handmade or hand-embellished textiles made up the bulk of the treasured items of the çeyiz, and while a few of these would traditionally be presented to the groom's family before the wedding, the rest were meant to furnish the new couple's home. They would also figure in the ritual itself. On the first day of the wedding festivities, the çeyiz would be carried publicly from the bride's house to the couple's new home and, once there, the textiles were laid out in an attractive display, often forming a kind of bower. The bride would sit among the cloths to receive her guests, who were able to inspect her handiwork and assess her technical and aesthetic skills. Public inspection of dowry textiles was also traditional in Hungary and nearby areas of Europe. The wedding ceremony included a parade through the village where embroidered cloths were piled high on a decorated wagon, and visitors were invited to take a close look at the holdings. In many places, fabric exchange between the families of the bride and groom took place before the wedding. On the Indonesian island of Sumba, as many as forty women's skirts passed from family to family.[37]

Special clothing is characteristic of the wedding ceremony the world over. The Western tradition includes gowns that are worn for one day only, marking the bride as a kind of queen (or princess) for a day (brides even have attendants). In other cultures, the bride would mark her transition from the unmarried to the married state by putting on a different kind of clothing on her wedding day. In Slovakia, she would cover her hair with an elaborate cap that she would wear from that time forward. In Burma, a woman of the Akha tribe would adopt a particular type of head cloth for the first time. At the point in the ceremony when the marriage was formalized, her friends would help her put it on, symbolically assisting her into her new status. The blue-black garments she had worn up until that point were also replaced with white fabric. (Among the Karen, the Akha's near-neighbors in Thailand, it was white that was worn until the wedding day.)

{below} *A Korean damask pojagi used to wrap gifts given to a bride by the groom's parents.*

{bottom} *Amazigh (Berber) bride riding to her wedding with her face covered, Morocco, c. 1990.*

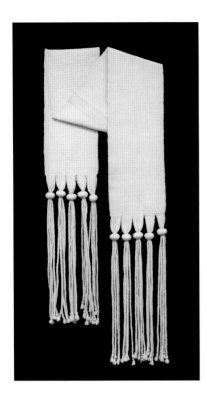

{above} *Wedding sash from Acoma Pueblo, New Mexico, 1920–40. This type of garment is often referred to as a Hopi wedding sash, but sashes were also made in other nearby pueblos. In many cultures fringes and tassels are associated with welcome, life-giving rain, and are thus often symbols of fertility.*

{opposite, above, left} *Couple united through cloth during a Tamil Hindu wedding, near Pondicherry, south India, 1977–78. A Brahmin priest presides.*

{opposite, above, right} *An Aztec couple tied together on a ceremonial mat during their wedding; painted by an indigenous artist for the* Codex Mendoza, *c. 1541.*

{opposite, below} *Wedding portal on Mirpur Road, Dhaka, Bangladesh, 1987. Portals like this are temporary gates put up just for the duration of the celebration; they are often lit up at night.*

Amish women in North America also wear a different type of cap from the time they are married, although theirs is unadorned.[38]

The bond of the marriage relationship is frequently made manifest with a literal kind of binding together or enfolding at the ceremony. The Kirghiz in China will in some instances playfully tie the couple to one another until family and friends give them gifts. In Lao Buddhist ceremonies, the officiator, and later the wedding guests, bless the bride and groom by tying white cotton strings around their wrists. This same kind of "handfasting" ritual was common in Celtic Europe and, until 1940, Scottish couples who handfasted were considered legally married. (This practice was probably the origin of the expression "tying the knot.") At Greek Orthodox weddings, both bride and groom are bedecked with ribboned crowns, and once the ceremony is complete, the strands from each of them are entwined together. At a Toba Batak wedding, the bride and groom are draped in the man's ceremonial life cloth; among Native Americans of the northern Plains, a couple might be wrapped or enfolded under a single blanket.[39]

The marriage space may itself be set off with a textile. In Morocco, an Amazigh (Berber) wedding takes place in a specially erected bridal tent, large enough to hold the whole community. In ancient Greece, the bride and groom sometimes stood under a kind of canopy—the bride's robe. The same cloth could also function as the canopy that covered the nuptial bed. Jews have been consecrating their marriage vows under a canopy, the *chuppa*, for thousands of years, and similar canopies are seen in India. In villages of the Carpathian Mountains in Hungary, it was traditional for a bride and groom to stand on a long, narrow wedding rug, embroidered with messages of good luck and motifs such as wedding rings. The rug symbolized the idea of prosperity (symbolically, the couple should never face poverty, standing on a bare earthen floor), and became part of their new home.[40]

Many of the textile-related wedding rituals refer—some more overtly than others—to sexuality and fertility. The Greek wedding cover was acknowledged this way; the phrase "to go under the same cloak" implied that the couple was bonded in a sexual union. In many cultures, the marriage bed was elaborately dressed to celebrate the union, and there was the well-known tradition of bringing back bloody sheets from the wedding night to prove that the bride came to the union as a virgin. Wedding garments and accessories also held sexual symbolism. The color red was so often associated with fertility that it was a symbolic element of weddings in many places, including India, China, and (traditional) Palestine. An Amazigh bride was brought to the bridal tent on a mule covered with a red carpet and red scarf, and she herself was sewn into a headdress that symbolized containment and fertility within marriage. Elsewhere in Morocco, brides often also wore silk—a sensual fabric—for the first time at their wedding.[41]

Cloth is integral to the celebration of regularly repeating holidays. The Toraja of Indonesia build a huge stairway with a bamboo ladder for their planting and harvest rituals, and drape it with rolls of imported Indian cloth that are believed to bring the blessings of the ancestors and ensure a

fertile crop.[42] Weekly, observant Jews put on special Sabbath clothes to mark their day of rest. Annually, they bring out dedicated tablecloths and matzo covers for Passover *seders* (ritual dinners). Christians, too, often keep Christmas tablecloths for their annual celebration. In Japan, the special cloths that are brought out at the New Year are used to call in the spirits. The Hmong traditionally marked the New Year—and its fresh beginning— with a new set of hand-embellished clothing.[43]

Finally, textiles routinely play an important role in the rituals that mark the end of the mortal journey. A corpse is almost always wrapped or covered with cloth. When an individual dies in bed, the sheet is pulled up over the face, symbolizing the fact that the person no longer needs to breathe. Body bags are used to cover those unfortunate enough to be killed in battle or who need to be transported to a morgue. Bodies are also wrapped in shrouds, and cloth is used to line coffins. Coffins in turn are further covered with other fabric (pall), sometimes in the form of a flag. Fine textiles may be used to honor the dead (the Asante of Ghana covered coffins with yards of prestigious and expensive kente cloth for this purpose) or because they are considered necessary to assist the passage to the next life. The Hmong believe that the souls of individuals buried without well-made funeral outfits might wander, eternally lost.[44] The Sumbanese help the soul move on by wrapping the dead in textiles that they know will outlast the flesh they enfold. The cloth will not only identify the deceased to the underworld, but also protect the soul from malevolent forces during the transition. The substance of the body is believed to pass through the fabric, eventually re-substantiating in the ancestral realm.[45]

Four Seal Miao festival. Exuberant outfits like this are made for the New Year by the Miao (Hmong) of China and their descendants in Southeast Asia.

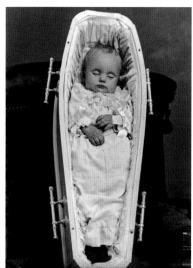

Just as with weddings, cloth is used to mark ritual space at the funeral. When Pope John Paul II died in 2005, his coffin was laid out on a large Oriental carpet on the stone floor of St Peter's basilica in Rome (this practice calls to mind the Hungarian wedding rug). The Toraja use the same ikats that cover the body of the deceased to wrap buildings near the grave. The Tai Daeng, a Lao people, liken the long banners that they hang outside the house of the bereaved for the duration (three to nine days) of a funeral ceremony to a ladder that the soul must climb to heaven.[46]

Although cloth does not survive well in most burials, the vast amount of it that has been unearthed in dry areas such as the Peruvian coast gives us a sense of just how much was sometimes provided for the afterlife journey. In pre-Columbian Andean burials, corpses were often wrapped in scores of garments and were further surrounded by fabrics woven especially as mortuary offerings. Some burial textiles were enormous; a typical single cotton shroud found on a mummy from the Paracas period measured about 300 square yards (250 square meters). (Production of the cotton for a single textile of this size required irrigation of more than two acres of land.) In ancient Egypt, preserved mummies were similarly wrapped in what amounted to several hundred square yards of linen, although that cloth was usually taken from the deceased's household and was not made just for burial. Fabric was involved in many of the steps of the Egyptian embalming process as well. As a corpse was prepared, linen pads were placed in hollow areas as it dried out. Arms and legs, and sometimes even fingers and toes, were bandaged separately, and then many layers of alternating shrouds and bandages were wrapped around the entire body.[47]

Textiles certainly also play a symbolic role for those left behind. I have cited the Ecclesiastes 3:1–7 verses that refer to the "time to rend" as a part of the human condition. They allude to the practice of tearing one's clothes apart when mourning someone's passing—it is a time when what had been whole no longer is. In Kendang, Indonesia, mourners hold a large

{above, left} *Detail of a man's* hinggi, *Sumba, Indonesia, 20th century. Hinggi (cotton wrappers with warp-ikat patterns) are brought to funeral services to assist the passage of the soul.*

{above, right} *Baby in a coffin, Black River Falls, Wisconsin, U.S., 19th century.*

{above} *Ceremonial tomb being built for the Kabaka, the King of Uganda, date unknown.*

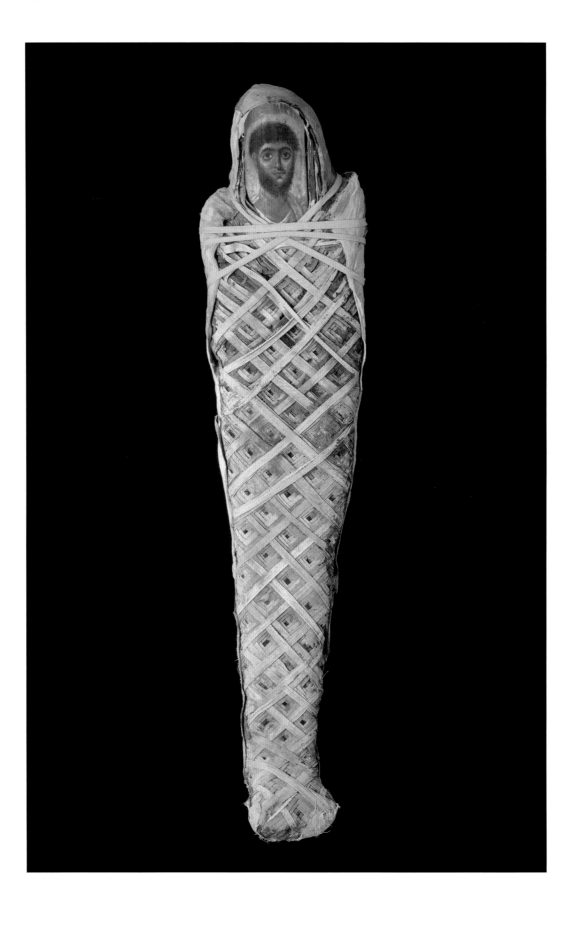

black cloth over the deceased, and then tear it into as many strips as there are surviving siblings.[48] Mourners in Western cultures may now be too restrained to tear their clothing, but they often wear symbolic black ribbons or armbands that mark their grieving state. Public mourning is marked in the West by flags flown at half mast.

A fitting place to end this tour through textiles and the mortal journey is to draw on the work of Elisha Renne, who studied the Bùnú Yoruba of Nigeria. In her 1995 book *Cloth that Does Not Die*, Renne points out that cloth frays and gradually disintegrates as it ages, tangibly mirroring the impermanence of mortal life. The Yoruba symbolically transcend time and mortality, however, by creating new fabric. They believe that every child represents an ancestor who has returned to Earth, and cloth, like children, must be continually reproduced. And, much as they value their children, they value cloth. They equate public nakedness (literally, in their language, "clothlessness") with insanity; a person without cloth is not considered a normally functioning human.[49] While people in most cultures do not go quite this far, the Yoruba make explicit an association or correlation that is often unconscious, but still salient.

Cloth and human needs

Textiles are equally central to the many parts of human activity that take place *between* important life passages—they are integral to every aspect of human experience—both the everyday incidents we may not often think about, and our more powerful, memorable moments. The following chapters build on the foundation established by this discussion of cloth and consciousness and the uses of cloth during the life journey, but they map the journey in a somewhat different way. Each chapter focuses on a specific realm of activity: basic survival (practical needs and physical and psychic protection); social interactions; economic interaction and differential power relationships; the exploration and expression of ideas and the creation of beauty (i.e., cognitive and aesthetic meanings); and interactions with the more transcendent, spiritual realms. This organizational strategy is loosely built upon (or, more accurately, inspired by) two well-known models of human experience, namely psychologist Abraham Maslow's "Hierarchy of Human Needs," first proposed in 1943, and the ancient Hindu/yogic concept of the chakras. The latter posits seven bodily energy centers that correspond to/interact with (some would say govern) particular aspects of human experience. Both systems share the premise that we humans have a natural tendency—a kind of hunger—to move "up" from basic survival mode to "higher" or more transcendent states of consciousness, but that all levels matter to us. (While I have not drawn on them directly, it is interesting to note that there are also other systems that posit a similar hierarchic model of human activity and the evolution of human consciousness. The Kabbalah refers to the seven levels of the soul, for example, and the Spiral Dynamics system proposed by Clare Graves and then further popularized by Don Beck, Christopher

Egyptian mummy wrapped in long strips of linen, 150–175 CE.

MASLOW'S HIERARCHY OF HUMAN NEEDS AND THE CHAKRA SYSTEM

Both systems begin with humans' most basic "animal" needs and activities, and move "up" through personal and social interactions into the realm of the transcendent.

MASLOW'S HIERARCHY OF HUMAN NEEDS

Definitions

Transcendence to connect to something beyond the ego.

Self-actualization to find self-fulfillment and realize one's potential.

Aesthetic needs to create symmetry, order, beauty.

Cognitive needs to know, understand, and explore.

Esteem needs to achieve, be competent, gain approval and recognition.

Love and belonging needs to affiliate with others, to be accepted.

Safety/security needs to keep out of danger.

Physiological needs to satisfy hunger, thirst, bodily comfort, etc.

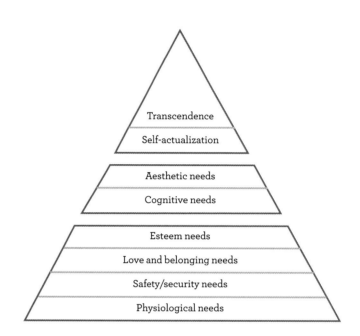

THE CHAKRA SYSTEM

Chakra number	Chakra name and corresponding place in the body	Related aspects of human experience
7	Crown *Sahasara*	Universal connection to Source (God); tapping into the "cosmic memory bank."
6	Third Eye *Ajna*	Transpersonal interface; seeing beyond the tangible plane.
5	Throat *Vissudha*	Expression and communication; truth-telling; hearing; discernment.
4	Heart *Anahata*	Love, compassion, emotional connection.
3	Solar Plexus *Manipura*	Personal power, autonomy; responsibility.
2	Pelvis *Svadhisthana*	Interpersonal relationships ("I and Thou"); inner child; sexuality.
1	Root *Muladhara*	Security, safety; food; money. Connection to the Earth.

Cowan, and Ken Wilbur considers not just individuals, but the broad sweep of human evolution.)[50]

I am not concerned with matching the fine points of any of these systems, and it is important to remember that they were designed for different purposes. Maslow was a psychologist concerned primarily with individual development. He argued that individuals must be able to meet fundamental "deficiency" (practical and emotional) needs before they could move on to a process of "self-actualization." (I do not find that these needs or arenas have to be sequential; often they co-exist.) Because Maslow's model has been highly influential in the West, the general framework has become familiar to many and remains a useful "handle" with which to think about the range of human activities and endeavors.

The chakra system, developed thousands of years before Maslow's model, was an articulation of Eastern philosophers' observations of the body's energy field. Each of its seven energy centers is located in a particular area of the body. The mystics who characterized the chakras were more concerned with spiritual rather than ego development, but the specific elements of their framework are nevertheless strikingly similar to Maslow's.

I am not the first or only one to use these systems or theories as a basis of thinking about other topics. I discovered recently that Maslow's hierarchy has already been mentioned in relation to textiles, although I had formulated my ideas long before I read Colin Gale and Jasbir Kaur's 2002 work, *The Textile Book*. Even if there is no one-to-one correlation with these systems, I am grateful for the overarching hierarchical framework they suggest. On one level, this organizational strategy is a practical way of handling and making sense of an overwhelming amount of detail. By stopping to look in turn at the different realms of human activity, I am able to "plug in" and integrate a wide range of disparate facts and stories about textiles, and to make cross-cultural comparisons. At the same time, I appreciate this organization because it helps me build another kind of cognitive map with which to explore the myriad roles that textiles play in our lives—one that alludes to a different kind of human journey (i.e., not one that moves temporally from birth to death, but through levels of activity and awareness). As we explore each of these arenas or domains and see how much of our lives—how much energy—involves textiles, we become ever more appreciative, not only of cloth, but also of the rich arc of human experience. Textiles are our constant companions through our journey. They help us relate to the Earth, to other people, to ourselves, and to something even larger than ourselves.

The arenas covered in the following chapters certainly overlap, and many of the examples or particulars I discuss could fit in multiple places. I try to focus on the given theme in each case, but inevitably there is some cross-referencing and some repetition of ideas. Where topics do crop up repeatedly, they serve as a reminder of the "interwoven" nature of our life with cloth. Now, I invite my readers to continue to follow this story with me—to delve even more deeply into the arenas in which textiles matter.

Living on the earth

Textiles and human survival

*Sewing [was] constantly necessary...on whaling ships. The length
of the cruises meant that the clothes, worn new at the beginning
of the voyage, would have worn out several times before home port
was again reached. Since the clothes were none too good to begin
with and replacement was only at exorbitant prices from the slop chest,
the whaleman became as adept at using the needle as the harpoon.
There is an old saying among sailors that a "whaleman can be told by
his patches; at the close of a cruise...[his] garments were 'a patch upon
patch and a patch over all.'"*

Hyatt A. Verrill, *The Real Story of the Whaler*, 1916

This chapter addresses the many ways that textiles help people live on the Earth and carry out their everyday activities. It begins with a look at the important way in which textiles literally connect or "root" us to our planet; for at least 30,000 years, people have made textiles from the materials of their environment. Textile activities have brought us to a deep knowledge of the Earth's plants, animals, and minerals and a close relationship with them. The chapter continues with a look at the myriad ways in which fiber and cloth are involved with survival, including how they help provide clothing, shelter, and various forms of bodily comfort; their critical role in securing, cooking, storing, and transporting food; the ways they have facilitated movement from one place to another (textile bridges, boats, saddle bags, etc.); and their indispensable role in miscellaneous tasks such as tying things together, wiping sweat from the brow, providing light, and writing. Textiles' meanings in terms of psychological safety and psychic protection are also discussed.

Animal, vegetable, and mineral: the sources of textiles

Textiles have always been part of the way that we human beings know and connect with the material planet we live on—the Earth. The fibers that go into cloth are made from the very substances of that planet, and throughout human history textile-making has been one of the ways in which we have directly connected with its animal, vegetable, and mineral kingdoms. Humans have been brought close to animals by learning to work with the materials they provide. We have used the fibers that keep us warm—we take wool and hair from sheep and goats, alpaca, buffalo, muskox, and dogs, turning it into other types of warmth-giving coverings. We sometimes use the relatively stiff hairs of a horse's tail as a fabric (sofas upholstered with horsehair were particularly common in the Victorian era), or even our own human hair as a kind of thread. We work with fur from creatures such as rabbits and beaver, shearing it and pressing it into a felt-like fabric, or using it whole, as skins. We appropriate the interior parts of animals as well, including the tendon fiber (sinew) that can stitch skins together. In the far north, the Inuit even used the intestine from walrus and similar animals, sewing it into fine-looking waterproof clothing.

{preceding page} *Fisherman casting a net on the Ubangi River, Central African Republic.*

{right} *The llamas seen in this detail of a Peruvian knitted purse remind us of the importance of the camelid animals (llama, alpaca, vicuña) in the Andes. This bag was made of alpaca, Chinchera, Peru, 1955–62.*

{left} *Eskimo (Inuit) woman sewing a gutskin parka, Kodiak, Alaska, 1904. The painted ice and igloo in the background indicate this was a staged photo.*

Warm and waterproof clothing is a matter of life and death in the Arctic, and it was traditionally made from the skins of the local animals. Inuit seamstresses who prepared the clothing developed an extremely intimate relationship with those animals—to the point that they literally took parts of them in their mouths. For example, they moistened the caribou sinew that they used for thread in their lips, and chewed skins in order to soften them. They even prepared eider duck skins (each one made a warm slipper) by sucking the fat out. The women came to understand the properties of the skins of every material and how it functioned in different conditions.[1]

Native peoples of the Pacific and North America used other animal parts for textile ornamentation, including boar bristles, moose hair, bone and, most unlikely of all, porcupine quills. The latter were flattened, dyed bright colors, and applied to leather garments and personal accessories. (A Frenchman visiting the New World in 1632 reported that the reds and blues of Huron quillwork were even more vivid than colors used in his country.)[2]

A FIRST ENCOUNTER WITH GUTSKIN

I remember the stunning visual beauty, the sensation that light was coming from within. I was astounded by the idea, by the totally unexpected possibility of someone using gut—the intestines and other soft digestive organs—as a clothlike material... That initial response remains a fresh one [many decades later].

Patricia Hickman

Inupiat or Yup'ik Inuit parka made of sea mammal (walrus?) intestine (gutskin), sewn with sinew and cotton cord, Western Arctic, 1919.

{above and left} *Close-ups of a decorative wreath made from human hair, U.S., 1850–75.*

Fish skins were also stitched together by Native Americans and Siberians, and fish scales were used as decorative embroidery elements. In the Blatná area of Bohemia, carp scales saved as waste from fish farming were cut into intricate shapes and applied to dark velvet that was later made into vests and aprons. Fish-scale embroidery was also recommended in Victorian ladies' magazines as a form of elegant fancywork.[3]

Birds were integrated into particularly stunning textiles. Small bird skins were occasionally stitched together as garments (thirty-eight eider skins were needed for one Ungava Inuit woman's parka), but plucked feathers were more commonly used for both decorative purposes and for insulation. The ancestral Pueblo people of the southwestern U.S. made glorious blankets (robes) of iridescent turkey tail feathers. Row after row of individual feathers were attached to yucca cordage and arranged in an overlapping fashion, like roof tiles. These blankets were not only warm, but also beautiful: the feathers rippled and caught the light as the wearers moved their bodies, creating an ever-changing play of color and light.[4]

SEWN SKIN CLOTHING IN THE ARCTIC

For a newcomer to the Arctic, slipping on a pair of skin boots and mittens and starting on a trip at –40 degrees C provides an exhilarating sense of freedom. At first the toes and fingers become uncomfortably cold, but soon a tingling sensation occurs as they begin to vasodilate; caribou stockings and mittens reradiate heat back into the extremities with unbelievable efficiency. Warmth surges slowly through the toes and fingers, and they become "warm as toast."

Jill Oakes

Pre-Columbian Andean peoples worked the brilliant feathers of Amazonian birds onto their tunics, helping their important people look as magnificent as the beings who flew through the air. Feathered cloth was so highly esteemed in the Inka state that it was routinely used in ritual sacrifice.[5] Like the Pueblo turkey feather blankets, many of those pieces were also made with iridescent feathers, some of which came from the tiniest of hummingbirds. Brilliant feather cloaks were also worn by royalty in Hawaii and other parts of the Pacific.

Mollusks and insects were surprisingly integral to textile traditions too. The brilliant carapaces of tropical insects have been used for millennia as adornments on cloth; in Southeast Asia, for example, green beetle bodies are sewn onto shawls and other special garments. Shells were also extensively sewn on as ornaments. More important in the history of humankind was the Chinese discovery of how to use the strong fiber produced by caterpillars. This happened in the Neolithic period, over 5,000 years ago. Having watched silkworms (*Bombyx mori*, which are technically caterpillars rather than worms) spin their cocoons from a strand they extruded from their own bodies, the Chinese learned to cultivate the insects and "capture" those strands before the creatures metamorphosed into moths. (The often-told legend is that the Empress Xilingji accidently dropped a silkworm cocoon into a cup of hot water or tea around 2500 BCE, and realized the fiber could be loosened and unwound. The story is apocryphal, but it is clear that silk was well established by that date.) Silk cultivation (sericulture) was a laborious process, involving weeks of feeding mulberry leaves to the voracious creatures (it takes about 3,000 cocoons to produce a pound of silk), but the lustrous thread was well worth the effort.[6]

{above, left} *Rabbit pelt quilt made in 1991 by Julia Nyholm, Ojibwa, who based it on quilts she remembered from her childhood in Michigan, U.S.*

{above, right} *Wild turkey underbelly and tail feathers.*

{left} *Kuba title-holder's hat worn as a sign of achievement. The base of the hat is woven from raffia palm and is adorned with cowrie shells and seed beads, Democratic Republic of Congo, 20th century.*

{opposite} *New Guinea* billum *(net bag) with feathers, 1900–50.*

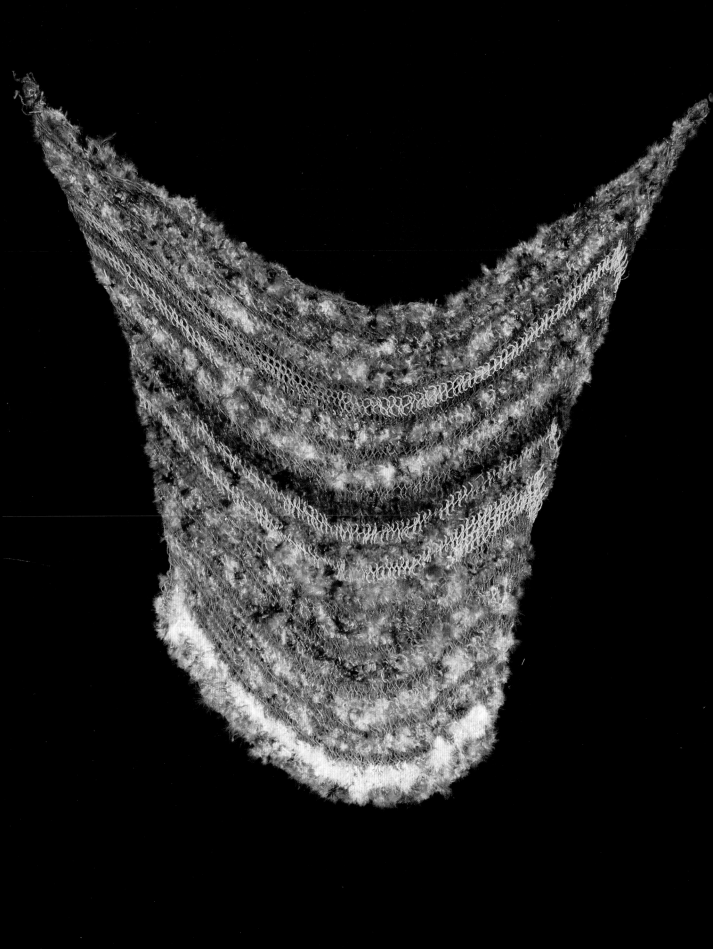

AN AMERICAN'S EXPERIENCE WITH SERICULTURE IN THAILAND, 1992

We were up by 5:00 to get ready for work at the silk farm... We pulled up to the concrete barn. Through the open, screened-in sides, we could see two three-level racks, 50 feet long, 6 feet high [about 15 x 2 meters]. On each level lay bare mulberry branches and thousands of silkworms—plump white caterpillars—just waking up.

"First, we feed," Chalerm instructed, loading fresh mulberry onto wooden carts. He demonstrated how to place the branches one by one on top of the caterpillars. With six people working, the task took an hour. [After breakfast] at 8:15, it was time to cut the mulberry... The sun burned our arms and neck a deep red as we cut branch after branch. When the trailer was full hours later, we headed to the barn to unload and give the worms their second feeding... In the afternoon we again cut enough mulberry to load the trailer and give the silkworms a last feeding.

Every day the silkworms ate more, and got bigger and bigger... They were ready [when] the two-inch caterpillars...had become translucent. The daily routine changed as the cocooning process began. The first step was to move the silkworms... For days [eight of us] picked up one worm after another, dumping bowlsful onto [special racks].

The cocoons needed three days to fully develop, then we pulled them from the wire. They are woven on tightly with a strong outside webbing. Timing was essential, or the moths would hatch... We carried the cocoons in buckets...[to] the factory, [which accepts] only perfectly oval, perfectly white cocoons with a live worm inside and the outside fuzz completely removed. We sat on the floor, rattling the cocoons, defuzzing, sorting the good from the bad.

Women in the factory, shrouded by steam, boil the cocoons in stainless steel sinks, [thus killing the pupae inside. The ends of the very fine fibers are pulled out from each cocoon, and then about twenty strands are reeled together to make a long, continuous strand].

Eve Waterfall and Kristin McGuire

{below} *Silkworm processing in Göreme, Turkey, 2009. After immersion in hot water, the completed cocoons are lifted out to loosen the ends so they can be reeled.*

{below, left} *This boy in Andhra Pradesh, south India, 1971, is standing between two large basketry racks where cultivated silkworms will spin their cocoons.*

{bottom right} *A silkworm in the early stages of spinning its cocoon.*

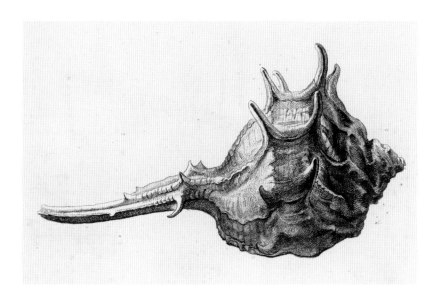

{left} Murex shell, *engraving by Wenceslaus Hollar, 17th century.*

{below} *Nopal cactus at a cochineal farm, Oaxaca, Mexico, 2006.*

To make our textiles even more beautiful, we also use animal products in the dye process. We have used animal dung and urine as fixative agents, for example, and crushed the bodies of insects and creatures from the sea to extract even small drops of color. Scale insects (cochineal and kermes) yield red dye. Small mollusks of the murex family yield blues and purples. (The famed "Tyrian purple" is discussed in chapter 4.) Ancient peoples found ways to attract these marine animals to suspended baskets, and then harvested them as a "crop." One of the latest discoveries of discard heaps (middens) of murex shells indicates production on the Arabian peninsula dating as far back as the 18th century BCE. The murex industry continued for millennia and its scale and importance is evident from the enormous remains of processed shells. Archaeologists uncovered a single undisturbed midden that was 120 yards (108 meters) long and 7–8 yards (6–7 meters) deep, for example, and, even today, one finds Mediterranean beaches and entire hillsides composed of crushed murex shells. There was also independent murex dye production in Mexico, where the people even learned to "milk" the mollusks for the precious drops of dye, returning them to the sea so they could produce more.[7]

The interface of the vegetable kingdom and the world of textiles has, if anything, been even more varied. In every ecological zone, people found native plants that could be used as textile elements, and literally every plant part

COCHINEAL IN PRE-COLUMBIAN MEXICO

Raising cochineal was demanding, as it was vulnerable to the elements and took enormous work and care. Cultivators had to "seed" or place nests of cochineal eggs onto cactus joints and protect the insects from predators. Harvesting was tedious; each tiny female insect had to be individually flicked off with a stick or feather quill. It took as many as 70,000 dried insects to make one pound of dye.

The Aztecs called cochineal *nocheztli*, or "blood of the nopal"—a significant name, for the nopal cactus was central to Aztec identity and culture. They collected staggering amounts of the dyestuff as tribute from the chief centers of production. By the time of the Conquest, some records indicate they were demanding over one hundred bags of cochineal a year from villages in Oaxaca and the Mixteca region; modern estimates suggest this may have amounted to over nine tons of cochineal, or more than a billion insects.

Amy Butler Greenfield

Nootka whaler's hat of cedar bark and spruce root, northwest coast of North America, 18th century.

was fair game. Tree roots, for example, could be turned into pliable cordage. The Tlingit and Haida peoples of British Columbia dug up spruce roots and wove them into baskets used for everything from fish traps to storage containers, shot pouches, and hats. Over time, they learned the best places to find the roots (sandy soil near the sea), the best weather conditions for collecting (rainy days, since the moisture helped keep the roots flexible), and the best way to treat the trees (carefully covering the disturbed ground, expressing gratitude) so more could be harvested from them in the future. Processing also involved awareness about their properties. The Tlingit learned to keep long roots (up to 20 feet or 6 meters) in coils in order to retain moisture, then roast them on hot coals so their tough outer covering could be peeled off, revealing a smooth, light fiber.[8]

This kind of intimacy with the local flora developed in every culture. In northern California, it was the grasses of the wetlands that were most important to the native people. They spoke of these plants as "water people," and treated them as respected relatives. Other peoples cultivated the inner stems of plants—the long bast fibers that carry life-giving water up the stalk. The ancient Egyptians learned to do this about 5,000 years ago, turning their native flax fibers into fine linen thread. Flax, like other bast fibers, must be put through a retting process to separate the usable material from the outer straw-like husk, and the Egyptians learned to soak the plants during the flooding cycles of the Nile until the straw disintegrated. In medieval and early modern Europe, retting was often done in rivers, and the process could be contentious. There were major confrontations between flax processors and shepherds who lived downstream, who said the decomposing chaffs polluted their water supply and poisoned their flocks. Henry VIII of England even passed a law stating that individuals who retted flax or hemp in a river where animals fed downstream would be fined 20 shillings.[9]

Textile fibers are also made from diverse kinds of leaves—the long leaves of the raffia palm that grows in swampy areas of the tropics, for example, or the tough leaves of the yucca or agave plants that grow in the desert—and even from plant seed hairs. The best-known seed hair is cotton, which comes from the short fibers of the cotton boll—a fluffy material that medieval Europeans once referred to as a "vegetable lamb." Before the invention of synthetics, kapok, a lightweight and waterproof seed hair, was commonly used as stuffing in life preservers, but it too could be spun into a usable yarn or thread.

Tree bark is a cloth staple in tropical climates: the inner bark of various species of mulberry, in particular, is pounded into a non-woven fabric or bark cloth (commonly known as tapa). Bark cloth was the single most important textile in parts of South America and Polynesia before foreigners brought other kinds of material, and it still holds important ceremonial and cultural meaning throughout the Pacific. The inner bark of basswood (linden) and cedar trees was also made into cordage, especially by the Native Americans. Even wood itself sometimes

SOME VEGETABLE MATERIALS USED TO MAKE CLOTH

Bast fibers (long fibers inside certain plant stalks) Linen (from flax plant), hemp, jute, ramie, hibiscus, lemba, milkweed, abaca, wild orchid, stinging nettle

Leaf fibers Palm (including raffia), pineapple (used in piña cloth), cattail, reed, yucca, agave, henequen, sisal, ixtle

Seed hairs Cotton, kapok, coconut hair (coir), devil's claw (martynia)

Bark fibers (usually inner barks) Either split and spun (e.g., basswood and cedar bark) or pounded into sheets, thus becoming bark cloth (tapa), e.g., mulberry, fig, hibiscus

Seeds For example, Job's Tears used as embellishments

Note: paper can be made from bark or any part of vegetable matter, once pulped and mixed with water.

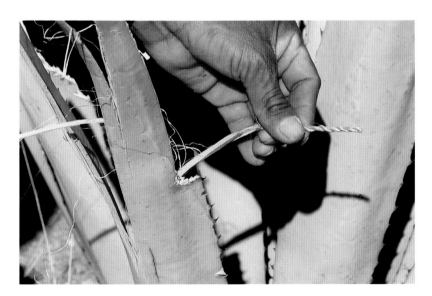

Spinning thread from an agave cactus, Mexico, 2004.

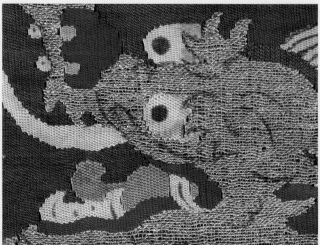

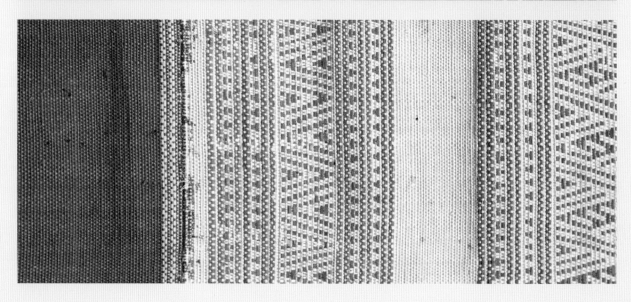

serves as a textile element. In the Preface I discussed a Shaker novelty cloth made with wefts of shaved poplar, and it is not uncommon today to find blinds or mats made from bamboo or other wooden strips. Baskets are often made from ash or oak splints. There are also woven wooden fences and house walls.

Plants have been critical to those concerned with coloring cloth. Again, every plant part has been significant in some way. Dyestuffs have been procured from the roots of mighty trees (e.g., mahogany roots, which yield a brown dye) or delicate vegetation on the forest floor (e.g., bloodroot, which yields a red-orange color). One of the strongest natural dyes, indigo, comes from fermented leaves. A wide variety of barks, nuts and seeds, flowers, and berries yield color as well, and people across the globe have been ingenious in determining how to extract it.

The mineral kingdom may come less readily to mind when we think of textiles, but it too is part of the story. Gold, silver, and other metals have been used in luxury textiles the world over. They could be formed into fine wire or flattened strips that functioned as textile elements, but most commonly, they were pounded into very thin sheets (foils), and cut into strips, which were then wrapped around a thread base. The supporting thread was typically silk, but in some very old textiles, gold was wrapped around animal sinew.

Asbestos is a broad term referring to a number of fibrous silicate minerals. Although we now know the fibers to be dangerous to our lungs, asbestos was once used to make cloth that seemed to have remarkable qualities. The material is lightweight, yet strong and fireproof (the name itself comes from the Greek for "inextinguishable"). The latter property was put to good use in the ancient world. Strabo and Plutarch wrote of perpetual wicks made of woven asbestos that were used in the sacred lamps of the Vestal Virgins (some believed they would burn for a thousand years), and Pliny described asbestos cloth used in cremation ceremonies as the "funeral dress of kings." The Egyptians sometimes wrapped mummies in the material. There are also stories from other parts of the world about powerful leaders who demonstrated their "magical" powers through the use of asbestos cloth. The Chinese king Kao Tsun (also called Wen Chen) of the Northern Wei dynasty, who reigned from 452–465 CE, was presented with a garment said to belong to the Cakyamuni Buddha. Kao Tsun was convinced of its authenticity when he exposed it to a violent fire for a full day and it was not consumed by the flames. Charlemagne, the powerful 8th-century European king, impressed guests from a rival kingdom by putting an asbestos tablecloth in the fire and removing it unharmed. A more humorous story comes from colonial America. Benjamin Franklin was known to have carried a coin purse made of asbestos so that his money "would not burn a hole in his pocket."[10]

Fiberglass is a more recent invention. Although glass-makers long experimented with thin glass strands, what we know as fiberglass was first produced in the 1920s as an insulation material. In the 1950s, molten glass

{opposite, top left} *Detail of gold embroidery on a wedding outfit from Hyderabad, Andhra Pradesh, India, 1960–80.*

{opposite, top right} *Detail showing gold woven into an emperor's qi-fu (dragon robe), Qing dynasty, China, late 19th or early 20th century.*

{opposite, centre} *Painted tapa (bark cloth) from an unidentified area of Oceania, 1900–75 (detail).*

{opposite, bottom} *End detail of a banana-fiber belt, Caroline islands, 1900–50.*

{above, left} *Fiber-optic threads are used in a series of intriguing contemporary garments by the company LumiGram. This one is called LumiStar13.*

{above, right} *Spinning glass thread for the manufacture of mats and baskets, Murano, Venice, Italy, 1905.*

threads forced through a sieve were made to resemble silk or cotton, and the fabric, which is also nearly flameproof, became a popular asbestos substitute. Fiberglass became well known in the 20th century as a drapery fabric, but it is also used now as insulating, corrosion-resistant material on items such as surfboards and boat hulls. Glass is also currently incorporated into fiber-optic threads that are bundled together into cables. While we might think of fiber optics in terms of information technology (the cables transmit light and data), its fibers are being incorporated on an experimental basis into fabrics. The trend is likely to continue. New carbon fibers, interestingly enough, mimic asbestos and fiberglass in that they will not ignite. They are being used in garments worn by people who must work near open flames, and are strong enough to protect against burning napalm.[11]

All of our synthetic "miracle fabrics" are, of course, derived from the mineral kingdom as well, as they are made from petrochemicals. A byproduct of the coal industry—the dark viscous liquid known as "coal tar"—also became the basis of our production of "chemical" or synthetic dyes. The process was discovered by accident in 1856, when a young Englishman trying to make artificial quinine from aniline was left with a purplish powdery substance that worked well as a coloring agent. Minerals had already been used for millennia to dye textiles. Some substances, such as malachite, could be applied directly to cloth to create color, but most often, mineral salts were combined with plant material. The salts allowed the dyestuffs to bond chemically with the fabric, creating a permanent hue. It is interesting to think of people discovering these reactions and learning to work with the materials they had at hand. Even a "primitive" coloring process involved complex interactions and a thorough understanding of the environment. To make their "mud cloth," for example, the Bamana people of Mali soak cotton cloth in a mixture made of pounded leaves from a local tree. Next, they draw patterns on the wet fabric, using mud from the nearby river. The iron oxide in the mud reacts with the tannin-rich leaf material, resulting in a colorfast black design in the patterned areas (this is actually done in the negative areas, creating a black background). Finally, they bleach the cloth, turning the foreground yellow areas white. Since the 1970s, mud cloth has become a symbol of African pride.[12]

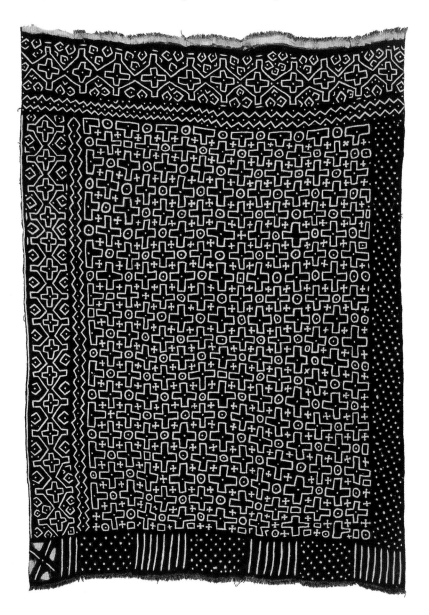

The Bamana people of Mali use iron-rich mud to make resist patterns on cotton. This type of fabric is known as bogolanfini *or mud cloth, 20th century.*

Clothing, shelter, and comfort

If asked to speak about the role of textiles in physical survival, most people probably think first of clothing and the way it protects us from the elements. This is certainly vitally important, especially in inhospitable climates. Garments can provide "micro-environments" to protect against extreme cold, heat, sun, wind, or excessive moisture. In the desert, cloth keeps blowing sand out of the mouth, nose, and ears, and it provides protection from the blazing sun. Ski masks protect vulnerable facial skin from sun, windburn, and frostbite. Once again, humans have been amazingly inventive. Our ancestors long ago learned how to manipulate and stitch cloth to create air pockets that would trap air, for example, creating warm yet attractive quilted fabrics. More recently, we have come up with battery-powered fleece jackets in which electricity literally flows through the threads, and remarkable new fabrics such as Gore-Tex®. The Gore-Tex membrane has about 9 billion pores per square inch, making it water and windproof, yet able to "breathe" by allowing water vapor to move through. It functions as a climate management system. The ultimate micro-environments, however, must be spacesuits, which even protect against a lack of earthly atmosphere. The newest models include temperature-modulating systems including undergarments that heat the body through a network of small water-conducting tubes.[13]

{top} *Tuareg man wearing protective cloth in the desert in Mali.*

{above, left} *Knitted woolen socks, Turkey, 1900–25.*

{right} *Man's quilted dressing gown, Marseilles work (also called boutis work), c. 1800. Quilted garments helped keep their wearers warm in unheated houses.*

{inset, above} *Gore-Tex® membrane seen through an electron microscope. It is made of a thin, porous fluoropolymer membrane which is bonded to nylon or polyester.*

{main image} *Astronaut Peter J. K. Wisoff on Discovery's robotic arm, 2000.*

Textiles also provide environmental shelter. We all know the importance of tents as temporary housing for refugees or people who have lost their homes during natural disasters. (After the devastating earthquake in Haiti in January 2010 left most of the population of Port-au-Prince homeless, it was vital that they find temporary shelter before the rainy season. "While they say they need food, water, and medicine," reported the *New York Times* about a week after the disaster, "when asked for their top priority, they shout 'tent, tent.'"[14]) Most people are also familiar with tents used in military campaigns or camping trips, but some are less aware of the fact that some people live in textile houses all the time. Nomadic cultures needed lightweight, portable shelters, and used textile coverings, even in seemingly harsh climates. Many settled down at night under fabric woven from goat or yak hair (some still do, although with shrinking grazing lands and modernization, the population of nomads is severely reduced). Other nomads slept in collapsible wooden frameworks that were covered in cloth. The North American tipi is one example of the latter; another is the Scandinavian Sami (Lapp) tent. The Central Asian trellis-tent (more commonly known as a *yurt*, or *ger*) also has a wooden frame, but it is made as an expandable latticework, which is covered with thick felts. This is a particularly ingenious shelter for its environment, which is plagued by freezing temperatures, snow, and ferocious winds of up to 90 miles an hour (145 kilometers per hour). The structure deflects the wind and snow, and the felts insulate so well that individuals inside are quite comfortable. At the other extreme, woven coverings are also used in the warmest climates. Houses made of straw and reed provide shelter from sun, rain, and insects.

Tents supplied by UNHCR (United Nations High Commissioner for Refugees) for Somalian refugees, Ifo camp, Dadaab, Kenya, December 2008. Other cloths are drying or being used as makeshift shelters.

{left} *Girl photographed outside a tipi, Deadwood, South Dakota by "Grabill," 1891.*

{below, right} *Carrying a roof to the home upon which it will rest, Sudan.*

{bottom left} *Yurt (trellis-tent) with decorated door, Mongolia, 1996. Newer yurts feature canvas covers over the insulating felts.*

{bottom right} *Nomad's goat hair tent, Saudi Arabia.*

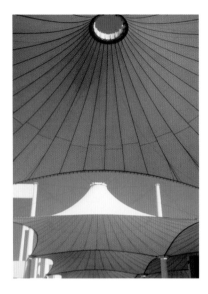

{above, left} *This terminal, which consists of tent structures, was built for the use of Haj pilgrims at the Jeddah International Airport in Saudi Arabia.*

{above, right} *Fabric roof, reminiscent of Bedouin tent architecture, at Elrey B. Jeppesen Terminal, Denver International Airport, U.S.*

Modern technology is helping to create a new generation of more permanent fabric-covered structures. Some feel these represent a revolutionary shift in architecture—that traditional gravity-bound building is being replaced with an "interwoven, floating new world." The tent-like structure that covers the Elrey B. Jeppesen Terminal at the Denver International Airport in the U.S. represents one kind of development in this emerging field. Its fabric roof, which is both inspired by and visually reminiscent of Bedouin tents, is made of fiberglass and glass filament, coated with Teflon®. It repels water, soil, and airborne chemicals, and absorbs sound. Because it is translucent and reflective, it also reduces the need for artificial lighting and lowers cooling costs. A model for an even more radical approach to "fabric architecture" was on display in the *Extreme Textiles* exhibition at the Smithsonian's Cooper-Hewitt, National Design Museum in New York in 2005. Peter Testa's forty-story "woven building" was supported not by a steel framework, but a flexible skeleton—a latticework of carbon fiber. It had a mesh-like "skin" covering.[15]

Textiles are equally important to human physical comfort inside a house. We probably think first of blankets and bedding materials, but we must not forget that the beds themselves often consist(ed) of textile structures. Beds in tropical cultures, especially in the New World, are often simply comprised of intertwined threads. Hammocks not only support the body, but also allow air to circulate around it. They are adaptable to indoor or outdoor spaces, and can be strung up or put away with ease. In the past they were particularly useful on sailing voyages, for the sometimes violent motion of a ship could easily toss a sailor out of a regular bed. Even when there is a more permanent wooden frame, interlaced textile structures sometimes support the body. The Indian *charpoy* consists of a frame with a resilient woven rope center. Like the hammock, it allows for good air circulation and is highly portable. There were similar "rope beds" in the West in the pre-industrial era, although unlike the charpoys, these were typically covered with mattresses. The ropes on these beds were periodically tightened if they began to sag, which is the genesis of our phrase, "sleep tight."

Interior comfort is also furthered in other ways. Textiles insulate the walls—the huge tapestries of medieval Europe, which we remember primarily in terms of aesthetics and narrative content, actually helped insulate the period's cold stone castles—and the floors. They also kept sleeping spaces warm; in the days before central heating was common, bed curtains provided comfort in drafty houses. Insulation could take unexpected forms. In medieval Europe, wooden bath tubs were often lined with fabric as protection against splinters, and they were at times enclosed under a cloth canopy which both provided privacy and kept the bather warm by trapping the steam rising off the hot water.[16]

The primary home furnishings in many cultures were made of cloth. In traditional Asian societies, in particular, people sat on cushions or mats on the floor and carried out all of their activities. Often, the houses were built with multipurpose rooms that were used in various ways throughout the day; it was the changing textile furnishings that delineated the different functions. In typical Ottoman homes, for example, a long cushion or divan with pillows and covers was positioned near the window of the main room. It was used for general seating and for working on light-dependent tasks such as needlework. The same space was transformed into a dining room when other textiles were brought in. A large cloth spread on the floor defined the dining area; meals were set up on a portable low table placed on the center of this fabric. The table was covered with another fabric and

{below} *Hammocks are routinely used for sleeping in parts of Latin America and also appeal to relaxing tourists. The beach in the left-hand photograph is Cozumel, Mexico.*

{right} *The sentimental image portrayed in this 1897 stereograph called "Praying for Dolly" illustrates how much bedding and other domestic textiles added to a sense of comfort.*

{below} *Woman and child seated on a charpoy (rope bed), India, 2005.*

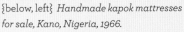

{below, left} *Handmade kapok mattresses for sale, Kano, Nigeria, 1966.*

{below, right} *"Overstuffed" upholstered chair manufactured by S. Karpen Brothers and exhibited at the World's Columbian Exposition, Chicago, 1893.*

outfitted with napkins and towels with which diners cleaned their hands. When those furnishings were removed and mattresses were spread on the floor, the space became a sleeping room. Textile "cabinets" provided storage space, especially for other textiles that were folded or rolled away when not in use. Other cultures also had textile-based interiors. Many of us are familiar with the futon mattresses that were brought out at night in Japan, and Koreans, too, relied on flexible space and this kind of "portable upholstery." Such an interior has many advantages: it allows versatility in limited space, and makes cleaning relatively simple—even allowing a house to be turned inside-out in summer, when furnishings are carried outside.[17]

In cultures where hard furnishings are the norm, we cushion much of our seating with fabric. The thickly upholstered ("overstuffed") chair almost stands as an icon or embodiment of comfort, but even in more austere interiors, chair seats are softened with woven rush, wicker or rattan, or cloth. Textiles also provide light in many dark interiors. Worldwide, candles and lamps have always relied on twisted or braided wicks to draw up the wax or oil to allow burning at an even rate. Today, fiber-optic technology is being used to transmit light as well.

On a sadder note related to textiles and physical comfort, we must remember those who do not have homes or even temporary tent coverings. Probably the most important possessions of many homeless people are the quilts and blankets that protect them from freezing. The city of Santa Cruz, California actually passed a law that made it illegal not just to sleep outside or in a vehicle at night, but also to cover up outside with a blanket. Protest was immediate and vociferous, as covering oneself seemed a primal human right. Ironically, the U.S. Department of Defense has been supplying blankets to homeless shelters since 1987. In 2001, a full $3 million of its budget was allotted to this activity.[18]

{above, left} *Carpet shop in Göreme, Turkey, 2009.*

{above, right} *Burning cotton wick in a Yahrzeit (a Jewish memorial candle).*

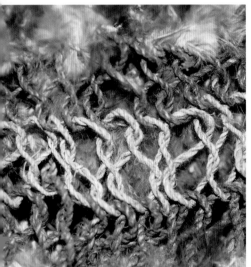

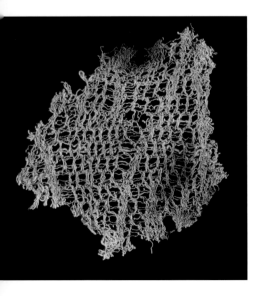

Procuring, preparing, storing, and carrying food

Textiles have been vitally important to human beings in terms of
procuring, preparing, and storing food. Archaeologists who knew how
to look at the evidence before them through textile-sensitive eyes have
recently shown us just how significant the development of cloth was to
the diet of Stone Age peoples. In 1994, Elizabeth Barber coined the phrase
"the string revolution" to describe what happened when our ancestors
learned to make cordage or thread, somewhere between 20,000 and
30,000 years ago (more recent research pushes the date back possibly even
further). Looking closely at the small statues that had long been essentially
dismissed as fertility figures of "primitive" peoples, Barber realized that
the women were not wearing skins or furs, but clothing made out of spun
thread, or string. Once people knew how to make string, Barber reasoned,
the door was opened "to an enormous array of new ways to save labor
and improve the odds of survival, much as the harnessing of steam did
for the Industrial Revolution." With string, people could make tethers and
leashes, handles, and fish lines. They could bind stone or wooden tools
together. They could weave baskets and make snares or nets to catch game
and fish—and snaring animals was, according to Barber, both an effective
and low-risk way to hunt. String-makers could also fashion slings and nets
to carry babies, and once their hands were freed up from this task, even
childbearing women became more mobile and able to participate in food
procurement—hunting, gathering, and eventually agriculture. Barber went
so far as to call string the "unseen weapon that allowed the human race
to conquer the Earth, that enabled us to move out into every econiche
on the globe."[19]

Barber's ideas were confirmed by Olga Soffer, who found that nets
had actually been in use at 29,000-year-old archaeological sites in the
present-day Czech Republic. Soffer had long been suspicious about the
prevailing belief that Ice Age people had sustained themselves by hunting
wooly mammoths, since she knew that no known living or recent hunter-
gatherer groups survived on game from large wild animals. Soffer also
determined that most of the mammoths had not been killed, but died of
natural causes, and she realized the assemblages in these sites were also
rife with remains of small animals such as rabbits and birds. It was the
smaller animals that must have provided the majority (70 per cent) of the
people's daily caloric intake. Once she started looking for them, she found
impressions of nets and baskets that were likely to have been used as traps,
and she saw that the bone and antler objects which had long been thought
to be used in hunting were in fact fiber-related tools such as awls, net
gauges, and weaving battens. Soffer understood that it wouldn't have been
necessary to be a strong or skilled hunter to help bring in smaller game:
children, nursing mothers, and others could easily participate, especially
when the hunt was communal. Furthermore, it was likely that the
women were the net- and basket-makers, so they had an additional role in
providing sustenance. Soffer thus gave agency to what she called the "silent

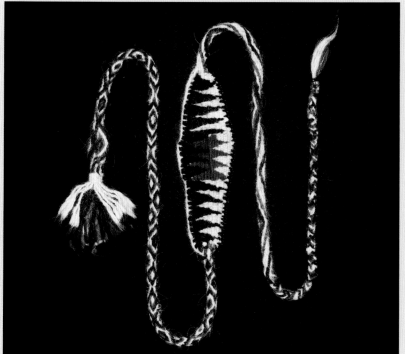

{opposite, top} *Packing twine.*

{opposite, middle} *Detail of a billum with feathers, New Guinea, 1900–50.*

{opposite, bottom} *Fragment of a pre-Columbian looped textile, 1000–1476 CE.*

{above} *Making nets for ocean fishing, Goderich Beach, Freetown, Sierra Leone, 1973–74.*

{left} *Peruvian sling, sometimes used as a projectile to hurl rocks when hunting small game, Paucartambo, Cuzco, Peru, 20th century.*

{above, left} *Bamboo chicken baskets, which each hold many birds, Guangxi Province, China, 1999.*

{above, right} *Nomadic Central Asian herders used salt bags to store the rock salt needed for their animals' survival. They were often given as wedding gifts, 20th century.*

majority" of the prehistoric world—she demonstrated that women, children, and the elderly were all actively involved in getting food with the help of textile structures.[20]

Nets and snares have been important in every culture. Long after the Ice Age, whole communities joined in directing animals into traps or casting nets in the ocean to catch fish. Farmers use nets to hold or protect crops; they cover fruit trees, keeping birds or insects away. In the pre-Columbian Andes, even the balance scales that weighed out foodstuffs were constructed from nets (netted bags hung from each end of a single string). Nets are still ubiquitous. The September 2005 issue of *National Geographic* pictured Mbuti (Democratic Republic of Congo) hunters who flush antelope and other animals into bark nets they have draped between trees.[21] Fishing nets remain vitally important, although now instead of being made of plant fibers such as hemp, they are usually made with synthetics that do not rot.

Cordage has also helped procure food in other ways—animals were hunted with arrows propelled by stretchable bowstrings, for example, or by slingshots. Rope was used in harpoons, and was part of the masts or sails that helped propel the boats used for fishing expeditions. Farmers also used it to stake plants, to mark trees that must be cut (or even to pull them down), and to tie up bales of hay.

Textile containers are universally used to hold and transport food. Among the nomadic people of Iran and Central Asia, salt bags were considered necessities, since the animals they depended on needed salt for survival. The design of these containers was quite practical—they were made with a narrow opening that, like a bottle neck, facilitated pouring and reduced spillage, and they were portable, so shepherds could carry them on their backs and pour out a handful of salt whenever their animals needed it. The bags also held emotional meaning. They were made for individual shepherds by the women of their families, and were often

beautifully worked. For women, they served as signs of love for the man who was gone for long periods of time with the flocks. For men, they served as a symbol of home. Filled salt bags were exchanged by families coming together through marriage.[22]

Even liquids, which are certainly critical for human survival, were (and are) held in textile containers. Tightly woven baskets functioned as milk containers in East and North Africa. Among the cattle-herding Borana of Ethiopia and Kenya, for example, one of women's important expressive forms were lightweight milk jugs woven out of local vegetable fibers.[23] We still use bags to transport liquid, sometimes over long distances, although we do so in a high-tech manner. The B.A.G. corporation has come out with a large flexible bag called a "Super Sack"® that can lift up to 12 tons of liquid or solid material. Huge textile containers ("Very Large Flexible Barges") that can even be towed across the ocean are in the development stage. Made of new composite fibers, a single bag would hold over 66 million gallons (250,000 cubic meters) of water. New materials have also been used in other ways to assist in food production and transport. Slings made of polyester monofilament, for example, can lift containers that weigh up to 50 tons.[24]

Textiles are equally important in food preparation and cooking. Nets, sieves, and winnowing devices help with many tasks, from separating wheat from chaff, to yogurt- or tofu-making or straining out curds and whey. Cooking is also done in textiles. Native peoples of northern California heated liquid by filling tightly woven baskets with water and dropping in fiery hot stones to bring it to the boil. Stews were made directly in these fibrous "pots." These traditions may be age-old. It is worth noting in this regard that archaeologists Richard Leakey and Glynn Isaac, like Barber and Soffer, realized the significance of the interlacing discoveries of early peoples. They focused on baskets rather than nets, claiming that the development of the basket was critical to moving civilization forward.[25]

{above, left} *Baskets used for cooking acorn mush at a Maidu feast, probably at Bidwell Bar, California, 1903.*

{above, right} *Unloading Super Sacks® used in international commerce.*

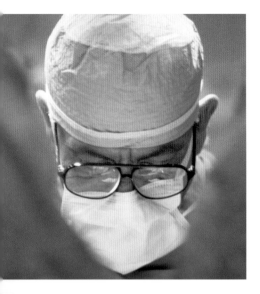

{top} *Cardiac surgeon wearing protective (surgical) mask and hat, San Francisco, 1996.*

{above} *Mother and child sleeping under a Vestergaard Frandsen mosquito net treated with the insecticide Iconet®; the photo was used on a press release by Syngenta, the Iconet manufacturer, for World Malaria Day, 2008.*

Hygiene, medicine, and physical protection

Textiles play a prominent role in maintaining health. At a fundamental, everyday level, we use cloth for cleaning both ourselves and our environment. We put washcloths and towels to our faces, dishcloths to our dishes, and rags and mops to the bathroom floor. Purification rituals usually involve cloth.

Cloth protects us from germs and unwanted pests. Doctors put on special "scrubs" and face masks for surgery, and sometimes wear Gore-Tex®, since it blocks bacteria. Surgeons and butchers wear gloves made of puncture-resistant fabric, policemen wear bullet-proof Kevlar® vests, and all of us put on bandages when we have been cut. Stitches are used to sew people back together after surgery. We also rely on nets to keep unwanted animals—insects, for the most part—away from our bodies. (The word "canopy" comes from the Greek *konopeion,* which originally referred to a net-covered bed that kept the gnats away.) The Lao-Tai people wove dense nets that they hung on dowels, essentially functioning as bed curtains. They were more successful at keeping out small blood-sucking insects than the commercial nets that have largely replaced them today.[26]

It is important to remember that mosquito nets not only protect from irritating bites, but also from debilitating diseases such as malaria. Since about a million people, mostly children, die from malaria each year, it is a matter of public health to make sure that sleeping under nets becomes standard practice in tropical climates. There are global campaigns underway to provide mosquito nets for every family that lives in an affected area. In 2008, the United Nations established World Malaria Day and called for universal coverage in two years (experts estimate that about 250 million nets are needed worldwide). Awareness about the issue in the U.S. has grown to the point that it has become fashionable to donate $10 to buy a mosquito net to save an African child; in June 2008, the *New York Times* even compared the movement to the March of Dimes campaign that targeted polio. One organization, "Nothing But Nets," had already raised $20,000,000.[27]

Recent developments in the field of medicine incorporate textiles in surprising and imaginative ways. For example, non-surgical facelifts are being achieved now with simple sutures made with strands of polypropylene outfitted with tiny cogs. These are inserted under the skin, and literally pulled up tight. The cogs hold up the sagging tissue, and over time the body generates new collagen around the threads. Scaffolds are also being engineered from silk protein that will soon be used in the regeneration or replacement of human knee ligaments (again, collagen builds around the silk, which is subsequently reabsorbed). Other innovations involve new fibers. Vectran™, a liquid crystal polymer that can be easily sterilized with gamma rays, is being used in implants, and woven carbon fiber composite has been made into a springy prosthetic device called the Flex Foot® (it was invented by an amputee runner). A promising material called

"Fluidic Muscle" is in development. Finally, there is great medical potential in the fiber applications of nanotechnology. Nanofibers—which can be 1/180,000 the breadth of a human hair, and have an almost infinite number of molecule attachment points—are already being used to make fabrics with anti-bacterial properties. These may soon be incorporated in bandage- or clothing-based drug delivery, or made into clothing with reactive molecules capable of sensing chemical hazards in the environment.[28]

Age-old textile structures are being put to new uses in the medical field, often as body implants. The scaffolding used during reconstructive shoulder surgery is actually stitched together. The threads mimic the organization of natural ligaments, and transfer the load evenly. Familiar textile forms are also proving helpful to cardiac surgeons. Knitted vascular grafts are being used to replace human arteries during bypass surgery, for example, and a warp-knit mesh bag is being used to enclose some weakened or enlarged hearts. The bag has just the right amount of stretch

{below, left} *Innovative textile structures like this assist in modern-day surgery. The snowflake device was custom-designed for a patient who needed extensive shoulder reconstruction. It has a wide range of possible attachment points for the damaged tissue.*

{below, right} *An embroidered stent used for the repair of abdominal aortic aneurysms. The illustration indicates how much the stent can be twisted without the lumen becoming closed.*

{bottom right} *Embroidered shoulder implant developed for the repair of the rotator cuff.*

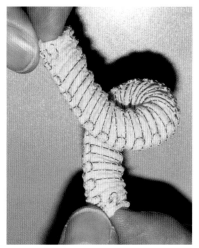

to constrain the heart muscle and prevent it from getting bigger while still allowing it to beat normally.[29]

Even in low-tech environments, cloth has provided physical protection in countless everyday contexts. A few examples of protective cloth from Japan demonstrate how effective it can be. People who lived in the moist climate of Awaji Island, for example, made aprons by stitching together water-shedding bundles of rice straw. Protective firemen's coats were in use throughout the country during the Edo period, when most buildings were made of wood and fire was a constant danger. The coats were constructed of many layers of quilted cotton that absorbed moisture. Before fighting a blaze, the firefighters doused themselves with water. Their garments remained wet enough to protect them from burning embers and keep them cool, since the heat of the fire gradually evaporated the water away. Samurai armor was also dependent on a fabric form. Its rows of overlapping metal or leather scales functioned as protective plates, but what made the armor work so well were the silk cords that laced vertically between the rows. The lacing allowed the strong and flexible surface to absorb the energy of a sword, even before penetration could begin.[30]

The Aztecs who battled Cortez in 16th-century Mexico wore padded cotton jackets, as did medieval knights (under their armor). "Poor-man's armor" in medieval Europe was made of heavily fulled (boiled) woolen cloth. While it may not have been as prestigious as knights' metal body suits, it was very effective against swords, for it was almost impenetrable to the weapon's thrusts. Densely woven silk was also used to deflect arrows and even bullets, and silk had other helpful properties. The Mongol ruler

{below, left} *Camouflage jacket worn during the Vietnam War, 1967–69.*

{below, right} *Image of a samurai in Kusakabe, Japan, attributed to Kinbei, 19th or early 20th century.*

Apollo 17 spacecraft being carried to a safe landing with the help of parachutes, 1972.

Chinggis (Genghis) Khan gave his warriors silk shirts to help protect against bleeding in the case of a stab wound, and to help stave off infection.[31]

There are many links between protective textiles and soldiers in the contemporary world. One familiar, iconic example is the use of camouflage fabric. Uniforms are routinely constructed with camouflage prints, but the cloth protects more than human bodies—it is also widely used to hide military vehicles and other equipment. Scientists are now taking the camouflage idea almost into the realm of fairy-tale and science fiction. Susumu Tachi developed a kind of "invisibility cloak"—an optical camouflage coat, which seems to make the wearer disappear. The rear surface of the material is fitted with photo detectors and the front surface with light emitters. The detectors record the intensity and color of light behind the wearer, which the emitters mimic exactly. An observer looking at the object thus appears to see right through it. This technique may one day have more than military applications. It may be used by surgeons, for example, whose own hands and surgical tools can block their view of the operations they are performing.[32]

Many airmen owe their lives to another kind of lightweight cloth— the parachute that literally served as a lifeline when they had to bail out of their planes. Parachute production was so important to the war effort during World War II that civilian use of silk and nylon was forbidden in the U.S.,

and there were heartfelt campaigns for the donation of old stockings that could be recycled for this purpose. A single parachute required fiber from thirty-six pairs of stockings.[33]

Parachutes rely on tethers, and we must remember that ropes and cords provide critical protection for hot-air balloons, mountain climbers, workers at construction sites, and rescue operations. Protection and support are also provided by seat belts and other restraining straps, and by various forms of trusses, ranging from bridge supports to jock straps and brassieres. Safety nets, used in contexts as diverse as the circus and high-rise construction projects, are protective, as are shade-giving cloth structures including awnings, parasols, and canvas overhangs on baby strollers.

Transport, travel, and the built environment

Parachutes represent a relatively recent kind of "transportation," but textiles have been used for a very long time to help people get from place to place. They were certainly essential for traveling on water. Sailing ships used textiles for the rigging and the sails themselves. At one time, large numbers of workers in seaport towns used "ropewalks"—devices about 400 yards (365 meters) long used to ply fiber into cordage—to produce the rope and cables needed on clipper ships. "Learning the ropes" was so important on such vessels that sailors became master knot-makers, and developed what later became known as the art of macramé. Sewing was another critical survival skill on long sailing voyages, since sails and protective clothing were in constant need of repair.[34]

Simple but effective boats have long been constructed with fiber and fiber techniques. Researchers theorize that Southeast Asian people built and navigated the first sea vessels—rafts—between 60,000 and 40,000 years

{opposite} *Inspecting parachutes after a test flight, 1942, Pioneer Parachute Company, Manchester, Connecticut.*

{below} *Reed boat on Lake Titicaca, Bolivia.*

ago. (If these dates are correct, the beginnings of the "string revolution" may be even older than previously thought.) These rafts would have been made by lashing together bundles of reeds. Similar buoyant boats were made in other marshy areas where reed is abundant. They are used on the Nile and the Euphrates Rivers, as well as on Lake Titicaca in the Andean highlands. Reed boats of this sort are surprisingly strong; the *Qal Ylumpi*, a 47-foot (14-meter) boat made in Bolivia in 2002, is said to be able to hold the weight of fourteen Volkswagen Beetles. In the far North, the Inuit stitched animal skins into waterproof kayaks. Coracles are bowl-shaped boats that are essentially large baskets. Made from grass, reed, cane, bamboo, and similar fibers, they are typically about 6 feet (2 meters) in diameter, and can hold several people. Coracles are still seen in India (where they ferry people and animals across rivers), the British Isles and Southeast Asia.[35]

Today, high-tech fabrics are making boats amazingly efficient. Glass fibers reinforce boat hulls, and braided structures made with carbon fibers are forming the bodies of contemporary racing yachts. Sails are also being made in entirely new ways. In one model, fiber is laid in grid patterns between sheets of Mylar that are laminated together. While this can be cut and sewn like any other cloth, it can also be molded to a precise shape for an individual boat.[36]

Textiles have always been involved with flight. The first airplane made by the Wright brothers depended on cloth: its wings were made of cotton muslin. The idea of fabric wings is actually resurfacing in "ultralight" planes. Inflatable flexible material is also being used on small aircraft intended for treacherous situations such as military and civilian rescue missions (including avalanches) and firefighting. And, as the discussion of the spacesuit above indicates, sophisticated fiber technologies are integral to space travel. Space shuttles have cloth insulation made of heat resistant alumina-borosilicate fiber, and thermal blankets made from ceramic fabrics protect the engines in booster rockets. NASA's 1997 Mars Exploration Rover Special was outfitted with special parachutes that slowed its descent to a mere 250 miles (400 kilometers) per hour (!) before it landed. As Susan Brown described it, the lander was for a moment suspended from "a narrow, braided tether— the world on a string."[37] In addition, the craft was cushioned with a "cocoon" made of twenty-four airbags, which were inflated with gas generators just before touchdown. The cocoon first hit the surface at 50 miles (81 kilometers) an hour, repeatedly bounced up and crashed back, and finally rolled to a stop. Since the bags were made from Vectran™, a fiber that actually gets stronger at colder temperatures, they did their job admirably well. Similar airbags were incorporated into later exploration missions. There have also recently been experiments with "solar sails," fabrics propelled by solar energy that are intended to move spacecraft between planets.[38]

SEWING SAILORS

To look into our Forecastle this afternoon one would think it was a Tailor shop, for one is making Pants another Shirts another is puzzling his brains over a Cap and the last Knight of the Needle is mending.

Journal of Henry Davis, 1862

Started the sewing society again, stitch on stitch, patch on patch is all the rage—here are half the ship crew below—going it hammer and tonge [sic] with their needles.

Journal of Robert Weir, *Clara Belle*, 1856

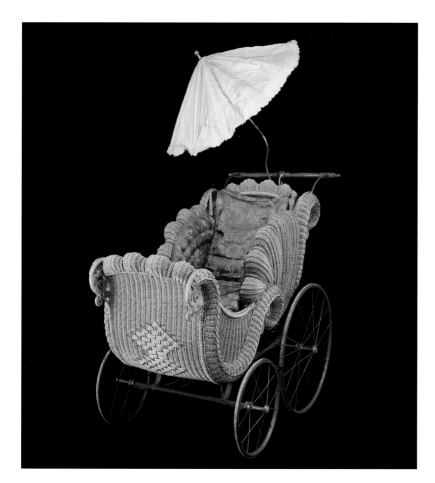

Baby carriage made by F. A. Whitney Carriage Company, Massachusetts, U.S., c. 1902 and used by a Wisconsin family. The body of the carriage is made of reeds worked around wooden dowels, and the carriage features elaborate silk upholstery and a silk parasol.

Lightweight materials are advantageous when speed is important. The same carbon fiber used to make racing yachts is also used to make rocket nose cones, and is incorporated into bike frames, racing cars, and speed-skiing helmets. The fiber is woven, and reinforced with polymer. It can be draped and tailored into variable chassis shapes, with no separate parts or seams.

Still other transportation devices that use fibers include snowshoes, which rely on interlaced webs to allow people to walk across deep snow by displacing their body weight, and baby carriers, which allow children to be taken from place to place. The carriers vary greatly—they range from nets to cloth slings or wrappers that secure the baby to the mother's back, to more solid basket-like containers or cradle boards. The body of the baby carriage (perambulator) introduced in Europe and America in the mid-19th century originally featured woven basket-like structures, which were later replaced with cloth stretched over a metal frame. The carriages also featured padded lining materials, which utilized sophisticated upholstery techniques.[39] Even our most up-to-date strollers (pushchairs) and bike trailers feature fabric seats and coverings.

Native North Americans of the Great Plains transported all of their goods in *travois,* devices made from two long poles that were joined at one

Emigrants Crossing the Plains, an engraving by Henry Bryan Hall, Jr., after a painting by Felix Octavius Carr Darley, c. 1869.

end by a kind of netting. The other sides of the poles were lashed to animals (dogs, and later, horses). The goods were secured in the netting, and were transported as the animals dragged the whole device along the ground. Another form of transport that traversed the Great Plains of North America in the 19th century was the covered (Conestoga) wagon. Its cloth cover was not essential to the actual workings of the vehicle, but it gave essential protection to the people and goods within. The horses that pulled the travois or wagons were themselves outfitted with reins, saddle blankets, and blinders (blinkers) to help keep away annoying flies.

Ropes and cords have had a strong imprint on the human landscape. The mighty pyramids of Egypt and the New World could not have been constructed without ropes, which were used to move their huge blocks of stone. Tent houses must be secured with rope, and more permanent structures are often built by workers standing on rope scaffolds. One of the surprising sights in relentlessly modernizing China is the tied bamboo scaffolding that is still used in the construction of even the highest skyscraper.

I have an early memory from a long-ago movie of people crossing a raging river by making their way over a swaying rope bridge. It made a deep impression—it was frightening to imagine looking down a deep ravine, supported only by twisted fiber cords—but the image lodged deep in my imagination. In fact, simple rope suspension bridges have served people and animals since time immemorial. They were common in areas with steep terrain, including such disparate places as the Near East, New Guinea, Northern Ireland, the Himalayas, and the Andes. Legend has it that Xerxes, King of Persia, had his subjects spin flax rope and use it to create a bridge they then stretched over the Hellespont. His armies crossed over it to invade Greece. The famous runners of the Inkan empire, who brought messages across the mountains in record time, also crossed many rope bridges. Up to 300 feet (91.5 meters) long, these were made of woven grass cables with "floors" of plaited branches. Reporting in 1604, Garcilasco de la Vega explained that three bridge-length ropes were twisted together to make a larger rope, which was in turn twisted with three others, and so on. The cables were quite strong (some were as thick as a man's torso), but because they would begin to sag over time, they had to be replaced regularly. Villagers fulfilled part of their service to the Inka state by doing bridge repair work. (Rope bridges do not work well for wheeled vehicles, so the Spanish conquerors tried repeatedly—and unsuccessfully—to span the Andean canyons with European-style arch bridges.) The Inka's descendants who live in the town of Huinchiri, Peru still maintain a rope bridge that spans the Apurimac River over a canyon more than 100 feet (30 meters) deep. The Huinchiris rebuild their bridge annually as part of a three-day festival that honors their ancestors and their relationship to the land.[40]

Fibers are used in bridges even in our more technologically complex society. Some pedestrian suspension bridges are actually made like the original rope structures, although their lightweight fiberglass components are resistant to rot and corrosion. These can be carried to remote locations and assembled on site. The cables for steel suspension bridges, too, are twisted together like rope. Crumbling concrete bridges are now sometimes strengthened with long, bandage-like reinforcing strips that combine carbon and glass fibers woven in tight crisscrosses. The interlace structure is the key to the strips' success, since they are stiff but not rigid, and can withstand nail holes without weakening. In the U.S., the development of these "super-bandages" was funded by the Army Corps of Engineers, with the idea that troops could quickly reinforce bridges to bear the weight of heavy military vehicles such as 113-ton tank transports.[41]

Engraving of a rope bridge from George Squier's Peru: Incidents of Travel and Exploration in the Land of the Incas, *1877.*

This photograph of Robert C. Pittenger at Anzio, Italy in May 1944 reminds us that both tents and sand bags were used for soldiers' protection during World War II.

Landscape and civil engineers are now incorporating textiles into the very ground we live on. "Geotextiles," heavy-duty porous fabrics, are literally woven into the earth. They are laid on or in soil surfaces, providing filtering and drainage layers, and plant roots become entwined in them, helping to protect against erosion. (Matilda McQuaid calls this a "soft armor," much lighter and easier to work with than traditional systems of rocks or concrete.) One type of geotextile even allows vegetation to grow in a textile matrix that floats on water; it forms living islands that can be moved from place to place.[42]

With so much of our landscape being covered in concrete and turned into highways, it is also notable that road beds themselves are routinely reinforced with strong, rot-resistant textile structures. Tires, too, are strengthened and held together with textile frameworks. Originally, canvas was used to reinforce the rubber, but today tire cord is made from steel and polyester that is loosely woven and heat stabilized.[43]

Textiles help protect landscapes as well. During World War II, citizens used blackout curtains to hide their cities from enemy bombers. Today, we use sand bags to fend off floods, and contain ocean oil spills with booms made of woven polyester with urethane coating. One scientist has even suggested that we protect an entire *mountain* with a textile in order to stave off the effects of global warming. Euan Nisbet, a greenhouse gas specialist, proposes draping the cliffs of glacial ice of Mount Kilimanjaro with white polypropylene in the summers until reforestation is possible. The cliffs are some 60 to 150 feet (18 to 45 meters) high. The sun's rays would bounce off the fabric, keeping the ice cool and thus preventing further melting. Nisbet claims this textile would "buy" the mountain several decades. It would also function as something of an art piece, as it "would look like a giant washing line: God's crisp, white sheets aired out three miles up in the sky." He feels the "effort to preserve a square mile of ice in the equatorial sky" would become a powerful local and universal symbol.[44]

Everyday uses and source of income

Textiles help individuals in myriad everyday ways. A piece of cloth is by nature multifunctional—one can use it to hold, wrap, protect, etc. We usually think of the Indian sari simply as a garment, but it does much more than cover the body. The *pallu*, the loose end that the woman drapes over her shoulder, also serves as a handy piece of fabric that can mop sweat from the brow or wipe off a dirty table surface. It can be held up to the face to filter out smog or serve as a modesty or sun shield, function as a potholder, or hold keys or money (they are tied into the end). The Moroccan *mendil* is usually identified as a "table cloth," but it too can also cover items such as bread, bottles, or glasses; protect a bride's clothes when henna is applied to her hands; be turned into a container (opposite corners are generally knotted together) for trousseaux or clothing being carried from one place to another; or swaddle a baby.[45] The Mexican *rebozo* and Guatemalen *tzute* similarly function as shawls or as carriers of everything from babies to firewood to food. Even the bandanna associated with the American cowboy, which is primarily remembered as a decorative neck cloth, was once critical as a wiping cloth and a facial protector against dust on the open range. In Japan, multipurpose textiles often consist of openwork bamboo. These structures hold and store clothing, and carry objects ranging from crickets to beer to building materials. Bamboo strips are also made into blinds and coverings for interior walls and exterior fences, and are fashioned into hats.[46]

Narrow woven or braided bands were, and to some extent still are, critical in tying up all kind of things—packages, documents, feed sacks, animal harnesses, blinds, mattresses, clothing, etc. In the European past, fashionable garments were often laced together, for sewing was laborious, and there were no zippers, Velcro®, elastic, steel hooks and eyes, or buttonhole-making machines. Even in the early 19th century, many households still had special looms to weave long yardage of "tape" that could be put to a variety of uses. Lengths were cut off to make apron or cap strings, for example, or to be used as garters or ties for storage bags. We think of the word "tape" today in terms of cellophane or other plastic materials, but the word used to refer to a textile, a narrow band that we might now call lacing, strapping or ribbon. Woven tape was such a ubiquitous part of everyday life that the Morristown, New Jersey National

USES FOR THE SCOUT NECKERCHIEF

In 1927, Commodore W. E. Longfellow wrote "Scouting with a Neckerchief" for the Boy Scouts of America. He listed forty-three different uses for the Scout Neckerchief, including:

- As an International Morse signal flag or for sending messages by Semaphore code
- For Troop and Patrol identification
- As a smoke mask
- As a dressing for a burned face and neck
- As a blindfold for games or a frightened horse
- As a substitute for a belt
- As a loin cloth or bathing trunks
- As a cover for a pail of water, or a dust cloth or cover
- As a pad for the head in carrying heavy loads or wherever needed to prevent chafing
- To lash poles together
- For making a life line, guard rope, or rope ladder
- For making a boat sail

Cloth used to carry cocoa and other objects and substances, Aymara people, Huancane, Peru, 20th century.

{opposite} Girl with Cherries, *1491–95, oil on canvas*, is attributed to Ambrogio de Predis and illustrates the way in which clothing was tied together with laces (then often called "points") in the Renaissance era. Laces were also used for decorative effect.

{left} *Saleswoman laying out handwoven belts and beaded narrow bands used primarily to tie on hats, Peru, 2007.*

{below} Effets Merveilleux des Lacets *(Marvelous Effects of Laces), a satirical image dating from c. 1810, reproduced in Dr. Ludovic O'Followell's* Le Corset, *1905.*

Historical Park, which interprets the American Revolutionary era, held an exhibition on the importance of the tape loom "to families of all financial positions."[47]

The simple non-woven textile form of felt has also been an almost invisible part of everyday human activities for hundreds of years. In addition to covering and keeping houses warm, it was used before synthetic non-wovens were common as an insulating lining for items ranging from snowmobile boots to railroad boxcars. Today, it is found in felt-tip pens and filters of all kinds.

In the past, the everyday tasks that are now handled in the developed world by paper or synthetics were usually handled by little scraps of fabric. The ancient Egyptians used small pieces of linen much as we use tissue paper, for example, and in Japan, worn-out futon covers were turned into scrub cloths. Scraps of absorbent fabric were and in many places still are being used as sanitary napkins; the expression "being on the rag" indicated

THE OUTPUT OF BRITISH INDUSTRIAL TAPE MAKERS

In the latter years of the 19th century, the weekly output of 230 people employed at Speedwell and Haarlem Mills in Wirksworth equalled the circumference of the Earth. Under the broad description of tape makers these workers were producing a wide range of narrow fabrics, from boot laces to ferrets (stout cotton or silk tapes) and smallwares (haberdashery).

The Peak Advertiser, 1999

{opposite, above} *Native Americans selling their baskets to summer tourists on Mackinac Island, Michigan, U.S., 1905.*

{opposite, below} *Beaded needlecase made by an unidentified Tuscarora (Iroquois) woman, Niagara Falls, New York, late 19th century. Sales of this kind of beadwork supported the entire tribe during that period.*

that a woman was menstruating. Goonj, a volunteer-run recycling center in New Delhi, currently turns scraps from worn-out garments into sanitary pads that are distributed to the poor.[48]

Textile-making has itself often functioned as an income-producing endeavor that helps people survive in difficult times. Turkish çeyiz was considered an investment, for example, for the fabrics could be sold off if a family's financial situation grew dire. The idea that textiles could, at need, be transformed into ready cash was so common that silver coins were sewn into dowry or wedding clothes in many cultures; "wearing one's wealth" in this way not only broadcast one's prosperity to others, but served as a form of security, a hedge against future poverty.

Struggling people who had some kind of access to ready markets often turned their textile skills into a source of cash. Iroquois women who lived near tourist areas such as Niagara Falls and Montreal developed lines of beaded "whimsies," for example, which were sold as souvenirs, and entrepreneurial individuals from other tribes made baskets and sold them along well-traveled highways. At the turn of the 20th century, these businesses were absolutely essential for the well-being of their communities. An 1894 U.S. government report "on the condition of the Indians" explained that:

> Basketwork...occupies the time of one or more in nearly every family, and...nearly one-sixth of the entire population have suddenly concentrated their energies upon this occupation. It guarantees good support, with prompt pay... [Sales] netted...nearly ten times as much as was realized from the sale of crops.[49]

There are equally compelling stories of individuals who found creative ways to turn waste materials into sale products. One comes from the memoirs of Hans von Luck, a German military officer who was held

Detail of Japanese kasuri (ikat fabric) made as a futon cover, 1975. When cloths like this wore out the patches were made into children's clothing and then eventually served as rags.

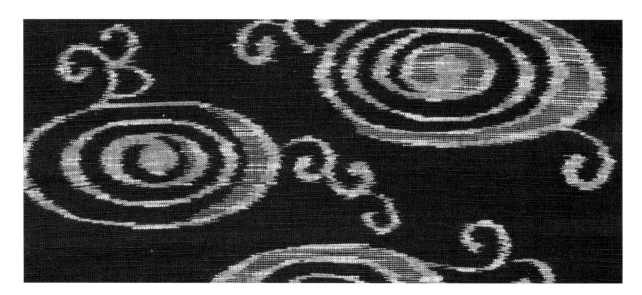

as a prisoner of war in the Caucasus mountains of Georgia during World War II. After local mine workers made him a pair of knitting needles, von Luck began to make stockings with insulation threads (probably silk) from stolen electric cable. These extremely warm socks were an immediate hit, and were purchased by both fellow prisoners and prison guards. Another example comes from South Africa in the 1980s. Elliot Mkhize came up with the idea of weaving baskets out of the colorful surplus telephone wire he found in the streets of Durban. The baskets sold well because they were strong and attractive, and customers found the novel use of the wire amusing. Others followed suit and started producing wire baskets of their own. The style is now well known throughout the world.[50]

In other cases, philanthropists and development workers have helped destitute groups come up with saleable textile products. This happened in Victorian Britain, for example, with projects revolving around embroidery and crocheted lace. In early 20th-century and Depression-era North America, a range of small scale textile "industries" were set up in remote impoverished regions: hooked rug workshops in rural New England and

maritime Canada; coverlet-weaving projects in Appalachia; lace-making and rug-weaving projects on Native American reservations; and so on. Sympathetic volunteers have also helped groups living in refugee camps to conceptualize new products that would appeal to potential buyers. Peace Corps volunteers helped create markets for many types of textiles, including the appliqué mola blouses of the Kuna Indians in Panama (see chapter 5), handwoven rugs in Turkey, and fancy huipils in Guatemala. In the late 20th century, organizations such as Pueblo to People, 10,000 Villages, and SERVV International established fair trade shops and mail-order businesses for marketing world handcraft. In addition, there is a spate of independent cooperatives around the world, where individuals learn new ways to support their families through cloth.[51]

{opposite, above} *Felt rug-making workshop in Turkmenistan, 2008. The women are laying out colored wool for the pattern that will be felted into the rug.*

{opposite, below} *Detail of a "De Venado" (Of the Deer) huipil made at a weaving cooperative founded with the help of a Peace Corps volunteer, Tactic, Guatemala, 1993.*

Decorative hooked mat of the type made in many development projects initiated by North American philanthropists in the early 20th century. This is dated 1925.

A Masonic apron found on the American Civil War battlefield of Stones River, Tennessee, January 1863. It was evidently carried into battle because it was believed to lend protection to the bearer.

Psychological safety and comfort

In addition to our physiological need for food, shelter, and protection, we also need psychological safety and comfort. Here, too, textiles play a universal role. Because cloth provides a visual screen, it is often used as a protective shield against unwanted energies or unseen forces—even against the wrong kind of social gaze.

While any cloth can be used for psychic protection, particular textiles are believed to offer special safety. Sometimes the protection comes from past ownership or history. Christians credited their Crusade-era battle victories to the sacred textiles they carried with them into the fray, such as a banner made from part of St. Cuthbert's shroud.[52] At other times protection stems from the material, construction or embellishment of the textile. Malian bogolanfini (mud) cloth, which (as described previously) involves iron in its manufacture, was traditionally worn by hunters, pregnant or menstruating women, or others who were in danger of losing blood. The traditional 19th-century Navajo handwoven dress, the *bi'il*, was felt to protect its wearer because its organizational pattern embodied a kind of cosmic harmony and kept her in psychological balance (see chapter 5). Eastern European women embroidered small zigzag lines known as "wolves' teeth" along the edge of their shawls in order to ward off negative energies (the "evil eye"), and zigzags or rows of small triangles were worked into textiles made by hill tribe peoples of the Golden Triangle area of Southeast Asia for the same reason. In North Africa, the Middle East and Central Asia, three-dimensional protective triangles are similarly attached to garments, cradles, and even horse trappings.[53] The triangle shape is itself considered powerful, but other helpful substances such as salt or coal, or pieces of paper with Koranic verses, can be enclosed in the pouches. Any cloth inscribed with the name of Allah has traditionally been considered powerful throughout the Muslim world. An essayist noted in 1937:

> If the whole of the sura Ya Sin be written on a white muslin shirt, no bullet can penetrate it. There is a story that when… [Irani] soldiers took aim to fire upon [the leader of a troublesome border tribe], their guns would not go off. This is said to have happened repeatedly, until… [they aimed at his hand, which was easily shattered.] They declared that he [had been "magically"] protected by one of these bullet-proof shirts, and only his hands were vulnerable.[54]

The Yakan people of Basilon, Indonesia also wore shirts with Arabic calligraphy for defense against bullets.

Painted designs on Plains Native American muslin "Ghost Dance" shirts, which originated in spiritual visions, were similarly believed to offer immunity from bullets. (The Ghost Dance Society was a religious movement that arose at the end of the 19th century, when native peoples had been displaced from their lands and their way of life, and were desperately trying to survive.) Masonic aprons, too, were associated

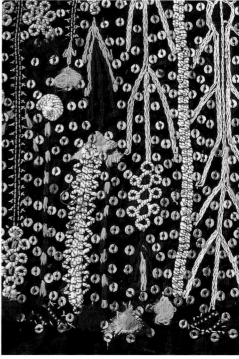

{above, left} *Embroidered protective triangular amulet of the type used in Afghanistan and Central Asia.*

{above, right} *The intricate embroidery hidden under the back hem of this woman's robe or* sana'a *from Yemen is believed to protect the wearer through its triangular amulets and sparkling sequins.*

with battlefield protection. *Freemasonry Today* tells of one of the survivors of the 1836 Battle of the Alamo in Texas who draped her dead husband's apron over herself and her child as a protective shield when she fled the ruined mission. An apron with a Masonic design was picked up on an American Civil War battlefield by Colonel Hans Heg. It had likely been dropped by a soldier who carried it into battle, feeling its watchful all-seeing eye would keep him safe. The belief in the Masonic apron's power may have gone back to its "ancestor," the Greek initiation robe. Cicero claimed that this white garment provided protection in every emergency.[55]

Other cloths with painted inscriptions essentially created protective "spells." In Thailand, men wore clothing covered with *yan* diagrams, magic squares that were believed to make them invulnerable to harm. In southern Morocco, cotton cloth is protected with a range of talismanic images applied in henna.[56]

Psychic protection is always critical in liminal periods when individuals are moving from one state to another, so protective motifs and materials are frequently found on textiles made for circumcisions, weddings, and other rites of passage. In Morocco, mirror-covered silk bands called *tenchifa* were considered especially important for nuptial chambers or in the dangerous period after birth (metal and mirrors are also considered

"THE THREADS THAT BIND"

[My seven-year-old son] approached me one morning last week, holding his blanket like it was a wounded animal… "Mom," his voice cracked. "There are more holes. Can you fix them?" I looked at the lifeless piece of fabric in his hands…careful not to pull on any of the life-bearing threads… Like a skilled surgeon, I carefully examined the patient… I felt I should have had him sign a medical release form before he left.

Kerrie Flanagan

{above, left} *Boy's hat in the form of a protective tiger which would deflect negative forces (the fierceness of the animal was thought to extend to the child), China, 1875–1911.*

{above, right} *Bamana hunter's shirt with protective/empowering amulets, Mali, 20th century.*

{opposite} *The long strands of beads that hang from this 20th-century Yoruba beaded crown shrouded the king's face when he was in a ritual trance, thus protecting onlookers from looking directly at his powerful visage.*

deflectors of the evil eye), and in Slovakia, large needles were inserted into shawls that were draped over the bed where a mother remained after childbirth. (These could also be represented by embroidered motifs that represented sharp objects.) Babies are considered particularly vulnerable to spiritual harm. The Turkmen swaddle their infants for the first forty days of life to keep them safe, and Moroccans cover their babies in protective embroidered outfits. The Chinese slipped bright tiger-shaped slippers on their babies' feet, symbolically "grounding" them with the cat's fierceness and strength, or fashioned hats with similar animals or brightly colored ornaments that would deflect the attention of spirits with evil intent. The Hmong made rooster-shaped hats for their babies. The cock or rooster heralds the arrival of the new day—the time when the forces of light overcome the darkness.[57]

Cloth provides a different type of spiritual protection in Yoruba culture. Kings are believed to hold so much power when they are in ritual trance that if one were to look them directly in the face, it might prove overwhelming (it would be akin to looking directly at the face of God). The kings wear beaded bird-topped crowns that not only proclaim their power, but also protect onlookers by shrouding their faces with pendant strings of beads.[58]

Sometimes the protection is more a matter of psychic comfort. Researchers have learned that this is unequivocally necessary to personal

{above, left} *Child interacting under his mother's pallu, Poona, India, 2008.*

{above, right} *Members of the Siddi Women Quilt Cooperative in Kendalgiri, northern Karnataka, India, in front of their workshop, 2006. Each wears a colorful sari with a pallu draped over her head.*

{opposite} *Pee-a-rat (Ute woman) with her baby in a cradleboard, c. 1899.*

well-being; those who do not experience a feeling of protection and safety when they are babies tend to fare very poorly in later life. In Western culture we are familiar with the way young children bond with their baby blankets; the cloth becomes associated with—actually seems to hold the energy of— the comfort and safety of peaceful sleep, protective parents, and perhaps even the contentment of nursing. In India, children whose mothers wear saris often form the same sort of attachments with the pallu. As explained in the wonderful book, *The Sari*, a pallu can become a physical embodiment of a mother's love—a form the child can literally take hold of:

> Most Indians have their first encounter with the sari as an infant, before the time of memory. Mothers use it as a multi-purpose nursing tool. When breast feeding they cradle the baby within it, veiling the operation from the outside world, and use the cloth to wipe the surplus milk from the baby's lips. The pallu retains this close association with the breast, as Mina observed of her son: "When he falls asleep he puts my pallu twisted around his thumb into his mouth. If I disengage my sari he starts wailing. Sometimes people give children pieces of cloth like a hankie or a scarf to get them out of the habit of their mothers' pallu. But I never have... He plays peek-a-boo with my sari... He keeps doing this until I smile back... He learnt to walk holding not my finger but my pallu."[59]

Author Mukulika Banerjee goes on to quote an Indian politician who recalled how she would clutch her mother's pallu while she was falling asleep. Her mother patiently waited until this happened, and then unwrapped the garment from her own body so that she could leave the room.[60] Interestingly, an Indian child's attachment is not with a *particular* sari, as is the case with the Western baby blanket. Rather, the child becomes attached to whichever cloth enfolds and extends from the mother's body on any given day; it functions as a literal part of her.

LEST THEY PERISH

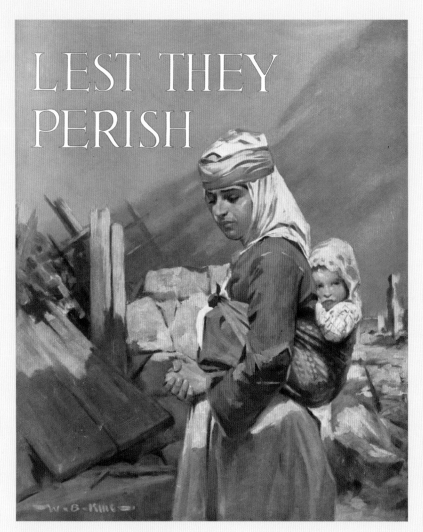

{left and below} *Across the world, mothers use cloth to tie their babies to their backs. Being tightly wrapped and close to the mother gives the child of a sense of security. The image on the left depicts Syria, Armenia, Greece or Persia, c. 1915 and below is Guangxi Province, China, 1999.*

{bottom} *These festive-looking needlecases were made for soldiers on the front during the American Civil War. They were known as "housewives" or "comfort bags" because they brought a sense of home to the embattled troops.*

In West Africa, where babies are tightly tied to the mother's back for much of the day, the concept of "backing" has come to stand for a sense of comfort, protection, and well-being. The image of mother and child tied together with cloth, according to Elisha Renne, is "projected out into the social world in broader, metaphorical ways... It is used to represent ideas about protection and support, about gratitude and obligation, and about affection." The concept is even incorporated into a Yoruba marriage-eve ritual, where the bride is symbolically "backed" by her new husband.[61]

The fact that textiles can seem to embody a feeling of comfort is poignantly demonstrated by the role that sewing kits played in the American Civil War. Soldiers were responsible for the upkeep of their own uniforms in the 19th century, and needed a portable sewing kit when they went to the front. The kits were not provided by the armed forces, but by families and charitable societies. Tellingly, these pouches outfitted with needles, thread and scissors were referred to at the time as "housewives" and "comfort bags." Their practicality must have been reassuring, but what made them especially comforting were their associations with domesticity, and home. Women were quick to provide the troops with this simple solace, and produced huge quantities of them. During the first half of 1864 alone, the western division of the Sanitary Commission (an organization akin to the Red Cross) distributed 38,393 to Union soldiers. A separate organization, the Christian Commission, distributed 500,000 through the course of the war. Similar gifts were given to Confederate soldiers. Textile-making as a way of expressing solidarity and bonding with one another will be examined in more detail in the next chapter. Here, the focus is on textiles' role in providing comfort and a kind of psychic survival.[62]

There are many contemporary examples of individuals who make textiles for people who are suffering, and thus do their bit to provide comfort. Some make quilts for children with terminal cancer or blankets for refugees fleeing natural disasters. Others make shawls for battered women or those with serious illnesses. Shawls made anonymously in conjunction with the "Prayer Shawl Ministry" are said to "wrap, enfold, comfort, cover, give solace, mother, hug, shelter, and beautify" the recipients. The feeling of other people's caring becomes embedded in these wrappers, much as they were in the comfort bags. One shawl recipient recounted this episode:

NO ORDINARY BLANKET

It was an unassuming wool blanket—red tartan plaid with fringe on each end. When new, it was starchy and its colors vivid; but after nearly twenty years of service, the colors were faded and so threadbare in places you could see right through it... My father's blanket began its distinguished career shortly after he and my mother were married. They were driving along a wooded highway when they noticed smoke rising in the distance... With no one around and no time to spare, they fought [a brushfire threatening a nearby home]... Dad said the discolorations gave the blanket "character."

A few years later, Dad passed a...[parked car where] a woman was having a baby. Dad lent a helping hand, the use of his blanket, and a ride to the hospital... [Still later, he] was the first one at the scene of a serious accident. Instinctively, he stopped and approached the mangled car where a young woman was inside, trembling and bloody. He thought of his own five daughters as he wrapped the blanket around her and comforted her. The warmth of the wool helped prevent shock from setting in and kept her calm until the ambulance arrived.

The car blanket ended its remarkable sojourn with our family one brisk December morning. A homeless man, a "regular" outside Dad's office building, asked him for some spare change. Almost as an afterthought, my father went back to his car, got the blanket from its resting place, and presented it to the man. The last time my father saw the red plaid blanket was around his shoulders.

Natalie Walker Whitlock

A few months ago, as I was pulling into the driveway, my thirteen-year-old daughter, Laura, came running out of the house towards me, crying... Something terrible had happened at school that day, and she couldn't wait for me to come home. She was wrapped in the prayer shawl. The first thing that she said through her tears was that she hoped I didn't mind that she was wearing it, but that it had made her feel better while she was waiting for me.[63]

Even the process of making such a shawl can provide comfort, both because it is good to feel one can contribute to the well-being of others, and because knitting and sewing engender a sense of calm and centeredness. This phenomenon is discussed more extensively in chapter 6, but a story told by 9/11 survivor Lisa Purdon illustrates how much textile-making can contribute to psychic survival. Purdon made a quilt in response to the World Trade Center collapse in 2001, and in describing what she went through, explained that it helped her deal with a constant bombardment of images, thoughts, and emotions. Through it, she found "containment from the chaos."

I needed to make a quilt for some reason. I think it was because it was a comfort object, I think I understood that, and suddenly I really needed something very close to the body, something intimate and that I could sit with... [The quilt] put things in perspective... I worked on it for the next...six months. It was very hard to work on...but it...really has continued to help me cope with what's happened... I use suture stitching in the quilt because it was very painful, like going through a terrible operation, a terrible injury, and trying to put it together, somehow make sense of...these things that were impossible to understand at the time.[64]

Purdon's quilt was primarily for herself, although she claims it was also important to the people around her that she finish it. The display of

{right} *"Comfort shawls" made for cancer patients and others in need of comfort by volunteers working for the "Prayer Shawl Ministry," 2005.*

{opposite} *In her 9/11 quilt, artist Jennifer Tenney Myers commemorated the attack on the Twin Towers of the World Trade Center in New York in 2001 by covering the Twin Towers with hundreds of tiny beads. It was completed in 2003.*

quilts like this helped others feel they could survive as well. Drunell Levinson, who lived within walking distance of Ground Zero, organized "September 11 Quilts," a memorial based on the model of the AIDS Memorial Names Project. Participating individuals contributed panels that were put together as a composite display, which other survivors found cathartic. Textiles clearly helped build community in this situation, and brought people together. This brings us to consideration of the social meanings of textiles, which are explored in the next chapter.

SEWING AS PSYCHIC SURVIVAL

The following is taken from political activist Ruth First's account of 117 days of confinement under the South African apartheid government. She writes of the sewn calendar she kept hidden behind the lapel of her dressing gown.

Here, with my needle and thread, I stitched one stroke for each day passed. I sewed seven upright strokes, then a horizontal stitch through them to mark a week. Every now and then I would examine the stitching and decide that the sewing was not neat enough... I'd pull the thread out and remake the calendar from the beginning. This gave me a feeling that I was pushing time on, creating days, weeks, and even months. Sometimes I surprised myself... I would wait for three days and then give myself a wonderful thrill knocking three days off the ninety.

The ties that bind

The social meanings of textiles

We are caught in an inescapable network of mutuality,
tied in a single garment of destiny.

Martin Luther King,
"Letter from a Birmingham Jail," April 16, 1963

{preceding page} *Woman threading a needle, unidentified 19th-century engraving.*

{right} *Peter Fendi,* The Poor Officer's Widow, *oil on panel, 1836.*

In chapter 1, phrases linking our mutual interconnectedness to cloth—our "interwoven lives," for example, or the "fabric of human relationships"— are listed. This chapter delves more deeply into the ways that textiles are involved in this "social fabric." It begins with a look at how textiles tie us together in our most intimate relationships, both in terms of emotional connections and sexuality. The discussion moves on to community on a broader scale, focusing on topics such as bonding through group-identified dress, shared textile-making, and textiles involved with leisure and play. The chapter ends with a look at the ways in which cloth can further cohesion in very broad groups, exemplified in stories about the sometimes surprising power of flags, and the many charitable efforts that involve textile sharing.

Family ties

As the previous chapters have intimated, many of our experiences with cloth take place in a social context. Textiles bond us to our families in varying ways. Sometimes, they "tie" individuals to the spirit of their ancestors. The Tuvan reindeer herders of Mongolia make this very literal; they use "magic" knots in their spiritual practices in order to keep themselves connected with ancestral energies. The Navajo made ties on their looms for the same purpose, and the Toraja of Sulawesi, Indonesia wove ceremonial garments featuring patterns believed to connect wearers with both the living and those who had gone before.[1] The textile connection with ancestors may be metaphoric, as in Ladakh, where the phrase "to be warp and weft" can be loosely translated as knowing one's lineage or place in the family (parental descent is known as "the warp," and the children are the weft).[2] The English phrase "cut from the same cloth" is often also used in relation to family heritage.

Families anticipating the birth of a child expend energy on amassing the appropriate baby textiles; they must lay in a supply of blankets, diapers, and clothing for a growing infant. The preparation process was particularly demanding in the era before mass production, as the recommendations in the 1838 manual *The Workwoman's Guide* make clear. Susan Hathorn, a sailing captain's wife who kept a diary of her daily activities in 1855, conformed fairly closely to these guidelines. Working almost daily, she started sewing in June for a baby born December 1.[3] In today's world, where necessities like diapers are readily available, relatives (especially grandmothers) often make one-of-a-kind blankets or quilts. Among native Hawaiians, these coverings are subsequently viewed as family treasures that hold the spirit and love of the maker. Junedale Lauwaeomakana Quinories remembers her mother grabbing the family quilts for this reason whenever there was a tidal alert; they, like the children, had to be taken to safety on higher ground.[4]

Mothers in Chinese minority cultures put inordinate attention on cloth carriers for their infants. As Yujiao Liu explained:

> Why would someone take so much time and put so much into the aesthetic design of a baby carrier, something that would wear away with frequent use, something that a baby would outgrow quickly?... Chinese minority [people do this] because they feel that the carrier is a physical symbol of the tie between mother and child. Most mothers are reluctant to give up their carriers to buyers and collectors. Under circumstances where they have to sell [them], most insist on cutting off the carrier ties to keep for themselves... I could not help but imagine that...these baby carrier ties might be the replacement for the umbilical cords we cut when our babies are born.[5]

A BABY'S LAYETTE

12–18 shirts
4–6 dozen Napkins (diapers)
4–6 bed gowns
4–6 robes
2–3 flannel shawls
1 cloak or pelisse
2–4 flannel bands
3–6 day caps
3–4 night flannels
4–8 socks
4–6 petticoats
4–8 socks
2–3 flannel caps
6–12 pinafores
3–4 day flannels
1–2 flannel cloak
1 hood

From *The Workwoman's Guide*, 1838

{below, left} *Detail of exceedingly fine tuck embroidery worked into a Miao baby carrier from Guizhou Province, China, 1950–89.*

{below, right} *Bai baby carrier, Dali, Yunnan Province, China, 2003.*

The story of the Hawaiian baby quilt reminds us that textiles often serve as family heirlooms. Cloth is portable and easily stored, so it is a possession likely to be passed down, especially because it seems to hold ancestors' energy. Sheldon Oberman tells of finding his grandfather's *tallit* (prayer shawl) many years after he had stored it away in a drawer when he was a teenager:

> In my late thirties, preparing for my own son's bar mitzvah [sic],
> I came across [it], still in the drawer, still waiting for me. As I held it,
> I smelled a faint trace of [my grandfather's] shaving soap. Then
> came a rush of memories—his whiskery face; his gentle voice; the
> softness of his shawl against my cheek when I would lean against him.
> I could see the way he wrapped the [fringe] around his fingers...
> I remember the way he would rise and rock back and forth in prayer
> and how the prayer shawl swayed with him, as if it might open and
> spread out like great white wings.[6]

Sometimes heirlooms are purposely created: textiles are made with the intention that they will become something important in a given family. Elsa Wachs asked fifty of her family members to contribute some personal item that could be sewn on the canopy she was making for her son's wedding. When asked to give a "piece of themselves," they provided objects like keys, gloves, and scarves. She also worked in items from the groom's childhood, and even pieces of the cantor's hat. That chuppa thus became a kind of family album, one with the potential to become even more meaningful over time, since it could be reused in future weddings. It was such a powerful object that others wanted similar albums for their own families, and Wachs found herself making personalized canopies for friends, even for couples who were not Jewish.[7]

Family memories are frequently embodied in textiles made with craps of everyday fabric. In the Siddi communities of India (the Siddi are a minority people, part of the African diaspora, who live south of Goa), women piece quilts from old sari scraps. Koreans sometimes make *pojagi* (wrapping cloths used to cover documents and sentimental items) from leftover fabric. In both cases, family members are reminded of those who had worn or used the textile.[8]

American scrap quilt traditions are rightfully world-renowned. Understandably, scrap quilts flourished where people were poor. This was true for the African-Americans of Gee's Bend and other southern coastal communities who stitched old overalls and leftovers from local clothing factories into bold abstract designs (their work has recently taken the worldwide art community by storm). It was true for many Native American groups who first embraced quilting in the 19th century. Mohawk quilter Doris Benedict reminisced:

In Jew Praying, *1875, Elia Efimovich Repin depicts a Russian man in a* tallit *(a traditionally patterned prayer shawl). Wearers sometimes bring the shawl up over the head, thus enclosing them in a private tent-like "house of prayer."*

TO WORK WITH LOVE

And what is it to work with love? It is to weave the cloth with threads drawn from your heart, even as if your beloved were to wear that cloth.

Kahlil Gibran

I remember as a child lying on the bed and sitting there looking at the big squares that my mom made out of my dad's coat or my grandfather's coat...it got to be a challenge to say, "That was Grandpa's and this was Mom's and that was Dad's," just from going through the patchwork as you lay there in the evening remembering who wore what and then what it looked like on them...it gave you a sense of warmth and closeness to other members of your family.[9]

Victorian "crazy" quilts incorporated fabric novelties that came from garments—pieces of dress silks, neckties, even hair ribbons. Some made great use of the silk badges that were then ubiquitous (they were printed for events ranging from fraternal meetings to Sunday School conventions to holiday parties). The badges were saved as personal mementos, and when put together into a quilt, they too functioned as family scrapbooks. The maker of one such quilt, now held in the Helen Louise Allen Textile Collection at the University of Wisconsin-Madison, remains unidentified, but we can follow her family story through the badges. Family members were apparently heavily involved in fraternal organizations, local politics, and the Methodist church. They traveled extensively through the region.[10]

The relatively new "passage quilt" is purposefully constructed from clothing left behind by a recently deceased loved one. These memorials contain everything from bath robes to evening gowns and golf shirts. They are made to help mourners get through their bereavement.[11]

When family members are far away and want to send a "piece" of themselves back home, they often choose a textile. It is lightweight and thus easy to carry or ship, but, again, the associative power of the cloth is more important than its practicality. Soldiers fighting in World Wars I and II often sent handkerchiefs or pillow covers to their wives or mothers because they could anticipate those items in use; a handkerchief sent to

Handwoven Peruvian belt made of alpaca fiber with the owner's name (Basilia Ticona Pari) and date (año de 1969) inscribed in a demanding pick-up weaving technique.

a lover might, for example, be worn close to her body. The cloth was a stand-in, an embodiment of the relationship between the individuals. The impetus for deployed soldiers to send souvenir handkerchiefs was so strong that businesses sprung up to supply them. During World War I, the French provided Allied troops with textiles marked with statements such as "Souvenir of the Great War," or "Souvenir de France." Other cloths included phrases such as "To My Dear Sweetheart."[12]

Love, sex, and friendship

Small textile gifts play many roles in furthering intimacy. Handkerchiefs were long used as love tokens or betrothal gifts. In the 16th century, when the Countess of Champagne indicated the gifts that ladies might properly accept from their suitors, she placed handkerchiefs at the top of the list. Even as recently as the early 20th century, it was customary for a Sicilian bride to send the marriage contract to her groom wrapped in a handkerchief. Among the Msinga, a Zulu people of southern Africa, it is traditional for lovers to give one another small decorative pieces of beadwork with personal messages woven in. The messages are not formed through actual words (in fact, some of the wearers may not be literate), but are embedded in the contextual interpretation of bead size, color, material, and placement. These "love letters" are typically worn as pendants, and if a man is seen with many around his neck, he is known to have many sweethearts.[13]

Intimacy also extends to friendship. Women who wanted to express their mutual regard in 19th-century Europe and America sometimes gave one another novelty handkerchiefs as well, or in the period when sewing was an everyday part of their lives, they offered handmade sewing accessories. Early in the century, friends sometimes gave maternity "pin pillows" to a mother-to-be. They inserted pins in attractive patterns, spelling out messages such as "Welcome Little Stranger" (in this pre-industrial period, pins were quite valuable, so the gift was practical as well as appealing). In 1823, Eliza Green received another sewing-related present, a needle keep, as a wedding present from her closest childhood friend. Green attached a note to the small case (it looked much like the comfort bags discussed in chapter 2), stating that she "valued it above rubies." Needlework and household tools were packaged in highly amusing forms in later decades; "trifles" such as the "Little Companion" featured in *Peterson's* magazine in January 1865 were often exchanged as gifts. "There cannot be a more appropriate or gratifying souvenir of affection [than a novelty sewing case]," noted *Ornamental Toys and How to Make Them* in 1870.[14]

Many of our most intimate relationships, of course, have a sexual component. The sexual symbolism of thread or string and some of the wedding customs that linked cloth with fecundity and sexuality have already been referenced. Red thread is equated with blood and the life force and, by extension, with human passion. Red threads appear in interesting ways in Buddhist contexts. A koan written by Chinese monk Sung-Yuan

"The Little Companion," Mrs. Jane Weaver's design for a dressed doll that incorporated a pincushion, a thread and needle holder, and a scissors' scabbard, appeared in Peterson's Magazine, *January 1865. Women often gave their friends this kind of amusing sewing novelty in the 19th century.*

{opposite, above} *Detail of an American pieced "crazy" quilt with silk souvenir badges, c. 1910.*

{opposite, below} *Detail of a crazy quilt square pieced together with rainbow-like ribbons.*

{below} *This outfit worn during a Caribbean carnival parade clearly plays up the sexuality of its wearer.*

{above, right} *Kathryn B. Gerry made this string skirt (apron), copying a prototype that is still found in vestigial form in some parts of the Balkans. The long tassels would cover a woman's pelvic area, and allude to fertility. The earliest evidence of these garments is on a Bronze Age archaeological site in Denmark, dating to the 14th century BCE.*

asks, "Why is it that even the most clear-eyed monk cannot sever the red thread of passion between his legs?" The image was literalized in early China, where courtesans wore red garters on their thighs. Rinzai Zen practitioners tie a red thread around a bride's wrist as a sign of a fruitful union and a frank acknowledgment of its sexuality. Red Thread Zen, a school started in Japan by the 14th-century master Ikkyu, went so far as to approach sexuality in a ritual manner, akin to Tantric Buddhism.[15] Even by itself, the color red stands for fertility, to the point that in many parts of the world a woman who has reached menopause is expected to forego the color and wear only somber hues.

When the color red is incorporated into fringe that sways on a woman's skirt (apron), it draws particular attention to the genital area. Elizabeth Barber argues that the string skirts found in Eastern European bridal clothing as recently as the 20th century are a continuation of a 25,000-year-old tradition. Patricia Anawalt claims the tradition can be traced all the way from the Paleolithic era to the present day.[16] Tassels and fringe hold the quality of sexual promise, even today. Amazigh brides are dressed in belts with hanging tassels, and Hopi brides carry sashes with long fringes that move gracefully and allude to life-giving rain (fecundity). Examples of sexual strings can be seen in contemporary Western culture as well: G-strings worn by exotic dancers, for example, and the tasseled "pasties" that might swing from their nipples.

The netted veils attached to women's hats in the mid-20th century also relate to string and sexual allure. These nets did not really hide the face, but cast over it a sense of mystery and drama. They were in essence like see-through lingerie, displaced to an area of the body that was not off-limits. These were related to the transparent veil of the Western bride, which was itself a modification of the ancient tradition of veiling the face with an opaque covering. In many cultures, the bride's face is not revealed to the groom until the wedding is complete, when she is available to him sexually.

I have talked about engagement rituals in which textile tools are involved in wedding negotiations. In fact, spinning activities were often part of the extended courtship process, and they carried overt sexual associations. (This makes sense when we think of the primal associations between creating thread and creating life.) Among the Dai of southwest China, a spinning-related courtship practice took place during the agricultural slack season. In the evening, young women would sit around a large bonfire just outside the village, quietly turning their spinning wheels. Groups of young men draped in red blankets would approach, playing guitars or other musical instruments as they walked around the circle. If one of them was interested in a particular woman, he would come up to her, and if the interest was reciprocated, she would take out a small stool from under her long skirt and invite him to sit down. When he did, he would draw his blanket around them both so they could talk privately. In pre-industrial Hungary, unmarried girls often spun together as they waited for boys to come and court. Legend has it that if a girl dropped her spindle while the boys were there, one of them would ask to kiss her. In Germany, the communal spinning house (also called a flax barn) expressly functioned as a courtship site on winter evenings. Boys would come to join the girls, "cheer[ing] the spinsters with song and recitations." (This reminds us that "spinster" was originally only a descriptive term, not a reference to an "old maid.") The German boys might escort the girls home, carrying their distaffs and spindles.[17]

In industrial-era America, too, the spinning wheel—or at least the young spinner—stood as a symbol of romance (implicit sexuality). Henry Wadsworth Longfellow's 1859 poem, *The Courtship of Miles Standish*, was well loved from the time of its release, but its heroine, Patricia Mullins, became a particularly important icon of the Colonial Revival movement several decades later. (It was only well after the Industrial Revolution that spinning became associated in the West with the leisure class and was regarded as a pretty or picturesque pastime.) Longfellow's portrayal of Mullins as the "May flower of Plymouth," a virtuous, thrifty, sweet, and docile woman who sang psalms while working at her wheel, completely captured the popular imagination. When she "f[ed] the ravenous spindle," according to Longfellow, she sent "electric thrills" through the body of her suitor, John Alden. It was the imagined quality of docility and calmness that resonated with Colonial Revival audiences, but Mullins's spinning was what gave her power. The thread she was spinning was likened to Alden's life and fortune.[18]

A staged photograph illustrating Henry Wadsworth Longfellow's poem "The Courtship of Miles Standish" which features the romantic tie between the characters John Alden and Patricia Mullins. It is a good example of the linkage that is often made between spinning and courtship. The image appeared in Nelle Mustain's Popular Amusements for In and Out of Doors, *1902.*

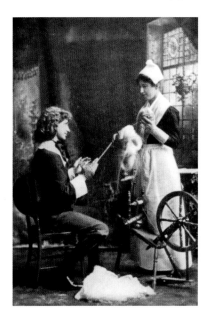

Women wave farewell to the hospital ship
Hope in Conakry, *Guinea, 1965. In his
2002 novel,* Middlesex, *Jeffrey Eugenides
envisages a scene where passengers leaving
on an ocean voyage bring balls of yarn
on deck, leaving shore-bound relatives
with the loose ends. As the ship moves out
to sea, the yarn ball runs out, literalizing
their separation.*

Creating community

Textiles also play a significant role in bringing groups of people together;
they concretize group relationships. In the Himalayan region, fabric gifts
are routinely exchanged on all social occasions, rather as flowers are
in Western culture. The Bhutanese offer cloths when they are greeting or
parting from friends, or celebrating events such as promotions. In Ladakh,
according to Monisha Ahmed, a skilled weaver must know how to distribute
her textiles so as to "tie her into the widest possible web of social relations,"
since her role is to help bind together the people of the community. In
Nagaland in northwest India, traditional cloths are now exchanged between
delegations of Christian communities. The Naga were formerly known
for their headhunting practices, and the cloths serve as a way of cementing
relationships among once-warring sub-groups.[19] In Tibet, a white scarf
or *kata* is given as an offering of good will to teachers, government officials,
or religious leaders. Katas are also exchanged among peers; they lend
a positive note to the beginning of any enterprise or relationship. In July
2006, on the occasion of the inaugural run of the train that connects China
with Tibet, each passenger arriving in Lhasa was greeted by a Tibetan
woman who placed one of these traditional textiles around his or her
neck. (The passengers were also greeted with Chinese flags, dramatically
indicating how the train was drawing Tibet further into the Chinese
orbit.) Another poignant kata story comes from a doctor who performed
an unsuccessful cataract surgery in Tibet under the aegis of the Seva
service agency in 2005. He explains that his patient, who had lost an eye,
nevertheless offered him a kata after the operation. The patient appreciated
the expended effort and the fact that many others had their sight restored.
To the doctor, the cloth now serves as a "reminder to strive for continuous
improvement."[20]

Groups offer textile gifts as expressions of communal esteem and affection. In 19th-century America, members of a particular church sometimes got together to make a "friendship" quilt for a departing minister, or for an individual who was leaving to homestead in the West. In other communities, "signature quilts" both represent and bond communities by featuring names of participating members. These could function at times almost as a local archive, and indeed have been used to track given church congregations or similar groups. Group solidarity was multiplied when, as was often the case, the finished textile was raffled off to raise money for the organization or its cause. Contemporary Native Americans use handmade quilts to bestow honor in a community context. High school graduates and star basketball players from northern Plains communities often receive a quilt (it functions as a robe that can be draped around the body) for their accomplishment, and honor quilts of this kind are given away in large numbers at funerals and other rites of passage.[21]

Henry Glassie describes a different kind of community bonding when he writes in *Turkish Traditional Art Today* (1993) of floor carpets in Anatolian mosques. The front or main section of these buildings is covered with uniform, commercially made textiles that "unify the floor, uniting the congregation that prays as one on Fridays." There is another level of meaning in the more intimate areas of the mosque, however, as locally made rugs cover the back of the floor and the balcony where women pray. The majority of these are woven in commemoration of a deceased loved one, whose name and village is inscribed in the border. They are conceived

{below, left} *Pieced star quilt made by Rae Jean Walking Eagle to honor a basketball player in her community, Brockton, Montana, U.S., 1999. (A basketball is featured in the lower right corner.)*

{below, right} *"Signature quilt" square, Louisiana, U.S., c. 1880–1900.*

{opposite, bottom left} *Palestinian woman in traditional dress at a gathering in Detroit, Michigan, U.S., 1975. Individuals who have emigrated from their homeland often wear garments that represent the community they came from, even when they are long out of date.*

{opposite, bottom right} *A Peruvian* chullu *(knitted hat) with decorative tassels and seed bead patterning distinctive to the Qero (Quechua) people of highland Peru, 1995.*

as pious donations to the mosque, and serve as a communal form of remembrance. To pray upon these textiles, Glassie says, "is to unify with the living congregation and with the congregation beyond."[22]

Some indigenous communities in Peru own and are responsible for a set of knotted strings or cords, *khipu*, which were made by their ancestors and passed on to successive generations in the same village. The khipu originally functioned as a thread-based record made by and about the town (see chapter 5 for a more detailed description). In the community of Tupicocha, they are lovingly maintained and ceremonially taken out at regular intervals. They are seen as the treasure—the "patrimony"—of the town; according to anthropologist Frank Salomon, they perpetuate age-old kinship relationships and village organization. A resident of Rapaz, another community that maintains an ancient khipu, says, "I feel my ancestors are talking to me when I look at [it]."[23]

Cloth imprinted with distinctive designs, or particular combinations or types of garments, may be used the world over semiotically to mark group identity. Many books have been written about European folk dress, for example, illustrating the distinctive styles worn in specific villages or geographical regions. These evolved differently because the villages were once relatively isolated, and individuals who lived in close proximity learned from and influenced one another. Over time, particular styles became ingrained in the community's sense of itself, to the point that when they were no longer used on a daily basis, these textiles became heritage markers for succeeding generations. The same phenomenon is evident in what are usually referred to as "ethnic" dress traditions. There were identifiable embroidery styles for each Palestinian village before World War II, for example; Bethlehem was known for its elaborate couching stitches, while Ramallah was characterized by trunk-shaped cross stitch. The Miao are so specific in their village designs that there is a saying that "if there are a hundred Miaos, there are a hundred different types of

Students at prayer in an Islamic school in Syria. The rugs that cushion their bodies are commercially manufactured.

{left} *Detail of a woven huipil from Cobán, Guatemala, 1930s. Gauzy white huipiles of this type are unique to the northern highlands (Alta Verapaz) and represent masterful backstrap weaving.*

{below, left} *The embroidery patterns on these Yao trousers show group identity and are quite distinctive, Thailand, 1986.*

{below, right} *Women and girls in the distinctive dress of the Long Horn Gejia Miao, Guangxi Province, China, 1999.*

A Sikh man wearing a turban, India, c. 2005.

costume."[24] Sometimes it is clan or ethnicity that is expressed, more than physical location. In Southeast Asia, Hmong clothing varied by clan affiliation—the Blue (sometimes translated as Green) Hmong were those who wore indigo-dyed skirts; the Redhead Hmong sported red pompoms on their hats.

The close association between garment pattern and community identity even became a problem for the indigenous Guatemalan people during the extreme political unrest of the 1980s. In order to prevent reform groups (cooperatives, leftists, etc.) from coming to power, the army began a counterinsurgency program to overcome so-called "communists." (The term was used to refer to almost anyone they wanted to contain, and the indigenous population became the primary target.) Because traditional dress (*traje*) had functioned almost like a heraldic banner that showed the local community the wearer came from, it became dangerous for individuals to appear in it in public; one might say they would essentially be "waving a red flag." "We have stopped wearing [traje] so they will not take us, so they will not kidnap and torture us," stated one refugee.[25] Under less extreme conditions, the patterns had signified a sense of belonging and community pride.

Distinctive dress also signals a sense of belonging to religious groups; sartorial symbols such as the nun's habit, monk's robe, and Sikh's turban abound worldwide. (While this book is primarily about textiles rather than forms of dress, it is in fact often the cloth that immediately stands out in these situations.) Individuals in separatist communities such as Hasidic Jews or Mennonites are also immediately recognized by their clothing, which is typically of a distinctive color as well as style. Although the dress signals distinctions such as marital status and religiosity to insiders who understand the subtle codes, outsiders typically see the believers as all dressing alike. They too are wearing red flags about their difference, to the point that their behavior is inevitably affected. A Hasidic Jew explained that their recognizable clothes cause them to function as "ambassadors" for their religion when they are in the outside world, and therefore they must always act properly in public. The garments constantly keep them tied to their community.[26]

Uniforms—outfits made of identical cloth—are given to soldiers to help shift their loyalty to the group or to schoolchildren to homogenize difference. Unifying textiles also foster a sense of belonging in groups that represent a more temporary or partial part of one's identity. We all know about the phenomenon of "team colors;" anyone who has gone to a football game and stood in the crowd of loyal fans creating a "sea" of red (or blue, or gold, etc.) cannot help being "pumped up" by the sense of solidarity. Uniform outfits can also help define one-time special occasions. The Yoruba of Nigeria celebrate weddings and commemorative events in garments made out of the same cloth (*aso ebe*)—cloth that has been specially printed for that purpose. Because everyone in attendance looks alike, the cohesion of the group is underlined (and because participants had to purchase

the cloth and have it made into garments, the honoree is shown a very high level of respect). In the West, printed T-shirts have come to express a similar kind of belonging at one-time events. The investment is not as great as with aso ebe, but when individuals put on a shirt proclaiming their participation in a family reunion or fundraising marathon, they are still expressing identification with a distinguishable group. Unifying cloth also identifies and connects individuals participating in more contentious activities, such as protest marches and demonstrations. The crowds of people wearing green to protest the apparently fraudulent elections in Iran in 2009 represent one recent example on the world stage.

{top} *Mongolia's annual three-day Naadam Festival features horse racing, athletic competitions, and general merry-making. The festivities kick off with a colorful parade, Ulaanbaatar, Mongolia, 1996.*

{above} *Football fans wear red to cheer on the University of Wisconsin "Badgers." This shot taken in 2006 captures the overwhelming feeling one gets seeing a vast crowd of sports enthusiasts wearing "team colors."*

Sharing work, forging bonds

The act of preparing a textile such as a friendship quilt is also an important way of furthering a sense of group cohesion. People bond easily with one another when they are engaged in shared work. Because textile production took so much of people's time in the pre-industrial period, this kind of experience was a significant part of daily life throughout the world. Elizabeth Barber found evidence that women in the Neolithic and early Bronze Ages worked together on textile tasks; building remains in early Europe indicate that there were inner courtyards where women and children spent their days spinning and preparing flax. Groups of women working together are also represented in classical Greek art, and large numbers of loom weights have been found in the women's sections of ancient Greek buildings, indicating that many women (probably slaves as well as wealthier householders) gathered there to spin and weave. The workplaces became community gathering spots, and as noted above, some evolved into courtship sites. There is also evidence in archaeological cloth remains from diverse areas of the world indicating that many different hands probably worked together on a single weaving. Here again, we can intuit that the proximity of shared work fostered socialization and fellowship.[27]

We can point to many more recent examples of shared fiberwork that bond communities together. Where textile tools are portable, women from a given town will often carry their equipment to a central location or to a friend's home so they can work together. They talk while they are working, and their children play together. Among the Yurok basket makers in northern California, according to Lila O'Neale:

> There was a sociable old custom of taking one's materials to the creek. Some women always worked with the same friend; others went every day to join any group of four or five. Working in the cool shade where supplies could be kept damp facilitated pattern-sharing as well as camaraderie.

{opposite} *This detail of Francesco del Cossa's* Hall of the Months *fresco illustrates a classical mythological subject—the people in the foreground represent* The Three Fates, or Moirae—*but the scene actually portrays a contemporary (1476) setting. We are reminded that large numbers of women worked together on textile-related tasks in both ancient Greece and Renaissance Europe.*

{below} *Detail of a pre-Columbian Moche-Huari-style (750–1000 CE) tapestry-woven border with figures holding double staffs. The division of space into rectangular units featuring repeated motifs is typical of this style and the orderly pre-Columbian approach to design. There is evidence that some of the larger Andean textiles were made by many individuals, working side by side. The figures on this piece may represent shamans. They echo images carved into stone at the Gateway of the Sun, Tiahuanaco (Tiwanaku).*

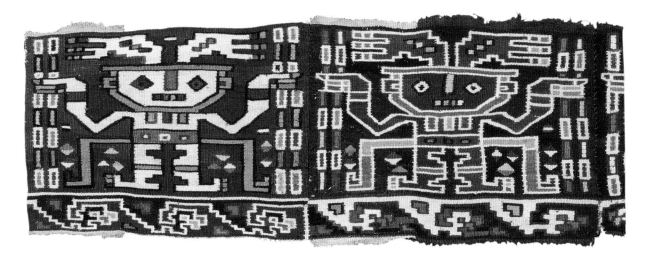

Such practices are still common among Mayan women in Mexico and Guatemala, and among Andean people, who get together with their spindles or looms.[28] It is important to note that relaxed socialization over textile tasks could include men. In Iceland, the *kvöldvaka* was a time of work and entertainment that traditionally took place in the evenings. Men would sit and card wool for the women as they spun, and all would engage in singing, storytelling, and conversation.[29]

Another moving description of communal textile production again comes from Henry Glassie. Writing about rug-weaving in an Anatolian village, he writes of a "quiet, sociable scene" in a home with a big loom:

> Talk rises and falls, work continues. A young woman is there with her baby, sitting near the loom to join in the weaver's conversations. An old gentleman...charged for the day with the care of his little granddaughter, comes and sits...in the back. [One weaver's mother] sits to one side, spinning... When their work enters a difficult passage, the weavers grow quiet, concentrating.
>
> Except at harvest when all hands are busy in the fields, a carpet is rising on the loom in every house, and when the sun is up, two women are at work. Most weaving is done by girls and ladies between the ages of 14 and 26 who form together a special collegial association and unit of affection with each neighborhood... They move fluidly in and out of each other's homes with no need to knock... They come to visit, and when they visit they sit and weave... [They] sit and tie knots and tighten the bonds between them.[30]

Not surprisingly, children who grow up in households where textile production is the norm like this invariably associate cloth with the community. They learn textile-making skills as a matter of course. Girls in pre-Columbian Andean cultures learned to spin soon after they were old enough to hold a spindle, for example, and they picked up weaving a few years later. Everyone in these communities feels ownership; even though boys may be less involved in some of the textile-making processes, it is all part of daily life. Among the Amazigh of Morocco, men do not weave, but their contribution to weaving is still recognized. They are involved in producing the wool used to make rugs; they herd the sheep, shear them, and sort and wash the fiber. They also help build the looms.[31]

The pleasure of working side by side creating textiles is equally evident in today's burgeoning craft groups. Knitters, whose work is especially portable, show up in large numbers to attend club or guild meetings, or even to cafes or shops that advertise drop-in knitting times. In 1999, instructors who organized a Knit-Out in New York City actually had to fend off would-be participants because so many had come. The resurgence of knitting engendered "In the Loop," a three-day international conference held in Britain in 2008. One of its amenities was a knitting lounge open to delegates throughout the conference so they could socialize

Frank Utpatel, The Quilting Bee, *Wisconsin, U.S., 1941. The artist's sentimental approach to the idea of women working together in the home to stitch a quilt is evident in this woodcut.*

as they worked. In the same vein, I noticed in 2009 that many of the cafes catering to knitters were staying open late to accommodate their patrons.[32]

European-based cultures developed "bees" for tasks that could profit from concerted group labor. Many of us may be familiar with the quilting bee, where a woman who had finished making a pieced or appliquéd quilt top would call together a group of community women to put in the actual quilting stitches. The bee usually entailed six to eight individuals who sat close to one another around a quilting frame and worked steadily for a number of hours. Before there were good roads, homesteaders in rural areas with severe winters on the American frontier had to wait until spring for these gatherings, and there are many references to the quilting bee as a harbinger of a more social season. When the actual quilting work was complete, the gatherings often ended with a kind of party that included husbands and other family members. A number of vernacular paintings of quilting bees celebrate the social pleasure of the event, and some specifically memorialize the moment when the party could begin.[33]

Bees for other textile tasks turned into parties too. Sadie Plant claims that many pre-industrial weaving activities involved singing, chanting, storytelling, or game playing.[34] It is certainly true that when a task is physically demanding, rhythmic motion and song help make the work easier. The people of the Hebridean islands, off the coast of Scotland, held "waulking" bees in which song was a central element. Waulking was a method of shrinking (fulling) woven woolen cloth through the application of moisture and heavy pressure (it is essentially a felting process). The women of the community would gather around a long trestle, pounding long lengths of fabric with their hands and feet. They had to work in unison and throw their full body weight into the effort, and the songs helped them keep up their energy and maintain a steady rhythm. There were separate specialists to lead the waulking, the singing, and the accompanying consecration ceremonies, and each area developed its own repertoire of anecdotes and music. Scholars consider waulking songs one of the main preservation vehicles of Celtic culture.[35]

I have been writing primarily about home-based activities, where women were most typically the fabric-makers. Men were (and are) more likely to make cloth when it is a particularly prestigious fabric or one that they themselves use. In West Africa, for example, men routinely weave the narrow "strip cloth" that is later sewn into important garments. Men are also the primary workers in professional workshops. The famed Kashmir (cashmere) shawls of early 19th-century India were woven in workshops staffed by men, for example, as were the European tapestries and luxury textiles of the 14th through 18th centuries. (Guild membership, a prerequisite for employment in many of these workshops, was often not even open to women.) The exquisite weavings and embroideries of dynastic China and Ottoman Turkey were similarly completed in court workshops, which only employed men. While these more formal settings with assigned overseers probably encouraged less socialization than domestic contexts, many of these men undoubtedly also experienced a sense of camaraderie and fellowship through their work.

Even when production was industrialized, people still worked side by side making cloth, and as the writings of the Lowell, Massachusetts "mill girls" make clear, meaningful friendships could certainly be made in those settings.[36] The noise of the equipment and the constant pressure to keep up with the machinery reduced the opportunities for sharing

WAULKING ON THE ISLE OF SKYE

Twelve or fourteen women, divided into two equal numbers, sit down on each side of a long board, ribbed lengthways, placing the cloth on it: first they begin to work it backwards and forwards with their hands, singing at the same time... When they have tired...[they use their] feet for the same purpose, and six or seven pair of naked feet are in the most violent agitation, working one against the other: as by this time they grow very earnest in their labors, the fury of the song rises; at length it arrives to such a pitch, that without breach of charity you would imagine a troop of female demoniacs to have assembled.

Thomas Pennant, 1772

This 1836 engraving, entitled Power Loom Weaving, *appeared in George Savage White's* Memoir of Samuel Slater. *The book introduced the idea of industrial production of cotton cloth to the general public. All of the individuals tending the looms are women, while the overseer is a man.*

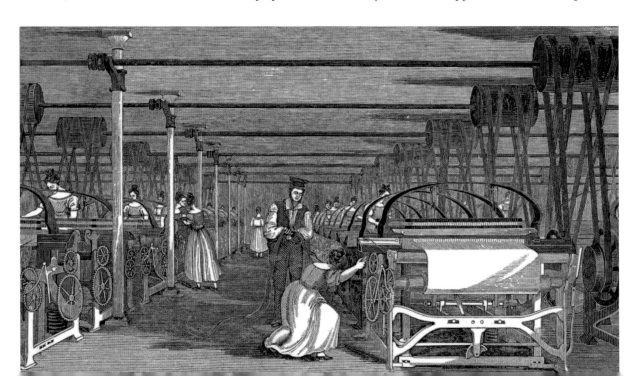

{left} Women at the Quern, and at the Luagh, with a View of Tayskir *was one of the illustrations in Thomas Pennant's* A Tour in Scotland, *which documents a waulking (fulling) "bee" on the Isle of Skye in 1772. The women are manipulating the woolen cloth with their feet, shrinking it down and making it stronger through the process. They sing as they work.*

{below} *Weaver and helper preparing cotton warp for weaving, Mali, 1960s.*

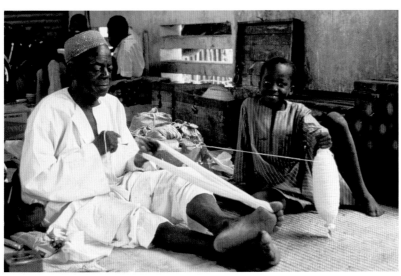

and socialization, but people usually find ways to connect with those they work with, and many photographs of mill workers from the turn of the 20th century show them posing together, either in the workplace, or at picnics or other social gatherings.

Socialization was equally salient in the work of selling textiles. (In some cultures or areas of the world, selling is considered men's work, although this is by no means universal.) In North Africa and the Middle East, rug and textile merchants have for centuries manned bazaar stalls that also functioned as social gathering places. Neighboring merchants visit with one another when business is slow, and customers are invited in for cups of tea and other refreshments. One gaily decorated carpet shop in Morocco provides musical entertainment to attract individuals who might be persuaded to come in and look at the merchandise. In other kinds of markets, salespeople ply their wares in a frenzy of competition. The crowded market in Benares, India is akin in feel to a scene from the floor of the stock exchange, as "commission boys" working for different sari

Musicians at a carpet stall in a bazaar in Rissani, Morocco, 2000.

dealers each try to be heard above the others. Women hawking embroidered *suzanis* in Turkmenistan wave their wares at passersby. In areas where markets are held in regularly rotating locations, market-going becomes a highlight of the week, not just as a source of needed income, but as an opportunity to visit with people of nearby communities and even interact with tourists.

Social bonding sometimes takes place around activities related to caring for textiles. In Homer's epic, *The Odyssey*, there is a scene where Odysseus is awakened by the cries of young women enjoying themselves as they are washing clothes in the river—they are stomping the textiles in the pools and making a lively contest of it. Community river washing is still seen today in places where there is no running water; the image of women washing clothes in the river is almost iconic for certain places, including parts of India and Latin America.

Leisure and play

To a much greater extent than we may at first realize, fibers and textiles are also part of leisure social activities, celebration, and play. Communal work can be turned into a party-like event, but when we turn to recreational pastimes, we find a wide range of other examples. Strings and cords are used to make musical instruments, and we play with ropes in tug-of-war contests and jump-rope counting games. Many sports are built around getting balls or other objects into or over nets—think of basketball, volleyball, tennis, ping pong, badminton, soccer, hockey, water polo, and lacrosse. Some of those sports "objects" involve textiles as well. Every baseball contains prescribed layers of (primarily woolen) yarn, which gives it resiliency and springiness. The cowhide cover of the ball is even today sewn together by hand, with exactly 108 stitches.[37]

{left} *Once the sail on this "desert fun car" catches the wind, the car is able to travel quickly across the sands, Turaif, Saudi Arabia, 1970.*

{below} *Piano hammers, made of dense and absorbent felt, help create the dynamic tonal quality of the instrument.*

{below, left} *Every baseball depends on fiber to make it "work." In addition to the stitches that hold the outside cowhide cover in the proper shape, the inside is filled with tightly stuffed yarn that gives it a great resilience. The specifications for American major league balls have remained largely unchanged since the 1930s.*

{bottom right} *The game of basketball is named after the textile (the net) that catches the ball as it falls through the hoop.*

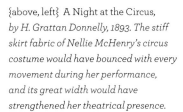

{above, left} A Night at the Circus,
by H. Grattan Donnelly, 1893. The stiff
skirt fabric of Nellie McHenry's circus
costume would have bounced with every
movement during her performance,
and its great width would have
strengthened her theatrical presence.

{above, right} Colorful hot-air balloons
rise over a snowy landscape at the 2006
balloon festival at Château-d'Oex,
Switzerland. Strong synthetic fabrics
help make this sport practical.

Other sports rely on particular fabrics too, whether it is in the
equipment, such as the covers of pool tables, or in players' uniforms. The
jockeys who race thoroughbred horses wear special "silks," and many of
today's more extreme sports rely on new fabrics that hold up to demanding
environmental conditions. Spandex, polypropylene, and other fibers have
enabled skiers, mountain climbers, and others to push themselves further
than ever before, and at the 2004 Olympics, members of Israel's judo team
hoped to increase their performance by wearing Zenash® fabric, which
contains silver ions that help regulate body temperature. In 2008, Olympic
swimmers were assisted by high-tech "supersuits" that reduced drag in
the water and increased their buoyancy.[38] Without the bright toreador's
cape, there would be no sport of bullfighting. Hot-air balloons also rely
on lightweight durable fibers, as do the racing sails mentioned in chapter 2.

Streamers, originally made of ribbon (crepe paper, initially treated
as an inexpensive fabric, was substituted in the last century),[39] were
wrapped around maypoles in northern Europe, and integrated into Morris
dancing in the British Isles. Streamers also helped transform ordinary
rooms into party spaces. They were used in early 20th-century parties as
"pulls" that might release presents or messages from a table centerpiece
(these were especially popular at wedding engagement "announcement
parties"). Cloth blindfolds are integral to games such as Blind Man's Bluff
or Pin the Tail on the Donkey, in which contestants have to cover their eyes.
Children make imaginary forts under stretched blankets, or hide under
the covers at night with a flashlight.

Dance and other performance outfits often involve some kind of expansive or mobile cloth that enhances movement. In Peru, indigenous women typically wear many-layered skirts as part of their festival attire. Blenda Femenias, who has studied contemporary embroidery practices in the Colca Valley, says that although the women complain about the heaviness of the garments, the heavy borders are in fact what give the skirts enough weight to fly out into space when the wearer is in action. They actually help the dancers keep spinning.[40]

Dress-up clothes are an integral part of play the world over. Children love to wrap themselves in grown-ups' garments, but adults also step out of their everyday, serious selves when they put on unfamiliar outfits. The "toga parties" sponsored by American college fraternities in the 1970s were infamous opportunities for revelry; students used bed sheets to turn themselves into imaginary Romans of an earlier day. At the turn of the 20th century, costuming was an accepted part of adult entertainment. Groups of friends loved to pose together as Greek maidens or people of the opposite sex, and took photographs to memorialize their happy experiences. Dress-up was even incorporated into party games, as at a "gingham party" described in 1908. Male guests were each given a piece of fabric with a different

{below, left} *Maypole dancers at the May Fete on the University of Wisconsin-Madison campus at the turn of the 20th century, U.S. The long ribbons attached to the poles wove in and out of each other in a picturesque pattern created by the participants' choreographed movements.*

{above, right} *Dancer performing the Rejang, a traditional Balinese welcoming dance, 1990s. The garments help exaggerate her body movements.*

{left} *The matador's red cape is essential to the drama of the bullring. This scene is from the final moments of a bullfight at Las Ventas Bullring, Madrid, Spain, 2008.*

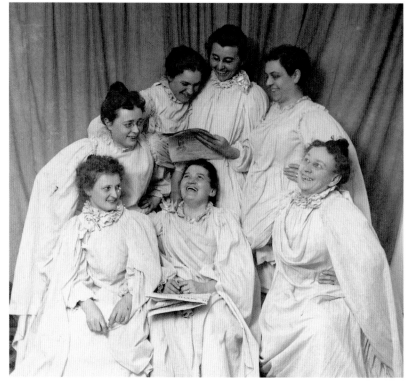

{above, left} *Photograph of a Japanese-themed party held as a church social, reproduced in Nelle Mustain's* Popular Amusements for In and Out of Doors, *1902.*

{above, right} *Annie Sievers Schildhauer photographed her friends striking "Grecian poses" in 1899.*

{opposite} *The fibers and construction of Robert Hillestad's "Meadowlark in Fiber" costume helped dancer Daniel Kubert "fly" during his performance at the 2007 season of the Meadowlark Music Festival in Nebraska, U.S. Hillestad made both an inner "suit" and a knitted outer layer that created a true feather-like effect.*

pattern, and told to look for the woman who was wearing the matching apron. They then had to hem the apron while the woman was wearing it. This slightly risqué interaction was the cause of much merriment.[41]

In our own time, carnival costuming is a central part of the social calendar for many people. Others' social lives are largely shaped by their membership in re-enactment groups built around costumed characters. Participants in the Society for Creative Anachronism, for example, dress up as imagined medieval characters. A website that serves as a clearinghouse for re-enactors of all kinds claims, "*ANY* time period you can think of is re-enacted today." Many of the groups re-enact wars of the past. These can be very specialized; there is one group that "re-lives" the 1879 Anglo-Zulu War. Increasingly common too are themed dress-up weddings, where both guests and members of the wedding party come in costume (e.g., as Renaissance maidens or Celtic heroes). These events are more informal than the standard "white wedding," and allow everyone to participate actively.[42]

Several contemporary artists produce a kind of dress-up clothing that intentionally fosters a sense of play and transformation. Robert Hillestad makes "celebration clothes" that allow individuals to access and express the most joyous part of themselves. Nick Cave's "soundsuits" (they enclose the body and do make noise) have a similar function. Cave delights in the way that people who put on these garments "rejoice in the experience." They "step outside their day-to-day existence," feeling "light within the moment."[43]

Rallying to the flag

Textiles even help much larger groups bond together. Flags, as an important case in point, both symbolize and function as tangible expressions of what are in some senses intangible entities—extensive and diverse geographic areas, political territories, and abstract concepts and beliefs. National flags become literal representatives of the national "body." This was evidenced in the U.S. by Congressional attempts to pass a constitutional amendment against flag mutilation, or army regulations against allowing a flag to become tattered. American citizens pledge allegiance to a flag first, and then to the nation for which it stands. Throughout the world, soldiers speak of willingness to die for their flags.

The emotional importance of these textiles is also clear from the huge amounts of money and attention that are invested in them. The "Star pangled Banner," the flag that inspired Francis Scott Key to write what became the U.S. national anthem in 1814, has had a place of honor in the Smithsonian Institution's National Museum of American History in Washington, D.C., since 1912. Over $18,000,000 was expended on its preservation between 1998 and 2002. More than 7 million people watched the Smithsonian conservators at work.[44]

The symbolic and emotional power that flags hold as a sign of broader group identity is also demonstrated in the American controversy about flying the Confederate flag over the South Carolina statehouse. It had first been raised over the building to commemorate the 100th anniversary of the Civil War—a decision that was made by an all-white legislature. For those men, the flag stood for regional pride. For others, it represented embedded racism, and symbolized division and hate. In protest, the National Association for the Advancement of Colored People (NAACP) organized a national boycott against South Carolina's $14 billion-a-year tourism industry in 1999. Feelings ran high; as one senator put it, "If you take that flag down, the next morning 10,000 flags just like it will be hoisted all over the state. The rebels will still yell."[45] Many conventions and business organizations complied with the boycott, costing the state millions of dollars, and the next year the legislators succumbed to pressure and agreed to remove the flag. Nevertheless, it was by no means a complete victory for the NAACP. A modified version billed as a "more traditional version of the battle flag" was still allowed to fly from a tall flagpole. Another boycott is ongoing at the time of writing in 2010, and some African-Americans have tried to introduce a flag of their own or to appropriate the Confederate flag by changing its colors to the red, green, and black of the African liberation movement.[46]

Flags that represent contested national identity have been powerful throughout the world. Examples from the 20th century include the flags representing the African National Congress (South Africa) and the Palestinian state. Both were once outlawed by the dominant political regime in their respective countries, and people who displayed them in any form were subject to punishment and reprisals. The Wiphala is a flag that represents Bolivian indigenous rights. It was dramatically displayed in May 2005 when thousands of indigenous people marched into the capital, La Paz, carrying the Wiphala and demanding nationalization of the country's natural gas resources. Under the leadership of Bolivian President Evo Morales, who is of Aymara heritage himself, this actually came to pass. The symbolic communicative message of the Wiphala is discussed in chapter 5.

There are now flags that represent an even broader global citizenship. The United Nations flag, which includes an image of the globe and symbolizes a world of peace and unity, has flown on every continent since the middle of the 20th century. In the 1970s, we started flying another textile symbolizing oneness: the Earth Flag. The NASA image of the Earth seen from space that was broadcast on television during the 1969 moon landing allowed us to see our planet—and ourselves—from a bigger, "outside" perspective. Visionary John McConnell had the image printed on a flag and put it into production. There were soon campaigns in America to get such a flag into every elementary school classroom, and while that goal was never realized, Earth Flags are often used now to celebrate ecological consciousness and ethnic diversity. Often, classes work to earn an Earth Flag in much the same way a Scout works to earn a badge. McConnell states:

> The Earth Flag is for all Earth people. Its purpose is to encourage equilibrium in nature, in social systems, and in the minds of men... Another purpose is to foster loyalty to Earth that will transcend national loyalties and differences... It tells us our most important task is to take care of our planet.[47]

An Earth Flag flying in a residential neighborhood in America, 2008.

Textile-making, charity, and community

As the discussion of comfort bags indicated, the very act of textile-making could itself be a way to express solidarity with a national or larger entity. American women made myriad types of textiles for the troops during the Civil War. Knitted socks and mittens were especially valued on the front, and women on both sides of the Mason–Dixon line provided a constant supply. Emma Le Conte, a Southerner, claimed she had become so adept at knitting that she no longer had to look at her work; she could read and knit at the same time. Catherine Edmondston noted with astonishment in her 1863 diary that Butler, the Union general occupying New Orleans, had even issued an order making "*knitting needles* Contraband of War."[48]

Women in the North also formed societies to provide for the soldiers. Most worked through the previously mentioned U.S. Sanitary Commission, which coordinated the efforts of the different societies and got the supplies through to the front on overcrowded military trains. (The provision of comfort bags was just a tiny bit of their work; for the most part they provided necessities such as bedding, clothing and bandages.) The output of just one small group is quite astonishing. When this is multiplied by the more than 10,000 active aid societies, it is clear just how remarkable this effort was. (Over time, the demands for particular societies became even more complex. As there were increasing numbers of wounded, more and more supplies

Albanian girls knitting, c. 1923. This photograph was taken by the American Red Cross so perhaps their work was for a relief effort.

OUTPUT FROM THE NORTHAMPTON, MASSACHUSETTS AID SOCIETY IN 1862

- 489 old towels and 359 new towels
- 482 sheets
- 39 pillows, 109 pillowcases
- 63 bedticks, 62 quilts, 3 blankets
- 765 shirts
- 432 pairs of socks, 230 pairs of drawers, 165 pairs of slippers, 91 pairs of mittens
- 53 double wrappers
- 53 enamelled cloth havelocks [hoods], 95 caps
- 1,205 handkerchiefs
- 1,006 rolls of bandage, 115 boxes of lint (for padding bandages); 40 compresses
- unspecified quantity of linen, cotton and woolen rag

Statistics from a clipping from the *Hampshire Gazette*, 1862 (exact date unclear), found in the Northampton, Massachusetts Historical Society.

were needed. Some had to be custom-made to meet special needs, including mittens with appropriate detailing on thumb and forefinger so the men could fire their muskets, and flannel shirts with one open sleeve for those wounded in the arm and shoulder.) Some of the items sent to the front were recycled, and they often arrived with personal messages such as, "Socks sent home in the knapsack of a dear brother who fell at Antietam," or "A pillow and sheet on which my wounded son was brought home from Cross Lanes."[49]

The same kind of solidarity and patriotism was demonstrated in other places and during other wars. New Zealand women formed aid societies two days after World War I was announced in that country. They too approached the task with fervor and sophistication, and supplied items ranging from comfort bags to hospital dressings, face cloths, and stockings. Girls as young as five knitted bandages. "Lady Liverpool" published a 193-page book with knitting patterns for other wartime needs. Socks were in particular demand: soldiers on the front reported that a single pair would last less than a fortnight. Despite the increasing presence of commercial goods, knitting campaigns were still significant during World War II. "KNIT NOW," insisted the New York-based Citizens Committee for the Army and Navy, which provided khaki yarns suitable for sweaters. The stories told by Elizabeth Erbe, who remembers "knitting all day for the soldiers" during that war, echo those of previous generations. She said knitters put their names in their completed sweaters, communicating clearly to the troops that the garments had been made with a sense of love.[50]

In more recent wars, expressions of support have been extended to the families of fallen soldiers. As a response to the conflicts in Iraq and

Afghanistan, three independent organizations arose in the U.S. with volunteers committed to supplying at least one quilt to each such family. They pledge to keep making quilts as long as soldiers are dying. The phenomenon is spreading; one of the groups, the "Home of the Brave Quilt Project," has fledgling chapters in Australia, Germany, and Britain that make textiles to honor their own war losses. These quilts too usually arrive with inscriptions of encouragement and other personal messages. The quilt-makers say that reaching out in this compassionate way gives them a sense of purpose and helps them feel part of the human family.[51]

Expressions of solidarity and community caring are of course not limited to times of war, and there are countless instances of people using textiles to help others in need. The North American efforts described are representative of a broader, worldwide phenomenon, and many of these projects are in any case global in scope. Donations of blankets and tents poured in from around the world to those displaced by the tsunami that devastated Asia in 2005. That same year, when Louisiana, Quilts, Inc. called for donations that could be distributed to New Orleans evacuees from Hurricane Katrina, they received almost 3,000 quilts and other bedding material in just over a week. Eventually the group had so many donations that it asked people to stop sending them. Blankets also started moving across the world after the 2010 earthquakes in Haiti and Chile. Similar ongoing relief efforts include "Warm-Up America," which collects 7 x 9 inch (18 x 23 centimeter) knitted sections that can be joined together into blankets donated to institutions such as battered women's shelters and group homes that serve those with AIDS; Project Linus, which delivers homemade "security blankets" to seriously ill or traumatized children (the 300 U.S. chapters have processed over 400,000 blankets), and Quilts From Caring Hands, which assembles quilts from high-contrast fabrics and donates them to visually impaired children. A particularly poignant cloth outreach project originated in my own department at the University

{above} *Detail of a quilt made by Operation Homefront Quilts and Caprock Quilters in Clovis, New Mexico, U.S., for the father of a soldier who died in Iraq in 2007.*

{below, left} *These outfits, small enough for a deceased premature infant, were made as part of a service project by a group of college students in Wisconsin, U.S.*

{below, right} *Cheerful "chemo caps" are lovingly created for people who are losing their hair as they undergo chemotherapy. They are usually made as a gesture of support—sometimes by friends, but also by anonymous strangers. This one, made in Hawaii by Bow Porter ("Bows Gallery"), features colorful fibrous "hair."*

of Wisconsin-Madison. Recognizing that parents who lost premature infants wanted to dress the babies nicely for their funeral but could not find clothes that were tiny enough, Textile and Apparel Design students drafted patterns for "micro-preemie" outfits and sewed prototypes for local hospitals. When requests for the pattern came in from other institutions, the students (and later the hospital) willingly obliged by providing it free of charge.[52]

While any object that had been made with such good intentions and sent to struggling people would likely be received with gratitude, the universality of textiles makes them particularly potent messengers in a global context. Everyone, in every culture, uses and understands cloth; everyone has kinetic experience with fabric and its comforting properties. An understanding of cloth-making processes may serve as another layer of connection. As knitting instructor Nancy Bush expressed it, "knitting is a means of binding my life together with the lives of all the knitters, men and women, who have knitted before me."[53]

In addition to sending and receiving complete textiles, individuals from different cultures may also come together by working together on the same cloth. This is not a new idea. When the city-states of Elis and Pisa were at odds with one another in ancient Greece, women helped resolve the conflict through a shared textile project. Sixteen wise representatives from each community collaboratively wove a garment for a statue of Hera, the goddess of marriage, every four years. Their joint effort symbolized a kind of intercultural marriage, and helped to untangle what had been tangled.[54]

In our shrinking world, these projects have an even more global reach. Two large textiles were part of the ceremony at the United Nations at the Millennial Peace Day in September 2000. The Cloth of Many Colors, originally envisioned by "peace troubadour" James Twyman, was described as a mile-long quilt, made from hundreds of swatches of fabric contributed by people throughout the world. The John Denver Memorial Peace Cloth similarly contained patches from around the globe. Several years later, after the 9/11 attacks on the World Trade Center in New York, Terry Helwig had a vision in which she saw people around the world tying their threads together. She initiated "The Thread Project: One World, One Cloth" that would represent the composite effort of thousands of "thread ambassadors." "Just as every thread makes a difference in the cloth," Helwig believes, "every person makes a difference in the world."[55]

Others are creating textile-related public art projects that draw attention to social and environmental concerns. Wertheim's Institute for Figuring in Los Angeles has initiated a Hyperbolic Crochet Coral Reef project that builds on Daina Taimina's crocheted model of hyperbolic space, which was mentioned in chapter 1. The Wertheim sisters elaborated on

SOME CHARITY TEXTILE PROJECTS

• Afghans for Afghans
• Binky Patrol: blankets for children and teens in need of comfort
• Blankets for Canada Society
• Chemo Caps; HappyHats and LapGhans; Kaps for Karing; Knitting Pals: chemo caps for cancer patients
• Children in Common: sewing for children in Eastern European orphanages
• Quilts 4 Cancer: given to children
• Stitches From the Heart: items for newborn infants from poor families

Listed in 2008 on the "Sewing Charity" website

Dr Taimina's techniques and developed a taxonomy of reef-life forms, including loopy "kelps," fringed "anemones," and crenelated "sea slugs." Crocheters from around the world contribute woolen elements that collectively create life-size reefs, which are being exhibited internationally. The project was designed to raise consciousness about the effects of global warming on the "world's largest organism," the Great Barrier Reef. In 2007, the International Fiber Collaborative's World Reclamation Art Project (WRAP) highlighted global dependence on oil. Founder Jennifer Marsh covered (wrapped) a long-abandoned gas station with stitched-together panels that had been contributed by more than 3,000 people from seventeen countries. Each panel commented on oil. When put together, they formed a "gigantic, fitted cozy" that enclosed the building, the gas pumps, and even the light poles. The next year Marsh invited people to submit fabric leaves to be attached to a full-size tree. Her comment echoes Helwig's idea of a greater whole. "Much as a tree is interdependent on its leaves and roots for survival," Marsh states, "societies are interdependent on the greater whole, family units, communities, and countries."[56]

I introduce these projects in this chapter in relation to textiles and community. Some of them also have to do with prayer and spiritual connection, however, and I will return to them in that context in chapter 6. First, though, we will look at more earth-bound activities. In chapter 4, I address how textiles are used in trade, and a less happy subject: the ways in which they are utilized to keep some people in positions of power over others.

The first initiative of the International Fiber Collaborative's World Reclamation Art Project (WRAP) spearheaded by Jennifer Marsh was intended to call attention to the world dependence on oil. An abandoned gas station was turned into a public art project when it was completely covered in fabric. People from seventeen countries contributed textile panels, commenting on the danger of relying on fossil fuels. These were stitched together at the New York State site in 2007.

Cloth and temporal power

Money, trade, status, and control

No Englishman other than the son and heir apparent of a knight,
or he that hath yearly revenues of £20 or is worth in goods £200, shall
wear silk in or upon his hat, cap, night cap, girdles, scabbard, hose,
shoes, or spur-leathers, upon forfeiture of £10 for every day, and
imprisonment by three months.

Articles for the execution of the Statutes of Apparell [sic]
(sumptuary law), issued May 6, 1562 by the Privy Council, Westminster, for Queen Elizabeth I

The previous chapters have shown that cloth has power—it holds energy and serves as a conduit of transformation. In addition, it holds value in a temporal, earth-bound sense, especially when it is made from materials that are difficult to obtain or it is extremely labor intensive to produce. In many cultures, textiles have literally functioned as money. Almost universally, they have been used to demonstrate and enhance status and wealth. This chapter explores the economic and political meanings of textiles, and the ways in which they have been used as a means or symbol of control and differential power.

The value of cloth

The value of a given fabric is dependent on a range of variables: the rarity and quality of the threads and other materials; the coloring agents applied to the fibers; the time spent on its production (usually related to the complexity of construction or embellishment); and sometimes the motifs it contains.

In this era, when we operate on the principle that "time is money"— i.e., we think about the hours put into a task and calculate its value as a kind of cost-benefit analysis—we can barely comprehend just how much time and human energy was once invested in every piece of cloth. There are astonishing stories of the time it would take to complete just one luxury textile: four to five weavers working steadily for at least a year for a Baroque tapestry, for example, or thirty men working for approximately nine months for a very fine Kashmir shawl. The magnificent Renaissance-era velvets were prestigious precisely because they were time-consuming to make; as three-dimensional fabrics that had an additional warp pile layer, they took more than twice as long to weave as a flat cloth.[1] These statements about production time are, in fact, only part of the story, for they usually consider only the weaving itself, which is one of the last steps in the creation of the textile. Prior to the moment when the weavers sat down to work, the fibers had to be prepared and made into thread, dyed, reeled, or wound onto bobbins, and set up on a loom. As the discussion of sericulture (silk production) in chapter 2 demonstrated, intense effort could be involved in even one of these preparatory steps. This might seem reasonable in the case of a luxury fiber such as silk, but even with a more ordinary woolen fabric, the flocks had to be attended to, the wool shorn and washed, fluffed or combed into a spinnable form, and then spun. It is important to remember (and hard to imagine) that every bit of cloth used in daily life— clothing, household linens, ships' sails, feedsacks, and so forth—involved this kind of preparation. Moreover, prior to the Renaissance, European handspinning was done on drop spindles rather than wheels, and it took about ten spinners to keep one weaver supplied. Spinning literally went on from dawn to dusk. Bette Hochberg estimates that in 14th-century Europe there were 1,700 spinners working for the textile industry in Venice; 30,000 in Florence; and 150,000 in Louvain. An equally large number of spinners in those cities probably spun yarn for domestic use.[2]

{preceding page} *Fresco detail showing the gold-ornamented clothing worn by Pope Pius II, c. 1460. The fresco is in the Piccolomini Library, Siena, Italy.*

{opposite, above} *The symbolic importance of purple in the ancient world is represented in this mosaic depicting Christ in the Sant' Apollinare Nuovo church, Ravenna, Italy.*

{opposite, below} *Detail of a Roman-era Coptic tunic dyed with what is probably an imitation Tyrian purple, Egypt, c. 200.*

Fibers that were rare or difficult to procure or process added to a fabric's value. Cloth made with gold and other precious metals is an obvious example. The process not only involved obtaining the ore, through mining or trade, but also converting it into thin strips or wire that could function in a flexible cloth. Silk was costly in part because for centuries the Chinese maintained control of its production. The textile material that was carried over the famed Silk Road—the network of trade routes that went from China to southern Europe (see below)—was exclusively finished fabric; the raw material was not allowed out of China because the government jealously guarded the secret of its manufacture. Legend has it that the monopoly was finally broken in the early 550s CE when monks operating on behalf of the Byzantine emperor Justinian I surreptitiously procured a supply of silkworm eggs in China and smuggled them back by hiding them in their canes.[3] Pashmina, the highest quality cashmere, is rare because it comes from a particular Himalayan mountain goat that only thrives at altitudes above 14,000 feet (4,500 meters). An even finer fiber from the Himalayan region comes from the Tibetan antelope (*chiru*). So many of these animals were slaughtered for their wool (*shahtoosh*) that textiles made from the fiber were banned in 1979 under the Convention of International Trade in Endangered Species.[4]

Rare coloring agents (dyestuffs) added value to cloth as well. Two dyestuffs described in chapter 2, murex and cochineal, were once highly coveted. It would be hard to overstate how vital the murex industry was in the ancient Mediterranean world, and how closely it was associated with temporal might. For many thousands of years—as long ago as the 18th century BCE according to recent discoveries—"Tyrian purple" was equated with wealth and power. ("Purple" did not always translate to a specific hue; murex actually produced a range of colors, including what we would call maroon.) One could be "born to the purple" (i.e., into the royal family) or be granted kingly power by receiving purple garments and status from the sovereign himself. In the Old Testament's Book of Esther, Ahasuerus, the King of Persia, "conferred the purple" on Mordecai in just this way. When Alexander the Great's troops captured Persia in 324 BCE, they found a vast store of purple robes in the royal treasury in Susa—a literal stockpile of power that could be manipulated by the ruler. The Greeks adopted purple for their own purposes.[5] There are many references in *The Odyssey* to women spinning "sea purple yarn." The ancient Egyptians (in the later periods) and Romans also used purple cloth as a mark of prestige. The *toga praetexa*, which featured purple stripes, could only be worn by priests and high officials in ancient Rome. Cleopatra is said to have sailed across the sea with this costly fabric—as Shakespeare imagined it in *Antony and Cleopatra*, "Purple the sails, and so perfumed that the winds were lovesick with them."[6] The "born to the purple" phrase was very suitable for imperial children of the Byzantine Empire, who were raised in rooms hung with perfumed purple drapes. Byzantine sumptuary laws regulated the sale, production, and wearing of purple, imposing severe penalties on those who disobeyed.[7]

Cochineal-dyed yarn drying on a line,
Oaxaca, Mexico, 2006.

W.W. Born claims that, to the people of the ancient world:

> Purple was the purest incarnation of red...the symbol of the sun and of
> fire... The conception...was bound up with magic, with ideas of fertility,
> of safety from demons, and of power.[8]

It was the fact that it was so difficult to extract the color, however, that really
gave purple such kingly associations. As described earlier, the mollusks
had to be lured to particular beds by the shore, and harvested at the
appropriate moment. Each animal yielded just a drop or two of color, and
an enormous number were needed for a textile of any size. Recently, one
experimenter calculated that 10,000 or more snails would be needed to dye
a garment weighing 1 kilogram (2 pounds 3 ounces) a deep purple; another
that 12,000 mollusks could produce 14 grams (5 ounces) of pure murex
dyestuff. The person who wore a purple garment had to be powerful enough
to afford such concentrated labor. (Not surprisingly, there were many "false
purple" dyes, but the counterfeit just reinforced the power of the purple.)[9]
   Red was never as rare as imperial purple, but it too had royal
associations in medieval Europe. Red shoes were always reserved for those
of power; Charlemagne wore them for his coronation in 800, as did Richard II

six hundred years later. Richard's garments were also red. After a 1467 decree by Pope Paul II replaced purple dye with scarlet, Catholic cardinals wore red. Although the color was associated with blood and was said to symbolize their willingness to die for the faith, their high position in the church hierarchy was pointedly evident in the expensive hue. Magistrates and other officials were allowed to wear red robes as well, as they represented the government. Reds were often explicitly forbidden to commoners, but it was unlikely they could afford such expensive fabric in any case. In the 15th century, a yard of scarlet cloth would cost the equivalent of one to two months of an artisan's wages.[10]

Amy Butler Greenfield recently recounted the story of the quest for "the perfect red" dye that obsessed Europeans in the 16th century. Because much of the economy was based on textile production (everyone from shepherds to nobles was involved in the business, and dozens of individuals might play a role in the production of single piece of cloth), control over dyestuffs could be a matter of life and death. Dyers' guilds, in particular, effectively functioned as secret societies that guarded their formulas and processes. "Members who violated the rule of secrecy were punished," Greenfield explains, "expelled from the guild, and—if the offense was grave—outlawed from the city." Members who compromised quality control standards faced dire consequences as well. The 1255 statutes of the dyers' guild of Lucca, Italy decreed that any member who used cheap red dyestuffs would be fined 100 lire, and might lose his right hand.[11]

Greenfield describes the intense rivalries and cut-throat competition that existed in the dye industry, and the ways cities and nations tried to corner the market on particular technologies. Cochineal, which yielded a particularly strong red, was the cause of espionage and international intrigue. When the Spanish took over the New World, they had access to this new dyestuff, and thus controlled the cochineal trade. They went so far as to keep the actual nature of the dried granules that yielded the color a secret and, well into the 16th century, other Europeans thought the insect bodies were some kind of grain or berry. Anyone who could get a store of cochineal would make a fortune—pound for pound, it was one of the most valuable goods a pirate could capture. (About 70,000 insects might be needed for a pound of dye.) Consequently, vessels carrying the material were vulnerable to attack, and cochineal piracy was a serious problem for the Spanish. Some raids yielded as much as 50,000 pounds (22,680 kilograms) of the treasured cargo.[12]

Another dramatic story involved Nicolas-Joseph Thiery de Menonville, who traveled undercover to Mexico to procure enough living cochineal to start a colony for France. After years of contending with disease and life-threatening escapades, he succeeded in covertly bringing a supply of nopal cactus and cochineal insects to the French colony of Saint-Dominique (later Haiti). The journey was horrific, beset with hurricanes and shipwrecks, and much of the material spoiled on the way. He established a small garden near Port-au-Prince, but it was not successful. Heavy rains rotted the cactus, and predatory ants went after the insects. There was also a native cochineal species that cross-bred with the Mexican specimens, ruining their effectiveness. Thiery died from a fever, and the business could not be saved. Cochineal dominated the market until about 1800, when lac, or Indian scale, was imported to Europe.[13]

The search for red dye is not the only espionage tale that centers around fiber processing and textile technologies. The Byzantines' alleged smuggling of silkworms out of China in the 6th century has already been mentioned. About 1720, Englishman John Lombe brought jealously guarded secrets about mechanical innovations in silk production from Italy to England, and then built a factory in Derby. The Italians were so incensed that they poisoned him for his treachery.[14] The British in turn jealously guarded their own knowledge of the workings of textile-producing equipment. In the late 18th century, the government not only prohibited the export of textile machines—or even diagrams of their construction—but also made it illegal for textile workers to travel. American entrepreneurs were so anxious to develop machines of their own that they offered bribes to anyone who might reproduce them. Samuel Slater, a twenty-two-year-old English apprentice, memorized the details of a device that sped up the cotton spinning process a hundredfold and, disguising himself as a farmer, sailed to America in 1789. By the next year, he had re-created the water-powered spinning frame and produced machine-made cotton yarn. His New England mill was soon churning out more yarn than local weavers could handle, and he began to nationalize distribution. Before long, a competitive American textile industry was in place. Using the same kind of tactic two decades later, Francis Cabot Lowell propelled that industry even further. He memorized the details of power looms he saw in Lancaster, England in 1810, and used them to design an improved version upon his return to the U.S. Lowell's processes and business acumen led to the creation of the first factory system—i.e., mills that incorporated various fiber processing tasks under one roof—and the creation of the first American factory town (Lowell, Massachusetts).[15]

Industrial espionage is by no means a thing of the past. Many lawsuits are filed by contemporary textile companies, claiming they are the targets of undercover agents seeking trade secrets. In 1998, for example, apparel manufacturer Johnston Industries sued its much larger competitor Milliken & Co., charging that it had stolen customer lists, product development research and, most importantly, its formula for a super-absorbent polyester fabric. One of its spies had posed as a graduate student seeking information for his thesis. In 2002, to cite another American example, John Berenson Morris was convicted of attempting to steal and transmit

TIME TABLE OF THE LOWELL MILLS,

To take effect on and after Oct. 21st, 1851.

The Standard time being that of the meridian of Lowell, as shown by the regulator clock of JOSEPH RAYNES, 43 Central Street.

	From 1st to 10th inclusive.				From 11th to 20th inclusive.				From 21st to last day of month.			
	1st Bell	2d Bell	3d Bell	Eve. Bell	1st Bell	2d Bell	3d Bell	Eve. Bell	1st Bell	2d Bell	3d Bell	Eve. Bell
January,	5.00	6.00	6.50	*7.30	5.00	6 00	6.50	*7.30	5.00	6.00	6.50	*7.30
February,	4.30	5.30	6.40	*7.30	4.30	5.30	6.25	*7.30	4.30	5.30	6.15	*7.30
March,	5.40	6.00		*7.30	5.20	5.40		*7.30	5.05	5.25		6.35
April,	4.45	5.05		6.45	4.30	4.50		6.55	4.30	4.50		7.00
May,	4 30	4.50		7.00	4.30	4.50		7.00	4.30	4.50		7 00
June,	"	"		"	"	"		"	"	"		"
July,	"	"		"	"	"		"	"	"		"
August,	"	"		"	"	"		"	"	"		"
September,	4.40	5.00		6.45	4.50	5.10		6.30	5.00	5.20		*7.30
October,	5.10	5.30		*7.30	5.20	5.40		*7.30	5.35	5.55		*7.30
November,	4.30	5.30	6.10	*7.30	4.30	5.30	6.20	*7.30	5.00	6.00	6.35	*7.30
December,	5.00	6.00	6.45	*7.30	5.00	6.00	6.50	*7.30	5.00	6 00	6.50	*7.30

* Excepting on Saturdays from Sept. 21st to March 20th inclusive, when it is rung at 20 minutes after sunset.

YARD GATES,

Will be opened at ringing of last morning bell, of meal bells, and of evening bells; and kept open Ten minutes.

MILL GATES.

Commence hoisting Mill Gates, Two minutes before commencing work.

WORK COMMENCES,

At Ten minutes after last morning bell, and at Ten minutes after bell which "rings in" from Meals.

BREAKFAST BELLS.

During March "Ring out"........at....7.30 a. m........."Ring in" at 8.05 a. m.
April 1st to Sept. 20th inclusive.....at....7 00 " " .... " " at 7.35 " "
Sept. 21st to Oct. 31st inclusive.....at....7.30 " " .... " " at 8.05 " "
Remainder of year work commences after Breakfast.

DINNER BELLS.

"Ring out"................12.30 p. m........."Ring in".... 1.05 p. m.

In all cases, the *first stroke* of the bell is considered as marking the time.

B. H. Penhallow, Printer, 28 Merrimack Street.

A time table of the Lowell Mills, Massachusetts, U.S., from 1851 indicates the long hours mid-19th century textile workers put in and reminds us that they were called into the factory with ringing bells. Similar bells were heard in pre-industrial European textile-producing towns such as Florence.

trade secret information about military fabrics from Brookwood [Textile] Companies. He was prosecuted under the Economic Espionage Act of 1996. There are also many cases of fraud in relation to present-day textile quotas.[16]

Textiles served as a currency or medium of exchange in many times and places. In the Western Zhou period in China (1027–771 BCE), one horse and one bolt of silk could be exchanged for five slaves. Through much of the Chinese dynastic period, in fact, silk could be used to purchase goods, livestock, or even government office. A yard of cloth was the principal medium of exchange in Benin by the early 16th century, and in 18th-century Madagascar, fine indigo-dyed silk cloth was worth the equivalent of six or seven slaves. Black-and-white check cloth functioned as the exchange medium on the Indonesian island of Buton well into the 20th century. In some parts of the Philippines, textiles can even today be used for transfer of property. Cloth was also used to pay ransoms. Fine French linen was considered so valuable in the late 14th century that the French king was able to send lengths of it to free his noblemen who had been captured by the Saracens during the Crusades. The ransom for the British King Richard the Lionheart was paid in wool.[17]

Citizens of many civilizations also owed fiber or cloth tribute payments to their leaders. This was true in China between 220 and 589 CE, when several different governments demanded silk as a form of tax. Set quantities were required from each family, with designated portions of household land given over to mulberry plantings to raise the worms. During the Tang dynasty (619–907) when the emperor Minghuang was fleeing from the capital, he took with him 100,000 bolts of silk that he had received as tribute payments from Sichuan, which was just one location in his vast empire. Marco Polo tells us that those who lived under Kublai (Qubilai) Khan several centuries later also had to tithe fiber or fabric. Spinners were required to send one of every ten skeins they made to the royal warehouse; weavers spent one day a week working in the royal workshop.[18]

The payments demanded by rulers in the New World were no less impressive. The Imperial Tribute Roll documented in the *Codex Mendoza* tells us that each of the millions of people who lived in the pre-conquest Aztec Empire had to give goods or services to the state up to four times a year. The cumulative annual total came to approximately 128,000 mantas (cloaks), 12,000 women's tunics or skirts, 4,400 loads of cotton, 8,000 reed mats, and 65 bags of cochineal. In addition, individuals were expected to provide the government with nearly 30,000 brightly colored feathers that were used to make the prestigious garments worn by nobles and warriors.[19] Although there were state-run textile workshops in pre-Columbian Peru, ordinary citizens also paid taxes in the form of cloth. (The authorities supplied them with the fibers and then collected the finished product.) This fabric supplied the Inkan army and was used by state officials, but there was so much of it stored in state warehouses that even after the Spanish conquerors had taken all they wanted from the floor-to-ceiling piles, one chronicler reported, "no dent was made in the pile."[20]

Clothes displaying status and wealth

In the Andes, as indeed throughout history and across the globe, powerful leaders displayed their status, power, and authority by displaying (wearing) what amounted to the wealth of the kingdom on their bodies. The finest pre-Columbian cloths, or *cumpi,* were prominently featured in every list of tribute. One type, which could also be used in ritual sacrifice, was covered with bright feathers laboriously procured from tropical birds (the same kind owed to the Aztec rulers). This fabric could only be worn by high-ranking local rulers or by permission of the Inka. It was specially made by the very finest weavers, "selected women," who were gathered in isolated temple workshops.[21]

Among the Asante and related people in Ghana, *kente* and other strip-woven cloth was part of the royal regalia. This cloth too is unnecessarily labor-intensive to produce; rather than make a wide piece of fabric, strip-weavers make separate woven bands about 6 inches (15.5 centimeters) wide, each of which includes complex pick-up patterns (patterns made by picking up individual threads one at a time by hand). These are then hand-stitched together into a composite cloth. Traditional kente was made with silk, an expensive trade good that further added to the value of the finished product. Kente was stored in special "ancestral" rooms, and left in the care of a dedicated official who was charged with maintaining the cloths and selecting them for public appearances (the king was, ideally, to appear in a different textile on each occasion). By one account, there were once 300,000 kente cloths in the Asante treasury.[22]

Textiles made with precious metals always functioned as a sign of power. Gold cloth is mentioned in the Bible; Aaron's priestly robes, according to Exodus 39, were woven with thin gold wires. The robes of Mary, consort of the 5th-century Roman emperor Honorius, were so laden with gold that when they were melted down in 1295, 40 pounds (18 kilograms) were

{below} *Detail of woven kente cloth strips, Ghana, 2005.*

{opposite} *Feather-covered cotton tunic, Chimú, Peru, 12th–15th century. The parrot and macaw feathers came from the Amazon, but were carried long distances to the desert-like Pacific coast. This is one of the reasons why garments like this were so prestigious and costly.*

Well into the 1970s, rolls or belts of feather-covered wooden platelets (tevau) were the major means of exchange on the Santa Cruz islands (part of the Solomon islands). They essentially functioned as money during traditional transactions such as marriage and the purchase of pigs or canoes. A double coil like this might contain 50,000–60,000 feathers from the scarlet honeyeater bird (Myzomela cardinalis). The value of the currency depreciated as the bright red color faded.

retrieved. About a quarter of the fabrics given to churches and popes in 8th- and 9th-century Europe included metals, and later, when fine velvets came into vogue, the clergy wore garments that mingled metals and silk pile.[23]

Often, it is a sheer abundance of costly fabric on a garment that indicates prestige. In Nigeria, "big men"—i.e., men who take up important social space, such as kings or chiefs—wear *agbadas* that are as large as 9 by 4 feet (2.75 x 1.2 meters). The Roman toga, worn only by male citizens with voting rights, functioned similarly. It was always made in proportion to the wearer's body, and during the Empire period sometimes reached dimensions of 45 square feet (nearly 5 square meters).[24] European luxury garments of the 14th to 18th centuries invariably included costly excess fabric—long, trailing sleeves and trains or conspicuous protuberances from the hips that pointedly flaunted the wearer's ability to consume, even waste, cloth. Some of the neck ruffs worn by Queen Elizabeth I were made of 25 yards (22.8 meters) of painstakingly detailed linen lace. A single yard of this fine fabric might take months to make. Although the lace was gathered into pleats that obscured the pattern when the ruff was worn, onlookers could easily "read" the encased neck as a sign of power.[25]

Powerful people might even be clothed for the next world with prodigious quantities of cloth. Hundreds of sheets of linen are typically found in unplundered tombs of ancient Egypt. These were the tombs of lesser-ranked people (few tombs of the most powerful have remained intact), and it stands to reason that those of very high status must have been supplied with an even greater quantity. Recent analysis of the material in King Tutankhamun's tomb (c. 1324 BCE) supports this idea. It included 145 loin cloths, 12 tunics, about 24 shawls, 15 sashes and 4 socks, wing-like sleeves, and even a faux leopard skin made of linen.[26] Linen at the time was considered as valuable a currency as gold or jewels,[27] so these body coverings represented a grand send-off indeed.

Rank is often directly marked on cloth that covers the body. In the West we see this through the complex code of military stripes and insignia sewn into specified places on otherwise unadorned uniforms. Such stripes are symbolic rather than extremely costly in themselves. However, we know that costly purple stripes (clavi bands) indicated rank in ancient Rome. Complex cloths denoting rank were also characteristic of imperial China. During the Qing dynasty (1644–1911), government officials wore large "rank badges" on both the front and back of their coats. These were silk, and very finely embroidered or woven with a standard set of symbols representing cosmic and temporal order. The center of each badge featured a bird or animal indicating the wearer's civil or military position. A fifth-rank civil official, for example, would sport a silver pheasant, while a third-rank military man would wear a leopard. Rank badges (sometimes known colloquially as "Mandarin squares") were produced in imperial workshops by highly skilled craftsmen.[28]

{above} *An important man, the "district head" of Katsina, Nigeria, rides a horse at the Eid-El-Fitr Big Salla celebration that marks the end of Ramadan. His high status is evidenced by his garments, which contain many yards of fine fabric.*

{left} *The vast amount of expensive fabric in this Elizabethan-era dress was a clear sign of conspicuous consumption and conspicuous waste. Having a portrait painted in such garments was also a way of demonstrating one's status to future generations. Attribution unclear (possibly Joachim von Sandrart), c. 1600.*

Woven Qing dynasty Chinese rank badge designed for the back of a surcoat, late 19th–early 20th century. The silver pheasant denoted a civil official of the fifth rank.

In much of the world, robes of honor (*khil'at* or *hil'at* in Arabic) marked status that was bestowed by a person of power. The antiquity of the practice is evident in what Jews know as the Purim story, documented in the Old Testament Book of Ruth, which was probably written in about the 1st century BCE. When the Persian king, Ahasuerus, asked his chief minister, Haman, to delineate a ceremony of honor, Haman described a ritual in which the honoree was clothed in the king's own robe. Robe bestowal also appears in 2,000-year-old Chinese literary sources and is known from medieval Iceland and other parts of Europe, but the practice was most ubiquitous in the Near East and South and Central Asia from the 9th or 10th century CE, until (in some places) the 19th century. Ottoman, Byzantine, Persian, and Mughal rulers and high officials awarded fine robes, much as Westerners awarded medals, to government and military personnel, visiting dignitaries, and ambassadors. They also used robes to reward particular activities—a strong wrestling match, a witty poem, or even a family celebration—and rulers sometimes exchanged khil'at among themselves for diplomatic purposes. A robe (usually accompanied by other items such as turbans, belts, pants, and shoes) was bestowed in a public setting (e.g., at court, on the battlefield) before an audience. Garment-giving of this sort bound donor and recipient, and was used as a way of wielding and manipulating political power. It also markedly demonstrated the might of the sovereign who bestowed it. In 9th- and 10th-century Turkey, the donor's name was usually worked right into the robe, so the wearer was publicly broadcasting his authority.[29]

Ibn Battuta, who documented ninety distinct incidents of this kind of bestowal in a narrative of his extensive travels, describes a 1332 ceremony in which he was honored by the Sultan of Delhi (this individual is said to have given out approximately 200,000 robes annually). The sultan was seated on a cushioned dais, surrounded by 100 guards and an array of officials and nobles. Ibn Battuta also received robes in Egypt, Persia, East Africa, and Constantinople. Ottoman leaders kept large stocks of robes on hand, but some events required so many of them that they had to be specially prepared. The quality of khil'at varied, and recipients could judge their current status by assessing the fineness of the gift. Sometimes the value was very explicit; the worth of the gold thread might even be sewn onto the robe on a label.[30]

The most fabulous of the robes could transfer great wealth. The same 14th-century Sultan of Delhi gave his brother-in-law a robe so encrusted with jewels that the base fabric was not even visible beneath it. When the Persian warlord 'Adud al-Dawla Fana Khusrao was invested, his robes of honor were so heavy with ornamentation that he was unable to prostrate himself on the ground.[31] Given the fact that these garments were so politically charged, it is not surprising that one finds countless stories of intrigue and betrayal associated with them. There are legends of poisoned robes used to trick a political enemy, for example, and many documented incidents of poor quality robes used as insults. It was also possible to use robes to denote dishonor. Captured enemies or individuals being disgraced might be publicly displayed in dirty or coarse garments associated with the poorest and least honorable people.

ROBES OF HONOR

The Christian Emperor was pleased with my replies and said to his sons, "Honor this man and ensure his safety." He then bestowed on me a robe of honor and ordered for me a horse with saddle and bridle, and a parasol of the kind that the ruler has carried above his head, that being a sign of protection.

The Travels of Ibn Battuta, 1325–54

Muhmud ibn Sebuktegin receives a robe of honour from the caliph al-Qadir Bi'llah in [the year] 1000, *miniature painting from the Jami' al-Tawarikh of Rashid al-Din, c. 1307.*

Jacques-Louis David, The Coronation of Napoleon, *1807 (detail). David was Napoleon's official court painter, and this work carefully documents the elaborate garments worn by Napoleon, Josephine (her garment is lined with ermine) and the officials of the church.*

In recent centuries, African leaders have pointedly offered the equivalents of robes of honor to visiting dignitaries, including American presidents. In the late 19th century, the Malagasy (Madagascar) queen bestowed two prestigious cloths on Grover Cleveland, thereby asserting her own authority and position on the international stage. When President and Mrs Clinton visited Ghana in 1998, they were wrapped by a governmental representative in fine strip-woven kente cloth. The Clintons' temporal power was recognized, but the cloth also underlined the ancestral power of the Ghanaian Asante chiefs.[32] Robing ceremonies also take place when an individual steps into an official new role, as the "mantle of office" phrase implies. Here, too, costly textiles signify power. The garments used at the coronations of the Holy Roman Empire were embroidered with gold and tens of thousands of pearls and other precious stones, and when Napoleon had himself crowned emperor in 1804, he chose a robe that alluded to those textiles. It was red velvet, worked with gold embroidery, and lined with white ermine. Today, ceremonial robes are still used for opening ceremonies in the British parliament—and in the parliaments of former colonies. Some robes (those worn by graduates or judges, for example) are now more symbolic than luxurious, but we can even find expensive fabrics in robes (*kesa*) worn by certain Buddhist priests. While most kesa are made of patchwork squares that allude to vows of poverty, some consist of precious cloth handed down from master to disciple and used in initiation ceremonies.[33]

Other textile displays

Conspicuous display of wealth and power was routinely demonstrated in textiles hung in public places. Wealthy individuals in the Middle Ages might commission a set of tapestries, for example, that could be displayed on castle walls or brought outside for a procession or encampment. These too were stockpiled as a kind of capital investment. (Philip the Good, Duke of Burgundy, had to build a new hall just to hold his tapestries, and then hire six guards to watch them constantly.) The importance of conspicuous textile display was dramatically demonstrated at the meeting that took place between King Henry VIII and Francis I in 1520 near Calais. The meeting was ostensibly held to cement a peace treaty between England and France; in effect, it was an event where rival powers might come together to reduce their enmity to a kind of spectacular drama. Henry set sail across the English Channel with nearly 3,000 horses and a retinue of more than 5,000 people, including noblemen, clergy, and servants. His ships were outfitted with magnificent fabrics, including banners and even sails made of gold cloth. The parties set up camp, creating a temporary city with elaborate pavilions. One of the main French tents was made of blue cloth adorned with golden stars to simulate the heavens. A statue of St. Michael was placed at its apex, and twelve rays (streamers) of velvet fanned out from this, each cascading down 30 feet (9 meters). More than 300 other tents in the French camp were also draped with gold, and the English structures were no less impressive. Henry not only covered his wooden pavilion with gold and silver cloth, but also lined its ceiling with costly tapestries.[34]

This "Meeting on the Field of Cloth of Gold" went on for more than two weeks, with ritual feasting, jousting, and performances. (Tournaments took place at a "Tree of Honor" that was outfitted with over 2,000 satin cherries, green damask and gold cloth leaves, and even silver fruit.) The thousands of individuals representing the two camps also tried to outdo each other in terms of their appearance. Nobles brought many elaborate garments—often constructed of gold cloth—and most changed their outfits twice a day. At the final high mass held to strengthen the peace treaty, the clergy too were resplendent in gold and red vestments made by the finest craftsmen. Even the chariots and horses were bedecked in fabulous fabric.

In the long run, this meeting proved very costly to France. The nobles essentially depleted their fortunes in order to pay for these extravagant wardrobes, and the event did not pay off politically. Despite the treaty, Henry did not honor his alliance with Francis. War broke out between the countries within two years.

Textile displays were equally impressive in the Near East. In the 17th century, experienced ambassadors to the Topkapi Palace in Istanbul could readily assess how their countries were currently favored by the Ottoman court, depending on the value of the throne cover that was selected for their visit. The palace was also outfitted with elaborate floor coverings, sometimes studded with thousands of gemstones and pearls, to the point that European ambassadors complained that they were difficult to walk on (in one case, an

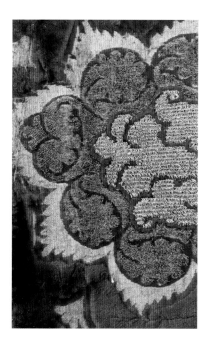

Even this small fragment of a 15th-century chasuble demonstrates how magnificent Renaissance fabrics could be. When similar textiles were used in non-ecclesiastical contexts, the fabrics were often arranged so that this large "pomegranate" motif was visible on the upper sleeve. Pile-on-pile silk velvet with gold and silver loops, Venice, Italy.

envoy lost his shoe during an audience with the sultan). Textile wealth was similarly flaunted in the Persian court. In 1599, Sir Anthony Sherley reported that the "wayes" of Isfahan were covered with velvet, satin, and gold cloth for about two English miles (3 kilometers), and the great Safavid ruler Shah 'Abbas I ceremonially rode his horse over them.[35]

These scenarios serve as extreme examples of the original "red carpet treatment," in which individuals demonstrate their public importance by literally crushing priceless textiles beneath their feet (admittedly, this has been reduced to a symbolic act today, since the red color is no longer costly). The practice of spreading textiles on the ground for triumphal processions may go back to nomadic practices in the ancient Middle East. The image appears in the Luke 19:36 description of Jesus's entry into Jerusalem: "And as he went, they spread their clothes in the way." (There is no indication that those were costly fabrics, but the symbolic meaning is unchanged.) Sometimes the red carpet treatment held associations with the glory not so much of an individual ruler, but of Islam. In Baghdad in 917, Caliph al-Muktadir laid out 22,000 pieces of fine cloth around the corridors and court to show the power of the faithful. A 1582 manuscript describing the arrival of Ibrahim Pasha at the Topkapi Palace in Istanbul alluded to Islamic symbolism in trodden cloth. "As the horses [sic] feet left the marks of their hoofs and nails on these priceless fabrics, hundreds of stars and crescents appeared...as if Heavens had honoured these satins."[36]

Cloth can be used to frame an event or set off physical space dramatically, and in medieval Europe, a "cloth of honor" was often hung

Hans Memling, Virgin and Child with Saints Catherine of Alexandria and Barbara. *The Virgin Mary is backed or framed by a "cloth of honor" in this early 1480s painting. It appears to be an expensive textile, similar to that worn by St. Catherine on the bottom left. The painting also shows the voluminous garments that fashionable women would have worn at this time, and reminds us of the importance of the color red, since that is what Mary is wearing.*

as a backdrop behind an important individual, adding ceremonial and visual weight to both the person and the occasion. This convention is frequently seen in religious paintings of the era: the Virgin, infant Jesus, and various saints are often depicted in front of expensive hangings. Cloths of honor also framed Asante kings and chiefs. When seated in state, they were positioned in front of strip-woven cloth and were covered by huge umbrellas. When moving from place to place, they were carried in palanquins of fine fabric. In ancient China, a man of power carried his mat with him when he traveled. Wherever he set it down, the place was marked as significant. Later, as off-the-ground furniture became more common in China, textiles could still transform ordinary seats into prestigious sites. Wooden chairs were draped with cloth hangings and, unsurprisingly, those of the highest quality cloth were reserved for the people of highest status. This kind of practice has parallels throughout the world. In Mongolia, respected elders and honored visitors to yurt homes were traditionally seated on the *tör*, a raised area covered with the best textiles; in Fez, Morocco, guests of honor were shown to the section of the long divan marked with a finely worked square napkin.[37]

Ikat hinggi (man's wrap garment), Sumba, Indonesia, 20th century (detail). The skull tree motif, which represents power over others, is visible between the crocodile-like animals.

Christian church buildings, too, were outfitted with elaborate textiles that demonstrated the power of the church. These ranged from curtains and wall hangings (including tapestries) to altar cloths and chalice covers. In the pre-modern period the fine fabrics made a strong impression on churchgoers, who came to equate their glory with that of the kingdom of heaven. All of this served to strengthen the influence of the institution.

The value or power of a given cloth could also come from its motifs or imagery, as was evident in the discussion of Ghost Dance shirts, Masonic aprons, and other protective fabrics in chapter 2. Images on prestige cloth typically alluded to strength and conquest. The coronation mantle of the Holy Roman Empire that Napoleon tried to imitate not only featured precious jewels, but a central image of a lion in the process of defeating a camel—a symbol of a ruler who was able to overcome his foes. Similar imagery was used for centuries on power cloths produced in the Sasanian Empire of Persia (241–654 CE). In China, it was the five-clawed dragon that represented undefeatable power. In the late dynastic period, only the emperor or members of his family could wear robes adorned with this creature. The dragon further represented the ideal leader, a kind of primordial force that united cosmic energies and embodied strength, wisdom, and benevolence.

On the Indonesian island of Sumba, important noblemen were the only people allowed to wear hinggi cloth with specific prestige images. Powerful among these were stylized "skull trees," representations of wooden structures that, in pre-colonial times, had been covered with the skulls of captured enemies and placed prominently in the center of the village. The heads were believed to hold a life essence that ensured fertility and prosperity for the community, and while headhunting practices have long been outlawed, the image of the skull tree maintains its power.

Mattibelle Gittinger tells us that the trees often were paired with male figures that probably represented slaves who had served the nobility—served to the point that they could be killed at the nobleman's funeral.[38]

Non-representational motifs sometimes held power simply because they were associated with those in authority. Among the Aztecs, for example, rulers wore robes with a special tie-dye design that communicated both privilege and ancestral heritage.[39] In other cases, motifs were adopted from foreign cultures that were perceived to be especially powerful; by using the same symbols, that mightiness could in effect be transferred and absorbed. Designs (and techniques) from Indian *patola* (double-ikat) cloth, for example, became the foundation of prestige cloth used in Indonesia. Patola had been brought to Indonesia by European traders in the 1500s, and was embraced there as an almost magical commodity. Some patola patterns were limited to Indonesian royalty and thereafter evoked royal privilege. They were treated as sacred heirlooms. A ruler's ability to control this valuable material resource became a sign of his power. In the case of the Toraja people of Sulawesi, a ruler who lost control of his patola cloth or allowed it to deteriorate was seen as someone who no longer had spiritual efficacy.[40]

People under colonial rule often acknowledged and appropriated the power of their colonizers by incorporating their imagery into their own indigenous textiles. The Sumbanese hinggi also included horses as power images. Horses could be almost deified as part of animal sacrifice, but in addition they were closely associated with the might of colonial armies, which were later honored in Sumba in annual mock cavalry battles. The Fante Asafo people of Ghana incorporated elements of British naval flags into banners they made for their own military companies. (The practice seems to have been adopted in the 17th century, soon after contact with Europeans.) Alluding to the power and might of the company, Asafo flags typically illustrate local proverbs but use European images such as the Union Jack (sometimes still included even after Ghanaian independence)

{below, left} *Detail of patola sari fabric, Patan, Gujarat, India, 1900–40. Patola is made using a double-ikat technique which is difficult to master. The cloth was so treasured in Indonesia that it took on almost sacred status there.*

{below, right} *Fante Asafo flag featuring the "Union Jack" (British flag) and a fierce, all-powerful mythic bird, Ghana, probably pre-1957.*

and heraldic motifs such as multi-headed creatures or confronting lions wearing European-style crowns. The military companies were organized for defense, but also functioned as male social organizations. Each group flew its flag at activities ranging from festivals to the commissioning of shrines or even funerals.[41]

Colonial-era rulers were themselves represented. Sumbanese ikats of the late 19th and early 20th centuries featured the Dutch Queen Wilhelmina, for example, and Nigerian prints often feature the British King George V and Queen Mary. Their likenesses were first introduced on stenciled *adire* fabric in 1935 in response to the monarchs' silver anniversary, but this so-called "jubilee cloth" is still popular as a power cloth today. Another, more three-dimensional, African textile relates equally directly to colonial authority. As illustrated in *Beads, Body and Soul: Art and Light in the Yoruba Universe*, beaded headdresses worn by Yoruba obas (kings) sometimes took the form of the curly white wigs worn by European kings and judges.[42]

World trade and politics

Because of their economic value, textiles have deeply affected the course of world trade and the history of nations and cultures. Cloth literally functioned as the backbone of many national and global economies. We know that silk trade was important to the Chinese from a very ancient time; strands of Chinese silk have been identified in the hair of an Egyptian mummy dating from 1000 BCE, in fact, and the presence of an embroidered silk saddle cloth in a tomb from southern Siberia, *c.* 300 BCE demonstrates that silk was already being exported to Central Asia.[43] Nothing is known about trade networks of great antiquity, although it is to be hoped that future scholarship will bring them to light. However, a great deal is known about the trade that passed over the Silk Road, which was well established by 200 BCE. (This "road" was actually a network or series of land and sea routes that together traversed over 5,000 miles, and many commodities other than silk were transported, including gold, ivory, paper, spices, and plants.) The trade route also served as a conduit for the exchange of beliefs and ideas. Notably, Buddhism spread from India to China across Central Asia. The Eastern Han Emperor Ming is thought to have first sent a representative to India to discover more about the Buddhist faith in the first century BCE, and soon monks, missionaries, and pilgrims routinely traveled with the trade caravans, bringing Buddhist scriptures, art, and practices along with them. The new religion took hold gradually. Christian and Near Eastern beliefs moved eastward across the world as well. When the Roman church outlawed the Nestorian Christian sect in 432, for example, some of its followers traveled as far as China, setting up churches along the way. Musicians also traversed the route in both directions, as did craftsmen bringing ceramics and metal-working technologies.[44]

Since trade is always a two-way exchange, it is not surprising that Chinese textiles were themselves influenced by the Central Asian cloth that made its way back along these same routes. The Sasanian pearl rondel motif appeared in China on sandstone carvings from the 5th century CE, and by the Tang dynasty (619–907), these motifs and a new twill weft pattern technique were integrated into Chinese silks. It is no exaggeration to state that the silk trade was directly responsible for the cross-fertilization of the art, knowledge, and cultures of Europe, the Near East, India, and China.[45]

The Silk Road fell into disuse by the 15th century. Many factors contributed to this, including the advance of Islam across Central Asia, the encroachment of the Gobi Desert into some of the settlements along the route, and the development of new sea routes. However, textiles were still central to world trade, and once again textile exchange led to new forms of cultural interface. Chinese silk made its way to South America, for example, where it was traded for silver. Much of the actual exchange of these goods took place in the Philippines, which, like South America, was under Spanish control. Textiles that were made in China, but shipped to Spain via Manila, were sometimes known in the mid-19th century as Manila shawls. When they were revived in the early 20th century, they were typically called "Spanish shawls."[46]

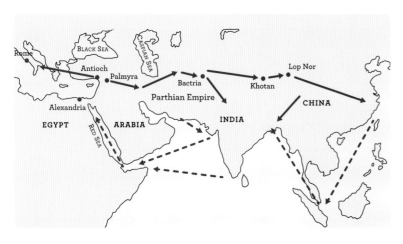

Schematic map of the "Silk Road," a series of interconnecting land and sea routes that carried cloth and other commodities—as well as ideas—between China and Europe. Individual traders did not usually traverse the full length of the route: rather, goods were transferred from one caravan to another, changing hands many times along the way. The Silk Road functioned from c. 1000 BCE to 1400 CE.

The global textile trade led to far-reaching changes in people's lives. The story of just one type of textile—chintz, or printed cotton—demonstrates the point. Now, when cotton prints are relatively inexpensive and taken for granted, it is hard to imagine that they were once such valuable commodities that they affected world events, but this was certainly the case. The people of India had early on mastered the art of weaving their native cotton, and developed techniques to apply colorfast patterns to its surface. Their cloth had an international reputation—even the ancient Greeks praised it highly—but cotton trade was not highly developed until the 16th century, when ships were regularly navigating the globe. Then, there was a particularly strong demand in Asia for Indian printed cloth. ("Chintz" was derived from the Indian *chitta*, meaning "spotted cloth;" it originally referred to any Indian cotton with a pattern or design.) Indian printers tailored their work for their different markets; designs made for the Japanese, for example, conformed to the Japanese aesthetic, while different-looking fabrics were made for the Burmese or Indonesians. As with the patola and other woven fabrics brought to Indonesia from India, the prints too became imbued with an aura of sacredness and served as a medium of exchange. The Mejprat people of Irian Barat (now New Guinea) sometimes used chintz to buy favor. One might loan the printed cotton for credit at more than 100 per cent interest, moreover, or even atone for a crime by giving enough of it to the wronged party.[47]

When Europeans became aware of the huge Asian appetite for Indian chintz, they quickly tried to get in on the market. Portuguese entrepreneurs arrived in India in 1498, setting up a trading company that soon controlled much of the sea traffic from that country. The Dutch and English arrived in the next century, establishing their own East India companies, and the French, Persians, Chinese, and Japanese later entered the fray. It was the British who eventually came to dominate the cotton trade, and this led to their eventual domination of India, as they took over political control and became an imperial power.[48]

Originally, there was not a huge European demand for chintz; rather, European traders brought their own goods—primarily metals—to India, exchanged them for cotton, and then shipped the cloth to the East Indies, where there was little interest in European goods. The cotton was in turn exchanged for spices. This was known as a "trade triangle" (also the

{above, left} *Palampore (bed cover or wall hanging), Coromandel Coast, India, c. 1775. The type of flowering tree motif that fills the central field of this textile originated in India, but was adopted by Europeans. Indian printmakers consistently adapted their work to fit their market, and by this point in time were following pattern modifications sent to them from French designers.*

{above, right} *Cotton chintz imported from India was made into this woman's two-piece gown worn by Ann Van Rensselaer in the Albany, New York area, c. 1790. (The textile was made earlier, and the fact that it was still fashionable when the gown was constructed attests to the appeal of chintz.)*

"triangle trade").[49] In time, however, Europeans themselves became enamored with the bright printed cottons—so much so that chintz eventually became a virtual obsession. One fabric that could be afforded only by the lucky few was the large *palampore*, which functioned as a bedcover, but could also be hung on the wall. Palampores were first mentioned in the records of the British East India Company in 1614. By the 18th century, they were such an important part of the European visual landscape that their flowering tree designs appeared in embroideries and dominated many non-textile media.[50]

The craze for printed cottons also extended to clothing, and here, the fact that the cloth was colorfast and washable added to its appeal (nothing like it was yet produced in Europe in the early 1700s). The demand was great enough that governments perceived the chintz trade as a financial threat to their own industries. French and later English authorities enacted laws prohibiting its use. It became so dangerous to wear Indian chintz garments on the streets of France that women often carried their cotton gowns with them to parties and changed into them once they were safe from public view. If they were caught, the garments would be confiscated, and wearers might be fined or punished. One account described the public burning of 800 Indian cotton garments. Eventually, European craftsmen started to make their own printed cottons. They adopted some aspects of the Indian process, but found other, speedier ways to get some of the same effects. European prints did not typically include hand-painted elements or use resist techniques. When printed fabrics came from European workshops, they were of course looked upon quite favorably by local governments, and were thus promoted heavily. The demand for imported Indian cottons fell dramatically. (This was not the first time that governments had passed sumptuary laws to try to protect their own textile interests. In order to preserve its wool industry in the 17th century, for example, Britain passed the 1667 British Flannel Act, which required everyone to wear wool at least part of the year, and corpses to be buried in wool.)[51]

There were a number of trade triangles revolving around textiles that were played out on the world stage in the 18th century. Several involved China. In one case, the British brought cloth to the native people of the Pacific Northwest of North America and exchanged it for furs (mostly sea otter pelts), which were then brought to China. There they picked up tea and sometimes silk, both of which were in high demand in London. Another had much more devastating social effects for the Chinese. After the British East India Company gained control over the opium-growing districts of India, it helped to create a new (artificial) demand for opium in China, first through illegal smuggling and later by forced imports. By the end of the century, the number of Chinese addicted to opium had grown to the point that the Company was importing over 2,000 chests of the drug a year. In exchange for the opium, Chinese silk textiles were brought back to Europe.[52]

The triangle trade that is perhaps best known in the West was the one that involved trafficking in human beings. Here, too, cloth played a central

role. Starting in about 1700, European ships sailed to
the west coast of Africa with cargoes of cotton fabric
(originally the cotton came from India, but later
from British mills), firearms, and liquor. The cloth
was sold to slave traders who in exchange captured
individuals, loaded them on ships, and took them
across the sea to provide cheap plantation labor
in the Americas. Once emptied of their human
cargo, the ships returned to Europe loaded with the
products of those plantations—rum, sugar, tobacco,
and, ironically, eventually cotton.

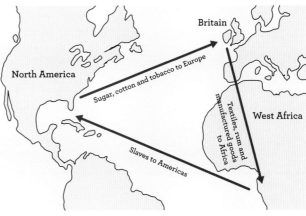

A schematic of the slave trade triangle.
This system of exchange began about 1700.

   Horrible as this trade triangle was, it was not
the only instance in which cotton was implicated in
the subjugation of African-Americans in the U.S. Cotton cultivation
can ultimately be said to be responsible for many of the racial wounds
and inequities that exist in the U.S. today. The slave trade had greatly
diminished by the late 18th century, but it was quickly reinvigorated with
the invention of the cotton gin, the machine that separated cotton seeds
from their fibrous seed pods or bolls. Almost overnight, the amount of
cotton that could be processed in a day increased about fifty-fold. In 1792,
prior to the invention of the gin, the U.S. was exporting about 140,000
pounds (63,500 kilograms) of cotton. Two years later, this figure increased
to half a million pounds. By 1796 it was 6 million pounds a year; by 1800, it
was nearly 18 million, and by 1820, close to 128 million. More and more land
was planted in cotton, and since someone had to cultivate, pick, and process
all of that extra material, the demand for slaves increased concomitantly.
(The speed of production also made it more cost-effective to keep a slave.
Before the gin was in use, it took up to sixteen months of a single slave's
dedicated labor to separate a 500 pound (227 kilogram) cotton bale,
and the cost of feeding and clothing a slave for that length of time had cut
deeply into slave owner profits.) It was the new ability to process cotton
quickly that made slavery vital to the economy of the southern states.

   Historian Margaret Washington remarked that for African-Americans,
the cotton gin represented the "antithesis of progress." The first federal
census of 1790 counted 697,897 slaves, but by 1810, the count had risen to
1.2 million—a 70 per cent increase in a twenty-year period. Before the gin was
invented, the South had agreed to stop importing slaves, but in anticipation
of this cessation, slave traders brought in even more individuals—39,000
between 1801 and 1808. (Others were smuggled in even after the trade was
officially made illegal, often through Spanish territories in Florida.) Moreover,
as the cotton economy spread, slavery was pushed deeper into the frontier as
new cotton estates, often run by the sons of the original plantation owners,
were set up in places such as Alabama. This expansion led to a further
breakup of slave families, as relocating owners frequently took male slaves
with them, but left women and children behind. (It almost led to a breakup
of the U.S. itself, as many Northerners—"free soilers"—objected to this

USE IT UP – WEAR IT OUT–
MAKE IT DO!

OUR LABOR AND OUR GOODS ARE FIGHTING

{top} *Slaves picking cotton, engraving by unidentified artist, c. 1850.*

{above} *This American World War II poster urged the public to make do with old clothing so as to save the supply of textiles for wartime use. It reminds us that cloth does wear out, and we cannot take it for granted. (On their concomitant posters, the British featured "Mrs. Sew-and-Sew.")*

expansion of slavery, and the disagreements helped precipitate the Civil War.) Cotton processing was, furthermore, particularly onerous work. Not only was it backbreaking, but also those who worked in the cotton fields could always be observed by an overseer, since—especially compared to tobacco—cotton didn't grow very tall. This meant less autonomy for the slaves, and more "gang style" labor management. For slaves, the rise of "king cotton" led to what Washington calls "a situation of despair."[53]

For slave owners who benefited from the slave economy, cotton stood as a symbol of prosperity. Scenes of cotton cultivation dominate the more than 126 images of slavery that were depicted on currency from the southern states and later the Confederacy. The bills were issued by banks and state governments expressly to promote the slave labor system. They were at their peak in the late 1850s, during the height of anti-slavery sentiment. One image was used on twenty-one different currencies.[54]

The availability of cheap cotton after the invention of the gin also had ramifications for others around the globe. Cotton was soon replacing linen, thus throwing linen spinners and weavers out of work, and it made sharp inroads into the wool trade as well.[55]

Cotton remained a strategic commodity during the American Civil War. Without it, the South had little to stand on economically, so Northerners did everything they could to destroy the crop. They established a naval blockade of Southern ports to keep cotton from being exported, even though the action cost the Union the support of the British, whose own industry was dependent on a steady supply of the raw material. Union officers stationed in the South were instructed to confiscate cotton when they could, and Confederates did everything possible to prevent them from doing so. Officers went so far as to destroy their own cotton crop, rather than let the Northerners get their hands on it, even though houses were sometimes inadvertently consumed with the burning bales. Cotton became so valuable in this period that Union soldiers "dreamed of adding a bale of cotton to their monthly pay."[56]

The shortages of all kinds of textiles that were felt during the Civil War remind us again of the role cloth plays in human survival. Soldiers needed cloth for tents, blankets, and protective clothing on the battlefield. Fabric was also needed in hospitals, where the ever-increasing number of wounded meant a growing demand for bedding and bandage material. Existing textile mills were forced to divert their usual operations to meet the soldiers' needs, so there was little cloth made for civilian use, especially in the South. Out of necessity, individuals "made do"—fashioning shoes from a canvas sail from a war-wrecked vessel, for example, or cutting up household sofa pillows to make warm shirts. This story of making do and inventive re-use was repeated during many wars, of course, when usual supplies became unattainable.[57]

Textile industries: fortunes and failures

The antebellum South was not the only economy that was dependent on textile production and then devastated by a loss of the industry. In the U.S. alone this story repeated itself again and again. New England, which had been the first center of American industrial production, lost its mills to the southern states at the beginning of the 20th century owing to cheaper labor costs; more than 100,000 northern textile workers were put out of work in a single decade as operations were moved south. About a century later, those southern mills were themselves closed as operations were moved to China, resulting in a loss of more than 300,000 jobs. By 2007, the American Manufacturing Trade Action Coalition stated that the U.S. textile and apparel-manufacturing industry as a whole had lost more than one million jobs since 1994, the year the North American Free Trade Agreement was

The women who work on production lines in Chinese textile factories are usually less than 25 years old. This factory is in Yixing city, in the Jiangsu Special Development Zone where clothes are made for Western companies. The photograph was taken in 2006.

Giovanni Battista Moroni, Il Tagliapanni
(The Tailor), *c. 1570. The Italian tradesman
in this painting is himself dressed in
fashionable clothing, including voluminous
"pumpkin breeches" and a doublet made
with slashed fabric. Cloth with so many
little slits would be inherently fragile,
which made it another sign of conspicuous
consumption. Moroni has rendered the
cloth in great detail, reminding us how
much attention the contemporary audience
paid to textiles.*

implemented. Trade agreements and globalization practices have
similarly affected textile manufacturing companies throughout the world.
China is not the problem in itself—in 1996, in fact, the *Philadelphia Inquirer*
reported that China was losing its own manufacturing jobs to countries
in Southeast Asia with even lower production costs—but many Chinese
cities have truly evolved into 21st-century textile towns. Datang, for
example, specializes in socks, producing about 9 billion pairs a year.
Shenzou specializes in neckties; Huzhou in sweaters; and Ningbo in other
sorts of knitwear. Ironically, due to the worldwide recession that began in
2008, many Chinese factories no longer have enough orders, so once again,
large numbers of workers are losing their jobs.[58]

The pattern of entire towns given over to textile production also
existed in pre-industrial Europe. To understand how deeply entwined these
economies were with the development of European culture, one might
point to the city of Florence, which in 1425 had a population of 60,000, at

least a third of whom were engaged in the textile trade. Most of the patrons of the art for which the city was famous had made their fortunes in textiles (they consequently favored detailed renderings of their beautiful fabrics when they posed for portraits). The fortunes of entire countries often depended on a single industry in the pre-modern period. In the 17th century, Thomas Wentworth, who was sent to Ireland as Lord Deputy by King Charles I, established the linen industry, which subsequently became integral to Irish identity. He brought master spinners and weavers from France and Holland, and introduced a treadle-flyer spinning wheel and new varieties of flax seed. By the end of the 18th century the Irish were exporting 25 million yards (over 22 million meters) of linen a year.[59] The effect of this kind of specialization was not always positive. If the demand for the particular product made in a given town was suddenly cut off, the impact could be disastrous. Severe displacement of a textile economy occurred in the late 18th century in Lyons, France when the bottom temporarily fell out of the worldwide silk market. While only about 40,000 people—about a quarter of the population—were said to be directly involved in the production of silk, the entire city was nearly paralyzed, since auxiliary businesses were affected as well. A similar problem befell the needleworkers of Marseilles, France who produced luxury textiles in the form of dimensional whitework that was displayed on beds in refined homes. Between 5,000 and 6,000 women were employed in the business in the 18th century, and their products were exported throughout Europe and the colonies. The British developed a way to imitate the effect of Marseilles embroidery on a loom, and their far cheaper textiles cut severely into the hand-worked market. Even today, the designation of a "Marseilles [bed] spread" can be confusing; it can refer to either the handmade variety or the manufactured version.[60]

Textile towns, and by extension sometimes national economies, were also deeply impacted by political and religious conflicts. When the Christians drove the Muslims out of Spain at the end of the 15th century, the skilled textile labor force that had supplied luxury textiles to Europe and the Near East for centuries was devastated. The Spanish textile trade never recovered. In the 16th century, it was Protestant textile workers—notably, lace-makers—who were driven out of Flanders. After a bloody massacre in 1572, Huguenots began to flee across the English Channel, depleting the workforce of that industry. There was a temporary reprieve in 1598 with the passage of the Edict of Nantes, which granted Protestants safety in France. However, Louis XIV rescinded the edict in 1685, resulting in another, even larger wave of refugees. France lost 500,000 citizens, many of whom were accomplished textile-makers. When they moved across the continent, they took their trade secrets with them.[61]

It is ironic that Louis XIV was partly responsible for this exodus, because in collaboration with his finance minister, Jean-Baptise Colbert, he had made a conscious decision to create a strong national textile economy in France. They established state-run textile workshops (silk and tapestry

{left} *A needle lace square medallion with a figure from classical mythology, Europe, 1870–1930. It is worked in a combination of rosepoint techniques.*

{below, left} *Detail of apparel fabric, Florence, Italy, 1620s. The raised velvet motifs are worked with several shades of purple, which were once set off against a silver-thread background. The silver must have been made of fine foil, since most of it is worn away.*

{below} *The exquisite silk brocade fabric in this pair of 18th-century shoes was probably produced in a French workshop.*

{bottom} *The spotted raised areas behind the flowers in this mid-18th-century apparel fabric are part of the complex brocade pattern.*

In this 1813 portrait, Marguerite-Charlotte David is posing in a fashionable satin Empire-style dress and is draped with a Kashmir shawl. Shawls were so much the rage in early 19th-century Europe that women took "draping lessons" to learn how to wear them. Painting by Jacques-Louis David.

weaving, embroidery, lace-making, and ribbon-making) in the 17th century, going so far as to "raid" other nations for their best workers. Textiles made in foreign countries were forbidden to French citizens, or at least severely taxed. In addition, the King kept the demand for French fabrics very high by pressuring his nobles to come and live at his new palace complex, Versailles. They were required to appear regularly there in formal court dress, and were literally forced to spend their fortunes on expensive fabrics—produced, of course, in French workshops.[62]

A few centuries later, the economies of towns built around the production of Kashmir and Paisley shawls were subject to a boom-and-bust phenomenon created by the vagaries of the very fashion industry that Louis XIV helped create. Kashmir (cashmere) shawls, which were made of the lovely soft hair of the pashmina goat discussed earlier in this chapter, functioned in India as prestige garments for male royalty (they were sometimes given as robes of honor in the Mughal period). When Napoleon's officers brought several of these intricate twill-tapestry shawls to Paris at the end of the 18th century, they took European society by storm. Napoleon's

One of the reasons these Indian (Kashmir) shawls were so expensive is that they were worked in a twill-tapestry weave and included individually pieced sections, as seen here in the multicolored border and the white outline of the curvilinear motifs. Indian workshops relying on labor-intensive techniques had a hard time competing with European workshops that made similar-looking shawls on Jacquard looms, 19th century.

wife Josephine owned hundreds, which represented a veritable fortune—these were the very kinds of shawls that took months to complete. Despite their cost, Kashmir shawls became the "must-have" fashion accessory in the early 19th century. Demand soon exceeded the supply, even though there were about 66,000 thousand shawl looms operating in the Kashmir region in the 1850s, and perhaps another 80,000 workers doing related tasks such as spinning, darning, washing, dyeing, and embroidering. The price of the already costly items kept going up.[63]

As a response to the insatiable desire for these Indian textiles, Europeans started producing "imitation" Kashmir shawls of their own. (This story indeed repeats the trajectory of printed cottons and Marseilles bedspreads.) Unable to import the goats that produced the supremely soft fiber of the Indian originals successfully, Europeans made their shawls with a combination of wool and silk. Unwilling to copy the labor-intensive Indian weaving methods, they sped up production by first using drawlooms and later creating patterns with the new and much faster Jacquard power looms. The European-made shawls have come to be generically known as "Paisleys," since the Scottish town of Paisley was the dominant production center. Paisley-type shawls coexisted with, but soon supplanted, the Kashmir weavings. (By the 20th century, the Paisley name became so associated with Indian-like patterns that people began to confuse Indian and European-made shawls, referring to them all as "Paisleys.")

Due to changes in fashion and displacements resulting from the Franco–Prussian War, the bottom fell out of the market for both kinds of shawls in the 1870s. The economies in both Paisley and Kashmir were ruined. Paisley workers kept trying to improve their equipment and change their designs, but to no avail; the industry collapsed altogether, and eventually even the looms were destroyed. The situation was worse still in India. The economic collapse in Kashmir was followed by a famine from 1887 to 1888, and the population was said to "die like flies." Fewer than 200 weavers survived.[64]

The story of devastation following changing textile markets recently repeated itself almost eerily in Kashmir. The weaving industry had recovered to some extent there after its low point in the late 19th century; although production of the twill tapestry shawls was never again globally significant, production of simpler designs continued on a reduced scale. While most of the fine shawls were and are still woven from pashmina, some Kashmiri weavers worked with shahtoosh, which as noted earlier comes from a Tibetan antelope that is now a protected species. Reuters News Service ran a story in 2003 with the headline, "Kashmiri Shahtoosh Weavers Struggle for Survival." It tells of Mohammad Gul and his two sons, who sit "hunched over a row of handlooms" in a small hidden building in Kashmir, "stealthily" weaving a shawl. Gul knows his illegal work might lead to a jail sentence, but he claims he doesn't have a choice—he "knows only shahtoosh weaving." The article claims that nearly 50,000 shahtoosh weavers became jobless after the fiber was banned in 1979. While this number seems exaggerated, the effect on existing weavers is undeniable. Although Gul's family was still working, its production was cut from about 200 to 40 shawls a year.[65]

One other story relating to the economic importance of a local textile industry reminds us that international awareness of the plight of unemployed cloth workers can make a difference. At the beginning of World War I, many Belgian families still worked as lace-makers, even though the availability of machine-made lace had reduced the industry to a fraction of what it had once been. When the German blockade cut off supplies, thousands of lace-makers began to starve. Rising to their aid, Americans formed the Commission for Relief in Belgium (CRB), which negotiated international agreements to allow thread into the country, found work for more than 20,000 individuals, and created markets for the product in Britain and the U.S. CRB personnel sometimes literally smuggled the contraband lace out of the country by wrapping it around their bodies and hiding it in their clothes. Lace smuggling was in fact nothing new. In the 18th century, the fabric was even smuggled into England in the bodies of starving dogs who were outfitted in the skins of larger animals.[66]

On a more optimistic note, we can describe how at least one local community has been recently revitalized through a new textile business.

This poster stating "Belgian Lace is not a luxury" was released by the Commission for Relief in Belgium during World War I. It was part of a campaign encouraging Americans to support starving Belgian lace-makers by buying their handiwork.

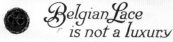

{below} *A yellow Star of David badge worn under the Nazi regime in the 1930s and 1940s by Jews.*

{bottom} *An inverted red triangle badge worn by a political prisoner under the Nazi regime, 1940s.*

Paducah, Kentucky had been struggling to survive economically, but in the last twenty years it has built itself up as a center of "quilt tourism." Now trademarked as "Quilt City USA," Paducah hosts an annual quilt exposition, has established a quilt museum, and offers subsidized artist studios in its revitalized downtown. Lest we think this new kind of economic development based on the enthusiasm of contemporary textile-makers is a fluke, we should remember that quilting was estimated in 2008 to be a $3.3 billion industry. Quilt enthusiasts can sign up for quilt-themed cruises and trips to China, Africa, Ireland, and Australia.[67]

Separation and subjugation

While cloth can in many ways bring people together, we know that it can also be used to separate, or reduce a sense of community. Cloth and cords can be used for sinister purposes. At the extreme, they can be used to kill— one can be smothered or suffocated with a piece of fabric, or strangled with a rope. (A strong image imprinted on the world's consciousness in recent years was the public execution of Saddam Hussein, the noose being tightened by two hangmen with black cloth covering their faces.) More often, they are implicated in the mistreatment and subjugation of a person or group. Nathaniel Hawthorne's novel, *The Scarlet Letter*, dramatically used as its central conceit the image of people in power marking an outcast with a cloth badge. Heroine Hester Prynne was condemned to wear a large red "A" on her chest, proclaiming her adultery to the world at large. The narrator claims that when the letter was touched it gave off a "burning heat...as if the letter were not of red cloth, but red hot iron." In the 19th century, American slaves were given rough, plain-weave textiles ("Negro cloth") with which to clothe themselves—fabric so coarse it was not considered suitable for whites to wear. It was a matter of law in South Carolina that slaves were visually distinguished in this way.[68] The most iconic example of subjugating fabric was the yellow cloth star Jews were forced to wear in Hitler's Germany. The Nazis were not actually the first to impose a cloth mark of separatism on the Jewish people. Some decrees had originated with Muslim leaders. Jews living under the rule of the Abbasid Dynasty in Iraq were ordered to wear a yellow belt and a tall, cone-like hat in the 9th century, and well into the 20th century, those living in the Tafilalet area of Morocco were required to wear black skullcaps. Other edicts came from the Christian church. In 1215, Pope Innocent III set forth a similar decree applying to Jews living anywhere in the Christian world. The markings were not uniform—in England they were required to wear an image of the Ten Commandments on their garments, while in France round yellow badges prevailed.

The branding practice fell into disuse for many centuries until Hitler reinstated "Jewish-yellow" patches in 1939. The immediate effect, as intended, was that Jews were put into a state of fear and shame. Although some tried to hide the badge, appearing in public without it was dangerous: one could be fined, beaten, imprisoned, or even picked up for forced labor.

Prisoners at Auschwitz in black-and-white striped uniforms, Poland, 1940s.

As a result, Jews placed posters on their apartment doors exclaiming, "Remember the Badge!" "Have you already put on the Badge?" "Attention, the Badge!" "Before leaving the building, put on the Badge!" The badges created an effective visual identification system that enabled the shift from haphazard persecution of this minority to organized destruction. As Ada June Friedman expressed it in "The Jewish Badge and the Yellow Star in the Nazi Era:" "One day there were just people on the street, and the next day, there were Jews and non-Jews." Gertrud Scholtz-Klink, a Berliner who was asked how she felt when she suddenly saw so many people in her city with yellow stars on their coats, said, "I don't know how to say it. There were so many. I felt that my aesthetic sensibility was wounded."[69]

It is important to note that Nazis used cloth badges to target other unwanted groups as well. Homosexuals were at first marked with armbands containing a black dot or the number 175, but later, when a system of colored patches was instituted, homosexual men were identified by an inverted pink triangle. Black badges denoted the developmentally delayed (what the Nazis referred to as the "retarded"), alcoholics, vagrants, and at first, the Roma (gypsies), although they were later coded in brown. Green was for criminals, purple for Jehovah's Witnesses, and red for political prisoners. Happily, the pink triangle symbol has recently been reclaimed by the gay pride movement, which has turned around its negative connotations.[70]

Another kind of cloth marking used in the Nazi concentration camps was the black-and-white striped prisoner uniform. Broad high-contrast stripes immediately branded the individual as a prisoner, and made him so conspicuous that escape was more difficult. Here, too, the Nazis were adopting a well-established code system, since stripes were long associated in European cultures with loss of freedom. The source may have been a misreading of Leviticus 19:19, which deals with forbidden mixtures. This passage was erroneously translated from Greek to Latin as "two colors"

{above, left} *Edward S. Curtis named his 1904 photograph of a Navajo girl,* A Child of the Desert. *Despite this rather romantic title, the predominantly white audience these images were aimed at would likely have been prejudiced by the enfolding blanket; a "blanket Indian" was typically considered backward and resistant to "civilizing" change.*

{above, right} *Embroidered shoe for woman's bound foot, Shandong, China, 1850–1900. The entire sole of the shoe is about three inches (8 cm) long. The Chinese practice of foot binding had many implications, but the most obvious is the fact that men were in a position of power over women as they were able to walk easily while women who wore shoes like this were not.*

rather than "two things" (two different fabrics). From about the 13th century, the Church prohibited the clergy from wearing stripes, and the Saxon government decreed that prostitutes, criminals, and other undesirables had to do so. The image of the striped uniform is still evocative; in addition to the Nazi death camps, it brings to mind prison chain gangs. It was however not the only visual coding system used to make prisoners stand out. In Britain, the prisoner was branded with a wide arrowhead that literally denoted "property of the crown." The phrase "broad arrow" came to stand for felony and shame. Today, U.S. prisons have largely switched over to the bright orange jumpsuit.[71]

Separating textiles are also present in the political arena. In prison executions in some American states, there is a curtain that visually isolates the witnesses from the inmate who is being put to death. (Sounds are still audible: after the prison team closed the curtain at one execution, "the witnesses could still hear...moans and groans for several minutes.")[72] The primary symbol of separation and groups being cut off from one another during the Cold War was the "Iron Curtain," the military, political, and ideological barrier established between the Soviet bloc and Western Europe from 1945 to 1990. The expression is credited to Russian philosopher Vasily Rozanov, who first spoke of an "iron curtain descending on Russian history" after the 1917 revolution. It came into popular use after British Prime Minister Winston Churchill applied it to what had happened in European politics after World War II.[73] There are many other evocative images of curtains as separators in popular culture, including (before security concerns made it largely obsolete) the curtain that was drawn across the aisle to separate first class airline passengers from those in coach, and the curtain hiding the Wizard of Oz and his elaborate machinery from view.

More encompassing fabric "barriers" also set one group from another. Sometimes it is primarily a matter of stereotype. In most Native American cultures, the practice of covering oneself in a blanket or "robe" held great meaning. Blankets were not only protective, but could be wrapped in a personally expressive manner. These meanings remained consistent, even when the textiles themselves were purchased, commercial products rather than handmade in a local context. To the people of the dominant culture in the late 19th century, "blanket Indian" was a derogatory term. It referred to an individual who was clinging to traditional ways and not accepting "progress" and "civilization."[74]

A woman's place?

Men and women are often separated by fabric barriers. A curtain has traditionally been placed between the male and female areas in places of worship in early Christian churches, Orthodox Jewish synagogues, and Muslim mosques. The dividing curtain is related to the practice of *purdah* or seclusion, practiced in many parts of the Muslim and Hindu world. Purdah is a Persian (Farsi) word, literally meaning "curtain." It involves separate spaces for men and women and proscriptions against interactions between the sexes. In practice, it means that women's activities are often restricted, since they are not to be seen in public. The body-covering veil that screens the woman from view is part of the purdah tradition. (It is essentially a portable tent that allows her to move into the public arena but still be hidden.)[75]

The *chadors* or *burkas* worn by women in the Middle East today are certainly multivalent, with different meanings to different people, but they are often seen by outsiders as a uniform of oppression. Critics see outfits that obliterate women's public selves as a symbol of their being "owned" or controlled by men, or by the prevailing government or ruling body, such as the Taliban in Afghanistan. The garments not only keep the women in social seclusion, but also literalize the idea that they are someone else's property. Many react viscerally to the presence of cloth coverings,

Girls waiting for a boat on Moheshkhali Island, Bangladesh.

particularly over the face. On the other hand, many women feel most comfortable in modest, body-covering garments; they say it represents their piety, religious identity, and freedom of expression. Such garments have polarized entire populations and set off political furor in countries including France, England, Italy, Germany, Norway, and Turkey.

A more humorous expression of the division between men and women that also involves curtains was described in the *Harvard Design Magazine* in 2002. Joel Sanders noted that curtains are the element of the domestic interior that embodies many of the tensions, prejudices, and the divergent approaches of architects and decorators:

> Architects typically repudiate curtains, believing that this element that modulates vision compromises the architect's conception, obscuring and softening the precise geometry of architectural forms. Decorators, for their part, consider curtains essential; veiling sunlight and views, curtains make domestic privacy possible and offer relief from the austere spaces created by architects often obsessed with form at the expense of comfort.

Sanders tracks the "curtain wars" back to the 18th century. Using fabric to soften or hide hard architectural elements was also manifested in a European-based practice that began in the 19th century, the covering of tables and other furniture with "skirts" that would literally hide their structural "limbs." The furniture was symbolically (and even literally) likened to a woman's body.[76]

Returning to the more serious issue of women being subjected or put "in their place" through cloth brings us to another complicated but important issue that must be addressed in a book about the roles textiles play in our lives. In the preface, when I explained why textiles are often unappreciated today, I made the point that women's textile work, especially sewing and embroidery, has often been devalued—even denigrated—in patriarchal societies, especially (but not exclusively) in the West. It is important to remember that fiberwork and cloth-making are not universally female pastimes. As the illustrations and stories throughout this book show, many men engaged in these activities, but typically men made cloth that had economic, ritual, or political significance, and worked in professional contexts. Nevertheless, even a cursory look at the chart listing the deities associated with textiles indicates (see chapter 1) that cloth-making is predominantly associated with women. In pre-industrial cultures, women were usually the spinners—the ones who created thread, much as they created children. They were also the ones who made the utilitarian household cloth such as clothing and bedding. This makes sense when we realize that beliefs about appropriate male and female work seem to come from pre-existing social attitudes about men and women. The rules are never fixed, and vary from culture to culture, but the general tendency is to follow the domestic/ordinary vs. public/extraordinary division.

In Ghana and other parts of West Africa where men weave and wear the prestigious strip cloth, women weave the everyday fabrics used for their own garments and for carrying babies, food, and other necessities. In the case of the raffia pile fabric for the ritually important dance skirts of the Kuba people of the Congo, the material is woven by men; women add the decorative embroidered pile. Men were the primary weavers among the Hopi and Pueblo people of the American Southwest and, significantly, they did the weaving in *kivas*, underground ceremonial spaces, that women did not usually enter. Women do most of the embroidery in the Middle East, but the embroidery on the all-important *kiswah* cloth used on the Ka'aba in Mecca is worked exclusively by men.

The type of equipment associated with men and women also often depended on what the cloth was used for. In West Africa, women typically work on vertical looms, rather than the horizontal ones used for strip cloth. In pre-conquest Central America, weaving had always been done by women on backstrap or body-tension looms. Once the Spanish introduced the floor or treadle loom, men who made cloth for sale rather than domestic use adopted the more mechanized equipment. (With the advent of economic development and modernization, these distinctions are no longer absolute.)

{above, left} *Men embroidering a panel which is wrapped around the kiswah (the textile that covers the holy Ka'aba in Mecca), Saudi Arabia, 1974. This is a highly prestigious job, and they are working with gold thread.*

{above, right} *Detail of raffia pile cloth of the sort used for ceremonial Kuba skirts, 20th century.*

Man weaving the goat-hair fabric used to make nomads' tents, Central Asia, 1850s–1860s. This kind of cloth was woven by specialists, and it was always a man's job.

THE PRAYSE OF THE NEEDLE

To all dispersed sorts of Arts and Trades
J writ the Needles prayse (that never fades)
So long as children shall be got or borne,
So long as garments shall be made, or worn…
Yea till the world be quite dissolu'd and past;
So long at least, the Needles use shall last.
…
And for my Countries quiet, I should like,
That women-kinde should vse no other Pike.
It will increase their peace, enlarge their store,
To use their tongues lesse, and their Needles more,
The Needles sharpnesse, profit yields, and pleasure,
But sharpnesse of the tongue, bites out of measure.

John Taylor, 1631

Another layer of complexity related to this subject brings us back to the culturally enforced isolation of women. In many Islamic societies in which women were expected to remain at home, fine textile work was something that filled their time. In homes where there were servants to carry out the harder domestic tasks, the pieces the ladies worked on became more and more embellished. Needlework, especially, was a socially approved activity, and it became a creative outlet as well. In a memoir of life in Istanbul in the early 20th century, Irfan Orga writes of his "elegant mother, always at home, always working at her beautiful embroideries that [brought her]…great comfort."[77] Such lavishly embellished Turkish fabrics exemplify the kind of labor-intensive elaboration and expensive materials that might go into these textiles. They could be shown off in certain contexts, such as the *hammam* or bathhouse, where they would be admired by other women. Skilled needleworkers thus gained respect from others within their accepted sphere.

Even without the custom of seclusion, European women also operated primarily in the domestic sphere until well into the 20th century. Domestic needlework played a similar role there, but, if anything, it was dismissed even more readily by men. John Taylor's poem, "The Prayse of the Needle," included in the preface of a popular pattern book in 1634, expresses a prevalent Western male attitude. Taylor, who was generally derisive about women, acknowledged that needles can be used to make practical garments and create beautiful images, and he commended women for their skill. At the same time, he stated that he approved of sewing because it helped keep women quiet, busy, and out of trouble—unable to interfere with men or be concerned with other kinds of tasks and matters.[78]

In *The Subversive Stitch: Embroidery and the Making of the Feminine*, Rozsika Parker argues that sewing came to be seen as an expression of

femininity in Western culture only after the Renaissance. The pastime became associated at that time not only with the domestic, but also with piousness and subservience; it was a sign of a constrained life. Although this was purely a cultural construction, it became so ingrained in public consciousness that by the Victorian era needlework was seen as an essentialized, natural part of femininity.[79] (Parker's argument can be extended beyond needlework to many forms of textile-making; this was the same era that produced Longfellow's poem, which equated spinning with female submissiveness.) The associations were so strong, in fact, that successive generations of feminists tried to distance themselves from needlework. Mary Wollstonecraft wrote in *The Vindication of the Rights of Women* (1792) that such work made women dull, sick, and self-absorbed. Others felt the energy that went into sewing would be better spent in more serious activities, such as mathematics.

Tellingly, we find that when men are kept in confined spaces like prisons or sailing ships, they too do "domesticated" crafts such as embroidery. Nevertheless, their work was never devalued. Women face much more of a double-edged sword: many, like Irfan Orga's mother, find pleasure in sewing and textile work, but may be defensive about it because of the way it is dismissed. Happily, feminists have in recent decades *used* sewing, claiming it as part of women's heritage and strength. This will be discussed further in chapter 5.

Corner of embroidered textile wrapper with silver thread and spangles taken to the hammam (bath) in Turkey, 19th or early 20th century.

I Sell the Shadow to Support the Substance.
SOJOURNER TRUTH.

*Sojourner Truth, the renowned American
ex-slave who became an abolitionist
preacher, made a famous speech at the 1851
Women's Rights Convention in Akron, Ohio,
where she kept asking, "Ain't I a Woman?"
It is significant that she posed in this
1864 photograph with her knitting, which
helped reinforce that very sentiment. Copies
of the image were sold as cartes de visite
to raise money for the abolitionist cause.*

In chapter 2 there is a description of how needlework was sometimes the only skill women could turn to when they needed to make money (i.e., step into the male-identified world of commerce), and how when circumstances demanded it, women sold their work. Irfan Orga's mother used her embroidery to keep her family from starving after World War I left the family penniless. Elizabeth Keckley, a one-time American slave, bought her freedom through her sewing work, eventually becoming a seamstress and personal confidante for Mary Todd Lincoln. Groups of women could also use their skills collectively. When the river silted up in Ipswich, Massachusetts about 1750, closing the harbor that had provided the town's livelihood, a group of women started a successful bobbin lace business. (Ironically, the Ipswich lace business failed in the 1820s when the men of the town tried to mechanize the industry by importing machines from England. The social prestige of the fabric declined rapidly and the market disappeared.)[80]

When textiles functioned as the center of Victorian reformers' philanthropic projects for indigent or needy women, the results were more equivocal. In terms of social betterment, 19th-century feminists may have been right to distance themselves from sewing, for the desperate situation of the poor was not often changed and the work could be brutal. Parker writes of the British philanthropic effort involving 500,000 women who were given whitework (Ayrshire) embroidery to do at home, on a piecework basis. They developed many physical problems from constantly bending over to do close work, and many who started as children (it was not unusual to begin at age three) were said to have eyesight problems or even go blind by the time they were twenty. A Nottingham doctor reported that in a fourteen-year period he had treated 10,000 cases of bad eyesight among these needleworkers.[81]

Some of the women "helped" in such charitable endeavors were also disadvantaged due to race, ethnicity, or cultural stigma, and it was even more likely that they would be limited to poorly paying textile work. Records of the African Free School set up in New York in 1821 indicate that freed slaves were given sewing lessons (good behavior was rewarded with sewing tools). While this training would ostensibly allow them to support themselves eventually, they were simultaneously kept subservient. Native American girls who were sent to boarding school in the early 20th century— they were forcibly taken from their families and expected to assimilate into non-Native American culture—were similarly given vocational training in sewing, weaving, and other textile crafts. Textile tasks were also imposed upon women in prisons. Bette Hochberg tells us that a House of Correction in England was known as a "spin house." "Poor, incorrigible, vagrant or lewd women" were forced to spin in these institutions that were part of the poorhouse system. London's infamous Bridewell prison included such a spinning school. Hochberg also describes the spinning and weaving that went on in Latin American jails. Finished articles were sold to shoppers through a small opening in the jail wall.[82]

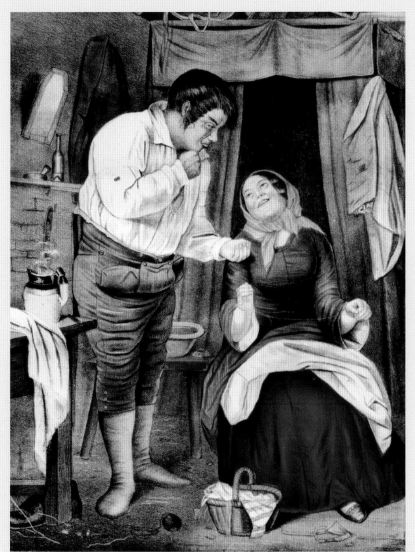

{left} The Blessing of a Wife *was typical of the Currier and Ives lithographs that were popular with Victorian Americans. The good and loving wife is sewing as she sits in front of what is presumably their bed, indicating how much the activity was a part of the expected female social role. The print was made between 1857 and 1907, but the scene seems to be set earlier in the 19th century.*

{above} *Sewing was considered "women's work" to such an extent that bags labeled "work" were immediately understood to hold sewing accessories. This was probably made from a pre-stamped pattern, 1900–30.*

{left} *This finely quilted card case represents the epitome of fine needlework, probably Italian, 1880–1920.*

Exploitation of textile workers

Of course, the instances of oppression associated with textile production went far beyond gender issues or attitudes about cloth-making as a feminine endeavor. The horrors associated with industrial textile manufacture, including the nightmarish conditions of the early English factory system, are well known. They affected men, women, and children. Dickens' novel, *Oliver Twist,* documented the lives of essentially enslaved labor to which even young children were subject during the 19th century in cities such as Manchester. Two hundred thousand children under the age of eighteen worked in cotton mills in 1839, putting in fourteen-hour days in dangerous and extremely unhealthy conditions. Sometimes they were chained to the looms to keep them from running away. While America did not have the same kind of workhouses forcing the very young into factories, the conditions were no better. Mill workers had to spend long hours on their feet in deafeningly loud, hot, airless, humid rooms (the humidity was kept high in order to reduce cotton breakage), working at numbingly repetitive tasks. Every worker inhaled a great deal of particulate matter, since the airborne lint was ubiquitous, but loom operators were particularly affected, since they had to suck the threads through the narrow ends of the weft shuttles. Doctors came to label this practice the "kiss of death." Respiratory illness was the eventual cause of death of 70 per cent of textile workers, compared to 4 per cent of people in other occupations, such as farming. In 1911, 146 garment workers employed by the Triangle Shirtwaist Company died when the factory caught fire, because they had been locked into the building.[83]

Sadly, the subjugation of textile workers is not just a part of long-ago history. In the 1990s, the story of Iqbal Masih brought the story of forced textile labor to world attention. Iqbal was born in Pakistan in 1973. When he was four, his desperate father, who needed money to pay wedding expenses for his older son and could not get a loan from a bank, essentially sold Iqbal

A young spinner in the Globe Cotton Mill,
Augusta, Georgia, America, 1909.

into slavery. He borrowed 600 rupees (the equivalent of $12) from the owner of the nearby carpet factory. Iqbal's labor was the collateral for the loan.

Although he ostensibly still lived at home, Iqbal went to the factory six days a week, staying from 4:00 in the morning until dark. Earning one rupee a day (about 3 cents), he worked with other children in a small, airless room (the windows were sealed to keep out insects that might damage the wool) outfitted with twenty looms and a small, bare light bulb. The children were verbally abused, frequently beaten, and often chained to their looms. They were not allowed to speak to one another. Iqbal's family was unable to repay the initial loan, and additional expenses such as charges for the meager lunch Iqbal was fed each day were constantly added to their bill. Eventually, the original 600 rupee debt grew to 13,000 rupees (US $260). There was no hope of paying it off—or of escape. Iqbal once snuck away to report the beatings and horrible conditions to the police, but the officers returned him to the factory. He was given another beating and told, "You are a working boy, a carpet weaver; you will remain a carpet weaver for the rest of your life."

Iqbal was granted a reprieve in 1983, when the Pakistani parliament passed a bill that abolished bonded labor contracts and canceled all debts owed in this system. He ran away from work to attend a rally sponsored by the Bonded Labor Liberation Front (BLLF), and learned that if he presented a "freedom letter" to the factory owner, he could be released. He was spotted at the rally by a BLLF organizer who brought him up on stage to exemplify the horrors of the bonded life. The audience was stunned that this was a ten-year-old, for the years of malnutrition and leaning over his loom had stunted his growth. Iqbal began attending a BLLF school and soon became a spokesperson for the BLLF cause. He was the first recipient of Reebok's Youth in Action Human Rights award. Visiting the U.S. in 1995 to accept this honor formally, he gave speeches urging President Clinton to put sanctions on countries using child labor.

Tragically, four months after receiving the Reebok award, Iqbal was killed while riding a bicycle with his cousin in a small village outside of Lahore. His murderer remains unidentified, but he was likely shot down by a mafia group associated with the carpet factories. Iqbal's death brought enormous attention to the subject of children and sweatshops, and an outpouring of protest led to major reforms, including the formation of Goodweave (formerly Rugmark)—an initiative for certifying that handmade carpets were made without exploitative child labor.[84]

Goodweave was an important step forward, but carpet slavery still exists. The American Anti-Slavery Group reported in 2007 what happened to Santosh, an Indian child who was kidnapped at age five and taken 400 miles away to Allahabad, the heart of India's "Carpet Belt." He reportedly worked nineteen hours a day for nine years, and when he was rescued at the age of fourteen, he was "almost catatonic."[85] A 2005 article entitled "The Stolen Childhoods of Asian Carpet Workers" cites data indicating 300,000 to 400,000 children are used by the carpet industry. Like Iqbal, most are caught in the debt bondage system. They too are fed little, and suffer from deteriorated eyesight, lung disease, kidney and liver problems, and deformation of the back.[86]

Forced labor of a different sort is also increasingly prevalent in the apparel industry. The so-called "quick response" system creates a no-win situation for seamstresses and other garment workers. With short-lived fashion trends and the ability brought about by new computer systems to track exactly what people are buying in retail stores, manufacturers are better able to predict what will and will not sell. Rather than mass-producing large numbers of given garments that they hope customers will respond to and buy (this is sometimes known as the "push" system), they order only short runs for which they essentially already have customers (the "pull" system). The stability of the work force was obviously much greater under the push system, since individuals could expect long-term work. With the quick response (now even called "just in time") model, manufacturers shop around for the very cheapest labor for each contract, thereby reducing wages even further.[87]

Also implicated in this change of the last few decades is the fact that piecework production is being integrated into textile and garment factories that once operated on an assembly line system. Piece-rate production has always been found in sweatshops and home-work systems, but this is new in factories, explains sociologist Piya Pangsapa in "The Piecework System and 'New Slaves' of the Apparel Industry." The situation is in some ways bringing textile workers back to the frightful conditions of the early industrial era. As more of the tasks are converted to piecework in countries such as Thailand, daily wages and overtime are eliminated. Workers now earn roughly half of what they earned a decade ago. Physical conditions have also deteriorated, and because the workers are in competition with one another, their social environment is no longer supportive. Pangsapa says:

> Working a disposable labor force to exhaustion, illness and disability for subsistence wages in unsafe conditions is brutal, but when the job in question is the only one available, it binds workers in *subjugation* and servitude to the factory. That is more akin to slavery than to having a job.[88]

Resisting oppression

There have certainly been times when textile workers have risen up to protest their working conditions or what they perceived to be a threat to their livelihood. Some of the very first inventions to mechanize textile processes were met with immediate resistance. A Danzig man built a power loom in 1661, but fearing riots among the spinners, the Polish government confiscated his plans and even drowned the inventor. The "spinning jenny," a device that greatly sped up the spinning process, evoked a similar reaction in the mid-18th century. Inventor James Hargreaves first tried to keep his invention secret from his neighbors, but understanding that it might mean they would be put out of work, a group of them found and destroyed the machine and threatened Hargreaves' life.[89]

The scene in this woodcut, which is credited to the Japanese Department of Education, features an angry Richard Arkwright sending his wife back to her parents because she deliberately broke his spinning wheel. Arkwright was the inventor of the spinning frame, which produced an even stronger thread than James Hargreaves's spinning jenny. He patented the device in 1764, but this print was made between 1850 and 1900.

Perhaps the best-known example of a textile worker protest has even yielded a word—"Luddite"—which is now used to describe someone who is resistant to new technologies. The Luddites were English weavers of the early 19th century who were bitterly opposed to the adoption of the Jacquard loom, which they rightly understood would threaten their jobs. Prior to its invention, complex weaving patterns were worked on a drawloom. Drawloom weaving was slow. It took a long time to set up the equipment for any given pattern, and then the weaving involved two people—the main weaver, and a "drawboy" who raised ("drew up") the pattern warp threads for each shot of the weft. French silk weaver Joseph Marie Jacquard devised a new kind of loom that used a series of punch cards to control the pattern threads. He attached groups of threads to hooks that could be essentially "programmed" to pass through the holes of these cards, and thus be raised up above or below the weft. (Each card represented one shuttle pass, and the cards were attached to each other like a ribbon.) The drawboy was no longer needed.[90]

Jacquard first demonstrated his invention in 1801, and by 1811, a formal protest movement had begun in England. According to a speech Lord Byron made to the House of Lords in 1812, the Luddites (named after a probably mythical larger-than-life leader, Ned Ludd) saw "the migration of control of the weaving process from human workers into the hardware of the machine" as a literal transfer of a piece of their bodies. They engaged in a kind of guerilla warfare. They met at night on the moors surrounding the industrial towns to practice their manoeuvers and, usually under cover of darkness, set about destroying wool and cotton mills and industrial equipment. Other cloth workers joined the movement, since the Jacquard loom was not the only new machine that would put people out of work, and violent protests took place throughout the industrial north. Luddites also engaged in several battles with the British Army; at one time, in fact, there were more British troops fighting the Luddites than there were fighting against Napoleon on the Iberian peninsula. Government reprisals were harsh. Legislation was passed that made "machine breaking" (industrial sabotage) a capital crime, and after a mass trial in York in 1813, seventeen men were executed. Many others were deported and taken as prisoners to Australia.[91]

Cloth itself has also been used as a sign and vehicle of political resistance. The phenomenon was dramatically demonstrated in the early 20th-century Indian struggle for independence and self-government. We have seen that Britain came to take over the Indian subcontinent because of its economic interest in Indian cotton, and sadly, as a colonial power, it pointedly destroyed India's indigenous cotton industry. By the early 19th century, the British forced the Indians to export their raw cotton to England, where it was spun and woven into yardage on the new mechanized looms. Indians then had to purchase the mill-woven fabric from England, paying not only for the finished goods made from their own material, but for import duties that were levied as it traveled back across the ocean. Between 1849

View of a drawloom still in use in Fez, Morocco in 1988. The complex arrangement of harnesses and cords was made obsolete by the invention of the more programmable Jacquard loom.

THE CROPPER'S BATTLE SONG

Croppers, who sheared the extra nap from woven woolen cloth, were among those who rebelled against textile industrialization when the "cropping frame" was introduced in 1812. They smashed many of the machines, and used firearms against the army.

Come cropper lads of high renown
Who love to drink good ale that's brown
And strike each haughty tyrant down
With hatchet, pike and gun!
(Chorus)
Oh the cropper lad's for me,
Who with lusty stroke,
The shear frames broke.
The cropper lad's for me.

and 1889, imports of British cotton to India went from 2 to 27 million pounds (about 1 to 12 million kilograms) a year. Besides losing economically, Indians' sense of competence was severely compromised.

Mohandas (Mahatma) Gandhi and his compatriots in the Indian independence movement recognized the semiotic power of cloth. Gandhi is said to have wept when he first realized what India had lost when forced out of its own cloth manufacture, and he articulated the importance of resisting the English policy in his 1908 book, *Hind Swaraj (Indian Home Rule)*.[92] The concept of *swadeshi,* the promotion of indigenous products, became central to the nationalist movement. It was officially adopted into the Indian National Congress (INC) program in 1921. The party called for a boycott of foreign cloth, and required its officers and supporters to wear hand-spun, hand-woven cloth *(khadi)*, which became known as the "livery of freedom." Every household was encouraged to spin its own cotton as a practical and patriotic gesture. By 1940, there were about 15,000 villages producing khadi, and they processed close to 16 million yards (over 14 million meters) in nine months. Gandhi made public appearances wearing simple khadi garments and spinning on a small, portable wheel *(charka)* that he had himself designed. The charka came to symbolize independence and was prominently featured on the INC flag.

Gandhi's khadi campaign was the result of decades of experimentation with cloth as a medium of communication. As a young, British-educated lawyer, Gandhi had worn fine Western clothes—suits, ties, tailored shirts, polished shoes—but gradually, he began to understand them as the clothing of a subjugating power, the uniform of colonialism. By abandoning the look of the English gentleman and the sartorial rules of the imperialists, he was visibly asserting his independence. He did this with an appropriate sense of drama, at one point burning his British-made garments on a bonfire. Wherever he appeared in public wearing nothing but a handwoven loin cloth, it had a huge impact. It made the English extremely uncomfortable, as their operating assumptions and rules were openly subverted (imagine him having tea with the King and Queen in Buckingham Palace, wearing only what they considered a "diaper" or "nappy"). It gave the Indian masses a sense of national pride and unity. The communicative message of the cloth was particularly effective in the early years of the 20th century when amplification systems were poor and many people would not have been able to hear speeches given in large gatherings (even if they could hear, Indians spoke a wide range of languages, and many would not have understood what he was saying). Much of the population was illiterate, and could not read slogans, signage, or treatises. Gandhi's appearance, however, was immediately understandable and empowering. Gandhi made a final political gesture with cloth shortly before his assassination in 1947. He sent a coarse khadi tablecloth that he had spun and woven himself as a wedding present to Princess Elizabeth and Prince Philip.[93]

The charka and khadi remained important symbols even after independence was achieved. Khadi is still being made in local villages and nationally supported workshops, although it tends now to be colorfully dyed and printed. Periodically, schools try to revive spinning among a new generation of Indians, thereby bringing the symbol of the charka back into public consciousness.[94]

On a smaller scale, boycotts of British textiles had also taken place as a symbol of resistance in the U.S. Those fighting for independence in the years leading up to the Revolutionary War felt it did not make sense for them to be wearing British goods, and after the passage of the Stamp Act in 1765, many started adopting "homespun" fabric as a symbol of patriotism. The senior class of Harvard appeared at graduation in this

{opposite} *Watercolor of cloth croppers in England, from George Walker's* The Costume of Yorkshire, *London, 1814. These men sheared the nap from fulled woolen fabric. The cropping frame was introduced in 1812, shortly before this illustration was made.*

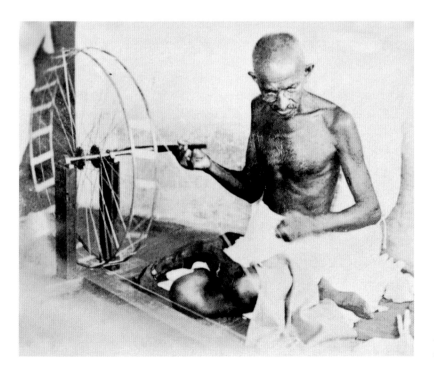

Mohandas (Mahatma) Gandhi spinning on his charka wheel, c. 1935.

kind of domestically produced cloth in 1768. Later, during the Civil War, patriotic Northerners similarly boycotted "imported luxuries," particularly targeting Britain, since the English were essentially siding with the Confederacy in order to maintain their supply of cotton. In late 19th-century China, civil officers of the Qing court expressed their frustration by modifying the images on their embroidered rank badges.[95]

Political resistance has also been powerfully expressed through cloth in a more recent independence struggle. During the first Palestinian *intifada,* or uprising, there was a significant revival of traditional dress among Palestinian women living in the occupied territories of Israel. Here, too, the outfit functioned as a sign of nationalism and protest against what they perceived as an occupying power. Heavily embroidered dresses, or *thobs*, had been typical women's garments in Palestine before the British arrived as regional administrators after World War I and, as discussed earlier, embroidered designs varied by village or community. These garments were gradually abandoned as life conditions dramatically changed, especially after the state of Israel was created in 1948. In the late 1980s and 1990s, however, when there was more of a concerted independence movement, a new generation of women wore thobs to indicate pride in their heritage. These "traditional" dresses actually featured new types of embroidery that stressed a kind of pan-Palestinian (nationalistic) identity rather than a particular village look. The *shawal* was an entirely new style that emerged, specifically referencing or promoting the intifada, and for a limited period, some of the dresses blatantly featured nationalistic motifs. There were "flag dresses" featuring the colors or even representational images of the (then) banned Palestinian (PLO) flag, and garments with motifs such as the Dome of the Rock mosque, maps of Palestine, or Arabic calligraphy embroidered on the chest or skirt panels. At this time individuals were being imprisoned for carrying the flag, so wearing the same image on one's dress was a potent snubbing of Israeli authority.[96]

Global recycling of fabrics

The last topic included in this chapter relates to the subject of contemporary trade and global economic imbalance. World textile trade now includes large amounts of recycled fabric, usually in the form of used clothing and household linens. Statistics on this rapidly expanding industry evolve constantly and rapidly, but in 2002, 822 million pounds (373 million kilograms) of recycled apparel was exported to the developing world from the U.S. alone, and Australia, Japan, and many countries in Western Europe were also active suppliers. The U.S. doubled its exports between 1990 and 1997, and the industry has been almost exponentially expanding since then. (An Oxfam Research Report of 2005 estimated that the global trade in second-hand clothing was worth more than $1 billion each year, but some estimates are even higher.) The significance of this is clear if we consider the fact that used clothing is currently America's single most important export to Africa.[97]

Wealthy countries have an incredible glut of usable clothing; garments
are relatively inexpensive to purchase and the international cosmopolitan
fashion system demands that we replace clothes quickly in order to stay
in style. We tire of these textiles long before they actually wear out. Some
people simply throw them away, sending them directly to the landfill, but
aware of how wasteful that is, others donate their unwanted items to charity
organizations. These groups distribute some of the donated material to local
shelters and needy populations, and sell another portion of it in their thrift
shops, using the profits to support their charitable activities. However, there
is far too much material to dispose of it all that way. At least half of the textiles
donated to these organizations are now shipped overseas, where they are
sold in thriving second-hand markets. First World discards have a second
(or third or fourth) "life" in Africa, Latin America, Asia, and parts of the
Middle East. The second-hand trade has created new systems of distribution
and exchange, new types of entrepreneurs (in the capital city in Zambia,
there were 2,500 such individuals in 1995), and even new local fashion trends.

Those who receive and distribute second-hand clothing are not
passive recipients—these developing world markets are not "dumping
grounds" where individuals feel grateful for any cast-offs they can get.
On the contrary, entrepreneurs in each market are very specific about what
they will be able to sell. In 2003, I visited Continental Textile Company in
Milwaukee, Wisconsin, an intermediary stop in this business. Continental
Textile picked up material from the thrift stores, sorted it thoroughly,
fumigated it, and compressed the sorted goods into regulation-size bales
that they shipped around the world. The proprietor had to stay abreast
of the constantly evolving preferences and demands in different markets.
(At that time, he was bemoaning the fact that there was no market in the
world that would accept cotton sweaters, and they had little choice but to
throw out the considerable number that came in daily.)

Used clothing goes by different names in Africa: in Zimbabwe it is
called *mupedzanhamo*, which can be translated as "where all problems
end." In Nigeria, the word is *okirika*, or "bend down boutique," and
Zambians use the descriptive term *salaula*, meaning "selecting from
a bale in the matter of rummaging." Tanzanians and Ghanaians use words
that translate as "dead white people's clothes." Despite negative labels,
the business is unstoppable. A 1996 article estimated that one third of the
population of sub-Saharan Africa was wearing second-hand clothing.
In 2002, 80 per cent of Ugandans were said to buy such apparel, and a 2005
report indicated it was over 90 per cent in Ghana. Even poor people can
afford high-quality used clothing, but not all of the purchasers are poor.
Many individuals appreciate the styles and the access the garments provide
to a seemingly exotic culture. A feature on the second-hand clothing
market in Kenya profiled a taxi driver who was pleased to pay $1.50 for a
T-shirt with the NFL logo on the sleeve and Budweiser emblazoned across
the chest. "I don't know what Budweiser means," he said. "I bought it
because I like foreign designs."[98]

Salaula (used clothing) market in Lusaka, Zambia, 1993.

The second-hand clothing business provides thousands of jobs in the developing world, from truck drivers to salespeople, to tailors who do modifications on clothes in the outdoor markets, to people who clean the clothes. Oxfam's research team in Senegal estimated that 24,000 people were active in the business in 2005. In countries where the local economy is weak, laid-off workers, widows, self-sponsored students, and others take to the trade because it requires little start-up capital and they can turn a small profit almost immediately. Often, family members will chip in with enough cash to enable a new entrepreneur to purchase the first 100-pound (45.4 kilogram) bale for resale. At the same time, there is a definite downside to the trade, including a loss to local textile industries and clothing producers. A decade ago in Nigeria, the textile industry was the largest employer in the manufacturing sector, providing 25 per cent of the total national employment. The number of jobs shrunk dramatically from 137,000 jobs in 1997 to 57,000 in 2003—almost 58 per cent of the industry workforce. While there are other causative factors for this shrinkage, including the same cheap imports from China that devastate the rest of the global market, the second-hand trade has clearly had an enormous impact.

My focus on Africa should not obscure the fact that this is a truly global phenomenon. It is worth mentioning how much used clothing regularly passes from the U.S. into Mexico on a daily basis. Although it is technically illegal for Mexicans to purchase second-hand clothes (the Mexican government bans this because it is seen as competing with their own local industry), one Texas supplier alone ships 50 million pounds (22.7 million kilograms) a year, and tons are said to be smuggled across the U.S. border every day. Sometimes it is individuals who do this, hiding clothing in special compartments in their minivans. There are also formal smugglers, or *pasadores*, who charge $10–$50 for a 50-pound (22.7 kilogram) bale. High profits make this illegal activity worth the risk, and the authorities are not always vigilant in policing the trade. Many obviously receive bribes. The goods get added value, or sell for more, as they move further away from the border and deeper into Mexico (the bribes, concomitantly, are also higher).[99]

The second-hand clothes trade is not illegal in wealthy Saudi Arabia, but it is also big business there, amounting to millions of riyals a year. According to the *Arab News*:

> The real buzz [in Jeddah] is seen on the weekends, when people of different nationalities make it a point to browse this market. You can find Filipinos, Indians, Pakistanis, Europeans and even Americans in search of a bargain. Some are buying in bulk to present to charities back home, some for their extended families and some for needy groups who use these second-hand clothes.

(The market is not a popular destination for Saudis.) Some of the regulars come to the market for its festive atmosphere as much as for the bargains. Interestingly, what isn't sold in Jeddah is in turn exported again to Sudan, Somalia and other African countries.[100]

This chapter has touched to some extent on the communicative power of cloth—the discussion of Nazi-imposed badges, khadi, and Palestinian flag dresses makes the point dramatically—but the subject will be explored in greater depth in chapter 5. The all-important aesthetic meanings of textiles will also be examined more closely.

Cloth as communication

Expressing meaning, messages, and beauty

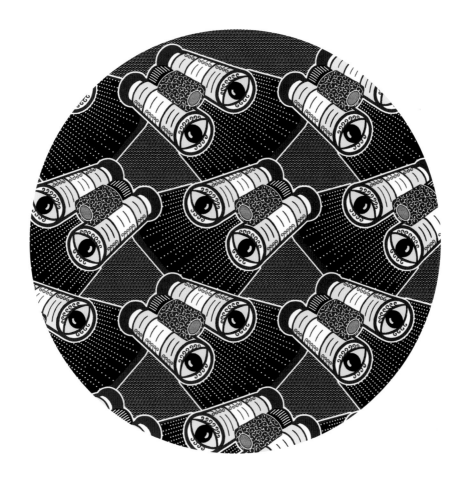

The aim of art is to represent not the outward appearance of things, but their inward significance.

Attributed to Aristotle, as cited in Will Durant,
The Story of Philosophy, 1926

{preceding page} *Detail of a genuine "Dutch wax" print from the Netherlands-based company, Vlisco, 2000s. The Dutch learned the batik (resist-dye) process in Indonesia when they were there as a colonial power, and started producing their own, cheaper imitations of Javanese batik in the mid-19th century. The mass-produced cloth did not appeal to the Indonesians, but it found a receptive audience in Africa. The Dutch then designed such prints with the African market in mind. Over time, "Dutch wax" became a respected and beloved cloth in West Africa, to the point where it became a symbol of African identity.*

We all have a need—a hunger—to express ourselves, and to share our ideas (communicate) with others. We are also hungry to understand what others are saying; we want to understand, learn more, and thus expand our individual horizons. We share information and ideas through many vehicles: speech, music, graphic signs, performance, and visual expression. Textiles help us communicate and learn, add beauty and stimulation to our days, and make our lives richer.

Threads that communicate

While this chapter is primarily about the way cloth helps us communicate, I will once again start with linear fiber elements such as thread and cording, for they too carry messages. The telegraph cable that was laid across the Atlantic in the mid-19th century made it possible to deliver a message from Europe to North America in a matter of minutes, and its presence helped end the isolation of the New World. The cable carried information of all kinds, from notes between political leaders to personal messages between friends and relatives. Today, similar messages are being sent over long distances through optical fiber filaments. In this case, high-speed pulses of laser light carrying digital information move through hair-thin strands of ultra-pure, transparent glass. The transmissions are extremely fast; it would be possible to send thirty-two volumes of the *Encyclopedia Britannica* across the southern hemisphere in less than a second! The optical fibers also have an astonishing capacity. A single pair can carry the equivalent of 37,000 simultaneous telephone conversations, or 800 video channels, at once.[1]

Cutting-edge technology is not necessary, however, for fiber-based communication systems. By the 9th century, the pre-Columbian Andean peoples had developed a sophisticated information storage system using knotted cords or string—the khipu mentioned in chapter 3. One khipu device consisted of anywhere from a few to several hundred hanging cords, which were attached to a horizontal holding cord. Each pendent element contained sequences of knots that might be tied in a number of different ways: some were tied right over left, and others left over right; some were looser than others; some were single and others double. Spaces between the knots, and cord color and composition also varied, and there might be added-in tufts of fiber or ornamental "knobs." These were all data "bits," variables that encoded different kinds of information and could be readily understood by those familiar with the system.[2]

Khipu were the means by which the complex Inka state was able to keep track of its huge administrative system. Early Spanish chroniclers noted that the cords documented a range of information, including tribute payments, censuses, inventories, calendars, and records of events. (The Spanish conquistador Francisco Pizarro himself realized the power of the khipu system; he saw that the Inka were using the knots to record what the invaders had taken from them.) In the 1570s the colonial Spanish government began to regulate the use of cords, and for a short while even

Ancestral Peruvian khipu illustrating various color arrangements and types of knots in camelid wool.

required khipu masters to keep specific records for them (the Spanish usually translated that information onto written documents). Ordinary individuals also used the threads at that time for their own purposes, including, as they were moving into an imposed Catholicism, itemizing points of the catechism or recording their sins. But the period of Spanish acceptance was short-lived. By the 1580s, when curates realized that the cords could also be used to keep track of more indigenous concerns such as offerings to pre-Christian deities, they discouraged their use. In extreme cases, they went out of their way to destroy khipu and suppress knowledge of how to make and use them.

While other pre-colonial Andean institutions fell apart, khipu-keeping knowledge remained intact for hundreds of years. Even without a central Inka state that needed to keep track of its empire, local villages still relied on the cords to document their activities, and individuals used the system for their own purposes. (It is touching to contemplate the image left by a 16th-century missionary who described converts memorizing prayers by using khipu-like devices made from materials they had at hand, such as small stones, or kernels of corn.) As the population became more attuned to writing systems, however, khipu "competence" gradually faded. A complete understanding of the "language" seems to have been lost during the 19th century. Even so, native communities treasured the cords that had been handed down in their villages, and still use them regularly in ritual activities.

When non-indigenous Western scholars of the modern era started looking at pre-Columbian Andean culture, some expressed surprise that such well-organized, advanced civilizations were without a written form of communication. They knew about khipu (there are hundreds extant from the pre-Columbian period alone), but the system was so different from the lexigraphic forms to which they were accustomed that they could not easily recognize its rich data. In the 1920s, anthropologist Leland Locke hypothesized that the cord sets were mnemonic devices based on a numerical decimal system, which were used primarily for book-keeping purposes. This was the generally accepted interpretation for decades. Recently, however, as we have begun to appreciate the highly abstract thinking of the Inka and as binary code has become an integral part of our approach to the world, we are beginning to understand that khipu may have functioned quite differently. One theory is that they worked like a computer language, essentially using zeroes and ones. Harvard professor Gary Urton argues in *Signs of the Khipu* that information appears coded on the cords in seven-bit sequences. The khipu-maker chose the length and color of each pendent string, and then worked the sequence of knots, incorporating the variables mentioned above. With all of the different combinations that were possible, Urton estimates the system may have provided over 1,500 separate units of information—more units than are required to read a newspaper in a pictographic representation of a language such as Chinese. He believes each knotted unit may have functioned similarly to a graphic sign—i.e., it stood for a value, object, or event. Although no one has yet deciphered the full code or found the equivalent of a Rosetta Stone, mathematicians are currently entering descriptive information on extant khipu into a database. Using tools developed to decode DNA sequences, they have identified thousands of repeating knot sequences that suggest distinct "phrases."

Frank Salomon, who has studied khipu extensively, argues that they were not connected to speech, but they functioned almost as a representation of reality, much like musical notation. Mirroring the structures of social practice and spatial understanding, they were dynamic devices, three-dimensional models with "working parts." Khipu records were kept by groups at different levels of the social network (for example, each *ayllu*—a subdivision of the community that functioned something like a landholding collective and fraternal organization—kept its own). Salomon believes the records were renewed each year, as part of the calendrical cycle.

It makes sense that the recording system used by these pre-Columbian people would have involved fiber, since they valued cloth so highly; it was for them not only a marker of status, but of sacredness as well. They came up with this language because they literally thought in textile terms. Fittingly, it was weavers—individuals who know how to think in those terms—who have been instrumental in helping to unlock the codes. Urton first began to understand the khipu in a holistic way after observing Bolivian weavers. For them, he realized, a fabric is:

> A record of many choices, a dance of twists, turns, and pulls that leads
> to the final product. They would have seen a fabric—be it a cloth or
> knotted strings—a bit like a chess master views a game in progress.
> Yes, they see a pattern of pieces on a board, but they also have a feel
> for the moves that led there.[3]

Another potential interpretative breakthrough came from Carrie Brezine, a researcher who is herself a weaver. When she found a pre-Columbian site with multiple khipu that seemed to have increasingly complex structures, she started to interpret them as a contextual system. She believes that a group of cords functioned as a set of related records, each kept by a successively higher level of Inka administrator.

"Smart" fibers

Examples of the newest developments in medical textiles remind us that fibers can now also be "smart"—"intelligent" enough to react to and communicate with their environment. "Smart textiles" are electronically programmed; they are engineered with internal sensors that react to stimuli from mechanical, thermal, chemical, electrical, or magnetic sources. Heat-modifying fibers that help regulate body temperature, for example, are currently being used in outdoor wear, including socks (one Australian product promises to keep wearers' toes at a constant 30 degrees centigrade), and undergarments. A Japanese lingerie company has come up with a line of thermal underwear made with thermo-regulating crystals that solidify and release warmth when the body cools down too far. Thermal-sensitive fibers have medical uses as well. Fiber sensors can also monitor vital statistics such as heart and respiration rate. The "Sensory Baby Vest" uses this technology to help parents of babies susceptible to Sudden Infant Death Syndrome. There are "life vests" for adults, too. They are still quite expensive, but the U.S. army has purchased several thousand as a first step in its plan to create a basic soldier's uniform that will one day continuously monitor all of the wearer's vital signs. Futurists also expect that every hospital patient will eventually wear an undergarment that continually transmits such information to a health professional.[4] A different kind of high-tech underwear with a range of desirable qualities —absorbent, anti-static, flame-resistant, odor-eating, and bacteria-killing— was recently field-tested in space. Astronaut Koichi Wakata wore a single pair for a month, apparently with good results. The idea is that future space travelers would not need as many clothes on their long journeys.[5]

When integrated with Global Positioning Systems (GPS) and mobile phone technology, smart clothing can be used to monitor location. This kind of surveillance has already been put to use in a high-tech prison in Yamaguchi prefecture, Japan: guards keep track of prisoners' movements through their RFID (radio frequency identification) tagged uniforms. More cheerful to contemplate are fiber monitoring devices such as smart cables or ropes that can track exerted stress and strain loads (these are being eyed by rock climbers); smart tents that would be able to collect the appropriate amount of energy needed by the inhabitants; and fabrics and composites integrated with optical fiber sensors that could monitor the stability of bridges and buildings. In production already are an iPod-controlling glove; a snowboard jacket with fabric-based MP3 controls; and interactive basketball jerseys capable of displaying information during play, {opposite} *Alyce Santoro's "Fish Dress" (also called "Jon Fishman's Musical Suit") was woven with audio tape that actually produces sound. It was used on stage as a musical instrument during a concert in 2004. The tape included a sampling of music that Santoro recorded from Fishman's personal music collection. During the performance Fishman ran a portable tape player over the cloth.*

including scores, fouls, player points, and time limits. The jerseys, which were invented by an Australian undergraduate, use conductive textiles to access a strapped-on computer and display the information on electro-luminescent panels integrated into the garments. On another communicative front, fabrics woven with acoustic filters may soon improve the speech heard on mobile phones.

I have mentioned fibers designed with anti-bacterial and odor-absorbing properties. Others include light-sensitive devices that change color depending on illumination. A "photochromic" shirt that responds in this way to ultraviolet intensity is being marketed in Japan to those who must not be over-exposed to sunlight. At the same time, electro-luminescent fiber is being used in textiles marketed to those who suffer from Seasonal Affective Disorder and need *more* light. The intriguing aesthetic possibilities of light-sensitive textiles are not forgotten. Polymers with attention-getting light emitting diodes are being incorporated into cutting-edge clothing and what is considered the "next generation" of displays and packaging.[6]

Smart textile innovations are designed to interact with all of the senses, and to affect emotions. Scentsory Design® fabrics emit fragrance in response to particular stimuli; they are being marketed as clothing that can increase well-being. Scentsory garments are made from yarns engineered with bits of perfume encapsulated in microscopic bubbles. On cue, they emit nano-sized droplets of uplifting scent. (Other substances, including bactericides or vitamins, can be microencapsulated in a similar fashion.) Light-sensitive fibers are used in "The Emotional Wardrobe" research project, in which garments change color in response to a wearer's feelings. Even more fantastic are the clothes being developed to convey a sense of touch over a long distance. There are sensors in the Hug Shirt™, for example, that detect pressure, warmth, and heartbeat. Someone wearing the shirt can actually receive remote tactile messages that mimic the sensation of being embraced. The British-based "Emotional Wardrobe" project is concerned with fundamentally changing people's relationships with their clothing and making garments more "emotively rich."[7]

Artists are also incorporating communication technology into some of their work. While they may not be technically "smart," they deliver messages *about* communication. Clothing made out of optical fibers, for example, "speaks" about our newest information systems. Alyce Santoro makes garments and installations incorporating audio tape as a woven element. When a magnetic tape head is run over the fabric, it makes sound. Her "musical suit" (also known as "Fish Dress") was commissioned by Jon Fishman, percussionist of the rock band Phish, for use as an instrument in a 2004 concert. Santoro recorded a densely layered sound collage from samples of music tapes in Fishman's personal collection. The recorded tape subsequently became the weft of the musical suit, which he wore during the performance. Admiring fans cheered as he ran the tape head over his body, producing different musical "messages."[8]

Playful cotton furnishing fabric featuring a design based on a sailor's semaphore signal, U.S., 1930–50.

Coded messages in flags and ribbons

In chapter 3, I discussed how shared textile designs or patterns can help groups feel a sense of solidarity or bonding. Specific combinations of pattern and color on cloth also communicate other messages. In the Middle Ages, heraldic banners and knights' tunics immediately identified the allegiances of their bearers. It was absolutely necessary to communicate with a visual code of this sort, since people needed to discern quickly from a distance whether approaching armies were friends or foes. Today, coded flag systems still function as quickly processed communicators. Ship pilots not only fly banners that announce their nationality on the open sea, but also use other flags as semaphores, that is, as textile signals that are not dependent on a shared language. Many are familiar with the idea that disabled vessels ask for help by flying an S.O.S. flag, but flags offer a much broader range of possible messages. Particular patterns indicate that there is a diver below a stationary vessel, for example, that a person is overboard, or that the ship is taking on or discharging explosives. Flag signals may go back and forth; in response to an S.O.S. signal, the pilot of a nearby ship might signal he has a doctor on board or is otherwise able to provide assistance. A different, alphabet-based semaphore flag system is used on land. In this case all the flags are square and carry the same red and yellow pattern, but signalers spell out messages by moving them through space. Holding a flag in each hand, they extend their arms in various positions, each of which represents a letter of the alphabet.[9] In wartime America, coded flags hung in front of family homes, indicating which of them had members serving in the armed forces. The number of blue stars in the center field indicated how many individuals were in service. Local organizations such as churches also flew these flags during World War II, denoting the number of their members on the front. The blue star flag tradition was introduced during World War I, was used during World War II, and has been revived in the last decade.[10]

Color-coded ribbons also convey a range of messages. The yellow ribbon signals remembrance for soldiers fighting far from home. For centuries, British women wore a ribbon for a loved one who was away and in potential danger; the idea was that the ribbon would come off only when the individual returned safely. American Civil War soldiers' wives are said to have worn yellow ribbons in the British fashion, and the practice took hold, as evidenced by the 1949 John Wayne film, *She Wore a Yellow Ribbon*, and the 1970s song, "Tie a Yellow Ribbon Round the Ole Oak Tree." During the U.S./Iran hostage crisis of 1979–80, yellow ribbons were a common sign of remembrance; people tied them to the front of their houses, to trees, and even to telephone poles. Ribbon-tying re-emerged after the destruction of the World Trade Center in 2001. In that case the ribbons no longer symbolized a vigil for people who were expected to come back, but represented remembrance and the act of vigilance itself. The form of the ribbons was altered as well, since cloth was increasingly replaced by magnets, which could be displayed prominently on cars, or by plastic bracelets. The ribbon nevertheless remains a powerful symbol, as evidenced by the fact that color-coded bands are now appearing as signs of vigilance for other causes. Pink ribbons represent the fight against breast cancer, and red ribbons the fight against AIDS. Purple ribbons represent the fight for the legalization of gay marriage. Black ribbons represent a state of grief or mourning. Orange ribbons were used "to remember" in Ukraine's 2004–2005 "Orange Revolution." Ukrainians wore the ribbons during strikes and acts of civil disobedience, broadcasting allegiance to their cause of independence from Russia.[11]

Giving a voice to the silenced

The communicative power of textiles was recognized by Sophocles, who, in a play that has now been lost, coined the phrase "the voice of the shuttle." He was recounting the story of Philomela, a young woman who was savagely raped and mutilated by her brother-in-law. To prevent her from telling what he had done, he cut out her tongue. Unable to express herself verbally, Philomela subsequently wove scenes of her violation into a tapestry. Her sister was able to interpret the weaving, and took revenge upon her husband. According to Homer's *Iliad*, Helen of Troy also used weaving to express her feelings about the destruction that had ensued after her abduction. As she worked on a large purple cloak, she incorporated images of battle scenes and the horrible wars the Greeks and Trojans suffered for her sake. One contemporary commentator who uses *The Iliad* verses to interpret what Helen must have felt writes that she went from "silent weaver to public speaker."[12]

Blue star flags like this would have flown in front of the home of someone serving in the U.S. armed forces during World War II. The single star indicates that the family had one person on the front. This one was displayed by the mother of James M. Hagman, who survived the war but died in an accident in 1945.

European myths express the same idea—that silenced individuals can speak through textiles. In one often-repeated fairy-tale, six brothers are changed into swans by a jealous stepmother. In order to save them, their sister must remain silent (she may not even laugh) for six years, and must make them shirts out of nettle fiber, which is notoriously difficult to work with. When she throws the completed shirts over the swans at the end of the allotted time, the textiles reverse the enchantment, allowing them to return to human form (because she had no time to finish the last sleeve, however, one of the brothers returns without an arm). Once the brothers' own power to speak is restored, they proclaim her innocence and in turn save her from a death sentence. The idea that textile-making is an important form of speech has been recently reclaimed by feminist scholars

We are healed of a suffering only by expressing it to the full.

Marcel Proust

A woman's ability to weave, cut, sew, or create with whatever resources were available were vital to not only her survival, but her remembrance in history as well.

Caroline Liebman

such as Patricia Klindienst, who in an essay entitled "The Voice of the Shuttle is Ours," argues that through the loom (or its companion part, the shuttle), women can find their voices and true power.[13]

Some of cloth's non-verbal messages function as alternative speech. In the previous chapter flag dresses that expressed Palestinian identity and resistance to Israeli authority are described. At other times, fabrics "speak" of atrocities or name names that cannot be said aloud. This is represented fictionally in Dickens's *A Tale of Two Cities*, in which the character Madame DeFarge incorporates the names of aristocrats targeted for the guillotine in her knitting. It is also seen in many real-life situations. In the 1990s in Bihar, India, women who had witnessed the horrors of female infanticide and wife-burning stitched images of their experiences into embroideries made from old saris. The textiles were exhibited in art galleries in North America and Europe, bringing the Bihari women's situation into the public eye. The exhibition organizers knew the potential power of this kind of exhibition, as they were well aware of the worldwide impact that protest textiles had had in preceding decades. For example, *arpilleras*, small pictorial embroideries illustrating the horrors that had taken place in Chile during the repressive Pinochet regime, had found a receptive audience in the 1970s. The arpilleras were made by women whose relatives had been arrested, tortured, or had "disappeared." Constructed with colorful fabrics in a three-dimensional folk art style, they at first looked fairly innocuous, until one really examined what the images depicted. Often, the names of the disappeared were included, as were expressions such as "Where are they?" Some of the cloth that was worked into the pieces came from articles of clothing that belonged to the missing.[14]

Arpillera workshops were initiated in 1975 by the Vicariate of Solidarity, an institution that operated under the protection of the Roman Catholic Church and therefore could not be dismantled by the Pinochet government. Women met in the workshops to stitch the textiles, which were subsequently smuggled out of the country and exhibited and sold overseas, often through church organizations. Making the arpilleras allowed the

women to deal with their grief and frustration. The money they earned from the sales helped sustain their families, a fact which was particularly vital, since it was often the former breadwinners who were missing. In addition, arpilleristas were empowered by the fact that they could "tell" their stories to outsiders who otherwise would not know what was happening in their country. As a result of this experience, many of them became political activists who worked to oust the repressive regime. Arpillera-making was so satisfying and effective that it spread in the 1980s to neighboring Peru, which had disappearances and political violence of its own.

The Hmong, a minority people, many of whom emigrated from Southeast Asia to the U.S. (and to a lesser extent, Europe) as refugees of the Vietnam War, began in the 1970s to stitch memories of their traumatic journey into small panels known as "story cloths." The Hmong had fought for the Americans during that conflict, sometimes working on covert operations with the Central Intelligence Agency. After the war, they were systematically targeted for annihilation by their Laotian and Vietnamese neighbors, and were forced to flee. Before displacement, Hmong women had embroidered "flower cloth," which featured stylized, abstract patterning and was solely used to embellish clothing. Beginning with their stay in refugee camps in Thailand and continuing through their resettlement in a very different culture, they used their needlework skills to communicate

A Peruvian arpillera, entitled Detenidos (The Detained)*, made by Felicita M. in the early 1990s. The cheerful-looking embroidery actually illustrates a grim scene: it includes gun-toting police and the truck in which prisoners suspected of assisting the Shining Path guerillas were taken away.*

what had happened to them. They were able to "speak" to outsiders who did not know their language. Story cloths were pictorial narratives with scenes such as planes strafing their villages and families escaping across the Mekong River. Like arpilleras, the cloths were themselves "witnesses," and they helped with Hmong survival in that they were saleable commodities.[15]

Under the auspices of sympathetic organizations, unemployed women who had suffered through the injustices of South African apartheid were also encouraged to tell their stories through embroidery. Their "memory cloths" helped ease the pain by illustrating some of the most difficult aspects of their "journey to freedom." Later, when the cloths were displayed in public exhibition venues in South Africa and around the world (often coupled with performative storytelling), they collectively provided a deeper understanding of life under repressive conditions.[16]

Another well-known example of a memory cloth is the composite NAMES Project AIDS Memorial Quilt, where each panel is made in honor of an individual who died from the disease. It has grown over time to immense proportions. When the first panels were made in 1987, HIV-AIDS was still a taboo subject. For the homosexual community whose members were dying in great numbers from the disease at that time, the cloth provided a particularly potent way of "speaking out" about their experience. Quilt panels are still accepted by the NAMES Project, although its memorial disproportionately represents losses from the First World. The ravages of the disease continue at a frightening pace in other parts of the world, such as Africa.

Other cloth communication systems routinely allow women to communicate non-verbally about more benign, everyday experiences. Many married women in East Africa, for example, wear colorful, commercially

Detail of a Hmong band with pompoms, Laos or Thailand, c. 1970, by an unidentified artist. The complex reverse appliqué and fine embroidery were typical of the paj ntaub *(flower cloth) the Hmong made for their own clothing before they were displaced from Southeast Asia.*

{left} *Hmong "story cloth," c. 1975–92, documenting the people's escape from Laos to Thailand over the Mekong River. The escapees are wearing their traditional clothing. Representational textiles of this sort originated in the Thai refugee camps and were sold to foreigners as a way of earning money and communicating the Hmong story.*

{above} *View of the NAMES Project Quilt (more commonly known as the AIDS Quilt) laid out on the Mall in Washington, D.C. The scale of this quilt becomes clear when one looks at the spectators in the lower right-hand corner of the photograph.*

{left} *Detail, informally known as "the Burning Man," from an embroidered wall hanging by Thembisili Mabizela, South Africa, 2004. This hanging was a product of the "Journey to Freedom Narratives," a collaborative project of the UNISA Visual Arts department, the UNISA Melodia Chorale, Intuthuko and Boitumelo Sewing Groups.*

A cotton kanga, a rectangular length of cloth which would be used as a wrapped garment, from Kenya, 2006. Kangas feature a brightly colored pattern as well as a printed proverb. Wearers may choose specific designs because of their proverbs; the textiles facilitate a kind of silent coded speech.

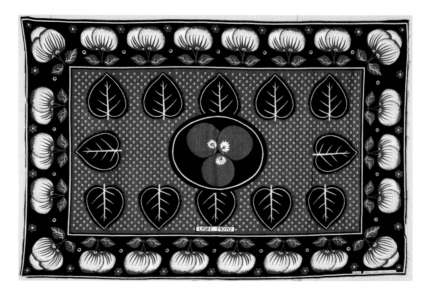

KANGA MESSAGES OR PROVERBS

(These are loose translations, and some proverbs may now be out of date)

- You can visit all the butchers, but the meat is the same.
- You are crossing my boundary, be immediately careful of my date tree [i.e., lay off my man].
- Don't feel jealousy, friends, for I have endured a lot.
- Education is an ocean (that is, it has no end).
- The one who loves does not take revenge.
- The person who laughs at another's scar has not been wounded yet.
- If you give to me, I will receive; I am not used to begging.
- You don't live without working.
- Life is the best gift; the rest is extra.
- The medicine of malaria is quinine. What is the medicine for wickedness?
- Thank you for your good deeds to me.
- Good luck begins in the morning.
- You will die poor if you rely on relatives.
- How did you know this if you did not go behind my back?
- You will get hurt by talking behind other people's backs.

printed wrapped garments called *kanga* (also called *leso*, *kikoy*, or *pagne*) which include both imagery and expressive text. The particular kanga a woman chooses on any given day may be used as a form of expression, since its printed motto or proverb (or its name, based on a proverb) communicates in a coded form. Rose Marie Beck, who has written extensively about these "texts on textiles," notes that there are many things that women in Swahili-speaking culture will not say out loud—they maintain a "restrained speech," since silence and forbearance are considered part of a woman's dignity. Because cloth is out of the spoken realm, it is outside of regular language conventions, so women can use it to express themselves and still remain within the bounds of propriety.[17]

The proverbs give women a chance to comment on subjects such as love, sexuality, politics, and gossip; they can allude covertly to disputes between married couples or in-laws, for example, or rivals for a man's affection. In an article entitled "Wearing Proverbs," Susan Domowitz tells the story of a man who began seeing another woman after his divorce:

> He noticed that she often wore a cloth in which the wild spider figured in the design...and suspected that she was trying to say something to him. Then he remembered a proverb that says, "What one does to cendaa (a small harmless spider), one does not do to bokohulu (a large spider considered dangerous)." The man interpreted this to mean that he should not mistreat this woman as she supposed he had mistreated

his first wife... [The woman] eventually confirmed that the message of that very proverb was indeed intended for him.[18]

Kanga text includes mockeries, puns, and ironic and humorous sayings as well as laudatory and didactic comments. Some are quite pointed. The sayings can be topical, and may become outdated; a woman would not choose to wear an "old message" if she could afford a new kanga. Interestingly, the power of the coded message is not based on the actual readability of the text when the textile is worn, for sometimes kanga are draped around the body in an upside down or even inside-out fashion. Because the proverbs are known and function almost as citations, however, the cloth is still "speaking."

Proverb cloths (*lamba hoany*) are also used in Madagascar. There, they function as a kind of lingua franca, for although there are eighteen different ethnic groups with distinct dialects, the cloths printed with Malagasy proverbs are understood island-wide. Women wear them throughout their adult lives.[19]

Well into the 20th century, women who could not speak freely in Turkey were similarly able to express their feelings through coded messages displayed on textiles. In this case, the communication was not based on proverbs; rather, it was the pattern worked into the needle lace or *oya* that bordered the woman's headscarf that spoke for her. As Patricia Hickman phrased it in *Turkish Oya*, "A woman could wear a scarf, and without saying a word to anyone, in complete silence, could publicly convey news as effectively as if she'd written a letter." Some patterns were used in prescribed ways. During the religious ceremony held the day after the marriage ritual, the bride traditionally wore the "sea-holly" pattern, which symbolically told her mother-in-law not to sting her like a thorn. A woman might make a pregnancy obvious to her community even before there was a verbal announcement if she appeared in a scarf adorned with the "good news" pattern. More often, Hickman explains, a woman's needle lace message would refer to something very personal.[20] Oya worked in green thread was generally understood to reflect satisfaction in marriage, while yellow might indicate unhappiness or annoyance. A scarf adorned with miniature pepper motifs might similarly communicate that a woman and her husband were not getting along or that things were "hot," and a pansy flower border implied that the husband was "roving." If a woman gave her mother-in-law a scarf with well-spaced meadow flowers, it indicated things were going well, but if it was adorned with "deathlike" dark projections, the news was not good.[21]

Coded messages about pregnancy and sexuality may also have been present in the magnificent medieval textiles that proclaimed the glory of the Christian church. Rozsika Parker argues in *The Subversive Stitch* that some of the imagery in the famed *Opus Anglicanum* or "English work" celebrated the power of women, although this idea went counter to the stance of the church fathers. Opus Anglicanum was a type of fine embroidery

Turkish oya (needle lace; sometimes also called "Arab lace") made in the form of different flowers and related shapes. The bands serve as edgings that are sewn on to head scarves that, in Pat Hickman's words, "surround the face like a refreshing garnish." In the past, each flower had a communicative symbolic meaning. The purple and white oya (below) was made before 1930.

Chasuble with Opus Anglicanum (English work) embroidery, c. 1330–50. The materials include silver-gilt threads, silk and silk velvet, and pearls.

featuring gold and other precious metals. In demand throughout Europe, it was used by royalty and church leaders, often in a ceremonial context; several extant examples are found on copes (circular capes) that were worn by cardinals and popes. The embroidery to which Parker refers was worked by nuns who lived secluded lives in convents, and much of its iconography honors the Virgin. Parker notes that while the church saw pregnancy, fertility, and childbirth as signs of women's sinfulness, Mary is actually portrayed in these stitched images as a fecund, sexual being. Using their needles as a form of coded speech, the medieval women communicated a story of their own choosing.[22]

Messages on textiles

Contemporary fiber artists like to point out the relationship between cloth and communication. They note that the word "text" actually derives from the Latin *texere*, which means "to weave." The association between weaving and words comes alive in the popular children's book, *Charlotte's Web*, in which an enterprising spider named Charlotte is able to save her porcine friend, Wilbur, by literally weaving words into her web. Wilbur is slated for slaughter—he will become Christmas dinner on the farm where they both live—but Charlotte spins words about him in her web, including "SOME PIG," and later "TERRIFIC" and "HUMBLE." Wilbur becomes famous, and his life is spared because of her actions.[23]

Words and symbols have certainly been written *on* or *in* textiles for millennia. Silk was chosen as a medium for written documents in China as long ago as 770 BCE. It was considered a superior writing surface to the stiffer alternative, bamboo, and once it was marked, the messages were permanent. The fabric was also lightweight and could be folded into small, transportable parcels.[24] Text was literally made part of cloth through weaving, embroidery, and once the technology allowed, printing. The messages might be didactic. Many people of medieval Europe learned Bible stories from the huge tapestries textiles hung in churches and draped on public streets during religious processions. The stories were first shown primarily through images, but text soon appeared at the bottom. With their pomp and sumptuous imagery, these hangings reinforced Christian precepts and ideology. As literacy increased by the 17th century, European girls learned the alphabet along with moral values as they fashioned needlework samplers. Girls as young as seven were often made to stitch lugubrious verses about mortality, virtue, and family piety.[25]

If they were wealthy enough to attend a young ladies' academy in the late 18th and early 19th centuries, girls were taught even more elegant needlework. As they painstakingly worked the delicate stitches on their "silkwork pictures," they learned about classical mythology and related subjects befitting current Enlightenment values. A completed embroidery

DIDACTIC SAMPLER VERSES

Loara Standish is my name
Lorde guide my hart that
I may doe thy will also
My hands with such
Convenient skill as may
Conduce to virtue void of
Shame and I will give
The glory to thy name

Loara Standish's work, made in Duxbury, Mass., c. 1653, is the earliest-known American sampler.

Though life is fair
And pleasure young
And Love on ev'ry Shepherd's tongue,
I turn my thoughts
To serious things
Life is ever on the wing.

Anonymous sampler, undated

This needlework of mine was taught
Not to spend my time for naught

Anonymous sampler, 1789

The pink will fade, the tulip wither
But a virtuous mind will bloom forever.

Anonymous sampler, 1816

Awake my soul and with the sun
Thy daily stage of duty run
Shake off dull sloth and early rise
To pay the morning sacrifice

Isabel Redie sampler, 1816

The verse that Mary Allen stitched on her sampler (England, 1821) was decidedly moralistic. In addition to the written message, the piece includes an image of angels in heaven and Adam and Eve in the Garden of Eden, further underlining its message about hard work, religion, and original sin.

Finely wrought, three-dimensional embroidered "terrestrial globe," probably made in the Quaker School in Westtown, Pennsylvania, U.S., c. 1820.

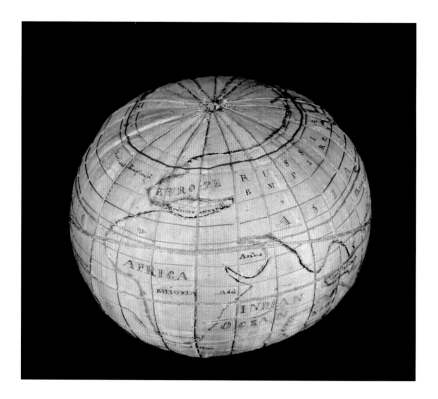

of this type was framed and typically hung in the family parlor, the way a diploma might be displayed on the wall today. Its presence communicated to the world that the family was prosperous and that the daughter was a refined and educated individual.[26] Academy students also learned geography and astronomy, and sometimes stitched their own terrestrial and celestial maps. Embroidered globes were used to demonstrate both sewing skill (each of the eight sections had to be cut, stitched, and stuffed perfectly to form an even sphere) and knowledge of the world.[27]

Sampler-type wall hangings continued to evolve over the next century, their messages changing with the mores of the times. By the 1930s in America, needlework was no longer a skill all women could boast about, but even so, a woman could display her own "handmade" sampler. Depression-era samplers fashioned from pre-stamped kits proclaimed very different values. Their primary message was about homeyness, and they were filled with saccharine homilies about the pleasures of the hearth.[28] Various ethnic groups had their own variations on the sampler theme. Czech immigrants, for example, embroidered bright wall hangings they called "kitchen helpers." Each featured a domestic scene with a proverb or word of advice, or a cheerful sentiment about women of that heritage ("where the Czech housekeeper cooks, there is good living" is one loosely translated example).[29]

Other textiles communicated messages about politics. In the 19th and early 20th centuries, many women who were fighting for social causes naturally turned to the medium they knew best—sewing on cloth—to get their message across; advocates of abolition and temperance, particularly, made their views known on fabric. Some of these didactic textiles, such as an "anti-slave [pot] holder," were used to raise money for the cause at hand. Signature quilts with didactic messages were also often sold to support specific causes. One, presented at the Women's Christian Temperance Union (WCTU) convention in Baltimore in 1878, featured about 3,000 names. The popular late 19th-century American quilt pattern, "Drunkard's Path," was often worked in the WCTU colors of blue and white.[30]

When printing technology advanced in late 18th-century Europe to the point that it was possible to print directly on fabric, the range of communicative textiles expanded, and since inexpensive cotton cloth became available about the same time, the manufacture of printed cloths exploded. One of the first affordable and popular cloths in Europe and America was the kerchief popularly known as the bandanna (the word is derived from the Indian term *bandhna* (*bandhana*), which refers to a tie-dye process that created dotted patterns). The earliest examples did not usually feature text, although they did communicate semiotically. I will digress for a moment to describe this. Bandannas were large red or blue squares, at first filled with spotted designs, and later with paisley patterns. As the mention of cowboy bandannas in chapter 2 reminds us, the cloths were at first associated with working men: they were worn by railroad engineers, farmers, and firefighters, in addition to cowboys. In more recent eras, bandannas have been used as part of the communicative code of specific groups. Boy Scouts indicate which troop they belong to with a tan or blue variety; Los Angeles gang members "show their colors" with red (the "Bloods") or blue (the "Crips") bandannas.[31]

Returning to the discussion of textual messages, I look first at the commemorative handkerchief. Containing both detailed renderings and text, these printed cloths were issued in limited runs to comment on topical political issues or recognize important events such as the coronation of Queen Victoria (1838), the commissioning of a warship, or the opening of a world's fair or exposition. Essentially, they celebrated and didactically communicated ideas about the grandeur of the "civilized" world. An extant commemorative of the Great (Crystal Palace) Exhibition of 1851, for example, depicts crowds of well-dressed English people in front of the glass building, bordered by indigenous peoples from various parts of the British Empire.[32]

Handkerchiefs were small and portable, and as I have shown, often functioned as gifts, tokens of affection, and souvenirs. Those with commemorative images remained popular for another century. They were produced for American events such as the 1893 World's Columbian Exposition in Chicago—birds-eye views of that fair indicated just how grand the "White City" was—and battles of the Spanish–American war. In England, the coronation of Queen Elizabeth II in June 1953 generated a commemorative handkerchief, as did many of her subsequent activities. In 1954, when she conducted a royal tour of Tasmania, a handkerchief created for the event was given to schoolchildren who participated in the honor guard. The practice of distributing these textiles to children was

{below} An anti-slavery potholder purchased during the American Civil War at the Great Northwestern Sanitary Fair. This 1863 Chicago event raised money for the U.S. Sanitary Commission which oversaw medical and other non-military needs of the Union soldiers. Household items with this political message were sold at anti-slavery events during this period.

{bottom} Detail of a Toile de Jouy (a French copperplate engraving), featuring scenes of military life, 1780–90.

{above, left} *Handkerchiefs with patriotic and morale-boosting messages were popular in both Britain and the U.S. during and after World War II. These date from 1948. The ubiquitous "V for Victory" in the central circle of the bottom example was surrounded with the dots and dashes of Morse code that stood for the same thing. The star shape of the top example was unusual, but since it was made after the war it could be slightly more lighthearted and less practical.*

{above, right} *"Conversation print" handkerchiefs were very lighthearted in the post-war era. Most conveyed information such as cocktail recipes or (as here) the rules of a card game, but they were primarily meant to be amusing. Made for the U.S. market, this canasta handkerchief (1949–50) was finished with a rolled edge and printed in the Philippines. Similar-looking handkerchiefs were made as far afield as Spain and Switzerland.*

actually of long standing. When King George V ceremonially "opened" a library in Manchester many years before, every child in that city was given a handkerchief that reinforced prevailing values. Featuring pictures of the king and queen, it bore the words, "Knowledge is power."[33]

Printed handkerchiefs with pointed commentary were ubiquitous in both England and America during World War II. The messages were in this case applied to silk or rayon squares worn as women's headscarves. The scarves were fashionable (*Vogue* magazine designated a "handkerchief of the month" throughout the war), but also communicated patriotism and served as a morale-boosting bit of propaganda. Some bore proud phrases like "Into Battle," "On to Berlin," or "Combined Operations" (referring to the Army, Navy, and Air Force); others offered cautionary slogans such as "Be Cautious, Be Careful, The Enemy Has Ears" or reminders about salvaging rubber and other materials. Still others bore images of battleships, tanks, or fighter planes (these could be used as a visual identification guide) or the ubiquitous "V" that stood for Victory.[34]

Soon after the war, printed handkerchiefs were even more ubiquitous, and much more lighthearted. Some, filled with cartoon-like animals and storybook characters, were made for children, but adults also used "conversation prints" as fashion accessories. This was a new type of printed commemorative in that it humorously addressed leisure-time activities or current aspects of popular culture. Even when denoting a civic anniversary or similar event, it was rendered with a light touch. Some functioned as souvenirs of travel—in America, there were handkerchiefs from each of the different states—which might be amassed as a collection. Perhaps the overarching message of these textiles was a sense of good cheer and amusement. They were particularly fitting as an emblem of the prosperity and optimism that prevailed in the post-war period.[35]

As my previous discussions of kanga and Nigerian aso ebe indicate, commemorative cloth and conversation prints are by no means an exclusively Western phenomenon. Africa abounds with its own "fancy prints." West Africans also use commemorative cloth to mark political, cultural, social, and religious events. These are large cloths—big enough to wear—and are often produced for distribution in a relatively local area. They are sometimes commissioned by local political figures or organizations, and broadcast government campaigns for initiatives like good nutrition or literacy itself.

African fancy prints may be made with an expensive and prestigious wax-resist technique, or a more ordinary (roller) printing process. Both varieties often include images of everyday objects such as fans, binoculars, whiskbrooms, or motorcycles; others include musicians or other figures from popular culture. The pictures may themselves comment on current issues, or the fabrics may include words or simple phrases that make the sentiments explicit. A print popular in Mali in the 1980s, for example, pictured a woman longing for money and material possessions. It was captioned "*Ce que femme veut*" ("What women want"). These prints are also time-bound; they are popular for a while, but most go out of style and are superseded by newer images.[36]

Topical prints have also been incorporated into Afro-Brazilian culture, particularly in the context of carnival costume. The *Filhos de Gandhy* (Sons of Gandhi), a Bahian parade group, is one example. They celebrate ancestral

{below} *An array of colorful "fancy prints" on sale in the market in Accra, Ghana, 2005.*

{opposite, above} *Woman's haori (a formal coat) with a design entitled* The Thrill of Flight, *Japan, late 1920s–early 1930s. Japanese men's and boys' garments were often printed with militaristic imagery in the first half of the 20th century as they were believed to help instill qualities of strength and bravery in their wearers.*

{opposite, below} *A woolen blanket,* Airplane Propellers, *made in Britain for the African trade in the 1940s. This was worn by a Basuto man in Lesotho, South Africa. In addition to the dramatic central image, the design includes British royal crowns.*

pride and West African tradition, albeit in an ostensibly Indian guise. New prints are devised for their outfits each year.[37]

Another kind of political print—one that did not include words—was seen in Japan during World War II. Some of the textiles used in men's and boys' clothing, especially jacket linings and under-kimonos, featured propagandistic images of tanks, planes, and violent war scenes. The masculine-identified imagery was thought to imbue wearers with qualities such as bravery, strength and power, and filial piety.[38] While the British did not themselves wear propagandistic imagery on anything larger than a kerchief, they did make such textiles for export. One blanket worn by a Basuto man in Lesotho, South Africa, featured an R.A.F. airplane propeller and incorporated the familiar British slogan, "V for Victory."

The modern Western version of the conversation or commemorative print is undoubtedly the T-shirt. Since the 1970s, "message" T-shirts have become relatively ubiquitous, proclaiming everything from personal or political opinion to advertisements for specific designers or branded products. Increasingly, the shirts are printed for one-time, temporal events, including the kind of family reunion or other social bonding event examined in chapter 3. Fans buy them when they go to rock concerts, and runners receive them when they tackle a difficult race. T-shirts are in such high demand at marathons, in fact, that they have become an assumed "perk" for those who compete; now, sponsoring groups have to factor in the cost of purchasing and printing them. According to one organizer, that amounts to about half of her annual budget. An interesting situation that has arisen is that those who run in multiple races wind up with a great many T-shirts and then have to deal with shirt maintenance. Some enterprising individuals are addressing this problem by sewing these mementoes into

{right} *Tunic with motifs reminiscent of Dahomey textiles, inscribed "Timba Lada Cordeiro da Paz." Timbalada is a musical group started by the beloved Carlinhos Brown, and Cordeiro is a region near Rio de Janeiro. Communicative "fancy prints" like this were made for the Afro-Brazilian market and worn by various carnival groups, Salvador, Bahia, Brazil, 2004.*

bed quilts. In 2002, Minnesotan Margaret Thatcher charged anything from $100 for a "nine-shirt throw" to $300 for a king size quilt. She was averaging about one T-shirt quilt order a week.[39]

T-shirts are also commonly purchased as souvenirs of travel, either to be worn by the traveler, and/or given as a gift to a friend or relative. The travel T-shirt gift is such a trope, in fact, that some years ago it generated a whole genre of souvenirs printed with the ironic comment, "My folks [*or fill in the relationship*] went to [*fill in the destination*] and all I got was this lousy T-shirt."

Beyond narrative content, textiles often express deep-seated, profound glimpses of cultural world views and beliefs. This can be seen in terms of kanga proverbs, Asafo flags, and Opus Anglicanum. Sometimes in their very layout or conception, textiles also served as actual embodiments of the way the makers see the world—as what I think of as "cosmological maps." The Bolivian Wiphala flag introduced in chapter 3 is one such example. "Wiphala" is derived from two Aymara words: *wiphay*, an expression of joy approximately meaning "Go;" and *phalax*, which refers to the sound produced by a flag floating in the wind. Every element embodies Aymara belief. The square form contains a 7 x 7 (49 square) patchwork design, arranged diagonally and worked in the seven colors of the visible spectrum, or rainbow. Each carries a symbolic meaning. The overall flag also represents the Andean lunar-solar calendar, and symbolizes the Andean "communitarian" system based on equality, equity, harmony, solidarity, and reciprocity.[40]

SIGNIFICANCE OF THE COLORS OF THE WIPHALA

Red The Earth and the Andean people

Orange Society and culture

Yellow Energy

Green Natural resources

Blue The heavens

Violet Andean government and self-determination

White Time

Persian-style garden carpets literally represent bird's-eye views of stylized outdoor spaces with regular flowerbeds and a central pathway, but beyond that, they serve as visions of Paradise. In Islam, Paradise is likened to a verdant but orderly garden, with life-giving, ever-flowing water in the center. To sit on a textile like this is to put oneself in alignment and harmony with the highest reward.

Textiles worn on the body are especially likely to be organized as a model of universal order, and many include the cardinal directions. The emperor's dragon robe of late imperial China functioned this way. Its construction and layout were aligned with the directions and the nine- and twelve-part divisions of the Chinese universe. Its consistently repeated imagery represented a controlled world, where everything was in its rightful place: dragons, the most powerful mythic beings, guarded the center and primary directions, and they were set in a field with the earthly elements: water at the bottom, a central triangular earth "mountain," bands of clouds in the sky, etc. Every motif had a specific beneficent meaning. The full symbolic power of the robe took effect, however, only when it was worn by the emperor. Clothed in this garment with his feet on the ground and his head rising above the clouds depicted on the cloth, he was believed to help unify the earthly and heavenly domains and thus maintain cosmic order.[41]

The layout of the traditional huipil or blouse from the community of Santo Tomás Chichicastenango, Guatemala, also symbolically represents the world. When it is opened out, it takes the form of a cross, alluding to the four cardinal directions much like the dragon robe. Added rosettes punctuate each of the four axes. Even though the huipil is worn by an ordinary woman, her head coming up out of the neck hole similarly completes the symbolic message—it is like a rising sun.[42]

Pre-Columbian weavings embodied Andean concepts of the cosmos and social organization. Their very materials—camelid wool, cotton, and feathers—consciously evoked the different realms of the natural world. There, too, the textile planes were often divided into quadrants that alluded to the four directions, and the designs included strong juxtapositions of light and dark, and motifs constructed as complementary pairs. The Andean world view was governed by binary oppositions such as male and female, high and low, open and contained, so each garment represented a state of balance and equilibrium.[43]

{opposite, above, left} *A Kazakh lali posh (food cover) embroidered by the women of a bridegroom's family and given to the bride's family. The repeating motif of a quadrisected circle alludes to the four directions and the sense of the continually moving and ever-returning sun.*

{opposite, above, right} *An opened-out huipil from San Juan Sacatepéquez, Guatemala, indicating the same four-part division of space as in the lali posh above.*

{opposite, below} *Chinese emperor's embroidered semi-formal court robe, 1723–35 (Qing dynasty).*

{below} *The entire conception of this Huari-style four-corner pile weave hat, from Peru, c. 800–1000, embodies the Andean world view. The shape of the camelid fiber hat and the designs on each of its sides reference the four directions, and there are repeating motifs which form complementary pairs as well as strong juxtapositions of light and dark.*

{bottom} *Tunic, or hanging, made from thousands—perhaps as many as a million—macaw feathers worked on a cotton base, Condesuyos, Peru, c. 700–850.*

Balance and harmony were also maintained by the Navajo bi'il, the handwoven dresses mentioned in chapter 2 in relation to psychic comfort. This style, which was primarily worn prior to the 1860s when the Navajo were forced into captivity by the U.S. government, was a simple two-panel rectangular tunic woven in a pattern of stripes and stepped diamonds. Again, the use of space and arrangement of dark and light reflected the people's concept of right relationship, and in a sense each garment reproduced the basic creation story, since the dominant dark center represented the place of emergence. Messages about the sky above, the world below, and the holy spirit were even embedded in the abstract designs of Great Plains bead and quillwork used on garments and personal accessories. Although their geometric forms may look to the casual viewer like the epitome of non-representation, they too encoded meaning. After interviewing beadworkers in 1903, ethnographer William Jones concluded that the work was a "graphic form of prayer."[44]

{top} *Border or fringe probably once attached to a mantle, early Nasca Culture, Peru, 200–50 BCE. The heads and tabs of this piece probably represent lima beans, which were an important food for the pre-Columbian elite. The "beans" are animated, indicating a belief that everything had a spirit. The tiny fringe tabs each also include interlocking (counterchange) motifs.*

{above} *A panel (i.e., the front or back) of a Navajo bi'il (dress), c. 1870s–1880s. The red yarn is "bayeta," a wool which was painstakingly unraveled from trade blankets and similar textiles. The central dark area surrounded by a balanced arrangement of stripes represents the place of emergence.*

Human ingenuity and aesthetic expression

We have seen throughout this book how much ingenuity, complex problem-solving, and creative thinking goes into textile-making. Even in something as seemingly simple as spinning, different adaptations were needed for different purposes: hard-twisted threads for sturdy trousers, cobweb-fine threads for lace work, and so on. Aesthetically exciting designs were often achieved with the simplest technologies—in many cases, with nothing more than sticks and string. The ikat textiles that have been mentioned several times are visually and intellectually sophisticated, yet the designs are made by nothing more than tying off sections of warp and/or weft to create a dye resist. Ikat patterning apparently arose independently in such far-flung places as Japan, Central America, and Indonesia, implying that people the world over have the same inventive propensity. Some scholars feel that the thought processes involved in coming up with these techniques have

had a huge impact on human culture—they have provided the impetus, in fact, for much of human advancement. Archaeologist Glynn Isaac claims that the invention of basket-making was the "watershed achievement of all time" that may even have helped expand the human brain.[45]

Many of the inventions or devices that sped up or simplified textile-making may also have led to new ways of thinking or doing. Sadie Plant, author of *Zeros and Ones*, believes these inventions were "very literally the software linings" of technology of all kinds. The mechanisms of even the earliest spindles and spinning wheels, she claims, formed the basis of later equipment based on axles, wheels, and rotations, and it was textile invention that drove the entire Industrial Revolution. In Plant's opinion these technologies helped create an almost "new people," more prone to capitalism, speed, and abstract thinking.[46]

Each new invention spurred on the next. The spinning wheel, which spread through Europe by the 13th century, allowed people to produce thread more quickly, and eventually led to the development of a faster loom. Englishman John Kay sped up the weaving process by which the weft threads passed through the warps with his 1733 device, the "flying shuttle." Before its invention, a weaver had to place the shuttle (the bobbin that held the threads) into the opening between the threads by hand, and his or her arm span determined the maximum width of the textile. (A large piece of cloth required two or more people.) The new mechanism allowed a single person to weave a wide fabric, as the shuttle was attached to a lever which when pulled sent the weft "flying" across a wheeled track. In turn, the flying shuttle created a new imbalance, as weavers could soon work faster than spinners could provide thread. James Hargreaves's spinning jenny helped solve this problem, as it allowed multiple threads to be spun simultaneously (as mentioned in chapter 4, Hargreaves was persecuted by neighbors who feared being put out of work). Incremental inventions kept refining the weaving process, but the major breakthrough came in the

{above, left} *This cloth was carefully stitched into a resist pattern before it was dyed yellow. When the threads are removed, a pattern of little dots would be revealed where the stitches kept the dye from penetrating. In India, where this stitch-resist textile was being worked, the process is called bandhani. The term is the source of the word "bandanna," since the earliest handkerchiefs featured dotted designs achieved with stitch resist.*

{above, right} *Detail of kain kebat warp-ikat women's skirt cloth made by the Kantu people, Kalimantan, Borneo, Indonesia, first half of the 20th century. The motif represents an omen bird, which is ritually sacrificed and used to determine future events.*

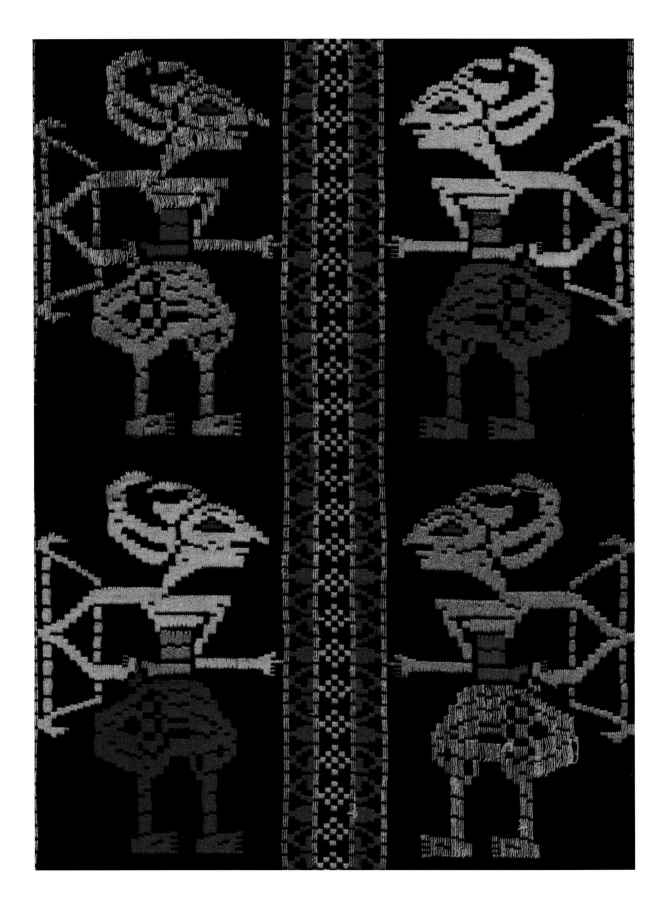

form of the Jacquard loom described in the previous chapter. Again, this machine essentially pioneered the 0/1 system that forms the basis of our contemporary digital world and is now recognized as the first "computer."

I have discussed the severe displacement of labor that resulted from the adoption of the Jacquard loom, and people today are well aware of the dangers of any such speeding-up process. At the same time, we must acknowledge Plant's idea of the "new people" that emerged with this textile technology. We have become comfortable with the way that individual "yes/no" bits of data add up to fully formed images and ideas, and we take it for granted that we will continually have to stretch ourselves and adapt to further innovations. Perhaps we can say that the Jacquard loom represented another aspect of generative textile-making. Interestingly, the cloth that came from this loom was at first called "spider work." Like the spider deities that were linked with both weaving and creating life, this technology also gave birth to something: a paradigmatically different way of thinking.[47]

The complex patterns that could be woven on Jacquard looms also brought—and continue to bring—visually appealing design to people throughout the world. It is in some ways perhaps superfluous to talk about the aesthetic importance of cloth, since there is an aesthetic dimension to almost everything we have discussed. Arpilleras and Hmong story cloths are worked in intensely colored threads, so that even if the story they reveal is a painful one, the textiles are cheerful enough for collectors to hang them in their homes as decorative accents. Crazy quilts communicated through their badges and souvenir textiles, but even more important was their explosion of color, pattern, and sensuous texture. The Czech "kitchen helpers" were didactic, amusing, and—as they often served as splash cloths that kept the walls clean—functional, but they were worked in saturated reds and blues that added a joyous feeling to the domestic environment. The patterns in Qing dynasty dragon robes and rank badges were exquisitely worked with brightly dyed silk and shimmering gold thread,

{top} *The shiny leather-like surface of this Miao jacket (back view) was created by repeatedly dipping cotton cloth into an indigo dyebath to achieve a very dark color, and then laboriously rubbing the surface. The patterned areas are worked in batik, China, 20th century.*

{above} *Woman spinning cotton, Bali, c. 1910.*

{opposite} *This example of supplementary weft patterning is from Indonesia, but the technique is used around the world. The detail here is from a nobleman's short saput (over-sarong) which would have been worn for festivals or public audiences in Eastern Bali, first quarter of the 20th century. The figures represent Arjuna, hero of the Hindu epic* Mahabharata.

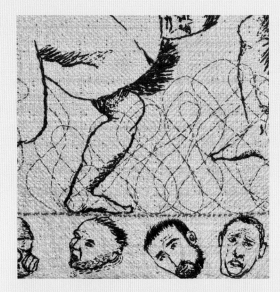

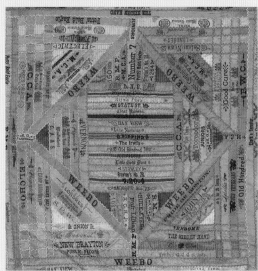

{left} *This outfit would have represented the finery of a Bedouin (Palestinian) woman. The photograph was taken about 1950.*

{below} *Dressed camel on the Great Nafud desert, Saudi Arabia, 1972.*

{opposite, above, right} *Jacquard loom punch cards on display in Lindesnes, Norway.*

and embellished with lustrous materials like pearls and coral; beyond helping to maintain cosmic order, they were beautiful to behold.

In many areas of the world where the physical environment is particularly dry, dusty or colorless, people add visual stimulation and excitement through bright, energetic textiles. In the arid desert region of northwest India, for example, Rabari and Kutch women routinely dress in intense oranges and reds, and stitch mirrors into their cloth. These catch the light of the sun and seem to dance with every step the wearer takes. Bright color is also central to textiles made by Moroccan people of the Sahara, and the Mongolian people of the Gobi desert. On the vast expanse of the Central Asian steppe—mostly treeless, and covered in the winter by an unrelieved blanket of snow—people adorned every surface of their traditional yurt homes with lively textiles with high-contrast hues. Pack animals were also adorned in cheerful hues, enticing pattern, and sensuous fringes.

Cheerful textiles were similarly important in 18th-century New England in the U.S., when colonists were struggling to get through winters that were far harsher than those they had known in Europe, and lived in dark interiors with little natural light. It is easy to understand why the printed Indian chintz that brought the look and joyful colors of a summer

{opposite, above, left} *Contemporary art piece made with a Jacquard loom interfaced with a computer-aided design program. Diane Sheehan's set,* Invention of Truth *and* Invention of Certainty, *was made in 2002–2003 as a political comment about the Iraq war and the U.S. presidency of George W. Bush.*

{opposite, centre, left} *In the late 19th century cigars were wrapped in small silk ribbons which identified the manufacturer. They were coveted and incorporated into crazy quilts. This piece functioned as a table mat, U.S., c. 1880–90.*

{opposite, below, left} *Corner detail of a personalized Jacquard-woven coverlet made by Harry Tyler, Jefferson County, New York for Sylva Hover, 1837.*

{opposite, below, right} *Recycled woolen fabrics that have been made into a braided rug, mid-20th century.*

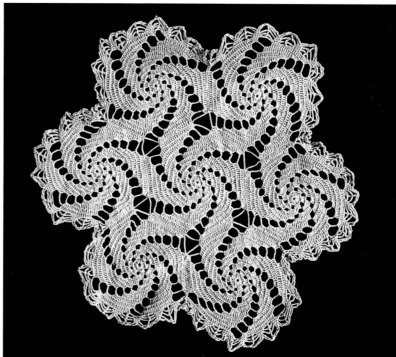

{above, left} *Beaded tassel fringe from a Peruvian belt, 1990s.*

{above, right} *Crocheted cotton doily, U.S., early 20th century.*

garden into the home would be a valued commodity, and why there was a near-riot on the Boston docks when a shipload of such fabric arrived. Housewives jostled one another quite aggressively to make sure they would receive part of the bounty. (Even when printed Indian cotton was banned in England, it was still made available to the colonies.)[48] The same impulse applied in Sweden and other parts of Scandinavia where the winters were long and very dark; bright textiles abounded in even very modest homes. Every table top was covered with a hand-worked textile, every plain towel was hidden by an embroidered "show towel" which would be removed when the functional object was in use.[49]

The impulse to outfit every surface with a cheerful textile also reflected the makers' need to fill their leisure hours with an expressive endeavor that would leave a lasting legacy. Highly decorated environments indicate that someone in the household had time to devote to this activity, so it is not surprising that these traditions reached their peak in the West only after industrialization provided ready-made threads and fabrics and freed up some of the time that had formerly gone to meeting survival needs. The "folk aesthetic"—essentially an explosion of color and pattern, the position that "more is more" when it comes to ornament—was a product of the Industrial Revolution, as was the 19th- and early 20th-century practice of filling the house with non-functional but decorative covers such as doilies, antimacassars, and lambrequins (shelf valances). These were much maligned in the modern period as a sign of old-fashioned fussiness, but we must remember they originated in the context of a new abundance of leisure and materials.

The urge to adorn (the body as well as the environment) is so universal that people the world over have gone to seemingly ridiculous extremes to meet it. Think of the human energy expended in milking murex mollusks or raising acres of cactus to feed a supply of cochineal insects, just to color cloth. The Navajo and Yoruba both went to a different kind of extreme to get bright red thread: they laboriously *un*raveled European trade cloth that contained the precious material, and then rewove the threads into textiles of their own design. The use of raveled yarns is not uncommon. There is an Akwete myth from southeastern Nigeria that tells of the group's legendary weaver dreaming of new textile patterns using recycled threads, and Jessica Hemmings speaks of African-American slave women who unwound threads from their owner's discarded stockings and fabric remnants so they could use them to arrange their own hair stylishly.[50]

We find numerous examples of handmade textile traditions that become more intricate over time because their makers develop an ever-more elaborated aesthetic. The Kuna, who live on islands off the coast of Panama and Columbia, first began to make their reverse appliqué *mola* blouses when missionaries supplied them with cotton cloth, needles, thread, and scissors. Kuna women translated the designs they had painted on their bodies into this new medium, in part because they were responding to missionary pressure to cover their bare breasts, but also because the materials offered a challenging new way to express themselves. Aesthetic pleasure, not shame, was the primary motivating factor. The earliest molas were made with simple two-color designs (these are now referred to as "grandmother" molas), but over time, the textiles grew more complex.

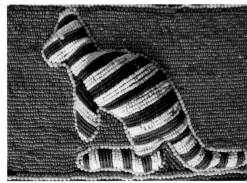

{top} *Detail of a silk kilim (flat-weave rug) with fantastic animals. Purchased in Turkey, 1980s; probably Kurdish from the Mount Ararat area of eastern Turkey.*

{above} *Detail of a beaded scabbard, Yoruba, Nigeria, 20th century.*

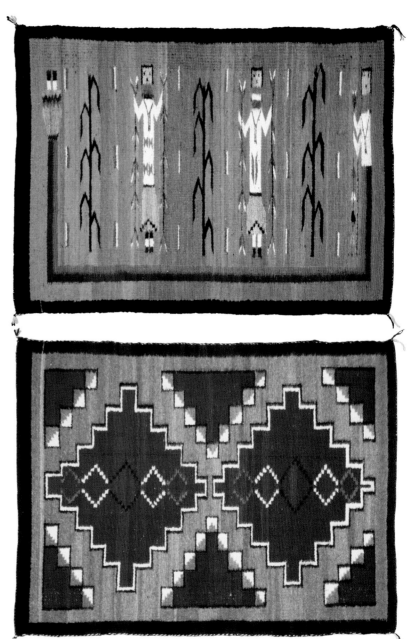

{above, left} *Mary Adams*, Wedding Cake Basket, *1995. Adams was born on the Akwesasne Mohawk Reservation on the U.S.-Canadian border in 1917.*

{above, right and right} *Navajo Bertha Bennally made this double-faced rug in 1979. One side features Yeibichai figures (dancers who represent holy spirits), while the reverse features a geometric diamond design.*

{opposite, above} *Kain lawon from Palembang, Indonesia, late 19th–early 20th century. Lawon were and still are used in a variety of ways, notably as display textiles in and around the ritual "stage" at weddings.*

{opposite, below, left} *Reverse appliqué mola panels like this are made as part of Kuna Indian blouses. When Kuna women tire of their old molas they sell them as decorative panels. This fanciful example features the Hindu elephant god Ganesh, Panama, 1970–90.*

{opposite, below, right} Subways of Paris, *furnishing fabric designed by Elsa Schiaparelli, 1936 (detail).*

More colors, more layers of cut-out fabric, and additional embroidered details were added. The Kuna judge each other's work on the basis of their fine workmanship and finesse in handling this very complexity.[51] Haitian vodou flags have also become more intricate over time. Although they have a very different look and purpose than the molas (they are ritual objects rather than everyday garments, and their imagery is much more prescribed), newer flags tend toward the inclusion of more colors, more sequins, and more pattern devices.[52]

Native North American textile traditions of the post-conquest era followed the same trajectory; textile-makers liked to show off their technical and design skill by executing highly difficult pieces, even when they were made for sale. Pomo basketmakers from California liked to weave "treasure" baskets that incorporated abalone shell and beautiful but hard-to-get feathers such as quail topknots. These were magnificent enough, but in the 19th century the Pomo also challenged themselves to see how tiny they could make the baskets (weaving on a miniature scale is much more difficult), and some were barely larger than a dime. Basketmakers from the eastern woodlands fashioned complex "fancy baskets" that evidenced the same kind of enthusiasm, humor, and consummate skill. There are extant examples of miniature and life-size ash splint teapots and wedding cakes, and wall pockets with their own tiny baskets jauntily hanging on woven chains. Navajo weavers, who in the 20th century were also primarily making sale goods such as rugs rather than textiles for their own use, similarly gave themselves technical and aesthetic challenges. Some figured out how to construct a completely reversible tapestry-woven rug with entirely different images on each side. The two faces were woven simultaneously—an extremely difficult technical feat.[53]

Textile-making afforded individuals an opportunity to experiment with and draw on an ever-increasing range of visual ideas. Because textiles were so portable, they traveled the world easily, and as the Indonesian adoption of Indian patola exemplifies, they served as inspirations to people from different cultures. Designs on Navajo rugs were taken from Oriental carpets, and mid-20th century Javanese artists incorporated science fiction themes from the American Flash Gordon comic strip into their batiks.[54] The Panamanian Kuna included such seemingly out-of-context images as Ganesh, the south Asian elephant deity.

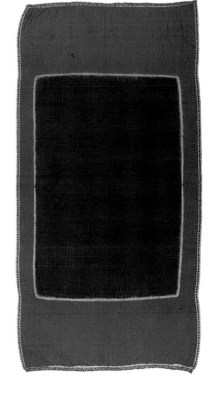

Claire Zeisler made many wall hangings in the 1970s which explored the qualities of fiber, including its linear elements and the way it can both wrap and be wrapped. This highly textured piece was made in 1972.

Many textile-makers received visions for their work through dreams. Native American weavers, basketmakers, and beadworkers all reported this, but parallel stories come from diverse cultures.[55] The fact that textile designs come through the unconscious reinforces both the importance of the creative impulse and the idea that textile-making is deeply embedded in human experience.

Contemporary textile art and activism

I could continue indefinitely to write enthusiastically about visually compelling textiles of all kinds—exciting commercial furnishing fabrics, batiks or brilliantly dyed color-field textiles from Indonesia, pile carpets or even humble hooked or braided rugs—but that is not my main purpose in this volume. (Happily, they are well documented elsewhere.) I do want to give at least passing notice (homage, actually) to the work of contemporary Japanese textile designers, particularly Jun-ichi Arai, who has been experimenting with and expanding the possibility of the textile surface—literally rethinking what a fabric is and can be. Jack Lenor Larsen describes Arai as someone navigating "the uncharted stratospheres between ancient and 3rd Millennium technologies."[56] Indeed, he combines new textile materials (e.g., nylon film worked with oxidized titanium, aluminum, and polyphenylene sulphate) with a reverence for and familiarity with traditional weaving techniques. Among his innovations are the integration of computer-aided design and Jacquard looms; the invention of "burn-out" designs, achieved by a chemical removal of one material in a multi-fiber fabric (this works on the same principle as paste or wax-resist prints, but uses new, engineered fibers); and the development of cloth woven with fibers with different rates of shrinkage which yield interesting puckered surfaces. He is fascinated by the possibilities afforded by slit film that is a fraction of a millimeter thick, and into which other materials—or digital information—can be inserted. As Reiko Sudo wrote in the 1992 exhibition catalogue, *Hand and Technology: Textiles by Junichi Arai*, Arai wants to "someday create a fabric whose pattern changes as subtly as the days in a lifetime, never exactly repeating." Arai's fabrics were first introduced into couture fashions made by designers such as Issey Miyake and Rei Kawakubo.[57]

Other innovative Japanese designers include Reiko Sudo herself, who is associated with the Nuno Corporation, which both markets state-of-the-art fabrics and exhibits at art museums around the world. (Arai was originally associated with this firm as well.) Nuno's fabrics are engineered for both aesthetic and "smart" properties. Those in the 2007 "Phosphorescent" series were woven with glow-in-the-dark threads that store sunlight, for example, while others achieve iridescence with stainless steel.[58] We seem to be poised on the edge of a new kind of textile revolution, the import of which we are just beginning to fathom.

The main subject I want to explore here is what has happened with hand textile-making in the last half century in relation to the art world.

After World War II, there was in the West a revival of interest in handcraft as a meaningful, expressive form, and by the 1960s and early 1970s many individuals were turning to fiber media to make the kind of personal artistic statement more typically associated with painting. These "fiber artists" were skilled craftspeople, but they used the medium in a new, non-functional way. The art textile movement came of age when a number of factors came together. Westerners were beginning to appreciate the varied textile traditions of the world in the 1960s, not just as ethnographic specimens, but as highly developed artistic expressions. The art world had by this time opened up to new kinds of abstract and symbolic forms, which made people look with new eyes at the kind of abstract cloth patterning so often seen on traditional textiles and, as I explained in the preface, information about and images of these traditions were suddenly much more available. As developing countries were beginning to gain independence, Western public awareness of them grew, and this led to a greater familiarity with their cultures and art forms. More individuals were able to experience the textiles in their native settings, moreover, because jet planes were increasing the accessibility of world travel. When these variables were coupled with the growing appreciation for traditional "women's work" being expressed by second wave feminists, interest in textiles exploded in the 1970s.[59] I'd like to point to some of the important ideas that have been explored by textile artists in the last several decades, and some of the attitudes that have changed our expressive landscape.

Individuals working with fiber in the mid-20th century felt the need to "rediscover the values peculiar to textiles"—i.e., they wanted to understand the properties of fiber and see what fiber could "do" or "say."[60] Soft, pliable threads and cloth not only behave differently from hard materials like stone and metal, but also carry inherently different messages—messages about tactility, flexibility or the ability to contain, for example, as discussed in

Jan Hopkins, Chicken Little, *2008. This teapot-like sculpture is made from cantaloupe peel, grapefruit peel, Alaskan yellow cedar, ostrich shell beads and waxed linen. Hopkins has found ways to work with surprising materials, stitching them like cloth or skin.*

{opposite} *John McQueen,* Ganesh, *2007. McQueen has pushed the idea of "basket" to its extremes; often his sculptures contain only space, with no openings.*

{left} *Jon Eric Riis, detail from* Icarus II, *2003. Riis is pushing the tapestry genre into the 21st century. His work often questions concepts of beauty and comments on the human condition. This piece includes silk, gold thread, and crystal beads.*

{below} *Mary Bero,* Chinese Lady, *embroidery, 1986.*

chapter 1. Textile artists invented new terms for their creations, such as "soft sculpture," "wall hangings," and "art fabric." They stretched the boundaries of their medium, experimenting with non-traditional materials that could be worked as linear elements or treated like cloth. Ed Rossbach coined the term "the new basketry" for his expressive containers made out of elements such as plaited newspaper and coiled cloth rags.[61] Others made baskets with videotape or film, strands of kelp, or hog casings. Some baskets played with the inside and outside of space, or surprisingly exhibited no openings. (Artist Michael Davis's definition of a basket—"a vessel that can breathe, that's filled with space"—is relevant here.)[62] The tradition of exploring the full range of fibrous materials continues unabated. Jan Hopkins stitches materials such as fruit rinds and sturgeon skin into haunting sculptures, ranging in form from chicken-headed teapots to life-size torsos. Her piece entitled *Tolerance* consists of a jaunty pair of high heels made with cantaloupe and grapefruit peels. The message "Judge her when you've walked in her shoes" is sewn into this "fabric." Sonya Clark's *Pearl of Mother* is constructed with strands of her own and her mother's hair. Sometimes

{above} *African-American artist Sonya Clark used both her own (black) and her mother's (gray) hair in* Pearl of Mother, *2006, a piece about the connection between the generations. Clark has long worked with hair as a textile element.*

{opposite} *Jeeun Kim's shoes reflect her experience of living in two cultures (Korea and America), which she likens to a "journey in a mismatched pair of shoes." Text is incorporated into the soles in fine lacework, 2007.*

the material *is* the message in contemporary textile art. David Cole's 2005 "Money Dress," made in the pattern of a Vera Wang evening gown, is knitted from a thousand shredded dollar bills. His huge woven fiberglass teddy bear (2003) confounds expectations about soft, comforting cloth.

Textile artists have also used traditional techniques in innovative new ways and pushed the boundaries of techniques that had had proscribed histories. Embroidery became much more free-form (one pioneer in this arena, Mariska Karasz, titled her 1949 book *Adventures in Stitches*). Crochet was freed from its heritage as a poor person's lace used in the aforementioned "fussy" items such as doilies, and was (is) instead used in irreverent figural sculpture. Lace was liberated as well, a legacy that was demonstrated in 2007 in the "Radical Lace" exhibition at New York's Museum of Arts and Design. Familiar old embroidery forms are now often used as a foil for disturbing stitched content. Quilts have been separated from their primary association as functional bedcovers; "art quilts" are more often made as freestanding hangings, functioning almost as sensual three-dimensional paintings. Felt was reclaimed from its practical life, too, and equally turned into an art medium.

Experimentation has pointedly extended to scale. Very large-scale pieces challenge the idea that textiles should be thought of as demure or only in intimate terms; Cole's 14-foot (4.2 meter) teddy bear is a case in point. Other artists call attention to the properties of textiles through environmental installations. Although they do not identify themselves as fiber artists, the work of Christo and his wife Jean-Claude comes to mind, for their pieces have over many decades left indelible public impressions about cloth. In 1976 they installed nearly 25 miles (40 kilometers) of billowing fabric in an 18-foot-high (5.5 meter) *Running Fence* in California. The fence undulated over hills and fields, following the contours of the landscape, and eventually descended into the sea. As the light hit the fabric at different times of the day, changing its opacity and hue, the installation reminded the public that cloth is not static, but a living presence. The 7,500 saffron-colored panels of *The Gates*, mounted in New York in 2005, explored many of the other textile qualities I have discussed, including cloth as pathway, curtain, and divider. Still more of their pieces evoked cloth as an enfolder. The wrapping of the Reichstag building in Berlin is perhaps the best known, but, as early as 1968, Christo had enclosed fountains and even medieval towers.[63] To understand how much more a part of our visual landscape environmental textile installations now are, we turn to an artwork that was actually commissioned by a French city council. In 2001, the town of Pont-Audemer charged artist Elisabeth Ballet with the task of "livening up" a busy road junction with a pavement pattern that would evoke the history of textile manufacture of the Normandy area. Ballet reproduced a lace-pattern on a huge scale in the pavement, making the intersection a memorable landmark and adding a bit of whimsy to the community.[64]

While most of the new textile art is non-functional, beginning in the 1970s there was an explosion of "wearable art" (more recently known as

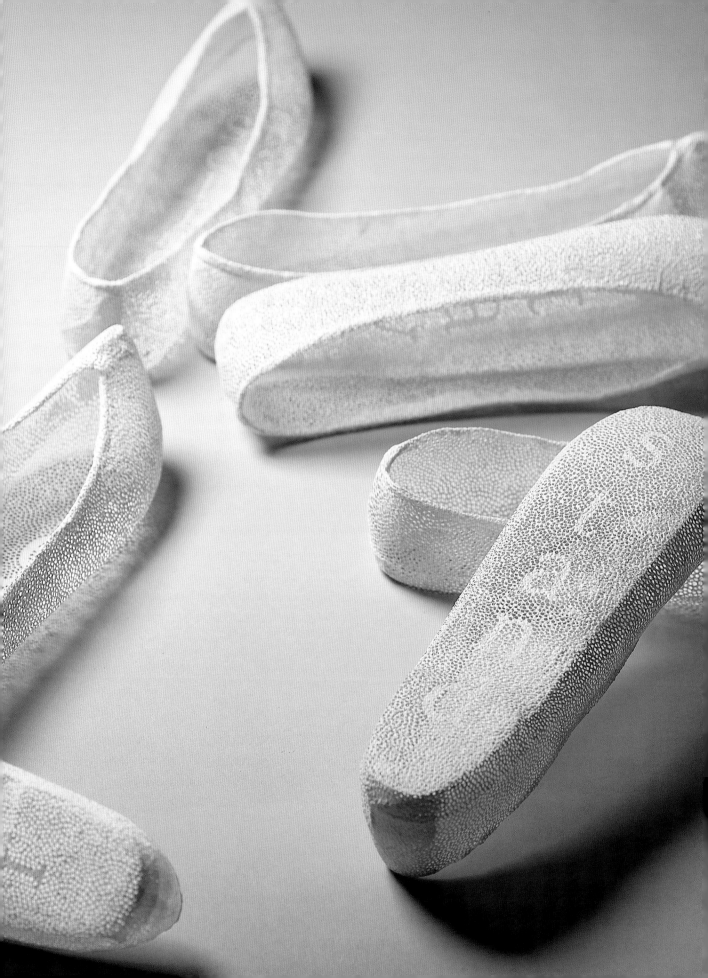

Carolyn Kallenborn's 2005 dress,
"Weighting." An example of "artwear," it
was constructed from taffeta, lead weights,
and forty pounds of river rock. It reflected
Kallenborn's feelings about the weighted
down, immobile quality of depression and
responsibility, although it also references
ideas about constriction and release.

"artwear") which was made to interact with the body, sometimes in performance settings. While it could be purely playful, the very fact that it highlighted the relationship between cloth and the body meant it was often turned into a vehicle for social commentary. Garment forms are used for non-functional pieces as well, further confounding expectations and asking us to think about the meanings of cloth. An early example was Yoshiko Wada's "Coca Cola Kimono" (1975), which included the logo of the soft drink company and wryly commented about globalization and commercialism overtaking Japanese culture. Jon Eric Riis still regularly uses the kimono template to contrast surface with what lies inside (his kimonos open to surprising revelations). His beautifully executed tapestry is frequently also covered with beadwork and embroidery.

I have explained that some of the 1970s artists purposefully reclaimed the rich textile heritage of the world as a feminist legacy. *The Dinner Party*, an installation work spearheaded by Judy Chicago, honored thirty-nine mythic and historical women with individual place settings featuring exquisite embroidered table runners, each worked in the style and technique appropriate to their era. Artists continue to use fiber to comment on women's lives. Canadian Janet Morton, for example, has made many pieces that allude to coziness and domesticity. Her 2004 *Femmebomb*, which covered the entire Human Ecology building at the University of Wisconsin-Madison, was a pointed comment on women's history and gender politics, as it referenced the generations of women who studied domestic skills—and textile design—in home economics programs in that building. Morton wrapped the structure in quilted pink recycled fabric. Large "buttons" were attached at regular intervals, and a 12-foot (3.6 meter) needle and spool of thread was positioned in front of the building.

There are some contemporary artists who draw (perhaps unknowingly) on the legacy of the 1970s fiber art revival but are uncomfortable with the associations made between women and art; they pointedly eschew any labels that limit the way people see their work. Despite the feminist repositioning of textile heritage, textile art is in many ways still taken less seriously than creative work made in other media. The deeply embedded hierarchies that posit some art forms as "higher" or "finer" than others continue to color Western attitudes. (Painting is always considered "real" art, but ironically, cloth plays a role even here, since most contemporary paintings are worked on canvas. To become a suitable painting surface, the fabric is

typically stiffened [treated with gesso] and stretched, which in effect cancels out its cloth-like suppleness and mobility.) Sculpture in hard media such as bronze, steel, stone or glass still tends to be valued more highly than work done in soft media, and fiber is particularly suspect because it bears a double prejudice: it is dismissed as both "decorative" and "feminine." (The feminine designation has often been notably absent, however, when the work was done by men who already had an established place in the art world, such as Christo or Robert Morris.) In a recent book that looks at the reception of fiber art in relation to the hierarchy of art and craft, *String, Felt, Thread*, Elissa Auther concludes that it is now possible to use the fiber medium without being judged by the art world as "too personal, quotidian, social, feminine, decorative, or utilitarian,"[65] but I do not agree that the stigma is fully gone. Several established institutions have renamed themselves so as to be distanced from negative associations. The Philadelphia College of Textiles changed its name to Philadelphia University in 1999, for example, and the American Craft Museum in New York changed its name to the Museum of Contemporary Arts and Design in 2002.

At the same time, there is a new generation of artists who passionately embrace the idea of craft, and a growing contingent of 21st-century "fiber activists" who are unconcerned with old hierarchies and operate largely outside the old venues. They are developing new structures that conform

Janet Morton, Domestic Interior, *2000 (detail).*

Janet Morton spearheaded an installation called Femmebomb *in 2004. It called attention to stereotypes of women and to women's traditional textile-making work.*

to their values. The Church of Craft, founded in 2000, is an international organization devoted to the "power of creating." Chapters hold meetings where individuals can work on "any and all acts of making," leaving behind any of the tensions between art and craft. Related to this is the "Do it Yourself (DIY) Movement," an open-ended community of designers that (in the words of documentarian/participant Faythe Levine) "recognize a marriage between historical techniques, punk, and DIY ethos while being influenced by traditional handiwork, modern aesthetics, politics, feminism, and art."[66] Most of these DIYers are technologically savvy, and both network and market their work through the internet. The majority are women who work with textiles. Some consciously eschew older values such as fine craftsmanship—a sign, to many, of female subservience. Simple embroidery stitches often prevail in their work, in part because the more amateurish look indicates that the piece was made by hand; the work emphasizes the making process itself, rather than the finished product. Whereas the 1960s and 1970s artists were often weavers, the new generation is more focused on knitting and stitching—both of which are more portable techniques that do not demand dedicated equipment. These techniques provide sensory satisfaction, which is particularly meaningful in a digital age.[67]

Also important in the emerging fiber scene is the rise of "New Wave knitting:" the explosion of "knitting rebels" who publicly flaunt their craft, sometimes in an edgy fashion. (They call attention to and re-imagine the gendered nature of fiber through titles such as "stitch and bitch" and "chicknit.") Sabrina Gschwandtner, who helped galvanize the movement, states that its advocates typically use atypical materials (leather, fiber-optic cable, medical wire), exploit digital technology, and combine collaborative performance art and activism with needlecraft. Such activists initiated a worldwide "knit in public day" in 2003, dedicated to "better living through stitching together," and a "Revolutionary Knitting Circle" in 2008 that coincided with the G8 (the group of the world's most powerful countries) Summit in Japan. They also collaborate on public art pieces. Liz Collins organized a series of performance-based installations under the rubric of "Knitting Nation," for example, and Laure Drogoul created the "Orchestral Apparatus for Musical Knitting," which amplified the sound of knitting needles operated by members of the audience. "Knitta," founded by Magda Sayeg in 2005, is a group that refers to its members as "tag crew knitters" or guerilla graffiti artists, who "bomb" cities with "vibrant, stitched works of art, wrapped around everything from beer bottles to public monuments to utility poles." Members outfit mailbox legs with knitted cuffs, or cover manhole covers and other quintessentially non-domestic parts of the environment with fabric that carries strong domestic associations. The work simultaneously challenges the male-dominated world of street art. The phenomenon of "yarn bombing" has caught on rapidly; other groups dedicated to knit graffiti have sprung up around the world (Japan, Ireland, Australia), and in 2009 Canadian artists Mandy Moore and Leanne Praine wrote a kind of how-to manual, *Yarn Bombing: The Art of Crochet and Knit Graffiti*, to inspire others to take to the streets with their own needles.[68]

Activist installations are not always based on knitting; other "craftivists" (craft + activists) use other fiber techniques. Swedish artist Ulrika Erdes "performs" "public embroidery" by leaving cross-stitched "tags" on bus and train seats. Australian Rayna Fahey has created both large and small-scale "interventions" in Melbourne. She has stitched over large steel grates in public spaces, for example, or, at the other extreme, has embroidered words such as "slave" or "corporate whore" onto men's neckties. Gschwandtner created an installation piece entitled *The History of String* in 2007 that referenced textile phenomena such as khipu and made connections between film-making and sewing.[69]

All of these artists use cloth as an aesthetic outlet—a way of expressing their personal creative vision. Like all textile-makers, they are drawn into the beauty and sensuous qualities of the materials, and the satisfying feeling of working with their step-by-step processes. "I forget to eat when I'm weaving," a Yurok basketmaker told Lila O'Neale in 1930,[70] expressing the almost hypnotic spell and sense of attentiveness that many feel when working with cloth. This subject will be addressed in the next, final chapter, which deals with textiles and the realm of the spirit.

Textiles
and the spirit

The sacred, spiritual, and healing
significance of cloth

There is perhaps no simpler way to create good merit in this troubled world of ours than to put prayer flags up for the benefit of other living beings... The silent prayers are blessings spoken on the breath of nature. Just as a drop of water can permeate the ocean, prayers dissolved in the wind extend to fill all of space.

Timothy Clark, "The Prayer Flag Tradition,"
Radiant Heart Studio, Redway, CA on www.prayerflags.com

Part of the universal human experience seems to be a deep longing to taste the state of timeless unity where the sense of individual self falls away. (In other words, part of the human condition is the desire to get beyond human limitation!) This brings us back to one of the first concepts introduced in this book, the idea that textiles serve as metaphors for transcendence; they are light, but tangible and material, and thus concretize an intangible, fleeting quality that we can't quite grasp. I discussed the Hindu metaphor of the veil of Maya, the web that keeps us in a state of illusion. Another important symbolic cloth that represents—even seems to capture—this evanescent quality is the "Shroud of Turin," a linen fabric imprinted with a full-size image of Christ. Many believe that it is the cloth that covered Christ's body after the Crucifixion, and that the image is an X-ray-like impression of the Resurrection process. The shroud is controversial. Some claim it more likely dates from the 13th or 14th century rather than the Biblical era; others point to evidence of pollen and coins from the earlier time. Whether it is "real" or not, the shroud has a great hold on public imagination. In 1978, three million people waited up to eight hours to see it. Pilgrims also come to Rome to venerate the *sudarium*, a cloth that reputedly belonged to Saint Veronica, who gave it to Jesus to wipe the sweat and blood from his face as he was on his way to the Crucifixion. When it was returned, it too miraculously bore his image. Veronica (the name is translated as "true image") does not appear anywhere in the New Testament, but the story persists. It was a popular artistic subject for centuries. Hans Memling (active *c.* 1465–94), El Greco (1541–1614), Bernardo Strozzi (1581–1644), and James Tissot (1836–1902) are among those who have painted her holding the imprinted cloth. Reproductions of the imprinted face also still abound.[1] The irrepressibility of these stories is a powerful demonstration and reminder of the fact that we use textiles to symbolize and further experience our most spiritual longings.

Bringing calm and recovery from trauma

Textile-making has a magical quality—it is a creative or generative process, associated with the life force—and the process can be comforting. It is an almost hypnotic, healing activity; engaging with the repetitive, rhythmic steps of sewing, knitting, weaving, and similar techniques create a sense of peace or calm. The action itself engenders this quality, but it is strengthened by the sensual pleasure of handling the thread or yarn, and watching a new form grow beneath one's hands. Cloth-making can create what Herbert Benson of Harvard Medical School calls the "relaxation response," a measurable state in which brain waves change and heart rate, muscle tension, and blood pressure decrease, and a feeling of serenity ensues. In her 2003 book, *Made From Scratch: Reclaiming the Pleasures of the American Hearth,* Jean Zimmerman claims that about one in three of the 38 million women who currently knit or crochet say they do it because it helps relieve stress, and Deborah Bergman, author of *The Knitting Goddess*, cites research that helps explain the phenomenon. Knitting is

{preceding page} *In this mid-20th-century photograph, the Samaritan High Priest is posing with an ancient scroll— the Samaritan Torah. Samaritanism is an Abrahamic religion closely related to Judaism; the Samaritans claim they maintain the true religion of the ancient Israelites.*

{top} *Woman knotting a Middle-Eastern patterned rug, China, 1998.*

{above} *Blue Hmong girl embroidering, Thailand, 1986.*

simultaneously stimulating and meditative, she explains. Working
with knitting patterns is a left-brained activity, but producing the stitches
is more right-brained. The process harmonizes the two sides of the
brain.[2] Reinforcement for this theory comes from meditative practice,
which involves a combination of repetitive behavior and single-focused
concentration. Hindus maintain that, used together, these activities
function as a path to free the mind and invite an inner tranquility.
(Fittingly, they also believe that making fabric can help individuals evoke
their spiritual nature and maintain a connection with the divine.) Cloth-
makers of all kinds allude to the double-pronged quality of the activity.
Weaver Kay Lawrence notes:

> It was the connection between the process of weaving and the rhythms
> of the body that drew me in: a contemplative quality in the practice
> of weaving that enables the mind to run free while your hands are
> engaged, a form of practice that encourages reflection... It's the still
> point of my life.

Teresa, a self-identified "geek knitter," tried to articulate the nature of
this focused concentration. She wrote of the joy of experiencing knitting's
"deep structural logic based on geometry and proportion, pattern and
shape and iterative processes," and the way knitting brings her into an
awareness and oneness with deep internal structures. She likened it to
engaging with the "morphology and underlying interrelatedness of plants."[3]
  Some rehabilitation centers acknowledge the therapeutic qualities
of textile-making activities, and wisely incorporate them into their
programs. Britain's Great Exhibition of 1851 included samples of "military
patchwork" that was being done by hospitalized soldiers. It was said to be
a workable alternative to drinking and gambling. In 1928, Gertrude Whiting
wrote of a "well-known sanitarium" that instituted bobbin lace-making

{above, left} *Prisoners in Sing Sing prison,
Ossining, New York, are shown knitting
in one of their classrooms in 1915.*

{above, right} *Man plaiting a bamboo
and raffia mat, Kuba-Kete village, Bakwa-
Tombe, Congo-Kinshasa, 1956.*

THE CALMING EFFECT OF LACE-MAKING

One who has never made lace—that is, the bobbin variety—cannot imagine the charm of the softly clinking, tinkling bobbins, like the singing of a simmering teakettle, or like a lullaby gently hummed in the twilight. Their merry little jingle is very soothing, and some physicians claim that the rhythmic effect is most beneficial to the nerves. Doubtless the regular, constant shifting of the bobbins...keeping the mind, eyes and fingers busy, proves a means of working off overwrought feelings and serves the same quieting purpose that piano-playing does for some [who are highly] strung.

Gertrude Whiting, 1928

Detail of a needle lace edging, Europe, c. 1870–90.

classes to help calm its patients. More recently, Colorado's Limon Correctional Facility introduced knitting and rug hooking to its inmate drug and alcohol rehabilitation program. It reports that alcoholics are able to calm themselves as they produce afghans, baby clothes, toys, and rugs.[4]

The soothing quality of rhythmic textile activities can be almost "catching" —those who sit close by, watching, may also experience a reduction in their heart rate and blood pressure. This is captured in "When Mother's Sewing Buttons On," one of the poems in Edgar Guest's 1921 sentimental collection, *When Day is Done*:

> When Mother's sewing buttons on
> Their little garments one by one,
> I settle down contented there
> And watch her in her rocking-chair.
> ...
> There's something in her patient eyes,
> As in and out her needle flies,
> Which seems to tell the joy she takes
> In every little stitch she makes;
> An hour of peace has settled down;
> Hushed is the clamor of the town,
> ...
> I chuckle as I watch her sew,
> For joy has set the room aglow,
> And in the picture I can see
> The strength which means so much to me.
> The scene is good to look upon
> When Mother's sewing buttons on.[5]

Sentimentality about the quietly stitching mother is not limited to Western culture, or to an earlier time. A Miao friend recently told Cecelia Chen that the "softest, most [heartwarming] scene he had ever [witnessed] was to see his mother, sewing and mending for her children under the pale glow of a lamp."[6]

In addition to relieving everyday stress, cloth-making is particularly helpful as a way of coming back to center after a traumatic incident. In chapter 2, I described how Lisa Purdon, who saw the falling of the twin towers of the World Trade Center from her apartment window, turned to quilting to deal with the chaos she was experiencing. Ollie Napesni, who had to deal with the heartbreak of a murdered son, found similar solace in her quilts. Following the Northern Plains Native American tradition, Napesni made a group of quilts to give away to others at the memorial

ceremony (it is not unusual for 100 quilts to be distributed at such a ritual).
The process was an intense but effective way to work through her grief.
To get ready for the memorial in Rosebud, she:

> Sat down to sew... I took an administrative leave and then every
> morning I get up at 4:00 and I just cry and sew...so a lot of the quilts
> I have there have teardrops on them I'm sure.

Sheree Bonaparte explains the process Napesni must have gone through:

> When you just sit there and quilt, all of a sudden things just start to
> calm down...[when you] finally get down to the last stitches, you've
> become a better person for it...the act of quilting is healing.[7]

"J.E.," a woman who was in a serious motorcycle accident in 1973,
used the sewing and embroidery skills she had learned as a child to deal
with both her emotional and physical trauma. She took the jeans she
was wearing at the time of the accident—jeans which had to be cut off
her body as she was rescued—and re-made them into an expressively
embroidered skirt. Working with her injured hands was essential to her
bodily recovery, but by turning the very fabric that had been "injured"
during the accident into something celebratory and appealing, she healed
other parts of herself as well.[8]

The making process can also function as a way of building self-esteem
and even getting in touch with a higher power. Ray Materson, whose drug
addiction led to armed robbery and a subsequent prison sentence, took up
embroidery with the materials he had on hand in his cell. He unraveled
tube socks to get a supply of colorful threads, and fashioned an embroidery
hoop out of a plastic bowl. He then stitched tiny pictures on caps, creating
a series of positive images inspired by sources such as Shakespeare and
the Bible. The process was meditative, and Materson found himself "talking
to God" as he worked at his embroidery. Other prisoners soon wanted
embroidered emblems of their own, to the point that Materson worked
with his needle up to twelve hours a day. The pieces also found a receptive
audience outside of prison, both before and after Materson was released.[9]

A related form of expression emerged independently in a Texas
prison, where a group of Mexican-American inmates found a related
way to make their lives "easier through art." Using ink or colored pencil,
the men make drawings on small pieces of cloth called *paños* (the word
can be translated as handkerchief, and most are handkerchief size). Paños
are easily mailed to the outside, and many are made as gifts for wives,
or girlfriends. The drawing style is akin to that seen in tattooing. Many
of the images depict "La Vida Loca" ("The Crazy Life")—the harsh reality
of life on the streets and in prison. Scenes of gang life, drug use, and
violence are evident, and repeating motifs include prison bars and clocks
representing the idea of "doing time." Other paños have religious themes

(these are often sent to older female relatives) or cartoon images. The impulse to experience this kind of "safe refuge" (recognized artists are often kept safe from prison violence) is so strong that these prisoners too have found innovative ways to work with available materials. When ink isn't available, some resort to making a puree from magazine pulp, coffee grounds, and Kool-aid. The artists were tearing up so much of the prison bedding for these pieces, also, that Texas prison officials finally started selling blank cloth in their commissaries. Like Materson's embroideries, paños have found an audience in art galleries and museums.[10]

As discussed in chapter 4, textile-making likewise served as a form of solace and release for women who lived under purdah-like conditions, and in the West as an amusement and comfort for Victorian women who spent most of their time at home.[11]

Spiritual power and blessing

Probably the central tenet of the Buddhist tradition is the idea that the human state is one of suffering. The Buddha brought a message of compassion and the idea that compassionate beings should work to help relieve the suffering of others. Buddhist practitioners build "merit" through compassionate action; the belief is that their accumulated good deeds will carry over into their next life, and ultimately help themselves and others achieve liberation. Many Asian women build merit by making textiles for Buddhist temples. When they have sons ordained as monks (this situation is not unusual: in Thailand, every male is expected to become a monk for at least part of his life), they are especially likely to do this. They weave cushions for them to sit or lean on, cloth to cover their begging bowls, and even the wrappings used to bind sacred scriptures. In Burma, the wrapping tapes typically have a prayer—itself a plea for mercy and compassion— woven into the cloth. The women also make clothing for the monks. In one small village in the Shan State, robes are laboriously woven from lotus-stem fibers. When this precious fabric wears out, explains Sylvia Fraser-Lu, its remnants are used to clothe Buddha statues. Finally, left-over threads are used as wicks for votive candles.[12]

In other cultures, certain individuals were allowed or expected to make textiles as a way of keeping spiritual energies in order. In Ladakh, women's weaving was believed to assure continuity in the world and keep negative forces at bay. Among the Osage people of North America, women who had been initiated into the clan priesthood were the only ones entitled to weave the cloth feast bags that held the ritual "fees" (e.g., knives, kettles, bison fat for anointing sacred objects, ceremonial foods) paid by advancing initiates. The bags helped build power through their imagery (zigzags represented lightning and the regenerative powers of the metaphoric bison) and their form (their wide rectangular shape alluded to a pregnant bison). The weavers sang ceremonial chants as they made these containers, further infusing them with sacred presence.[13]

{top} *A young Burmese monk poses with a fan, 1887–90. Cloth for East Asian Buddhist monks was sometimes provided by women of the community.*

{above} *Sutras (holy texts) wrapped in beautiful and protective silk brocade cloth, Deer Park Buddhist Center, Wisconsin, U.S., 2009.*

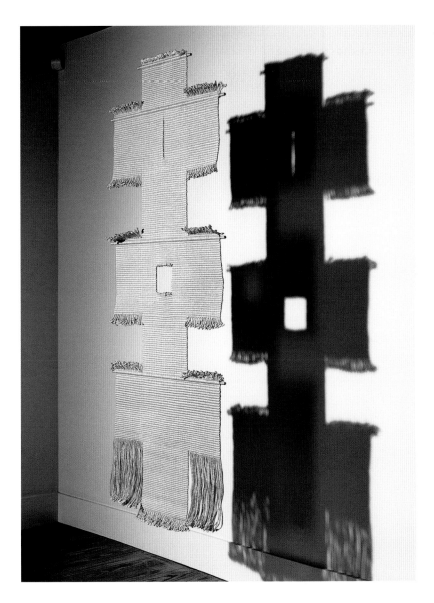

Lenore Tawney, Path II, *c. 1965–66.*

Some individuals take it upon themselves to express a spiritual vision through their textile-making, offering the finished works to the world at large. Lenore Tawney, one of the first artists to turn to fiber as a sculptural medium in the 1960s, made pieces from what she called her "inner landscape," and created a meditative space with her profoundly moving weavings. They bore titles such as "Path" (1965), "In Fields of Light" (1975), "Waters Above the Firmament" (1976), and "Woven Field with Deity" (1994). "Throughout the work," wrote Kathleen Nugent Mangan in a 1996 exhibition catalogue, "Tawney's intention [was] the same—to represent what is *not seen*, to express the essence." (It was after being inspired by Tawney's work that I dreamt of making the veil of Maya installation described in the preface.)[14]

The prayer that goes into making many traditional textiles bestows blessing on others. In Turkey, those who make the traditional tall felt hats worn by the whirling dervishes chant during the process so as to increase

Scene from the 1979 Eka Dasa Rudra ceremony held at Besakih Temple in Bali. Functioning as a major "realignment" of the balance of energies at play in the seen and unseen worlds, the ceremony is only held once a century. The three main shrines— for the Hindu deities Shiva, Vishnu, and Brahma—are outfitted with cloth.

the beneficent power of the garments. Consecrating prayer was also part of making cloth in Scotland. At the end of a waulking bee (see chapter 3), an elder woman lifted the fulled cloth and gave it a turn sunwise (i.e., turning to face God), intoning "in the name of the Father." After assistants repeated the process in the name of the Son and Spirit, the intended recipient was mentioned by name and blessed:

> May the man of this clothing never be wounded,
> May torn he never be
> What time he goes to battle or combat,
> May the sanctuary shield of the Lord be his.[15]

Sarah Jacobs worked alone to transmit a blessing when she prepared a *challah* (Sabbath bread) cover for her daughter's Bar Mitzvah. She printed photos of the girl's female ancestors on the cloth and combined them with words from the book of Proverbs: "Strength and glory are her clothing, and she shall rejoice at the end of the days." Plains Native American women such as Ollie Napesni who make star quilts to give away also do this as a way of spreading love and spiritual power. In the case of a memorial feast, the newly made quilts are displayed in ceremonial structures as part of the process of releasing the spirit of the deceased. When a family gives away many handmade quilts to honor others (this is done at baby-namings, graduations, and weddings as well as funerals), it is seen as a spiritual act.[16]

Pure white cloth

Finished fabric plays multiple roles in spiritual experience. We can begin to explore this interplay by looking at the symbolic meanings and practical uses of white cloth. "Snowy white" fabric has a near-universal association with spiritual purity. "Without sins," said the Prophet Muhammad, "a soul is like a polished mirror or a white piece of cloth."[17] A similar image is used in the Old Testament. In Malachi 3:2, the people are asked, "Who may abide the day of his coming? And who shall stand when he appeareth?" The lines are familiar from the often-heard verse in Handel's *Messiah*, but few know the next line from the scripture, or would even be able to understand its meaning. "For he...is like fullers' soap" is a reference to the cleaning agent used by those who finish woolen fabric. Other Biblical examples abound. When the Sanhedrin (a council of seventy elders appointed to help Moses govern the Jews) judged the background and level of purity of potential priests, the ones who passed the test were "clothed in white;" those found lacking were clothed in black. In the New Testament, Revelation 3:5 states, "He that overcometh [temptation], the same shall be clothed in white raiment; and I will not blot out his name out of the book of life." Revelation 4:4 describes twenty-four throned elders sitting around the Lord's throne in heaven, all dressed in white.[18]

Christians wear white in many contexts today. Catholics dress this way for their Holy Communion, for example, and Mandeans, members of

{top} *Women participating in a ceremony with the k'allu (spirit medium), Shoa Province, Ethiopia, 1965–66.*

{above, left} *Christian procession on Good Friday, Pondicherry, south India, c. 1971.*

{right} *Xhosa doctors dancing, Transkei, South Africa, 1967–68.*

Young Catholic woman in a white nun's habit modeling the prayer position. Date and location unknown.

a small Gnostic Christian sect that still has some followers in the Middle East, wear white during all religious ceremonies. Their garments symbolize "the heavenly dress of light" worn by angels and pure souls. Those who go through Mandean baptism are told to "Cover yourself in white like the garments of radiance and coverings of light. Put on white turbans like resplendent wreaths."[19] Most baptismal and communion garments are white as well.

Almost all altar cloths in the Christian church are made of linen, in part because that is what Jesus' grave clothes were made from, but also because linen bleaches to a bright white in the sun, and the altar can be symbolically dressed in a robe of purity. The white napkin draped over the communion chalice and brought to the celebrant's lips is fittingly known as the "purificator." As a priest puts on his white linen alb he prays, "Make me white, O Lord, and cleanse my heart; that being made white in the Blood of the Lamb I may deserve an eternal reward."[20]

Muslim pilgrims who go to Mecca for the Haj are said to enter a state of *ihram* (purity) when they arrive at the city's boundary, about 6 miles

(10 kilometers) from the holy center. To mark the transition into this sacred state, they change into white garments. Mormons wear white for temple services as well; there are special lockers in most temples where believers can leave their street clothes when they enter the finer realm. White is used to wrap the deceased at a Muslim funeral, marking the transition to a permanent state of purity. (An Islamic funeral prayer asks that the individual is "purified of wrongdoings, as a white cloth is purified of grime.") Zoroastrians (Parsis) dress in white at both funerals and weddings, and ritually wash their white clothes after each ceremony.[21]

Sacrifice ritual at the Pura Dalem temple, Ubud, Bali, Indonesia, 2000.

The ritual dress of followers of the Santería (primarily found in the Caribbean) and Condomblé (primarily found in Brazil) religions, which both have roots in West African Yoruba culture, is also white. The associations with white are very strong in Africa. Some Yoruba weave white fabric specifically to mediate between ancestor spirits and humans. Metaphorically, the white thread descends from heaven. It is able to attract good spirits and repel evil ones, and has healing power. Yoruban white cloth is also involved in a ritual in which diviners determine which ancestors are reborn in young children. The fabric used in this ceremony is so special that it must be woven in a single day (this brings to mind the Rumpelstiltskin story, which similarly relates to supernatural creation). Eventually, the ritual cloth is worn to shreds and disappears, symbolically representing the dust-to-dust idea. It must be replaced with a new cloth that starts the cycle again.[22]

Comparable meanings prevail in Indonesia. Before constructing a house on the island of Sumbawa, the Wawo people pour water from a pot containing white cotton yarn into the post-holes, essentially blessing the structure with purity and health. In Bali, white cloth stands for peace, compassion, and a longing for unity and harmony. At an interfaith service held after the 2002 terrorist bombing at Kuta Beach, hundreds of Hindus, Muslims, Christians, and Buddhists came together to pray for the souls of the 184 victims. They began with a procession along the beach, carrying a 197-foot (60 meter) white cloth stretched above their heads. The Tibetan kata described in chapter 3 represents purity as well. In offering an unblemished cloth to another, one symbolically indicates that the gesture is not marred by corrupt thoughts or ulterior motives.[23]

White cloth has a role in ceremonies of atonement. Jews traditionally wear white on Yom Kippur, the holy day when believers atone for any transgressions they or their community have committed in the previous year. The source of the practice is Isaiah 1:18, where the power of God's forgiveness is promised: "Though your sins are like scarlet, They shall be as white as snow; Though they are red like crimson, They shall be as [white] wool." For Catholics, Ash Wednesday functions as the day of humility when believers are reminded of their sins. In parts of France, children dress in white before the communion mass in order to ask for a pardon.[24]

While it is somewhat parenthetical to this chapter, it is worth pointing out the strongly held association of white cloth and purity in non-spiritual

An enormous thangka (cloth with a painted or embroidered picture of the Buddha and other deities) laid out on a hillside as part of the Tibetan Buddhists' annual Great Prayer Festival. The cloth is rolled up into what looks like a giant snake and monks carry it aloft, over their heads, as they climb a steep hill. It is then dramatically unfurled and allowed to hang down over the landscape. The scale of this 20th-century piece is evident from the small size of the spectators beneath it.

contexts. The white wedding dress, as a case in point, is linked with the idea that the bride is pure in the virginal sense. This issue may be less important in Western culture than it once was, but the fact that many jokes still make reference to it indicates the association is still resonant. (The white wedding tradition is in fact spreading, and the princess-like dress has become a global symbol of the bride; in Japan, according to a tourist-oriented website, "all young people imagine a bride [wearing the] snow white dress of the West.")[25] White coats are also associated in the public mind with cleanliness and purity, and they are worn by physicians. They were first adopted in the 19th century, when a group of doctors donned the lab coat as a sign that they were up-to-date and "scientific." While many physicians actually prefer other colors, patients frequently expect them to wear white.[26]

Creating sacred space, containing sacred energy

We know that fabric defines space and helps create a sacred environment. Cloth held aloft, like the long white strip used at Kuta Beach, often represents protection, and as it is positioned above the head and below the heavens, can symbolize a conduit to God. The Jewish wedding chuppa is an age-old example of this potent symbology. According to the Midrash (interpretations of the Talmud), in fact, it represents God's sheltering presence at both the wedding and the home that is being created.[27] Tall banners flying outside Balinese temples announce that a festival is taking place, and crossing under these cloths, one enters the ritual space. Textiles hanging overhead are also important in Buddhist ritual. In a particularly dramatic annual ceremony in Tibet, the first day of the Great Prayer Festival traditionally began at dawn with a procession featuring an enormous fabric *thangka* (a depiction of the Buddha and other holy figures). These thangkas could be as large as 75 x 115 feet (23 x 35 meters). A long column of monks

This vertical banner serves as a portable shrine at the Sumiyoshi Festival, Tsukuda Island, Japan, 1857; woodcut by Ando Hiroshige.

streamed out of the temple carrying the rolled thangka aloft like a giant overhead serpent. They moved through the monastery complex, praying continuously, and threaded their way through excited crowds trying to touch the sacred fabric. Then, they moved up the side of a steep, rocky hill and, at the top, unfurled the cloth so that it faced the monastery and the crowd below. (Although these huge thangkas are considered important national treasures, many were destroyed during the Chinese Cultural Revolution and occupation of Tibet, when the ceremonies were forbidden. The tradition is being reclaimed now—some new giant thangkas are being created—although recently, monks at one of Lhasa's most prestigious monasteries refused to take part in the ceremony because they felt coerced by Chinese authorities to do it in what they considered to be an inappropriate manner.)[28] Even on ordinary days, Buddhist temples are alive with layer upon layer of cloth. Walls are covered with smaller embroidered or painted thangkas mounted on bright brocades and satin fabrics, and sculpted images are dressed and positioned under fabric canopies. In India, Afghanistan, Central Asia, and China, temple walls may be filled with cloths featuring repeated images of the Buddha. The "Thousand Buddhas" are the visual counterpart of the repeated mantras and prayers that inscribe the space with compassion and love.[29]

Some Islamic mosques featured a cloth completely covered with calligraphic representations of the name of Allah (God). In this case, too, the cloth was a visual form of prayer, and the constant repetition of the name was a reminder that God is the one and only reality. This held true for the weavers who worked the repeating calligraphy into the fabric, who must have experienced the cloth as a form of meditation. It also helped those who sat in the space to focus their attention on this fundamental Islamic precept.[30] Sacralizing fabric is familiar in Hindu contexts as well. In one 9th-century temple in Java, the textile reference is literally embedded in the architecture, as its walls are patterned with designs from sacred cloths. In Gujarat, India, hangings themselves set off a shrine. This custom was started by nomadic people who worshipped the mother goddess. Once they settled and built more permanent structures,

TABERNACLE CURTAINS

The Bible gives a long list of prescriptions relating to the curtains of the tabernacle, from which the following are excerpted.

1 Moreover thou shalt make the tabernacle with ten curtains of fine twined linen, and blue, and purple, and scarlet: with cherubims of cunning work shalt thou make them.

2 The length of one curtain shall be eight and twenty cubits, and the breadth of one curtain four cubits: and every one of the curtains shall have one measure.

3 The five curtains shall be coupled together one to another; and other five curtains shall be coupled one to another.

4 And thou shalt make loops of blue upon the edge of the one curtain from the selvedge in the coupling; and likewise shalt thou make in the uttermost edge of another curtain, in the coupling of the second.

5 Fifty loops shalt thou make in the one curtain, and fifty loops shalt thou make in the edge of the curtain that is in the coupling of the second; that the loops may take hold one of another.

6 And thou shalt make fifty taches [clasps] of gold, and couple the curtains together with the taches: and it shall be one tabernacle.

From Exodus: 26.

{right and opposite} *Mata ni Pachedi (large temple cloths) are made in dedication to the Hindu mother goddess, Ahmedabad, Gujarat, India 2004–2005. The printed and hand-painted imagery tells the goddess's story.*

the cloths framed the goddess statue
in their temples.[31]

The sacralization of temple or church
space is sometimes intensified by the
presence of priestly robes. The vestments
worn by Catholic priests during Mass, such
as the previously discussed alb, are intended
to increase the efficacy of the ceremony.
The amice, to give another example, is
imbued with a prayer related to the crucifixion, and brings the energy
of the sacrifice into the room.[32] The robes that high officials of Buddhist
monasteries wear on ceremonial occasions function similarly. Some, like
the temple hangings, include a "thousand Buddhas," reflecting the idea
that the cosmic consciousness of the Buddha is limitless. They are reminiscent
of the dragon robes worn by the Chinese emperors, in that they function
almost as a religious map during the ritual and represent another kind
of "refuge" for the congregants. When they are not being worn by living
priests, they are sometimes also spread over the throne of the Buddha.[33]

A SUFI'S DESCRIPTION OF SETTING THE SPACE FOR THE KORAN

At that time the Archangel brought to the Prophet two green pieces
of cloth from heaven, one of which was decorated with all kinds of precious
stones from the earth, and the other with precious elements from heaven.
He opened the first cloth and told the Prophet to sit on it, and he handed
him the second one and told him to open it. When he opened it, he received
the Holy Koran with words of light, and the secret of that tree in the seventh
Heaven was revealed to him.

Shaykh Muhammad Hisham Kabbani

Textiles also temporarily transform more personal environments into holy spaces. It was noted earlier that the weekly Sabbath is welcomed in many Jewish households with a special tablecloth. The fabric symbolically sacralizes the time (the twenty-four-hour Sabbath day) as well as the family home, which during that period becomes a house of prayer, rest, and spiritual renewal. Muslims may unroll a personal prayer mat five times a day, orienting themselves to Mecca, and using the cloth to cushion their bodies and keep them clean as they bend in supplication. Henry Glassie tells us that in Turkey, small prayer rugs with the mihrab motif may also be hung on the wall. One prays *through* these textiles, Glassie explains, so they need not be placed underfoot.[34]

Prayer shawls define personal space by effectively surrounding the body in a tent of holiness. Jews often draw their tallit up over their heads and faces when they are deep in prayer, shutting out the mundane world. (Many interpret the New Testament verse in Matthew 6:6, which discusses entering one's "room" or "closet" for prayer, as referring to a shawl.) Jewish tallit always include fringes (*tzitzit*), which serve as a highly tactile reminder of the covenant with God. Prescribed in Deuteronomy 22:12, the fringes are worked into each of the four corners. They are tied with an intricate series of knots, which are said to spell out His unpronounceable name. Symbolically, prayer shawls also signify robes of heavenly or primal light. Rabbi Zalman Schachter-Shalomi had a vision in the 1950s of a shawl woven in vibrant colors, each of which corresponded to the mystical levels of the kabbalistic Tree of Life. His rainbow design gained a following throughout the world, and opened the door for Jews to feel free to personalize their prayer shawls, making them individualized "houses of light." (These shawls are now marketed as the "Joseph's Coat tallit.")[35]

Prayer shawls are used in other, non-Jewish contexts. Founders of the shawl ministry mentioned in chapter 2 specifically conceive of their textiles as prayer shawls, and many who make and receive them see them the same way. "To me, it's like having God's arms around you," says one woman who makes shawls for others.[36] Hindu Shiva worshippers who use shawls are now able to go online to purchase a large cloth that, when worn, is promised to facilitate communication with that deity. Prayer shawls even function as prominent props in the online fantasy world. In the magical realm of "Everquesters," where players from around the world create characters who travel through different "planes of power," there are graduated levels of shawl quests involving ever-more powerful textiles. For those who make sufficient progress, there are shawls of "awakenings" and heightened perception.[37]

The cloth that sets individual sacred space may be as small as a handkerchief. Christian Sunday School teachers encourage children to make their own prayer cloths by painting manufactured napkins. Handkerchief-size prayer cloths are also recommended for travelers. They are easily tucked in a suitcase and thus, like Muslim prayer mats, make convenient portable devices for personal ritual.[38] Small prayer cloths

Rabbi Avram reading scrolls, Yemen, c. 1934–37. His tallit (striped prayer shawl) is drawn up over his head.

are particularly used for healing purposes, a topic which will be discussed in detail below.

As shawls contain people, other textiles contain sacred objects. Holy manuscripts such as Buddhist sutras are wrapped in cloth. The Torah scrolls that contain Jewish scriptures are also "dressed" in fabric, and housed in a cabinet (ark) behind a curtain. When it is time for a Torah reading, the curtain is ritually opened so that the scrolls can be removed (it represents the moment of revelation, when the veils are parted), and the Torah cover is carefully slipped off. Medieval Christian manuscripts were not only wrapped in textiles, but sometimes also had protective cloth sewn right into the pages. Illuminations depicting scenes such as Christ ascending to heaven might, for example, be covered with pieces of precious silk. The coverings were particularly important if the book was displayed on an altar and exposed to light, but they also carried symbolic meaning. They too often took the form of little curtains, which literalized the concept of revelation. One book featured a page with angels kneeling in each corner, pulling back an actual drapery to reveal an image with the words, "Jesus of Nazareth, King of the Jews," written in Hebrew, Greek, and Latin.[39]

North Africans protect yet another sacred manuscript with fabric. The Orthodox Church of Ethiopia claims it holds the original Ark of the Covenant, the container for the Ten Commandments. It is kept under strict guard in a bunker-like building, but at the annual celebration of *Timket* (also spelled *Timkat*), a three-day Epiphany festival commemorating the baptism of Christ, ceremonial replicas of the tablets (*tabots*) come out in colorful processions held throughout the country. Beautifully bedecked priests carry tabots wrapped in fine silks, and they are further protected with large umbrellas. The processions end at a nearby body of water, where after an all-night vigil, the tabots are given a symbolic baptism. Celebrants may jump in as well. On the third day, the priests reverse the procession and return the tabots to the churches.[40]

Oromo and Amhara men standing near the spirit medium at the Timket celebration, Ethiopia, 1965–66. Their beautiful umbrellas are part of the protective fabric that surrounds the replicas of the Ark of the Covenant tablets.

In some parts of the Middle East, individuals kept their copies of the household Koran in lovingly decorated cloth bags. These gave honor to the scripture and, when put on display, proclaimed the piety of the family. The "holy of holies" in the Muslim religion is also covered with cloth. The Kaa'ba is a cubical building in the center of the al-Haram Mosque in Mecca. It is believed to have been built by Abraham and Ishmael on the spot where Adam uttered his first prayers to God. Inside is a black stone, probably a meteorite, said to have been given to Adam on his expulsion from paradise. The Kaa'ba is protected by a huge black cloth (7,083 square feet or 658 square meters), which cascades down over the sides of the structure. It features an encircling band woven with silver and gold threads, spelling out the Islamic creed and the holy names of God, as well as a panel over the door with Koranic verses rendered in beautiful calligraphy. This holy and costly fabric, known as the *kiswah*, is replaced every year.[41]

{above, left and above, right} *The Kaa'ba, the cubical building in Mecca, Saudi Arabia, is one of the holiest sites in Islam and is covered with an enormous and exquisitely made cloth called the kiswah. It is replaced each year during the Haj. The photograph on the left dates from 1910. The photograph on the right, from 1989, documents the process of the cloth being lifted up over the brick structure. Note the gold band that encircles the cube, which is seen being embroidered on page 185, and the great number of pilgrims bowing down in prayer.*

{right} *A (Shi'ite) Hazara prayer cloth used to wrap prayer stones, Afghanistan, 20th century. The cloths are themselves considered to be holy.*

{above} *The Black Madonna statue in the Église Notre-Dame de Dijon, France is dressed in crisp crewel-embroidered garments. They not only honor her, but also keep her power protected.*

MADONNA OF THE PROTECTING MANTLE

Mary, spread out your mantle,
make of it a shield and screen,
Let us all stand safely under it,
'till all dangers are past.
Merciful patroness,
Come to our aid, Mary.

O mother of compassion,
your mantle is already spread out;
Whoever diligently places himself under
will not be brought low in any danger

Your mantle is so very broad and wise...
It covers the whole wide world,
It is our refuge and cover.

Found on an Innsbruck print, 1640.

In spiritual traditions that do not focus on written texts, other kinds of sacred objects are similarly contained. Indian Sinarth Brahmins cover their prayer beads with an embroidered glove-like mitt. The Akan people of Ghana cover spirit figures and shrine houses that honor the power of their river, the Tano, with prestigious kente cloth. Native Americans wrap their drums, which represent the "heartbeat" of the people, in protective fabric (sometimes even a star quilt). In South American shamanic traditions, spiritual leaders carry stones, herbs, and other powerful objects in a woven *mesa*. The mesa can be spread out on the ground, creating a temporary altar for ceremonial use, but otherwise it maintains the energy of the objects of power. "Medicine bags" and prayer bundles are familiar to many other cultures as well. In most cases, the skin or cloth that holds the objects comes to take on a sacredness of its own.[42]

Physical and spiritual healing

In addition to offering protection and blessing, cloth is frequently used to heal the physical body and the spirit. The distinctions between these categories are arbitrary, of course, and I have already discussed psychic protection in chapter 2. Here, I focus on textiles that play an active role in healing rituals or are specifically designated as healing cloths. The healing is invariably felt to have a spiritual component.

Sometimes it is threads that are used for healing. Shamans from
Siberia to Latin America are believed to travel along threads as they move
between worlds, and actual strings are used in many restorative rituals.
A Moroccan story has it that if a man takes a thread from the garment
of a sick person and places it under his pillow, he will dream of a female
spirit who will give him advice about possible cures. Strings that
symbolically secure the soul to the body are tied around the wrists of the
person undergoing healing at the Lao "Soothing the Souls" ceremony
(*Suu Khwan*), which is performed to call the soul back to the body in case
of illness, accident, or dangerous passage. In Muang Phuan, where the
ceremony often takes place in a private home, everyone present adds a
string to the patient. A long string also connects the patient to a steaming
basket of rice. Together, the strings create a circle of healing energy.[43]

In Bali, the same Indian silk patola cloth used to maintain temporal
power is believed to heal mental illness. Small pieces are cut from the
sacred fabric and burned, and the patient inhales the pungent smoke.
(Thus, it is not unusual to find some of these highly valued cloths with tiny
missing sections.) Villagers from Tenganan Pegringsingan in Eastern
Bali weave their own double-ikat cloth (*geringsing*) that echoes patola
patterns. The name of the cloth implies its curative properties: *gering* means
"plague" or "epidemic;" *sing* means "not." Believed to keep sickness, harm,
or misfortune away from individuals and the community as a whole, it is
used in a variety of rituals. Usually, it is worn by individuals, but statues
of the deities may also be draped in geringsing for additional protection.
The fabric is labor-intensive to make (up to three years for a single cloth),
but it is not splashy; its dark tones are dyed with local plants. (There is a
widespread false rumor that the reddish brown color is achieved with human
blood.) The Tenganan villagers have a distinct and apparently ancient
culture; they are known in fact as "Bali Aga," or "old Bali." They maintain
that the Hindu god Indra came to them and gave them this type of sacred
cloth as a form of magical protection. Geringsing is made nowhere else.[44]

A variety of textiles are used for healing and spiritual passage on
other Indonesian islands. At funerals in Bima, the powerful fabric is the
same white cloth that greets a newborn baby. In Sumba, hinggi (see chapter
4) are placed on boulders around the funeral site to help the spirit of the

*Geringsing double-ikat cloth is made only
in the village of Tenganan Pegringsingan,
Bali. Considered to be extremely powerful,
it is used in healing rituals. During
ceremonies the fabric may be draped over
a person's chest. It takes up to three years
to make a single cloth of this type.*

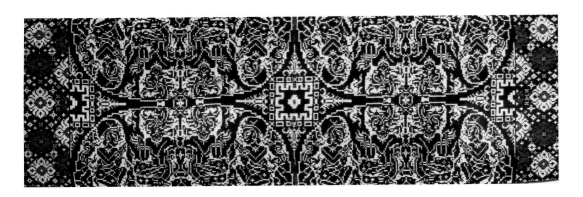

A Balinese balian (traditional magic healer) in the 1980s. The requisite black-and-white cloth is generously wrapped around the shrine behind him, but, in this case, it is actually a cheaper, printed version, which, unlike wastra poleng, features a "chessboard" design with no shades of gray.

deceased leave safely; the cloths in that context are likened to sails that carry the soul away. The Tinguian people of the Philippines cover corpses with fabrics with particularly complex weaves. They believe that evil spirits must first count all the threads and holes in a textile before they can penetrate it and cause harm.[45]

Special nets have been used to "catch" illness. In Queensland, Australia, healers attached a net worked with ostrich feathers to the aching part of an individual's body. The Patani, a Malay tribe, used nets against smallpox, and in Borneo, an ill person undergoing an exorcism was wrapped in a fishing net.[46]

Moroccans specifically "charge" many of their fabrics to give them healing qualities. They may put a cloth in a spiritual shrine for some time, helping to imbue it with a spiritual blessing (baraka) that can then be transferred to a person. Other cloth is charged when covered with the name of God or "magic squares" or hexagrams painted on with henna.[47] In Rajasthan, in western India, individuals who attend performances that involve painted rectangular cloth scrolls called phads are believed to be protected from disease. The phad is covered with images of religious epics, and is set up as a temporary shrine for a night-time performance by itinerant storytellers. From sunset until dawn, they move down the scroll and sing the story of the narrative it depicts, illuminating the sections they are recounting with a small lamp. The triumph of good over evil represented in the story is extended to the life of those who participate in the ritual.[48]

The Bunu Yoruba use the white cloth associated with the spirits of the sky in healing rituals. People who are ill or prone to emotional outbursts may be told to wear the textile, which will help connect them to the spiritual world. Yoruba medicine also includes fabric made with equal numbers of black and white threads, which keep each other in balance and extend that equilibrium to the patient. The Balinese use a black-and-white check cloth (wastra poleng) in a similar fashion, draping it over guardian shrines or wearing it for dance performances. It represents a perfect, harmonious balance between opposite forces (good and evil, light and dark, etc.) that depend on each other to exist, and thus helps keep the world in order. The cloth is considered so powerful that a local environmental NGO was able to protect Balinese forests by wrapping it around thousands of trees across the island. The campaign was successful because no Balinese would dare fell a tree covered with this cloth.[49]

The Lao Neua people of Laos used special shoulder cloths during ceremonies for the sick and dying, one end of which was woven in a concentric diamond pattern with an "eye" in the center. This symbol represented the third eye in Tantric Buddhism. During healing invocations, the shawl was wrapped around the head of the priestess in such a way that the diamond sat over her forehead. (These lozenge cloths have not been woven for over a century, but were so special that they were securely stored and taken out when needed. Sadly, economic necessity forced many Lao Neua to sell their family heirlooms in the 1980s.)[50]

End detail of a Lao shoulder cloth worn by a priestess during ceremonies for the sick and dying. The concentric diamond woven into one end represents the third eye in Tantric Buddhism. During the healings the diamond was positioned over the priestess's forehead, just above her own third eye. These cloths have not been made for about 100 years.

There is a long tradition in the West of healing with a cloth that has been prayed over by a person of spiritual authority. The Bible speaks of cloth that was touched by the apostles and then used to heal the sick: "And God wrought special miracles by the hands of Paul, so that from his body were brought unto the sick handkerchiefs or aprons, and the diseases departed from them, and the evil spirits went out of them" (Acts 19:11–12).

Prayer cloths are used in multiple ways. A supplier addressing a Catholic clientele says it is customary to lay out the cloth on a table, and place petitions and pictures of those in need of spiritual or physical healing directly on it. Alternatively, the cloth may be placed on a sick person or held by the petitioner.[51] Catholics refer to prayer cloths as sacramentals, that is, material objects that have been consecrated by the church and that increase devotion and bestow spiritual grace. One type, the Green Scapular, is particularly associated with the Virgin Mary. It is typically blessed by a priest, and then worn or carried by the person in need of assistance. Ideally, this individual will also pray to Mary every day, but the efficacy of the cloth is such that even if it is surreptitiously placed in his or her vicinity—even in the clothes or bedding—the person may continue to receive benefit. The scapular is said to have great power, as "the devil knows he is powerless to hurt" anyone who wears it.[52]

Mormons used prayer handkerchiefs in the 19th century. Historian Michael Quinn explains that when a group of believers asked Joseph Smith to come to heal them and he was unable to go, he pulled a red silk handkerchief out of his pocket and sent it to them with one of his evangelists. The people were healed. This took place in the 1830s. By the 1880s the practice had begun to fade among Mormons, but was taken up by Pentecostals. Indeed, American evangelical Christians make great use of prayer cloths. High-profile preachers such as Oral Roberts provide them upon request, but there are also many quiet organizations devoted to their distribution. Healing Room Ministries, which focuses much of its energy on this activity, now buys large quantities of fabric and cuts them in bulk. The cloths are anointed with oil and prayed over before shipping. Vineyard of Love Ministry offers free prayer cloths through the internet, which are said to be blessed with tailor-made prayers ("for you and your intentions"). Prayer cloths are routinely brought to non-sectarian hospitals as well. An American nurse is working on a campaign to make sure that children undergoing surgery are allowed to bring them into the operating room with them to help minimize their fears.[53]

While there have been some scandals in recent years surrounding the authenticity of prayer cloths sent through the mail, most practitioners are sincere in their use of these textiles, and many attest to their efficacy. R. Marie Griffith, a teacher of religion at Northwestern University, explains the "metaphysics" of the cloths:

> The evangelists would take a handkerchief and pray fervently over it, maybe pray so hard that they would be sweating. They'd wipe the sweat of their brows onto the handkerchief, and then send it off to someone as a sacramental object of divine grace and prayer... We think of prayer...in the Protestant evangelical tradition as being above materiality. But these objects themselves were thought to be saturated with a kind of power through these signs of intensive prayer.[54]

Individuals who make small quilts for a project similar to the Prayer Shawl Ministry explain that prayers are "literally part of the fabric" they bestow, for "from the time the fabric is purchased to the time it is given away, a...quilt is prayed over by scores of people." Each adds energy. Kathy Cueva, president of this Prayer Quilt Ministry, reports that she has often experienced the quilt she is working on becoming "almost too hot" to touch.[55]

THE GREEN SCAPULAR

The doctor explained to me that [a very sick patient] would very probably die within three days without regaining consciousness. He and a nurse escorted me to the room. I addressed the sick woman but she gave no indication whatsoever that she understood a word I was saying. Thereupon I took a green scapular from my pocket, applied it to her forehead, and repeated the invocation, "Immaculate Heart of Mary, pray for us now and at the hour of our death." And what happened? The woman immediately regained consciousness, joined her hands and very devoutly asked God to forgive her sins. I was amazed. The doctor and the nurse, both non-Christians, were also flabbergasted.

Reverend Leo Steinbach, 2006

Intercession and communication

Cloth is also used for intercession on a broader scale. The Himalayan prayer flags that carry requests and blessings on the wind are usually made of small rectangles of colored fabric, strung together horizontally. Most are printed with texts, either Sanskrit mantras that are believed to affect invisible energies (the most common is *Om Mani Padme Hum*) or shortened versions of Buddhist sutras, and they are placed everywhere: on the tops of high mountain passes (pilgrims add new strings when they arrive); on monasteries, stupas, or shrines; on bridges, rooftops, and around houses. They are allowed to weather and eventually dissolve, for it is believed that the prayers become a permanent part of the universe. In tune with the natural cycle of life, the Tibetans continually place new flags alongside the old.[56]

The prayer flag tradition probably dates back thousands of years to the shamanistic Bon religion of pre-Buddhist Tibet. Bonpo priests used colored flags to correspond to the elements—earth, water, fire, air, and space. Believing that health requires a balance of these elements, they arranged flags around a sick patient to help harmonize the elements in her body and bring her into a state of physical and mental health. They also used flags to help harmonize and appease the elemental spirits of mountains, valleys, lakes, and streams, who could cause disease if unfavorably provoked. The prayer flag tradition and its color code system were retained as Buddhism came in.[57]

When the Chinese took over Tibet and tried to erase Tibetan culture and religion, they discouraged—though never completely eliminated—the use of prayer flags. The tradition has been revitalized there, however, and

Prayer flags flanking the stupa at Deer Park Buddhist Center, Wisconsin, U.S., 2009. They are imprinted with mantras praying for the release of all beings' suffering, and as they wave in the breeze, the prayers are carried upward.

A view of the Nigerian Yoruba Egungun Society masquerade costume in action. The many lappets hanging from these outfits whirl as the dancers turn, creating an energy that helps the dancer contact the spirits of the ancestors.

is flourishing in other places as well. Tibetan refugees living in India have a thriving business producing them for worldwide distribution (they are increasingly popular in the U.S. and Europe). New types are also emerging. After the attacks of 9/11, Catherine Cartwright Jones created a "Prayer Flag for Peace, Reconciliation, and Ramadan," for example, with the word "peace" written in Arabic, English, Hebrew, and Hindi. English-language "peace prayer" flags are also proliferating. When the Rubin Museum of Art in New York, an institution devoted to Buddhist art, asked artists around the world to create "modern" versions of the flags in 2004, more than 120 individuals complied. At the International Sarcoma Patient Advocate Network meeting in 2005, a "Prayer Flags for Sarcoma" initiative resulted in a string of thirty-two flags that hung at the front of the meeting room—one for each type of sarcoma the group was dealing with.[58]

Ironically, the prayer flag idea is also being adopted for more personal intercession, and sometimes carries commercial overtones. One company that advertises its flags as "ideal gifts" includes some with universal prayers for peace and others with sentiments such as "Follow Your Heart, Honor Your Wisdom" or "May we be inspired, creative, free, grateful." There are even prayer flag expressions that invoke more materialistic desires, including bigger breasts and a flat screen TV.[59]

Textiles that increase communication with other realms by moving with the wind are used in spiritually focused dance garments. The robes of the Sufi whirling dervishes of the Mevlevi order, who perform their *Sema* ritual as an experiential journey—a union with God—are designed to catch and magnify the spiritual energy. The white skirt represents purity. Its hem is weighted, so as the semazens spin, the fabric billows out in a graceful, ever-moving circle, and like the Peruvian dance skirts described in chapter 3, enhances their turning. The breeze created by the skirt also makes the mystical experience tangible.[60] Long strands of ribbon, yarn, or fabric strips that whirl with every movement are similarly part of many Native American dances. Grass Dance regalia, for example, is covered with long strands of yarn that represent the swaying of long grass on a windy day. The regalia symbolize and express a state of harmony with the universe and Mother Earth. Swirling cloth lappets add to the transcendent experience of the Nigerian Yoruba Egungun Society masquerade, in which the vortex the fabric creates as it moves assists individuals to connect with ancestral spirits.[61]

Shamans use different kinds of textiles to help them move into an altered state of consciousness. In addition to string, they sometimes incorporate sewn-on elements on their garments. Among the Inuit, a shaman's clothing traditionally included finely pieced skins and actual parts of protector animals—wings and claws of birds, in some cases, or whole skins of weasel. The garments of a Mongolian shaman usually incorporated metal implements. In Manchuria, the outfits invariably included mirrors, bells, and iron antlers, as well as streamers and cowry-adorned collars.[62] Because of their energetic charge, pieces of cloth are

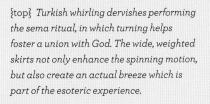

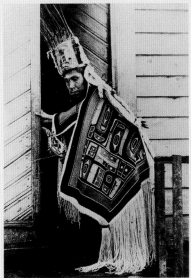

{top} *Turkish whirling dervishes performing the sema ritual, in which turning helps foster a union with God. The wide, weighted skirts not only enhance the spinning motion, but also create an actual breeze which is part of the esoteric experience.*

{above, left} *Frederic Remington's 1903 painting,* An Indian Dance, *indicates how much the fringe and feathers on a dance outfit would enhance the mystical quality of the experience.*

{above, right} *The man in this 1888 photo, labeled "Kitch Hawk alias Jake the Bracelet Maker," is wrapped in a Chilkat dance blanket made with cedar bark and goat hair. The long fringes would spin out while he turned.*

"Wishing tree" near Geghard Monastery, Armenia.

frequently left as an offering to a higher power. Native American people often leave prayer ties and/or bundles, typically filled with tobacco, for what is usually translated as the Great Spirit. They serve as expressions of thanks and are believed to increase the efficacy of any request. While Native American practices vary, prayer ties are generally made from red, yellow, white, or black cloth, colors that correspond to the four directions. They are frequently attached to trees or bushes. Some are filled with substances other than tobacco—cornmeal, perhaps, or a stone, or shell— and some are plain, "filled" only with prayers and gratitude. Feathers are sometimes tied in, again to help carry the blessing out into the air.[63]

Trees draped with fabric are, in fact, found around the world. In Madagascar, people who seek help from the spirits wrap the trunk of a sacred tamarind tree with red or white cloth, for example, and Druze and Muslim Arabs cover trees growing near the tombs of holy men or women with cloth ties not unlike those left by the Native Americans. Each strip is put there in conjunction with a request or healing prayer. "Rag trees" (also called raggedy bushes or wishing trees) are seen throughout Europe. In some places, tree ties are associated with female power. In Lebanon the tradition can be dated back to the worship of fertility goddesses, and there is still a 375-year-old oak in Rachaya known as "the mother of cloth bands." One may also find strips dedicated to the female deity at the top of Mount Tai, a holy site in China. In Shinto Japan, mothers fashioned red cotton into breast-shaped forms and hung them from yew trees to ensure a good supply of milk. Wherever such ties are used, the cloth is allowed to disintegrate, much as it is with prayer flags.[64] Honoring the rag tree tradition, artist Donna Henes created a healing installation at Manhattan Psychiatric Center on Wards Island in 1980. She asked people to donate their "favorite item of soothing lucky energy filled clothing," and tore what she received into strips that she and some of the hospital patients then knotted onto the island's trees. As they tied the 4,159 knots, passersby told stories of cloth-hung trees in far-flung areas of the world, including Armenia, Ireland, and Morocco.[65]

The church of the Señor do Bonfim in Salvador, Brazil has long functioned as a place of healing ("bonfim" is roughly translated as "happy outcomes"); pilgrims go there to pray for cures or good fortune. After making a request, it is customary to purchase a small colored ribbon stamped with the name of the church, and tie it around one's wrist or ankle. It, too, is worn until it essentially wears away, by which time the issue should have been resolved.

The Yoruba practice of sacrificing cloth to maintain spiritual harmony is a dramatic example of textile intercession. When someone is sick, according to Elisha Renne, their clothes might be burned or buried. She recounts the following story in *Cloth That Does Not Die*:

> One woman described an incident in which a diviner advised her that some people were trying to harm her children. The woman swore that she would be willing to sacrifice anything to save them: "Later, when I opened my box to use one of my marriage cloths, I found that all had been eaten by termites... My children were spared."[66]

Since many cultures maintain that the seat of the soul lies in the head—it is the part of the body that is literally closest to the heavens, and the centers that guide spiritual energies are located there—textile head coverings often represent a relationship with spirits. A covered head signifies obedience to God, and men of many religions wear skullcaps to acknowledge that the divine presence is always above. Skullcaps were known in ancient Egypt, and were common among Zoroastrians (they believed the cap kept harmful cosmic rays away from the pineal gland, the center of spiritual awakening and creative thought). Muslim and Jewish men both wear them today, as do Catholic priests. The caps can be made

{below, left} *Tunisian man's hat, 1965.*

{below, right} *Crocheted cotton Jewish skullcap (called yarmulke in Yiddish; kippa in Hebrew) made in Guatemala, c. 2006. The Mayan women who make such caps have little idea about Jewish custom or ritual; volunteer development workers who help them to come up with saleable products give them prototypes and the weavers then make their own choices about color and pattern.*

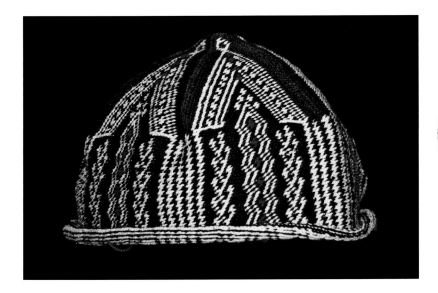

{right} *A batik head cloth from Jambi, Sumatra, Indonesia, mid-20th century, featuring images derived from Ottoman Islamic calligraphy. It would probably be used in a religious context. Some Sumatran families also use the cloths to wrap or drape the Koran, or as wall decorations.*

{below} *Kayapó feather headdress, Brazil, c. 1990. Wearing a halo of this sort extends a person's energy field or aura. Feathers are particularly thought to lead to transcendent states, as they come from creatures who can fly.*

in a variety of ways, but when sewn, they typically consist of several rounded triangles attached together. In the Syrian Orthodox church, the seven sections of the skullcap symbolize the seven levels of the Mithraic priesthood.[67] Slightly less form-fitting caps are worn by men of different faiths in West Africa—Christians, followers of indigenous religions, and Muslims. They are referred to with the same word (*kufi* or *kofi*) that is used to describe a skullcap. Residents of the Nazir Monastery, a holistic spiritual community in the U.S., crochet colorful kufi that they offer as "cosmic crowns" to people of different religions. They make the point that the Islamic kufi, the Jewish yarmulke or kippa, and Yoruba/Candomblé fila are essentially the same.[68]

Larger head coverings are also used to indicate respect and obedience. There are multiple references in the Old Testament to turbans worn for this reason (see for example Leviticus 8:9, Exodus 29:6). The Sikh's turban marks commitment to the religion and its gurus. When a believer puts it on, "the turban ceases to be just a piece of cloth and becomes one and the same with the Sikh's head;

he carries the power of the Guru wherever he goes."[69] Large head coverings serve an additional function, however, in that they may augment the wearer's spiritual power. The energy of an Ottoman-era Muslim Turk's turban was considered so great that when it was not in use and was stored in the home, it was sometimes covered with another cloth to keep its power contained.[70]

At the annual Klepdzo festival of the Dangme tribe of southern Ghana, senior priests put on a raffia straw hat that "places them in the midst of the gods." It is carefully stored away the rest of the year. In the Philippines, individuals are able to "converse with the cosmos" when they wear head cloths pieced from scraps of many other prestigious cloths.[71] Head coverings of Tibetan Buddhist lamas vary by lineage and spiritual rank, but all carry symbolic power. The Black Hat of the Karmapa is even said to be the physical representation of a spiritual crown woven from the hair of 100,000 female deities. Chimù high priests in pre-Columbian Peru also used human hair to increase the efficacy of a ritual headdress. Their llama wool cap was adorned with 160 braids taken from people who had been ritually sacrificed (in all, this amounted to about 4 pounds or 1.8 kg of hair). The head covering carried an enormous power from their accumulated energy.[72]

As a side note, it is interesting to point out that men's religious head coverings, much like women's, have strong semiotic power. Sikhs believe they must always wear their turbans, and this has created great problems for believers trying to go through contemporary airport security. After much discussion of religious profiling, the U.S. Transportation Security Administration (TSA) revised its procedures relating to headwear in October 2007, effectively allowing Sikhs to keep their turbans on during a personal search. Muslim Americans who wear skullcaps have also been subject to discrimination. The New York Civil Liberties Union argued in a 2006 lawsuit that a corrections officer who was barred from wearing his kufi while on duty was unfairly treated. The suit was settled after several months in favor of his religious freedom.[73]

Uniting and uplifting the world

A fitting place to end both this chapter and this book is to delve more deeply into the communal cloth projects introduced in chapter 3 which hold the intention of changing the energy of the planet. I focus here on their spiritual dimensions and consider how these projects bring together many of the themes explored in this book.

The Cloth of Many Colors project unveiled in 2000 was conceived as a "living prayer." James Twyman dreamed of the cloth while leading a prayer vigil at a refugee camp on the border of Kosovo and Macedonia in 1998. Thirty thousand displaced people were present at that event, and Twyman saw a cloth pieced together from contributions from diverse people as a way of bringing the inspiring energy of the prayer vigil into physical form. When the mile-long cloth was first presented at the United Nations, thousands more gathered to pray. The next day, when it was wrapped around the U.S. Capitol building, still more thousands prayed around it.[74]

The John Denver Memorial Peace Cloth, conceived as a visible expression of the vision of one world that Denver had been working for before his death, also held the power of collective prayer. Its patches too were charged with the energy of accumulated memories and individual spirits. One woman offered pieces of crib sheets that had been used by her now-grown children, for example, and another sent a square made of yarn unraveled from the sweater of her recently deceased best friend. Several mothers sent garments from children who had died. There were even patches that had "witnessed" John Denver concerts, as fans contributed parts of their embroidered shirts from the 1970s. This composite fabric was used at the annual Prayer Vigil for the Earth, where rituals continued unabated for thirty-three hours. The temporary "peace village" set up on the mall in Washington, D.C., featured a ring of tipis, and altars and shrines from different religions. The Peace Cloth circled the perimeter, symbolically enfolding all the traditions together and uniting them as one unit.[75]

When Terry Helwig conceived of her Thread Project, she said she

kept thinking our world is hanging by a thread. I wondered if that precarious thread was enough to hold us. Could a thread of hope or compassion matter in the larger scheme of life? Should we let go of that thread, or hang on? It occurred to me that every human life begins with us dangling from a thread in our mother's womb. It is from that place that we are born; maybe a thread is no small thing.

Her "thread ambassadors" also contributed textile elements that evoked memories of loved ones, and some that related to world spiritual leaders. One woman wrote:

I'm sending a strip of fabric woven by lepers from one of Mother Teresa's leper colonies outside of Calcutta. If people who have no fingers or toes can learn to weave, any of us can learn whatever we must to make it through. So weave on.[76]

These contributions were incorporated into forty-nine woven panels, which were made into seven cloths (the 7 x 7 number communicates completion, and recalls the arrangement of the Wiphala flag). Panels were woven by indigenous peoples from Guatemala, Australia, Canada, Ghana, and Afghanistan, who in many cases added their own ideas and materials. Even after the panels were completed in 2006, individuals hearing about the project still wanted to contribute. Helwig promised that new donations would "be tied end to end and wound into a large, earth-like ball" that would travel with the panels when they are exhibited. She has wide-ranging ideas for the display of the cloths, including an exhibition where viewers would stand enfolded inside an 8-foot (2.4 meter) circle of the fabric.[77]

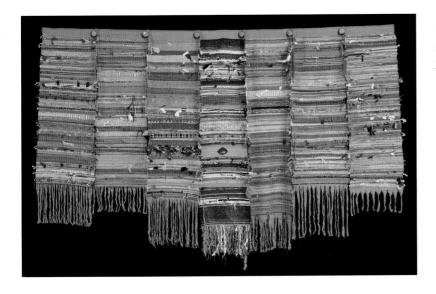

"Dawn Looming," one of seven large cloths woven from individual threads collected from people around the world. This is part of Terry Helwig's "The Thread Project: One World, One Cloth," 2006.

Many writers on spiritual matters have commented on the Thread Project, and their words bring me back to concepts introduced in earlier chapters. Jungian psychologist Jean Shinoda Bolen remarked:

> The Thread Project is tangible and mystical. Each cloth is woven from thousands of threads, every thread is a connection to someone in the world who wanted to be part of this vision of wholeness, reconciliation, and healing. These cloths are likely more than symbols. Where quantum physics and spirituality meet, a parallel weaving of all these threads of intention is probably taking place.

"Within these threads," author Jean Houston commented, "lies the Soul of the World."[78]

These statements also bring me back to the preface of this book, when I described my own vision for a textile installation representing the veil of Maya, and my overall conviction and excitement about the meaning and power of textiles. There are others now who have realized something akin to my long-ago vision, acknowledging and recognizing the symbolic and literal importance of cloth. They, too, have come to understand why textiles matter: how they can be joined together to help bond us with one another; how they provide protection; absorb and transmit energy; allow us to express ourselves and create beauty; serve as embodiments of scientific concepts, creation myths, and the very generation of life; and help us attain different states of consciousness. Because industrialization, mechanization, and now globalization have taken the production of cloth far away from most of us, we have collectively lost our awareness of its power—lost our understanding of its magic. Hopefully, this holistic consideration of the meanings of textiles in human life will help reawaken that understanding in those who have not yet thought much about it, and help us all feel a new sense of connection and appreciation.

NOTES

Preface pp. 6–15

[1] Jeremy Lange, "Air Conditioned Clothes," Lifestyle section, *React*, Sunday supplement, *Parade*, Apr. 10–16, 2000.

[2] Gordon, *The Saturated World*, esp. 14–16.

[3] Gordon, *Shaker Textile Arts*, 45–48; Gordon, "Victorian Fancy Goods."

[4] Kopp and Kopp, *American Hooked and Sewn Rugs*; Crockett, *Card Weaving*; Newman, *Contemporary African Arts and Crafts*.

[5] Torimaru and Torimaru, *One Needle, One Thread*.

[6] Barber, *Women's Work*; Weiner and Schneider, *Cloth and Human Experience*.

[7] Gale and Kaur, *The Textile Book*.

[8] Bergman, *The Knitting Goddess*; Judith, Chakras: *Eastern Body, Western Mind*; "The Problem of Maya or Illusion and How to Deal with It," hinduwebsite.com/beliefinmaya.asp.

1 The Very Fabric of Existence pp. 16–57

[1] J.R. Minkel, "String is the Thing," *Columbia*, Spring 2006: 16–21; Taimina, *Crocheting Adventures*; www.math.cornell.edu/~dtaimina/; Smolin, *Three Roads to Quantum Gravity*, 186.

[2] Jasleen Dhamija, "Woven Incantations," presentation at TSA Symposium, 2000; Budge, *The Gods of the Egyptians*.

[3] Watts, *The Joyous Cosmology*, 31–32.

[4] "Hermetic Philosophy and the Mystery of Being," www.plotinus.com; Kapp, *Rigmaroles & Ragamuffins*, 107.

[5] Foster, *New Raiments of Self*.

[6] Bausum, *Threading Time*, 29; Barber, *Women's Work*, 238.

[7] Weiner and Schneider, *Cloth and Human Experience*, 2.

[8] Julia Parker, "Old Ways, New Ways," Keynote address, TSA Symposium, 2004.

[9] Stallybrass, "Worn Worlds," 36.

[10] Bausum, *Threading Time*, 52; personal memory of a story about Lila O'Neale; Altman and West, *Threads of Identity*, 26; personal conversation with medievalist Valerie Garver, Madison, WI, Apr. 14, 2009; Murra, "Cloth and its Function in the Inka State," esp. 281, 289.

[11] Elliott, *Tying Rocks to Clouds*, 111–12; Stallybrass, "Worn Worlds," esp. 46.

[12] Banerjee and Miller, *The Sari*, 28–29; Robert S. Carlsen and Martín Prechtel, "Weaving and Cosmos amongst the Tzutujil Maya of Guatemala," *Res: Journal of Anthropology and Aesthetics*, 15 (Spring 1988): 122–32.

[13] Richard Preston, "Capturing the Unicorn," *The New Yorker*, Apr. 11, 2005: 28–33.

[14] Korolnik-Andersch and Korolnik, *The Color of Henna*.

[15] Maxwell, *Sari to Sarong*, 115.

[16] Strasser, *Never Done*, 105.

[17] Kathleen Jenks, "Weaving Arts and Lore: Cosmic Webs, Spinning, Spindles, Embroidery, Quilts, Clothing" on "Myth*ing Links: An Annotated & Illustrated Collection of Worldwide Links to Mythologies, Fairy Tales & Folklore, Sacred Arts & Sacred Traditions," www.mythinglinks.org/ct~weaving.html.

[18] Bergman, *The Knitting Goddess*, 40, 20; Budge, *The Gods of the Egyptians*; Susan Starr Sered, "Rachel's Tomb and the Milk Grotto of the Virgin Mary: Two Women's Shrines in Bethlehem," *Journal of Feminist Studies in Religion* 2, no. 2, Fall 1986: 7–22.

[19] Gail McMurray Gibson, "The Thread of Life in the Hand of the Virgin" in "The Distaff and the Pen: Woman and the Distaff" in Holloway, Bechtold and Wright, *Equally in God's Image*.

[20] Thorskegga Thorn, "Spinning in Myths and Folktales," www.thorshof.org/spinmyth.htm; Gail McMurray Gibson, "The Thread of Life in the Hand of the Virgin" in "The Distaff and the Pen: Woman and the Distaff" in Holloway, Bechtold and Wright, *Equally in God's Image*.

[21] Quoted in Celestine Bohlen, "O Say Can You See What That Flag Means," *New York Times*, Dec. 16, 2000: B11.

[22] Ahmed, *Living Fabric*, 76, 90.

[23] Robert S. Carlsen and Martín Prechtel, "Weaving and Cosmos amongst the Tzutujil Maya of Guatemala," *Res: Journal of Anthropology and Aesthetics* 15 (Spring 1988): 122–32; Schaefer, *To Think with a Good Heart*, 237.

[24] Robert S. Carlsen and Martín Prechtel, "Weaving and Cosmos amongst the Tzutujil Maya of Guatemala," *Res: Journal of Anthropology and Aesthetics*, 15 (Spring 1988): 122–32; Wesley Thomas, "Sil Yool T'ool: Personification of Navajo Weaving," in Bonar, *Woven by the Grandmothers*, 40; Barre Toelken, Lecture, University of Wisconsin-Madison, Mar. 2000.

[25] Thorskegga Thorn, "Spinning in Myths and Folktales," www.thorshof.org/spinmyth.htm; Thorskegga Thorn, "The Spindle and the Well," www.thorshof.org/spinwell.htm; Schaefer, *To Think with a Good Heart*, 193–94.

[26] The information in this chart was compiled from a wide range of sources, including: *Stories to Tell*; Gail McMurray Gibson, "The Thread of Life in the Hand of the Virgin" in "The Distaff and the Pen: Woman and the Distaff" in Holloway, Bechtold and Wright, *Equally in God's Image*; Weigle, *Spiders and Spinsters*; "Temple of Spider Grandmother, www.angelfire.com/nc2/cybertemples/SpiderGrandmother.html; "The Goddesses," www.goddess.com.au/goddesses/; www.theisisproject.org/soul_spirit/; "Hrana's Gallery of Goddesses," www.hranajanto.com/GoddessGallery/GGF-all.html; www.wic.org/artwork/spiderw.htm; and www.bigisland.com/~stony/lore38.html.

[27] Lakota story told by Jenny Leading Cloud (White River, Rosebud reservation, SD) to Richard Erdoes in 1967, www.aaanativearts.com/article939.html.

[28] Francesca Bray, "Womanly Work: Ideals and Realities of Textile Production in Imperial China," keynote address, TSA Symposium, 2002; Bray, *Technology and Gender*, 183–91; Ahmed, *Living Fabric*, 96.

[29] Hitchcock, *Indonesian Textiles*, 136.

[30] Schaefer, *To Think with a Good Heart*, 193–94, 251; Atasoy, Ipek, 20; Kate Fitz Gibbon, "Turkoman Embroidery and Women's Magic," presentation at TSA Symposium, 2000.

[31] Atasoy, *Ipek*, 20; Lester, *Autobiography of God*, 32.

[32] Patricia Williams, entries on Slovak and Czech ethnic dress in Eicher, *Encyclopedia of World Dress*, vol. 9; Hitchcock, *Indonesian Textiles*; Alit Kertaraharja, "Singjara, Bali" in *Jakarta Post*, Mar. 21, 2002; www.threadsoflife.com/; "Balinese Dress and Textiles," www.murnis.com/culture/articlebalinesedressandtextiles.htm.

[33] "The Caste System and the Stages of Life in Hinduism," www.friesian.com/caste.htm; Krishakok, "Sacred Threads," Aug. 28, 2007, krishashok.wordpress.com/2007/08/28/sacred-threads; Becker, *Arts, Gender and Changing Constructions of Amazigh (Berber) Identity*.

[34] Taped interview conducted by the New York Historical Society with Lisa Purdon in preparation for *Home Sewn: Three Centuries of Stitching History* exhibition at New York Historical Society, Nov. 18, 2003 to Apr. 18, 2004; Pamela Scheinman, "Graduation Rituals in Portugal," *Fiberarts*, Nov./Dec. 2000: 16.

[35] *Whiting, Old-Time Tools and Toys of Needlework*, 211; sherpe.com/carving/index.html; Lisa Kies, "Traditional Russian Tools and Activities," www.strangelove.net/~kieser/Russia/villagetools.html; "Traditional Hand-Made Souvenirs," www.villaggioilgabbiano.com/calabriaartigianato_en.asp; Hochberg, *Spin, Span, Spun*, 21.

[36] Mika Toyota, "Clothing and Courtship: Akha Textiles in a Social Context" in Dell and Dudley, *Textiles from Burma*, 125; Sandra Dudley, "Textiles in Exile: Karen Refugees in Thailand" in Dell and Dudley, *Textiles from Burma*, 78; Wu, *Life Styles of China's Ethnic Minorities*, 103–4.

37 Zinn, "The Values and Meanings of Çeyiz;" Glassie, *Turkish Traditional Art Today*, 738–40; *Dowry: Eastern European Painted Furniture, Textiles and Related Folk Art* (video); Gáborján, *Hungarian Peasant Costumes*; Gittinger, *Textiles for This World and Beyond*, 72.

38 *Dowry: Eastern European Painted Furniture, Textiles and Related Folk Art* (video); Mika Toyota, "Clothing and Courtship: Akha Textiles in a Social Context," in Dell and Dudley, *Textiles from Burma*, 125–29; personal conversation with Jennifer Angus, Madison, WI, Mar. 2009; Scott, *Why Do They Dress That Way?*

39 Wu, *Life Styles of China's Ethnic Minorities*, fig. 137; personal conversation with Larry Fenske, Madison, WI, Sept. 2007; A.E. Anton, "Handfasting in Scotland," *Scottish Historical Review*, 37, no. 4 (Oct. 1958): 89–102; Chapter 4: "Religion and Cultural Factors," *Adolescent and Reproductive Health in Southeast Asia: Thailand*, www.unescobkk.org/fileadmin/user_upload/arsh/Country_Profiles/Lao_PDR/Chapter_4.pdf, "Wedding Traditions and Folklore," www.pibweddings.com/traditionsorigins.html; www.celticatlanta.com/weddings/handfast/index.htm; personal conversation with Patricia Loew, Madison, WI, Jul. 2010.

40 Bausum, *Threading Time*, 31; Scheid and Svenbro, *The Craft of Zeus*, 86–90, 125; "The Wedding Rug," www.iarelative.com/wedding/wrug.htm; jlissy.home.mindspring.com/tradit.htm; "Marriage in the Jewish Tradition," adapted from "Judaism 101" in "Your Guide to Jewish Weddings," *Monthly Reporter*, Madison, WI, Jan. 2005.

41 Bausum, *Threading Time*, 31; "Marriage in the Jewish Tradition" adapted from "Judaism 101" in "Your Guide to Jewish Weddings," *Monthly Reporter*, Madison, WI, Jan. 2005; Denamur, *Moroccan Textile Embroidery*; Seng, "Two Middle Eastern Wedding Costumes as Vehicles of Traditional Culture."

42 Maxwell, *Sari to Sarong*, 115.

43 Lewis and Lewis, *Peoples of the Golden Triangle*.

44 Gittinger, *Textiles for This World and Beyond*, 97; Maxwell, *Sari to Sarong*, 116; Cheesman, *Lao-Tai Textiles*, 176–78; Hitchcock, *Indonesian Textiles*, 142.

45 Ross and Adedze, *Wrapped in Pride*; Forshee, *Between the Folds*.

46 Cheesman, *Lao-Tai Textiles*, 176–78; Maxwell, *Sari to Sarong*, 116.

47 Murra, "Cloth and its Function in the Inka State," 280; "Egyptian Mummies," *Smithsonian Encyclopedia*, www.si.edu/Encyclopedia_SI/nmnh/mummies.htm.

48 Hitchcock, *Indonesian Textiles*, 143.

49 Renne, *Cloth That Does Not Die*, 47; Henry J. Drewal, "Pageantry and Power in Yoruba Costuming" in Cordwell and Schwarz, *The Fabrics of Culture*, 190.

50 Maslow, "A Theory of Human Motivation;" *Maslow's Hierarchy of Needs* on www.edpsycinteractive.org/topics/regsys/maslow.html; www.spiraldynamics.org/Graves/colors.htm; rationalspirituality.com/articles/Ken_Wilber_Spiral_Dynamics.htm; Judith, *Chakras: Eastern Body, Western Mind*; Gale and Kaur, *The Textile Book*, 3.

2 Living on the Earth pp. 58–113

1 Oakes and Riewe, *Our Boots*, 30, 41, 47, 109.

2 Robin Odle, "Quill and Moosehair Work in the Great Lakes Region," in Odle, *The Art of the Great Lakes Indians*, xxxi.

3 Patricia Williams, "Ethnic Dress in the Czech Republic," in Eicher, *Encyclopedia of World Dress*; Hartley, *The Ladies' Hand Book*.

4 Oakes and Gustafson, "Coats of Eider," *American Indian Art Magazine*, Winter 1991: 68–72; "Reconstructing the Anasazi Turkey Feather Blanket," documentary video, New Mexico: Bandelier National Monument, c. 1970 (no longer extant).

5 Murra, "Cloth and its Function in the Inka State," 281.

6 Reina and Kensinger, *The Gift of Birds*, 11–12; Vainker, *Chinese Silk*; Peter Ross Range, "Spin Cycle," *Smithsonian*, Jul. 2008: 78.

7 Born, "Purple in Classical Antiquity;" Ehud Spanier, "The Royal Purple and Biblical Blue: An Interdisciplinary Study," presentation at Chazen Museum of Art, Madison, WI, Sept. 14, 2005; Scott, "Millennia of Murex;" Abbott, *Kingdom of the Seashell*, 176; Greenfield, *A Perfect Red*.

8 Busby, *Spruce Root Basketry*.

9 Robert Laures, "A Medieval Response to Municipal Pollution," presentation at Mid-America Conference on History, Lawrence, KS, Sept. 1992, reprinted eserver.org//history/medieval-pollution.txt.

10 James E. Alleman and Brooke T. Mossman, "Asbestos Revisited," *Scientific American*, Jul. 1997: 70–75; Thomas B. Lemmon, "The Historical Significance of the Salamander and its Relationship with Asbestos," presentation to International Association of Heat and Frost Insulators and Asbestos Workers, Apr. 15, 2003, www.awlocal5.com/history%20of%20salamander.html; Maines, *Asbestos and Fire*, 30; www.unrv.com/economy/asbestos.php.

11 "Fiberglass," www.aecom.yu.edu/ehs/Industrial%20Hygiene/Fs_Fibergls.htm; "Fiber Optics," www.webopedia.com/TERM/F/fiber_optics.html; Alyssa Becker, "High-Performance Fibers," in McQuaid, *Extreme Textiles*, 74; Braddock and O'Mahony, *Techno Textiles*, 25–26; Quinn, *Techno Fashion*, 106.

12 Rovine, *Bogolan*; Kimberly Michelle Jones, "History, Origin and Significance of Mud Cloth," www.library.cornell.edu/africana/about/mudcloth.html.

13 Matilda McQuaid, "Introduction: Stronger, Faster, Lighter, Safer, and Smarter," in McQuaid, *Extreme Textiles*, 24–27; Cara McCarty, "NASA: Advancing Ultra-Performance," in McQuaid, *Extreme Textiles*, 138–61; Amanda Young, "The Spacesuit," in McQuaid, *Extreme Textiles*, 162–79.

14 Ray Rivera and Damien Cave, "Haiti Struggles to Find Tents to Put over the Heads of its Displaced Masses," *New York Times*, Jan. 22, 2010.

15 Philip Beesley and Sean Hanna, "A Transformed Architecture" in McQuaid, *Extreme Textiles*, 104; Armijos, *Fabric Architecture*.

16 See "Master Giles de Laval" (Mark Calderwood), "Tubbed and Scrubbed: An Overview of Bathing in the Middle Ages," 2002, reproduced on www.florilegium.org.

17 Scarce, *Domestic Culture in the Middle East*; Zinn, "The Values and Meanings of Çeyiz;" Jan Stuart, "Portable Upholstery: Textiles for Chinese Furniture," presentation at Elvehjem Museum of Art, Madison, WI, Nov. 30, 2001; Serim Denel, "Statements from the Loom and the Needle: Woven and Embroidered Anatolian Textiles in the Home Environment," presentation at TSA Symposium, 1992.

18 thehomelessguy.blogspot.com/2005/10/blankets-and-such.html; "Legalize Sleep," www.huffsantacruz.org/articles/UCSCsleepingban.pdf.

19 Barber, *Women's Work*, 45; Richard Harris, "These Vintage Threads Are 30,000 Years Old," [U.S.] National Public Radio broadcast, Sept. 10, 2009, on www.npr.org/templates/story/story.php?storyId=112726804.

20 Kate Wong, "Profile: Olga Soffer—The Caveman's New Clothes," *Scientific American* 283 Issue 5 (Nov. 2000): 32–33.

21 *National Geographic Magazine*, Sept. 2005: 83.

22 Landreau, *Yörük*; Tanavoli, *Bread and Salt*, 41–42.

23 Marco Bassi, "Every Woman an Artist: Milk Containers in Borana," in Silverman, *Ethiopia*, 64–87; "Basketry Milk Container," www.museum.msu.edu/exhibitions/Virtual/afcon/7557-283.html.

24 Matilda McQuaid, "Introduction: Stronger, Faster, Lighter, Safer, and Smarter," in McQuaid, *Extreme Textiles*, 14–15.

25 Larsen and Freudenheim, *Interlacing*, 18.

26 Cheesman, *Lao-Tai Textiles*, 218–20.

27 Donald H. McNeil, Jr., "So Many Mosquitoes, Only So Many Nets: U.N. Calls for 'Universal Coverage,'" *New York Times*, Apr. 29, 2008: D6; Donald H. McNeil, Jr., "A $10 Mosquito Net is Making Charity Cool," *New York Times*, Jun. 2, 2008: 1, 13.

28 "Facelift with Threads," www.faceliftthread.com/contourlift.html; "Spider Webs Could Help Treat Injured Knees," Oct. 18, 2006, reported on MSNBC, www.msnbc.msn.com/id/15253292/. Info. on Serica Silk

Technologies from www.sericainc.com/en-intl/about/technology-overview.php and email correspondence with Dr David Kaplan, Tufts University, 6/08; Susan Brown, "Textiles: Fiber, Structure and Function," in McQuaid, *Extreme Textiles*, 48, 53–55, 57, 60.

29 Susan Brown, "Textiles: Fiber, Structure and Function," in McQuaid, *Extreme Textiles*, 48–50, 54–55, 60.

30 Takeda and Roberts, *Japanese Fishermen's Coats*, 39; Hochberg: *Spin, Span, Spun*, 24; Bottomley and Hopson, *Arms and Armour of the Samurai*; Kure, *Samurai*.

31 Kapp, *Rigmaroles & Ragamuffins*, 118.

32 "Japanese Scientist Invents Invisibility Cloak," *BBC News*, Feb. 18, 2003; "Invisibility Cloak Edges Closer," *BBC News*, Apr. 30, 2009, news.bbc.co.uk/2/hi/sci/tech/8025886.stm; Oliver Graydon, ed., Optics.org (optics.org).

33 Gordon, "Showing the Colors: America."

34 Ashley, *The Ashley Book of Knots*; Graumont and Hensel, *Encyclopedia of Knots and Fancy Rope Work*.

35 Bruce Bower, "Erectus Ahoy: Prehistoric Seafaring Floats into View," *Science News*, 164, no. 16 (week of Oct. 18, 2003), 248; www.data-wales.co.uk/coracle1.htm; www.worldofcoracles.co.uk.

36 Re high-tech modern boats: Matilda McQuaid, "Interview with Eric Goetz," in McQuaid, *Extreme Textiles*, 78–101.

37 Matilda McQuaid, "Introduction: Stronger, Faster, Lighter, Safer, and Smarter," in McQuaid, *Extreme Textiles*, 21–24; Susan Brown, "Textiles: Fiber, Structure and Function," in McQuaid, *Extreme Textiles*, 35.

38 Cara McCarty, "NASA: Advancing Ultra-performance," in McQuaid, *Extreme Textiles*, 138–61, esp. 151; Susan Brown, "Textiles: Fiber, Structure and Function," in McQuaid, *Extreme Textiles*, 35, 37; en.wikipedia.org/wiki/Mars_Exploration_Rover#Airbags.

39 Hoffman, "The Pride of the Block."

40 Hochberg, *Spin, Span, Spun*, 10; "The Last Inka Suspension Bridge," www.rutahsa.com/k-chaca.html; Ric Finch, "Keshwa Chaca: Straw Bridge of the Inca," *South American Explorer*, 69 (Fall/Winter 2002): 6–13; D.W. Gade, "Bridge Types in the Central Andes," *Annals of the Association of American Geographers*, 62, no. 1 (1972): 94–109; Squier, *Peru*; John Noble Wilford, "How the Inca Leapt Canyons," *New York Times*, May 8, 2007: D1, D4.

41 Philip Beesley and Sean Hanna, "A Transformed Architecture," in McQuaid, *Extreme Textiles*, 133; Renee Meiller, "Polymer Bandages May Give New Life to Old Bridges," *University of Wisconsin News*, Aug. 15, 2005.

42 Philip Beesley and Sean Hanna, "A Transformed Architecture," in McQuaid, *Extreme Textiles*, 122.

43 Matilda McQuaid, "Introduction: Stronger, Faster, Lighter, Safer, and Smarter," in McQuaid, *Extreme Textiles*, 15.

44 Oliver Morton, op. ed. column, "The Tarps of Kilimanjaro," *New York Times*, Nov. 17, 2003: 21.

45 Banerjee and Miller, *The Sari*, 99.

46 Bess and Wein, *Bamboo in Japan*.

47 Gehret, *Rural Pennsylvania Clothing*, 242–43; "Bygone Industries of the Peak: Tapes and Narrow Fabrics," www.genuki.org.uk/big/eng/DBY/BygoneIndustries/Tapes.html; morristown.areaparks.com/parkinfo.html?pid=5968.

48 Barber, *Women's Work*, 200; Hastreiter, *Kasuri*; "Not Just a Piece of Cloth," documentary about New Delhi recycling project shown on Link-TV, Jan. 2009.

49 Henry B. Harrington, "Condition of Indians—New York," in *Report on Indians Taxed and Not Taxed in the United States, Eleventh Census of the United States*. Washington, D.C.: Government Printing Office, 1890: 481.

50 Von Luck and Ambrose, *Panzer Commander*, 243; Arment and Fick-Jordaan, *Wired*.

51 Gordon, *Bazaars and Fair Ladies*; Gordon "Spinning Wheels, Samplers and the Modern Priscilla."

52 Bausum, *Threading Time*, 56.

53 Gillow, *African Textiles*, 87; Maureen Trudelle Schwarz, "The Bi'il: Traditional Female Attire as Metaphor of Navajo Aesthetic Organization," *Dress* 21 (1994): 75–80; Wesley Thomas, "Sil Yool T'ool: Personification of Navajo Weaving," in Bonar, ed., *Woven By the Grandmothers*; Welters, *Folk Dress in Europe and Anatolia*; Lewis and Lewis, *Peoples of the Golden Triangle*.

54 Bess Allen Donaldson, "The Koran as Magic," *The Muslim World*, 27 (1937): 254–66.

55 "Texas and the Alamo," *Freemasonry Today*, 44 (Spring 2008), www.freemasonrytoday.com/44/p12.php; *Bespangled, Painted and Embroidered*; Oliver, *Signs and Symbols*; catalogue info. re V1998.1.639 at Wisconsin Veteran's Museum, Madison-Wisconsin, online at collections.dva.state.wi.us/Unicgi/mwebuni.exe?request=keyword; keyword=masonic;dtype=d

56 Hitchcock, *Indonesian Textiles*, 135; Bobbi Jo Innamorato Williams, "The Native American Ghost Dance," 2002, on njnj.essortment.com/nativeamerican_rmqk.htm; Susan Stem, "The Magic of Yantra Clothing," thailand.wowasis.com/es/tb_yantramagicclothes.php; Korolnik-Andersch and Korolnik, *The Color of Henna*.

57 Denamur, *Moroccan Textile Embroidery*, 11; Wendy Moonan, "The Dowry: Where Love Meets Money," *New York Times*, Feb. 19, 1999; Kate Fitz Gibbon, "Turkmen Embroidery and Women's Magic," presentation at TSA Symposium, 2000; "Princesses of Morocco in Morocco's Traditional Dresses and Belts," www.theroyalforums.com/forums/f234/morocco-s-traditional-dresses-and-belts-1659.html; Patricia Williams, "Ethnic Dress in Slovakia," in Eicher, *Encyclopedia of World Dress*; Lewis and Lewis, *Peoples of the Golden Triangle*; Kanomi, *People of Myth*, 198.

58 Drewal and Mason, *Beads, Body and Soul*, 26, 28, 64, 203–6.

59 Banerjee and Miller, *The Sari*, 32–33.

60 Ibid.

61 Renne, *Cloth That Does Not Die*, 123, 192.

62 William Brewster, "Sewing Soldiers: An Examination of Sewing Kits Used by American Soldiers, 1861–1865," unpublished class paper, University of Wisconsin-Madison, May 1998; Gordon, "Textiles and Clothing in the Civil War."

63 Marites N. Sison, "Shawls Encircle Owners in Prayer," *[Canadian] Anglican Journal*, Apr. 2004 on www.shawlministry.com/Articles/Anglican_Journal.htm.

64 Taped interview conducted by the New York Historical Society with Lisa Purdon in preparation for *Home Sewn: Three Centuries of Stitching History* exhibit at New York Historical Society, Nov. 18, 2003 to Apr. 18, 2004.

3 The Ties that Bind pp. 114–47

1 Lecture and documentary film on the Tsaatan (Duha) Reindeer People, Rubin Museum of Asian Art, New York, Jul. 19, 2005; Pearl Sunrise, "Navajo Weaver as a Teacher of Traditional Textile Arts," presentation at TSA Symposium, 2000; Maria Christou, "An Ethnographic Interpretation of the Smoke Rising and Smoke Descending Ceremonial Attire of the Sa'dan Malimbong Toraja," presentation at TSA Symposium, 2006.

2 Ahmed, *Living Fabric*, 11.

3 Karen Crocker, "What One Woman's Diary Reveals about Preparing for the New Arrival," unpublished research paper based on Hathorn's diary (reproduced in Petroski, *A Bride's Passage*), University of Wisconsin-Madison, 2005.

4 Marsha L. MacDowell, "A Gathering of Cultural Expression," in MacDowell and Dewhurst, *To Honor and Comfort*.

5 Liu, Lan and Lin, *Bonding via Baby Carriers*, 21.

6 Sheldon Oberman, "The Gift of the Prayer Shawl,"
www.sheldonoberman.com/doc15.htm.

7 Musleah, "Weaving Meaning and Memory into the Chuppas of Hope," 5.

8 Henry John Drewal, "Stitching History: Patchwork Quilts by
Africans (Siddis) in India," lecture, University of Wisconsin-Madison,
Sept. 18, 2005; Chong, *Pojagi*.

9 Interview with Doris Benedict by Alex Jacobs at St. Regis
Reservation, New York, 1996, in MacDowell and Dewhurst, *To Honor
and Comfort*, 19.

10 Beverly Gordon and Laurel Horton, "Turn-of-the-Century Quilts,
Embodied Objects in a Web of Relationships," in Goggin and Tobin,
Women and the Material Culture, 93–110.

11 Sabrina Gschwandtner, "Passage Quilts," *Fiberarts*, Nov./Dec. 2008: 48–51.

12 Francine Kirsch, "Embroidered Handkerchiefs and Handkerchief Cases
for Those They Left Behind," *Piecework*, Jul./Aug., 1999: 49–51.

13 Capellanus, *The Art of Courtly Love*, 17; Peri, *The Handkerchief*, 32;
"Nothing to Sneeze At;" Morris and Whyte, *Speaking with Beads*, 55–56;
Anawalt, *The Worldwide History of Dress*.

14 Swan, *Plain & Fancy*, 123; Vincent, *The Ladies' Work Table*, 6;
Ornamental Toys and How to Make Them, 3.

15 Guy, *The Red Thread of Passion*; Subhana Barzaghi, "Red Thread Zen:
The Tao of Love, Passion, and Sex," 1993 lecture, New South Wales,
Australia, on www.sacred-texts.com/bud/zen/red-thrd.txt.

16 Barber, "On the Antiquity of East European Bridal Clothing," *Dress*
21 (1994): 17–29, esp. 25–26; Barber, *Women's Work*, 56–57; Anawalt,
The Worldwide History of Dress.

17 J.R. Johns, "Spinning Parties," *Pennsylvania Dutchman*, May 1949;
www.nzgirl.co.nz/articles/6008; Lindsay, *A History of the Reformation*,
94; Hochberg, *Spin, Span, Spun*, 17.

18 Celia Betsky, "Inside the Past: The Interior and the Colonial Revival
in American Art and Literature, 1860–1914," in Axelrod, *The Colonial
Revival in America*, 261–64; Longfellow, *The Courtship of Miles
Standish*; Christopher Monkhouse, "The Spinning Wheel as Artifact
Symbol, and Source of Design," in Ames, *Victorian Furniture*, 155–59;
Hochberg, *Spin, Span, Spun*, 48.

19 Bhutanese U.N. ambassador Ugyen Tshering interviewed in
conjunction with Peabody Essex Museum exhibition of Bhutanese
textiles, Salem, MA, 1995, www.peabody.yale.edu/; Ahmed,
Living Fabric, 100; Vibha Joshi, "Design, Meaning and Identity
in Naga Textiles: Continuity and Change," in Dell and Dudley,
Textiles from Burma, 123.

20 Edward Cody, "Train 27, Now Arriving Tibet, in a 'Great Leap West',"
Washington Post Foreign Service, Jul. 4, 2006: A01; www.seva.org/blog/
arch/13.html.

21 Lipsett, *Remember Me*; MacDowell and Dewhurst, *To Honor and Comfort*.

22 Glassie, *Turkish Traditional Art Today*, 572–73.

23 Frank Salomon, "Patrimonial Khipu in a Modern Peruvian Village,"
in Quilter and Urton, *Narrative Threads*, 293–319; Gallardo quoted
in Simon Romero, "High in the Andes, Keeping an Incan Mystery Alive,"
New York Times, Aug. 17, 2010: A6.

24 Weir, *Palestinian Embroidery*; Torimaru and Torimaru, *One Needle,
One Thread*, 7.

25 Gordon and Fitzgerald, *Identity in Cloth*, 1–8.

26 Solomon Poll, "The Hasidic Community," in Roach-Higgins, Eicher
and Johnson, *Dress and Identity*, 225.

27 Barber, *Women's Work*, 86–90; Mary Frame, "Orientation and
Symmetry: The Structuring of Pattern Repeats in the Paracas
Necropolis Embroideries," presentation at TSA Symposium, 1988.

28 O'Neale, *Yurok-Karok Basket Weavers*, 134; Nilda Callañaupa,
"Quechua Textiles: Preserving a Living Tradition," presentation
at TSA Symposium, 2000.

29 Hochberg, *Spin, Span, Spun*, 22.

30 Glassie, *Turkish Traditional Art Today*, 702–3.

31 Becker, *Arts, Gender and Changing Constructions of Amazigh
(Berber) Identity*.

32 Zimmerman, *Made from Scratch*, 224; www.intheloop.soton.ac.uk.

33 Weissman and Lavitt, *Labors of Love*, 44–45.

34 Plant, *Zeros and Ones*, 65.

35 "Sunwise Blessing: Living the Sacred Celtic Spiral,"
www.celticspirit.org/sunwise.htm; Gordon, *The Final Steps*, 5–6.

36 Larcom, *A New England Girlhood*.

37 Diane L. Fagan Affleck, "Textiles and Baseball," *Shuttle, Spindle &
Dyepot*, Spring 2008: 16–18.

38 "Israeli High-Tech Fabric to Debut at Olympics," Globes Online,
Aug. 10, 2004, www.zensah.com/globesreview.html.

39 Gordon, "'One of the Most Valuable Fabrics'."

40 Blenda Femenias, lecture at University of Wisconsin-Madison, Mar. 2008.

41 Gordon, *The Saturated World*, esp. chapter 4; Mary Mckin Marriott,
"Social Affairs for March Evenings," *Ladies' Home Journal*,
Mar. 1908: 47.

42 Theresa M. Winge and Joanne B. Eicher, "The American Groom Wore
a Celtic Kilt: Theme Weddings as Carnivalesque Events," in Foster
and Johnson, *Wedding Dress across Cultures*, 207–19; www.reenactor.net/.

43 "Art in Motion," video profiling Nick Cave, it.truveo.com/nick-cave-
art-in-motion/id/180144029559826741.

44 The Star Spangled Banner websites: americanhistory.si.edu/
starspangledbanner/ and americanhistory.si.edu/news/
pressrelease.cfm?key=29&newskey=80.

45 Stephen Braun, "South Carolina Moves to End Stalemate on
Confederate Flag," *Los Angeles Times*, Apr. 13, 2000; K. Michael Prince,
Rally 'round the Flag, Boys!: South Carolina and the Confederate Flag
(Columbia: University of South Carolina Press, 2004): 232.

46 Robert Bonner, "Transforming a Flag—and its Meaning," *Los Angeles
Times*, Dec. 30, 2000; "South Carolina's Confederate Flag Comes Down:
Controversial Confederate Flag Removed from the Statehouse,"
Information Please® Database, © 2006 Pearson Education, Inc.,
www.infoplease.com/spot/confederate4.html.

47 John McConnell, "The History of the Earth Flag," *The Flag Bulletin*,
Mar./Apr. 1982; www.earthflags.com.

48 Gordon, "Textiles and Clothing in the Civil War," 43.

49 Gordon, "Textiles and Clothing in the Civil War," 45.

50 Heather Nicholson, "Warm Socks from Warm Hearts," *Piecework*,
Jul./Aug. 1999: 34–39; Erbe as cited in Gordon, "Showing the Colors:
America," 252–53.

51 Gregory, "Communities of Comfort."

52 Zimmerman, *Made from Scratch*, 224–25, 230; "SoHE, Meriter Distribute
Patterns for Infant-Bereavement Gowns," *University of Wisconsin-
Madison News*, Nov. 16, 2004.

53 Bush, *Folk Socks*, 6.

54 Scheid and Svenbro, *The Craft of Zeus*, 10–11.

55 threadproject.com/asp/default.asp; www.johndenverpeacecloth.org;
www.earthrainbownetwork.com/MiscelSubjects24.htm.

56 www.internationalfibercollaborative.com; Jennifer Marsh, "Gas Station
Cozy," *Fiberarts*, Nov./Dec. 2008: 34–37.

4 Cloth and Temporal Power pp. 148–99

1 Campbell, *Tapestry in the Baroque*; Eric Hansen, "Pashmina: Kashmir's
Best Cashmere," *Saudi Aramco World*, Jul./Aug. 2002: 23; Roberta
Orsi Landini, "The Triumph of Velvet: Italian Production of Velvet
in the Renaissance," in de Marinis, *Velvet*, 216–26.

2 Hochberg, *Spin, Span, Spun*, 31; Kapp, *Rigmaroles & Ragamuffins*, 109.

3 Feltwell, *The Story of Silk*; Vainker, *Chinese Silk*, 58–73.

4 Sheikh Mushtaq, "Kashmiri Shahtoosh Weavers Struggle for Survival,"
Reuters News Service, Srinigar, India, Jan. 03, 2003, www.tibet.ca/en/
newsroom/wtn/archive/old?y=2003&m=1&p=4_4.

5 Scott, "Millennia of Murex," 34–35.

6 William Shakespeare, *Antony and Cleopatra*, Act II, Scene ii.

7 Born, "Purple in Classical Antiquity;" Scott, "Millennia of Murex;" Sandberg, *The Red Dyes*, 21.

8 Born, "Purple in Classical Antiquity," 115.

9 Born, "Purple in Classical Antiquity;" Sandberg, *The Red Dyes*, 20.

10 Greenfield, *A Perfect Red*, 24–25.

11 Greenfield, *A Perfect Red*, 6–7, quote on 17; Sandberg, *The Red Dyes*, 67.

12 Greenfield, *A Perfect Red*, 116.

13 Sandberg, *The Red Dyes*, 67.

14 Hochberg, *Spin, Span, Spun*, 22.

15 "Immigration and Emigration: Industrial Espionage," BBC Legacies, www.bbc.co.uk/legacies/immig_emig/england/derby/article_1.shtml.

16 Penenberg and Barry, *Spooked*, 15–17; "Guilty Plea to Economic Espionage," Oct. 17, 2002, www.usdoj.gov/criminal/cybercrime/morrisPlea.htm; Melody Peterson, "Lawsuits by Rivals Accuse Textile Maker of Corporate Espionage," Business News, *New York Times*, Oct. 13, 1998.

17 Whitfield and Farrer, *Caves of the Thousand Buddhas*, 108; Renne, *Cloth That Does Not Die*, 10; Hitchcock, *Indonesian Textiles*, 134–43; Hochberg, *Spin, Span, Spun*, 30, 39.

18 Kapp, *Rigmaroles & Ragamuffins*, 147; Vainker, *Chinese Silk*, 55, 82.

19 Hochberg, *Spin, Span, Spun*, 44; Frances Berdan, "Matriculá de Tributos y Información de 1554," Appendix C in Berdan and Anawalt, *The Codex Mendoza*, 63.

20 Sophie Pommier, "The Fabrics of Ancient Peru," in Thomas, Mainguy and Pommier, *Textile Art*; Murra, "Cloth and its Function in the Inka State," 287.

21 Reina and Kensinger, *The Gift of Birds*, 11–12.

22 Doran H. Ross, "Asante: Kingdom of Cloth," in Ross and Adedze, *Wrapped in Pride*, 33.

23 M. Braun-Ronsdorf, "Gold and Silver Fabrics from Medieval to Modern Times," *CIBA Review*, Issue 3 (1961): 2–16; Martin, *Textiles in Daily Life in the Middle Ages*, 11–40.

24 www.adireafricantextiles.com/agbadainfo.htm; Russell, *Costume History and Style*, 74.

25 Hochberg, *Spin, Span, Spun*, 32.

26 Brenda Fowler, "Forgotten Riches of King Tut: His Wardrobe," *New York Times*, Jul. 25, 1995.

27 Barber, *Women's Work*, 191, 200.

28 Robert A. Portnoy, "Chinese Imperial Rank Badges: A Language in Thread," *Piecework*, Jul./Aug. 1994: 69–74.

29 Stewart Gordon, "Ibn Battuta and a Region of Robing," in Gordon, *Robes of Honour*, 1–30; Gavin R.G. Hambly, "The Emperor's Clothes: Robing and 'Robes of Honour' in Mughal India," in Gordon, *Robes of Honour*, 31–49; Gordon, "Suitable Luxury," 10–17; Atasoy, *Ipek*; Rice, *The Illustrations to the "World History" of Rashīd al-Dīn*.

30 Atasoy, *Ipek*, 34.

31 Hambly, "The Emperor's Clothes: Robing and 'Robes of Honour' in Mughal India," in Gordon, *Robes of Honour*, 34.

32 Mary Jo Arnoldi, "Gifts from the Queen: Two Malagasy Lamba Akotofahana at the Smithsonian Institution," in Kreamer and Fee, *Objects as Envoys*, 99; Ross and Adedze, *Wrapped in Pride*, 50–51.

33 collectionsonline.lacma.org/MWEB/about/cost_about.asp.

34 Fletcher, *Splendid Occasions in English History*, 3–10; H. Wescher, "The Textile Trades in the Reigns of Francis I and His Successors," *CIBA Review*, 69 (Jul. 1948): 2532–2540; *Anglo, Spectacle, Pageantry and Early Tudor Policy*, 138–50.

35 Louise W. Mackie, "Jeweled Islamic Textiles—Imperial Symbols," presentation at TSA Symposium, 2002; Atasoy, *Ipek*, 32–34.

36 Atasoy, *Ipek*, 30–1.

37 Denamur, *Moroccan Textile Embroidery*, 42; Ross and Adedze, *Wrapped in Pride*, 33; Jan Stuart, "Portable Upholstery: Textiles for Chinese Furniture," lecture, Elvehjem Art Museum, Madison, WI, Nov. 30, 2001; Vainker, *Chinese Silk*, 161.

38 Gittinger, *Textiles for this World and Beyond*, 68.

39 Patricia Rieff Anawalt, "Riddle of the Emperor's Cloak," *Archeology*, May/Jun. 1993: 30–36.

40 Maxwell, *Sari to Sarong*, 3, 116.

41 Gillow, *Traditional Indonesian Textiles*, 75; Adler and Barnard, *Asafo!*

42 Gillow, *Traditional Indonesian Textiles*; Forshee, *Culture and Customs of Indonesia*, 145; Drewal and Mason, *Beads, Body and Soul*, 209.

43 Scott, "Millennia of Murex," 34.

44 Feltwell, *The Story of Silk*; Vainker, *Chinese Silk*; "The Silk Road," www.ess.uci.edu/~oliver/silk.html.

45 Whitfield and Farrer, *Caves of the Thousand Buddhas*, 111.

46 Vainker, *Chinese Silk*, 169, 192–98; Robinson, "'Mantones de Manila': Their Role in China's Silk Trade," *Arts of Asia*, 17, no. 1 (1987): 65–75; Susanna Worth, "Embroidered China Crepe Shawls," *Dress* 12 (1986): 43–54.

47 Gittinger, *Master Dyers to the World*, 153–55.

48 Gittinger, *Master Dyers to the World*, 15–17.

49 Sona Hairabedian, "All the Rage: Cotton in Europe in the 17th and 18th Centuries," firstulster.org/Pages/3_1_2_cotton_essay.html.

50 Kotz, *Dallas Museum of Art*, 58.

51 Sandberg, *The Red Dyes*, 138; Hochberg, *Spin, Span, Spun*, 50.

52 www.frommers.com/destinations/britishcolumbia/1236020044.html; www.geopium.org/drugtradeinasia.html.

53 Yafa, *Big Cotton*, 81–86; "Margaret Washington on the Impact of the Cotton Gin," in *Africans in America*, www.pbs.org/wgbh/aia/part3/3i3126.html; Hochberg, *Spin, Span, Spun*, 30.

54 "The Color of Money: Depictions of Slavery in Confederate and Southern States Currency," exhibition, Franklin G. Burroughs-Simeon B. Chapin Art Museum, Myrtle Beach, SC, Aug. 17–Oct. 29, 2006; www.colorsofmoney.com/comoverseer.htm.

55 Hochberg, *Spin, Span, Spun*, 30.

56 Gordon, "Textiles and Clothing in the Civil War," 42.

57 Gordon, *ibid*; Gordon, "Showing the Colors: America."

58 Yafa, *Big Cotton*, 183, 333; Forrest Laws, "Job Loss to Textile Imports Surpasses 1 Million," *The Farm Press*, Jun. 8, 2007; Michael F. Martin, *U.S. Clothing and Textile Trade with China and the World: Trends since the End of Quotas*, C.R.S. Report for Congress, Jul. 10, 2007, at www.fas.org/sgp/crs/row/RL34106.pdf; Jennifer Lin, "China Losing Textile Industry to Southeast Asian Nations," *The Philadelphia Inquirer*, reported on *Knight Ridder/Tribune Business News*, Jul. 1996, findarticles.com/p/articles/mi_hb5553/is_199607/ai_n22318314; David Barboza, "In Roaring China, Sweaters Are West of Socks City," *New York Times*, Dec. 24, 2004.

59 Hochberg, *Spin, Span, Spun*, 50; *Cloth Merchants of the Renaissance as Patrons of Art*, special issue of *CIBA Review*, 47 (Oct. 1943).

60 Lesley Ellis Miller, "Meeting the Needs of Manufacturers: The Education of Silk Designers in 18th-Century Lyon," presentation at TSA Symposium, 1998; H. Wescher, "The Textile Trades in the Reigns of Francis I and his Successors," *CIBA Review*, 65 (Mar. 1948): 253–58; Jacqueline Atkins, "From Lap to Loom: The Transition of Marseilles White Work from Hand to Machine," *Chronicle of the Early American Industries Association*, Mar. 2001.

61 Hochberg, *Spin, Span Spun*, 53; Sandberg, *The Red Dyes*, 136; Jackson, *A History of Handmade Lace*.

62 Pamela Parmal, "La Mode: Paris and the Development of the French Fashion Industry," in Grumbach, Parmal and Ward, *Fashion Show*: 14–17; A. Latour, "Colbert's Reorganization of the French Wool Industry," *CIBA Review*, 69 (May 1948): 2446–2452.

63 Ames, *The Kashmir Shawl*; Jis Lal Kilam, "A History of Kashmiri Pandits," *Kashmir Information Network*, 2001, www.kashmir-

information.com/Kilam/chapter10.html; Eric Hansen, "Pashmina: Kashmir's Best Cashmere," *Saudi Aramco World*, Jul./Aug. 2002.

64 Rossbach, *The Art of Paisley*; Reilly, *The Paisley Pattern*.

65 Sheikh Mushtaq, "Kashmiri Shahtoosh Weavers Struggle for Survival," Reuters News Service, Srinigar, India, Jan. 03, 2003, www.tibet.ca/en/newsroom/wtn/archive/old?y=2003&m=1&p=4_4.

66 Elaine Merritt, "War Lace: Commemorating Victory and Determination," *Piecework*, Jul./Aug. 1999; hoover.archives.gov/exhibits/Hooverstory/gallery02; Jean K. Dilworth, "Allied Laces for Food," abstract of presentation to Ars Textrina International Conference, www.eiu.edu/~famsci/faculty&staff/research.htm; Jackson, *A History of Handmade Lace*, 78.

67 Meg Cox, "Stitching up the Future: The Revival of Quilting Brings a Kentucky Ghost Town Back to Life," *Wall Street Journal*, Apr. 12–13, 2008: W1, W5.

68 Hawthorne, *The Scarlet Letter, Introductory Sketch*, 41; "Textile Firm Linked to 'Negro Cloth' for Slaves," *USA Today* online, Feb. 21, 2002, www.usatoday.com/money/general/2002/02/21/slave-westpoint-stevens.htm; Shane White and Graham White, "Slave Clothing and African-American Culture in the Eighteenth and Nineteenth Centuries," *Past and Present*, 148, no. 1 (Aug. 1995): 149–86; Becker, *Arts, Gender and Changing Constructions of Amazigh (Berber) Identity*: unpaginated copy.

69 Friedman article in Friedman, *Roads to Extinction*, 18; statement by Scholtz-Klink from Koonz, *Mothers in the Fatherland*, xxi.

70 www.glbtq.com/arts/symbols.html; en.wikipedia.org/wiki/Nazi_concentration_camp_badges; history1900s.about.com/od/holocaust/a/yellowstar.htm

71 Lizou Fenyvesi, "Reading Prisoner Uniforms: The Concentration Camp Prisoner Uniform as a Primary Source for Historical Research," presentation at TSA Symposium 2006; Pastoureau, madcat.library.wisc.edu. ezproxy.library.wisc.edu/cgi-bin/Pwebrecon.cgi?SC=Title&SEQ=20070617144630&PID=QtIh_2RknTOnazzqTUJwDfGTn&SA=Etoffe+du+Diable.+English; Pastoureau, *The Devil's Cloth*.

72 Jim Provance, "Ohio Won't Make Major Changes in Execution Process," www.toledoblade.com/apps/pbcs.dll/article?AID=/20060629/NEWS02/60629022.

73 users.tinyonline.co.uk/gswithenbank/sayingsi.htm.

74 Kapoun and Lohrmann, *Language of the Robe*.

75 Denamur, *Moroccan Textile Embroidery*, 11; dictionary.reference.com/wordoftheday/archive/2000/10/18.html.

76 Joel Sanders, "Hard/Soft, Cool/Warm," *Harvard Design Magazine*, 16 (Winter/Spring 2002); Gordon, "Woman's Domestic Body."

77 Caroline Stone, "The Skill of the Two Hands," *Saudi Aramco World*, May/Jun. 2007: 30.

78 John Taylor, *The Needle's Excellency: A new Booke wherin are diuers Admirable Workes wrought with the Needle.* London: James Baler, 1631.

79 Parker, *The Subversive Stitch*, esp. 103–50.

80 Caroline Stone, "The Skill of the Two Hands," *Saudi Aramco World*, May/Jun. 2007: 5; Sarah Booth Conroy, "Keeping Mary Todd Lincoln on Track: Elizabeth Keckley, The First Family's Seamstress and Confidante," *The Washington Post*, Mar. 29, 1999; Ferrero, Hedges and Silber, *Hearts and Hands*; Wendy Monnan, "Tales of Ipswich Lace and Stitches of Salem," *New York Times*, Aug. 1, 2008.

81 Parker, *The Subversive Stitch*, 175.

82 *Home Sewn*; Kapp, *Rigmaroles & Ragamuffins*, 108; Hochberg, *Spin, Span, Spun*, 36, 57.

83 Yafa, *Big Cotton*, 67, 96.

84 Iqbal's story is recounted in Pharis J. Harvey, "Crucifixion at Easter: The Redemptive Death of a 12-Year-Old Boy," ilrf.org/publications/iqbal.htm; Clare Holohan, "Slave Labour: A Reality in the 21st. Century," www.studentxpress.ie/features/slavery.html#slave.

85 www.iabolish.org/slavery_today/slave_experience/mental.html.

86 Rob Payne, "The Stolen Childhoods of Asian Carpet Workers," Nov. 2005, ihscslnews.org/view_article.php?id=41.

87 Gale and Kaur, *Fashion and Textiles*, 136–40; Collins, *Threads*.

88 "Textile Piecework System Called 'New Slavery': Study Finds Global Industrialism Fueled by Forced Labor," University of Buffalo News Service, 2007, www.buffalo.edu/news/fast-execute.cgi/article-page.html?article=74370009

89 Hochberg, *Spin, Span, Spun*, 62.

90 The story of the Jacquard loom and the Luddite reaction is taken from Plant, *Zeros and Ones*, 15; www.spartacus.schoolnet.co.uk/PRluddites.htm.

91 Gordon, *The Final Steps*, 13.

92 Susan S. Bean, "Gandhi and Khadi, the Fabric of Indian Independence," in Weiner and Schneider, *Cloth and Human Experience*, 355–73.

93 Susan S. Bean, "Gandhi and Khadi, the Fabric of Indian Independence," in Weiner and Schneider, *Cloth and Human Experience*, 355–73; Yafa, *Big Cotton*, 310; Blum, *The Loom Has a Brain*, 23.

94 Madhumitha Srinivasan, "Spinning a Revival," www.spinayarn.aseematrust.org.

95 Yafa, *Big Cotton*, 72, 74; Gordon, "Textiles and Clothing in the Civil War;" Diana Collins, "From Protest to Persuasion: Chinese Textiles as Political Tools from the 19th and 20th Centuries," presentation at TSA Symposium, 2004.

96 Jeni Allenby, "Re-inventing Cultural Heritage: Palestinian Traditional Costume and Embroidery since 1948," presentation at TSA Symposium, 2002.

97 Oxfam America Research Report, "The Impact of the Second-hand Clothing Trade on Developing Countries," 2005; www.oxfam.org.uk/what_we_do/issues/trade/research_shc.htm; Palmer and Clark, *Old Clothes, New Looks*; Hansen, *Salaula*; Shantha Bloemen, "T-Shirt Travels," Filmmakers Library, 2001.

98 James C. McKinley, Jr., "Old Clothes Are Hot Item in Kenya," *New York Times*, Mar. 14, 1996.

99 Melissa Gauthier and Jean-Sebastien Marcoux, "Cross Cultural Trade of Used Clothing and the Fabric of the Border," presentation at TSA Symposium, 2004.

100 Hassan Adawi, "Second-Hand Clothes Sell Briskly in South Jeddah," *Arab News*, May 30, 2005.

5 Cloth as Communication pp. 200–45

1 Emily McPherson, "Homework Help: Science: Physics: Fiber Optics," www.jiskha.com/science/physics/fiber_optics.html.

2 Khipu information compiled from Salomon, *The Cord Keepers*; Frank Salomon, "Patrimonial Khipu in a Modern Peruvian Village," in Quilter and Urton, *Narrative Threads*, 293–319; John Noble Wilford, "String and Knot, Theory of Inca Writing," *New York Times*, Aug. 12, 2003: Science section 1, 4; Urton, *Signs of the Inka Khipu*; Gareth Cook, "Untangling the Mystery of the Inca," *Wired*, Jan. 2007: 142–47; Gary Urton and Carrie J. Brezine, "Khipu Accounting in Ancient Peru," *Science*, 12 (Aug. 2005): 1065–67; Harvard khipu database project khipukamayuq.fas.harvard.edu.

3 Urton, *Signs of the Inka Khipu*, 147.

4 Smart textiles information compiled from Patricia Wilson, "Textiles From Novel Means of Innovation," in McQuaid, *Extreme Textiles*, 183–211; Gale and Kaur, *Fashion and Textiles*; Colchester, *The New Textiles*; Colchester, *Textiles Today*; Braddock and O'Mahony, *Techno Textiles*; www.smartextiles.info/news_events.htm; www.ualberta.ca/~jag3/smart_textiles/Page_5.html; www.abc.net.au/catapult/indepth/s1435357.htm.

5 "Astronaut Koichi Wakata Didn't Change Underwear for a Month," *The (London) Times*, Jul. 31, 2009.

6 Rachel Joanna Wingfield, "A Surface Dialogue: Electronically Responsive Surfaces in the Built Environment," M.Phil thesis, 2002,

Loop.pH R&D Site (posted Jan. 26, 2004), www.loop.ph/bin/view/ Openloop/ASurfaceDialogue; www.talk2myshirt.com/blog/ archives/826; Rao Tummala, P. Markondeya Raj and Venky Sundaram, "Next-Generation Packaging Materials," www.electroiq.com/.../ display/packaging...display/...packaging/.../next-generation-packaging-materials.html.

7 www.cutecircuit.com/products/thehugshirt/; www.emotionalwardrobe.com/overview.htm.

8 Video of the performance on www.youtube.com/ watch?v=HbNR7bT0yyE&feature=channel_page.

9 www.anbg.gov.au/flags/signal-meaning.html; www.anbg.gov.au/flags/semaphore.html.

10 Gordon, "Showing the Colors: America."

11 Jack Santino, "Apply a Ribbon Magnet to the Ole Humvee: The Yellow Ribbon Tradition Reborn," (American) Folklife Center News (U.S. Library of Congress), 27, no. 3 (Summer 2005); "Ribbon Campaigns," www.gargaro.com/ribbons.html.

12 Barber, Women's Work, 153; N.S. Gill, "Helen of Troy in the Iliad of Homer," and "Iliad's Portrayal of Helen According to Hanna M. Roisman," from Your Guide to Ancient/Classical History, www.ancienthistory.about.com/od/helen/a/Helensportrayal.htm.

13 Aristotle, Poetics 16.4; Klindienst, "The Voice of the Shuttle is Ours;" "The Annotated Six Swans," www.surlalunefairytales.com/ sixswans/index.html#THIRTY3RET.

14 Morrison and Caldwell, Stitching Women's Lives. Re arpilleras, see Betty LaDuke, "Chile: Embroideries of Life and Death," Massachusetts Review, 24, no. 1 (Spring 1983): 33–40; Agosín, Tapestries of Hope; Agosín, Scraps of Life; Cooke and MacDowell, Weavings of War; Billie Jean Isbell, "Public Secrets from Peru," ecommons.library.cornell.edu/ bitstream/1813/2196/1/Public_Secrets.pdf.

15 Dunnigan and Catlin, Hmong Art; Cooke and MacDowell, Weavings of War, 63–68.

16 Marsha MacDowell and Marit Dewhurst, "Stitching Apartheid: Three South African Memory Cloth Artists," in Cooke and MacDowell, Weavings of War, 77–87; Gwenneth Miller, "The Embroidery and Digital Project," in Andersson, The Journey to Freedom Narratives.

17 Information on kanga: Rose Marie Beck, lecture, "Texts on Textiles: Proverbial Communication," University of Wisconsin-Madison, Apr. 30, 2001; Rose Marie Beck, "Aesthetics of Communication: Texts on Textiles (Leso) from the East African Coast (Swahili)," Research in African Literatures, 31, no. 4 (Winter 2000): 104–24; David Parkin, "Textile as Commodity, Dress as Text: Swahili Kanga and Women's Statements," in Barnes, Textiles in Indian Ocean Societies, 47–67; De Proverbio: Electronic Journal of International Proverb Studies, Issue 11: 2000 and Issue 12: 2000, www.deproverbio.com/journal.php.

18 Susan Domowitz, "Wearing Proverbs. Anyi Names for Printed Factory Cloth," African Arts, 25, no. 3 (1992): 84.

19 Rebecca L. Green, "Lamba Hoany: Proverb Cloths From Madagascar," African Arts, Summer 2003, online at www.findarticles.com/p/ articles/mi_mo438/is_2_36/ai_111847723.

20 Hickman, "Turkish Oya," 44.

21 Hickman, "Turkish Oya," esp. 47, 54; lace.lacefairy.com/International/ Turkey.html.

22 Parker, The Subversive Stitch, 52.

23 White, Charlotte's Web.

24 Vainker, Chinese Silk, 40.

25 Bolton and Coe, American Samplers; Watts, Divine and Moral Songs for Children.

26 Ring, Girlhood Embroidery, 20–25; Parker, The Subversive Stitch, 137; Swan, Plain & Fancy, 44–83.

27 Humphrey, Friends. A Common Thread.

28 Gordon, "Spinning Wheels, Samplers and the Modern Priscilla."

29 Rosie A. Walker, "Louisiana's Living Traditions: Textile Uses in the Homes of Central Louisiana Czechs," www.louisianafolklife.org/ LT/Articles_Essays/creole_art_textile_czechs.html.

30 Gordon, Bazaars and Fair Ladies; Ferrero, Hedges and Silber, Hearts and Hands.

31 "Nothing to Sneeze At;" "Necktie through the Ages," www.twilightbridge.com/hobbies/festivals/father/necktie.htm; Susan S. Bean, "The Indian Origins of the Bandanna," The Magazine Antiques, Dec. 1999: 832–35; Weiss, The American Bandanna.

32 Museum of London, Access. No. 81.532.

33 Wall signage, "Commemorative Events on Cloth" exhibition, Art Institute Chicago, May 6–Jul. 16, 2006; "The Joy of Libraries," The Guardian, Jan. 6, 2007; catalogue.nla.gov.au/Search/Home?lookfor=handkerchief; "Nothing to Sneeze At;" Gustafson and Chester, Hanky Panky.

34 Michelle Boardman, "Shoulder to Shoulder: Women's Patriotic Scarves of World War II," Dress, 25 (1998): 3–16; Peri, The Handkerchief.

35 "Nothing to Sneeze At;" Murphy, Children's Handkerchiefs.

36 Picton and Becker, The Art of African Textiles, 25–30, 128–30.

37 Pravina Shukla, "The Mahatma's Samba," in McDowell and Shukla, Dancing the Ancestors, 2002, 13–23.

38 Jacqueline Atkins, "Propaganda on the Home Fronts: Clothing and Textiles as Message," in Atkins, Wearing Propaganda, 62–66.

39 Matt Mullins, "Sweating to a T," Wisconsin State Journal, Nov. 1, 2000: D-1; "Quilt Patches Together Runner's Mementos," Wisconsin State Journal, Nov. 1, 2000: D-1.

40 Juan Forero, "Bolivia Epitomizes Fight for Natural Resources," New York Times, May 23, 2005: A8; en.wikipedia.org/wiki/Wiphala; www.katari.org/wiphala/wiphala.htm.

41 Vollmer, Five Colours of the Universe, 24; Vollmer, Ruling from the Dragon Throne, 104, 111.

42 Gordon and Fitzgerald, Identity in Cloth, 23.

43 Denise Arnold, "Making Men in Her Own Image: Gender, Text and Textile in Qaqachaka," in Howard-Malverde, Creating Context in Andean Cultures; Vanessa Drake Moraga, "Geometry as Metaphor: Ancient Andean Textiles," in Ancient Peruvian Textiles, 9–19; Lois Martin, "Nasca Needlework and Paracas Procession," and Mary Frame, "Elemental Pathways in Fiber Structures: Approaching Andean Symmetry Patterns through an Ancient Technology," presentations at TSA Symposium, 2006.

44 Maureen Trudelle Schwarz, "The Bi'il: Traditional Female Attire as Metaphor of Navajo Aesthetic Organization," Dress, 21 (1994): 75–80; Jones cited in Ruth Bliss Phillips, "Great Lakes Textiles: Meaning and Value in Women's Art," in Phillips, Penny and Wooley On the Border, 6–7.

45 Isaac cited in Larsen and Freudenheim, Interlacing, 18–19.

46 Plant, Zeros and Ones, 61, 64.

47 Plant, Zeros and Ones, 15.

48 Jane Nylander, presentation at Old Sturbridge Village, MA, c. 1975.

49 Plath, The Decorative Arts of Sweden.

50 Lisa Aronson, "Akwete Weaving: Tradition and Change," in Engelbrecht and Gardi, Man Does Not Go Naked, 42; Jessica Hemmings, "Appropriated Threads: The Unpicking and Reweaving of Imported Textiles," presentation at TSA Symposium, 2002; Whiteford, North American Indian Arts, 72; Judith Wilson, "Beauty Rites: Towards an Anatomy of Culture in African American Women's Art," International Review of African American Art 2, no. 3 (1994): 13.

51 Salvador, The Art of Being Kuna.

52 Polk, Haitian Vodou Flags, 23.

53 Berlo and Phillips, Native North American Art, 29–30, 135; Gordon, American Indian Art, 55.

54 Gittinger, Textiles for This World and Beyond, 61.

55 Ruth Bliss Phillips, "Great Lakes Textiles: Meaning and Value in Women's Art," in Phillips, Penny and Wooley, On the Border, 6–7;

O'Neale, *Yurok-Karok Basket Weavers*; Musleah, "Weaving Meaning and Memory into the Chuppahs of Hope," 25.

56 Larsen quoted on "The Statement" newsletter for professional designers, "Personalities" section, www.wilsonart.com/design/statement/viewarticle.asp?articleid=114.

57 McCarty and McQuaid, *Structure and Surface*; Paul Makovsky and Mary Murphy, "Jun-ichi Arai: The Futurist of Fabric," *Metropolis Magazine*, Nov. 2, 2004; Sudo quoted on "Modern Fashion Encyclopedia: Junichi Arai" on www.answers.com/topic/junichi-arai.

58 McCarty and McQuaid, *Structure and Surface*; www.nuno.com.

59 Gordon, *Domestic American Textiles*; Auther, *String Felt Thread*; Larsen and Constantine, *Beyond Craft*; Larsen and Constantine, *The Art Fabric*.

60 Albers, *On Weaving*.

61 Rossbach, *Baskets as Textile Art*; Rossbach, *The New Basketry*.

62 Quoted in Marilyn Millstone, "Moving Outside the Lines," *American Style*, Winter 2009–2010: 78.

63 www.christojeanneclaude.net.

64 *Selvedge*, Spring 2004: 6, www.vulgare.net/elisabeth-ballet-pavage-pour-la-place-du-pot-detain-pont-audemer-haute-normandie.

65 Auther, *String Felt Thread*, 167.

66 churchofcraft.org and reavel.blogspot.com/2009/02/handmade-nation.html; Levine and Heimerl, *Handmade Nation*.

67 Joanne Turney, "Fashion's Victim," *Crafts*, Jan.–Feb. 2010: 46–49.

68 Gschwandtner, *Knit Knit*; www.knitknit.net; Bret McCane, "Musical Apparatus for Orchestral Knitting," www.citypaper.com/news/story.asp?id=14738; "Knitta, Please," www.magdasayeg.com/home.html; Moore and Praine, *Yarn Bombing*.

69 www.craftivism.com; www.ulrikaerdes.se; "Knit...with Grit," radicalcrossstitch.com/wp-content/uploads/2009/05/issue-7_radical-knitting-story_12.pdf.

70 O'Neale, *Yurok-Karok Basketmakers*, 138.

6 Textiles and the Spirit pp. 246–79

1 Gary Habermas, lecture at CRC Crossroads Church, Madison, WI, Oct. 22, 2000; Habermas and Stevenson, *The Shroud and the Controversy*; Kuryluk, *Veronica and Her Cloth*.

2 Benson quoted in Zimmerman, *Made from Scratch*, 222–23; Bergman, *The Knitting Goddess*, xiv.

3 Bergman, *The Knitting Goddess*; Kay Lawrence and Lindsay Obermeyer, "Voyage: Home is Where We Start From," in Jefferies, *Reinventing Textiles*, 64–65; Virginia Hall, interview quoted in *Home Sewn*; Yafa, *Big Cotton*, 21; "Making Light: Geek Knitting," at nielsenhayden.com/makinglight/archives/004347.html.

4 Zimmerman, *Made from Scratch*, 222–23; *Selvedge*, 32 (Jan./Feb. 2010): 9; Whiting, *Old-Time Tools and Toys of Needlework*, 201–2.

5 Guest, *When Day is Done*, 100.

6 Cecelia Chen, quoted in Liu, Lan and Lin, *Bonding via Baby Carriers*, 12.

7 Lisa Purdon, interview for *Home Sewn*; Ollie Napesni interviewed by Yvonne Lockwood, and Sheree Bonaparte interviewed by Kurt Dewhurst, East Lansing, MI, Nov. 23, 1996, cited in MacDowell and Dewhurst, *To Honor and Comfort*, 48–51, 75, 76; Beatrice Medicine, "Lakota Star Quilts: Commodity, Ceremony and Economic Development," in MacDowell and Dewhurst, *To Honor and Comfort*, 114–15.

8 Bobbie Sumberg, "Remade and Recovered: A Garment as Personal Narrative," presentation at TSA Symposium, 2006.

9 Materson and Materson, *Sins and Needles*.

10 Jessica A. Lussenhop and Victor A. Sorell, "Pocket Tapestries: Chicano Prisoners Confront the Past and Endure Confinement," *The Outsider*, Fall 2005: 10–13; "Paño: Art from the Inside Out," Museum of International Folk Art exhibition, Jul. 21, 1996–Jan. 7, 1997, featured on www.internationalfolkart.org/exhibitions/past/panos/index.html.

11 Gordon, "Victorian Fancywork in the American Home."

12 Dell and Dudley, *Textiles From Burma*; Hastreiter, *Kasuri*; "Thailand's Monks," thailandparadise.com/thailand-monks.htm; "Religion in Thailand," on "Sacred Destinations," www.sacred-destinations.com/thailand/thailand-religion.htm; Sylvia Fraser-Lu, "Stemming from the Lotus: Sacred Robes for Buddhist Monks," presentation at TSA Symposium, 2006.

13 Ahmed, *Living Fabric*, 96; Bailey and Swan, *Art of the Osage*, 93.

14 Judith E. Stein, "The Inventive Genius of Lenore Tawney: Reflections on a Lifetime of Art," *Fiberarts*, Sept./Oct. 1997: 29–34; Kathleen Nugent Mangan in *Lenore Tawney*, catalogue for Tawney's exhibition at the Stedelijk Museum, Amsterdam, 1996, cited on janhaag.com/osleta.htm; Kaufman, *New American Tapestry*.

15 Mara Freeman, "Sunwise Blessing," 1995 at www.celticspirit.org/sunwise.htm.

16 *Home Sewn*; Marsha MacDowell, "North American Indian and Native Hawaiian Quilting," in MacDowell and Dewhurst, *To Honor and Comfort*, 48, 51; Bea Medicine, "Lakota Star Quilts," in MacDowell and Dewhurst, *To Honor and Comfort*, 114–15.

17 "Islam by Question: Examples of His Prayers," islambyquestions.net/moreAbout/prayers.htm.

18 The New John Gill's Exposition of the Entire Bible at philologos.org/bpr/files/w004.htm.

19 Segelberg, *Masbuta*, 120; "And Life is Victorious: Mandaean Ritual Clothing," *ASUTA: The Journal for the Study and Research into the Mandaean Culture, Religion, and Language 3* (2001).

20 "Vestments of the Traditional Catholic Priest," Catholic webmasters, www.angelqueen.org/mass/vestments.shtml.

21 "Rituals and Sites of the Hajj," www.sacred-destinations.com/saudi-arabia/hajj-pilgrimage.htm; Massoume Price, "A History of Moharram and Other Rituals of Death in Iran," *Iranian Culture*, Dec. 2001, at www.iranchamber.com/culture/articles/rituals_of_death.php and www.islam1.org/iar/imam/archives/2004/12/30/the_basic_rules_of_islamic_funerals.php; Al Ghazali, *Remembrance and Prayer*; Modi, *The Marriage Ceremony of the Parsis*; Isaiah Bennett, "Inside a Mormon Temple," *This Rock Magazine*, Jun. 1995.

22 Brown, *Santeria Enthroned*, 354; Renne, *Cloth That Does Not Die*, 21–23, 29.

23 I Wayan Juniartha, "Service Unites Interfaith Communities in Prayer for Peace," *The Jakarta Post*, Oct. 21, 2002, www.seasite.niu.edu/flin/prayer-service_jkp20okt02.html; www.tibet.com/Buddhism/katas.html.

24 "Ash Wednesday Rituals and Observances," www.helium.com/tm/381527/although-wednesday-traditions-emanated.

25 www.geocities.com/Tokyo/2888/celebration-e.html.

26 Joe Wright, "The New White Coat," National Public Radio, *All Things Considered*, Nov. 29, 2002, studentweb.med.harvard.edu/JMW16/html/whitecoat.html.

27 Musleah, "Weaving Meaning and Memory into the Chuppahs of Hope," 23–24.

28 Anthony Anderton, "Monlam Chenmo—The Great Prayer Festival," *Asian Geographic*, 17 (*Xplorer Collector's Edition*, May 25, 2003), published by the Canada Tibet Committee for World Tibet Network News, temp.phayul.com/news/article.aspx?id=4235&t=1&c=1; Terris Temple and Leslie Nguyen, "The Giant Thangkas of Tsurphu Monastery," www.asianart.com/tsurphu/; "Tibetan Monks in Protest over Opera Ban," www.monitorchina.org/english_site/document_details.php?id=4859.

29 Vainker, *Chinese Silk*, 149–52.

30 Piotrovsky, *Earthly Beauty, Heavenly Art*, 25.

31 Mary-Louise Totton, "Virtual Cloth in a Javanese Candi," in Barnes, *Textiles in Indian Ocean Societies*, 110–29; Leidenfrost, *Unconscious Eloquence*; gujaratkalamkari.blogspot.com.

32 www.religionfacts.com/christianity/.../vestments_resources.htm; Vainker, *Chinese Silk*, 152–55.

33 Watt and Wardwell, *When Silk Was Gold*; Vainker, *Chinese Silk*, 154.

[34] Glassie, *Turkish Traditional Art Today*, 580.

[35] scheinerman.net/judaism/Tallit/index.html; Richard A. Murphy, "The Talid," maranthalife.com/teaching/jew-dres.htm; Yonassan Gershom, "Wrapped in a Robe of Light: The Story of the B'nai Or Prayer Shawl," 1983, revised 1998, www.pinenet.com/~rooster/tallis.html.

[36] Heather Felton, "Shawl Ministry Comforts Those in Need," *Florida Catholic*, Venice, FL, May 2003.

[37] www.exoticindiaart.com/product/SR53; Coldain Shawl #2: Cloth Coldain Prayer Shawl, everquest.allakhazam.com/db/quest.html?quest=978.

[38] "We Create a Sacred Place for Prayer," www.sundayschoollessons.com/pcloth.htm.

[39] J. Paul Getty Museum exhibition, "Shrine and Shroud: Textiles in Illuminated Manuscripts," Jun. 28–Oct. 2, 2005.

[40] Personal conversation with Judith Thompson, Madison, WI, May, 2008; Chuck Missler, "Ethiopian Expedition," www.travelmgmt.com/ark/ark1.htm; www.indo.net.id/mbs/Over_the_Trail_of_the_Lost_Ark.htm; "Timkat-Feast of the Epiphany, 19 January," www.selamta.net/Festivals.htm; www.peace-on-earth.org/Ethiopia/1st.pdf.

[41] www.mecca.com/modules and "Changing of the Ka'bah Kiswah 1429" on www.youtube.com; Sanders, *In the Shade of the Tree*.

[42] Gillow and Barnard, *Traditional Indian Textiles*, 9; Raymond A. Silverman, "The Gods Wear Kente," in Ross and Adedze, *Wrapped in Pride*, 66.

[43] Kapp, *Rigmaroles & Ragamuffins*, 126–27; Cheesman, *Lao-Tai Textiles*, 86, 169.

[44] Hitchcock, *Indonesian Textiles*, 136; Maxwell, *Sari to Sarong*, 117–35; Hauser-Schäublin, Nabholz-Kartaschoff and Ramseyer, *Balinese Textiles*; www.baliblog.com/travel-tips/geringsing-balinese-weaving-at-the-bali-museum.html; Susi Johnston, personal correspondence, 3/09.

[45] Hitchcock, *Indonesian Textiles*, 143; Warief Djajanto Basoni, "Geringsing, Bali's Magic Cloth," *The Jakarta Post*, Apr. 12, 2009.

[46] Jacqueline Davidson, *Nets through Time: The Technique and Art of Knotted Netting*, unpublished manuscript, 1995.

[47] Korolnik-Andersch and Korolnik, *The Color of Henna*, 143.

[48] Vandana Bhandari, "Wandering Minstrels—The Tale of the *Phad*" and "Textile Narratives + Conversations," TSA Biennial Symposium, Toronto, 2006, Proceedings, 433–37.

[49] Renne, *Cloth That Does Not Die*, 21–23; Hauser-Schäublin, Nabholz-Kartaschoff and Ramseyer, *Balinese Textiles*, 81–94; personal correspondence with Susi Johnston, 2009.

[50] Williams, *Persistence of Image*, 181; Fraser-Lu, *Handwoven Textiles of South-East Asia*, 127–28.

[51] www.cukierski.net/prayercloth.htm.

[52] "Mary's Gift of the Green Scapular," www.olrl.org/pray/gscapular.shtml; Robert MacDonald, "The Green Scapular," www.fatima.org/essentials/requests/grnscapleaf.asp; "The Green Scapular Leaflet," www.olrl.org/pray/greenscapular.shtml; "The Green Scapular," www.theworkofgod.org/Devotns/scrmntl2.htm; Mott, *The Green Scapular and its Favors*.

[53] christianityfreebies.com/freebies1/Ministry/A71QPMB24CE.cfm; healingrooms.com/; Griffith, "Material Devotion," www.materialreligion.org/journal/handkerchief.html.

[54] Griffith, "Material Devotion," www.materialreligion.org/journal/handkerchief.html.

[55] Winston, *Fabric of Faith*, 2, 23, 24.

[56] Beer, *The Encyclopedia of Tibetan Symbols and Motifs*.

[57] Beer, *The Encyclopedia of Tibetan Symbols and Motifs*; www.sphosting.com/reverndbunny/peacehealing.html; www.dharmashop.com/display.mgi?CAT=pf&T=Prayer%20Flags.

[58] "Prayer Flags for Sarcoma," sarcomahelp.org/newsletter/v02/ispan; www.joyflags.com.

[59] "The Prayer Flag Project," Maxi Boyd blog, Nov. 18, 2006, prayerflagproject.blogspot.com/.

[60] Friedlander, *The Whirling Dervishes*.

[61] Thomas Vennum and Richard LaFernier, "Dressing for the Wisconsin Ojibwe Powwow: Embodying Community," in *Cultural Survival Quarterly*, 20, no. 4 (Winter 1997): 45–50; "The Grass Dance," *Saskatchewan Indian*, Jun. 1997, www.sicc.sk.ca/saskindian/a97jun17.htm); vtvt.essortment.com/americanindian_rnyw.htm; Henry John Drewal, "Pageantry and Power in Yoruba Costuming," in Cordwell and Schwarz, *The Fabrics of Culture*, 189–230; Mary Ann Fitzgerald with Henry Drewal and Moyo Okediji, "Transformation through Cloth: An Egungun Costume of the Yoruba," *African Arts*, 28, no. 2 (Spring 1995): 54–57.

[62] Znamenski, *Shamanism*, 237; Berlo and Phillips, *Native North American Art*, 158; Cheesman, *Lao-Tai Textiles*, 188; Issenman, *Sinews of Survival*, 210; E.J. Lindgren, "The Shaman Dress of the Dagurs, Solons and Numinchens in N.W. Manchuria," *Geografiska Annaler*, 17, Supplement: Hyllningsskrift Tillagnad Sven Hedin (1935): 365; www.museum.state.il.us/exhibits/changing/journey/hunters-spiritual.html.

[63] www.eaglespiritministry.com/pd/howto/hcp.htm.

[64] Sarah Fee, "Cloth in Motion: Madagascar's Textiles through History," in Kreamer and Fee, *Objects as Envoys*, 70; A. Dafni, "Why Are Rags Tied to the Sacred Trees of the Holy Land?" *Economic Botany*, 56, no. 4 (2003): 315–27; Hannah Wettig, "Lebanon's Trees Immersed in Myth and Cultural Pride," *Daily [Lebanon] Star*, Aug. 9, 2004; Renne, *Cloth That Does Not Die*, 21–23; Jacqueline Ruyak, "A Tree Blooms in Tono," *Fiberarts*, 28, no. 3, Nov./Dec. 2001: 15.

[65] Henes, *Dressing our Wounds in Warm Clothes*.

[66] Renne, *Cloth That Does Not Die*, 45, 47, 48.

[67] Rev. Antonio Hernández, *My Kingdom for a Crown: An Around-the-World History of the Skullcap and its Modern Socio-Political Significance* (n.d. but *c.* 2003): 20, 29–32, 54, online at www.hatsuk.com/skullcaps.pdf.

[68] Nahziriyah Monastic Community, www.nmcnews.org/kufi/crochet.html.

[69] Sikh Theology, www.sikhcoalition.org/Sikhism11.asp.

[70] Biebuyck and Van den Abbeele, *The Power of Headdresses*.

[71] E. Nii Quarcoopome, "Self-Decoration and Religious Power in Dangme Culture," *African Arts*, 24, no. 3 (Jul. 1991): 56–65, 96.

[72] Linda Beeman, "Conversing with the Cosmos," presentation at TSA Symposium, 2000; Julian Gearing, "India, Sikkim, China and a vexing Tibetan lama," www.atimes.com/atimes/China/FG21Ad06.html; Rev. Antonio Hernández, *My Kingdom for a Crown: An Around-the-World History of the Skullcap and its Modern Socio-Political Significance* (n.d. but *c.* 2003): 8, online at www.hatsuk.com/skullcaps.pdf.

[73] Gabriel Haboubi, "TSA Revises Turban Search Procedures after Sikh Criticism of 'Religious Profiling,'" *The Jurist*, Oct. 17, 2007; Andy Newman, "Manhattan: Religious Garb Spurs Lawsuit, *New York Times*, Oct. 6, 2006; "To Settle NYCLU Lawsuit, State Prison Officials Abandon Policy Barring Religious Accommodations for Correction Officers," NYCLU website, May 9, 2007, www.nyclu.org/node/1001.

[74] "The Cloth of Many Colors: Twenty-Four Hours that Will Change the World," Global Renaissance Alliance, Aug. 2000, www.renaissancealliance.org/issact/isspers/society/cloth.htm.

[75] johndenverpeacecloth.org/; "Prayer Vigil for the Earth," oneprayer.org/.

[76] threadproject.com; Terry Helwig, "Materialize Your Visions," *Spirituality and Health*, Jul./Aug. 2004: 48–51.

[77] Terry Helwig, "Materialize Your Visions," *Spirituality and Health*, Jul./Aug. 2004: 48–51.

[78] Bolen and Houston cited on threadproject.com.

WORKS CITED

"A Lady," *The Workwoman's Guide.* London: Simpkin, Marshall, 1838

Abbot, R. Tucker. *Kingdom of the Seashell.* London: Crown, 1972

Adler, Peter, and Nicholas Barnard. *Asafo! African Flags of the Fante.* London: Thames & Hudson, 1992

Agosín, Marjorie. *Scraps of Life: Chilean Arpilleras, Chilean Women and the Pinochet Dictatorship.* Trans. Cola Franzen. Trenton, NJ: Red Sea Press, 1987

Agosín, Marjorie. *Tapestries of Hope, Threads of Love: The Arpillera Movement in Chile, 1974–1994.* Albuquerque, NM: University of New Mexico Press, 1996

Ahmed, Monisha. *Living Fabric: Weaving among the Nomads of Ladakh Himalaya.* Bangkok: Orchid Press and Trumbull, CT: Weatherhill, 2002

Albers, Anni. *On Weaving.* Middletown, CT: Wesleyan University Press, 1965

Al Ghazali, Muhammad. *Remembrance and Prayer: The Way of the Prophet Muhammad.* Trans. Yusuf Talal DeLorenzo. Beltsville, MD: Amana Publications, 1996

Altman, Patricia B., and Caroline West. *Threads of Identity: Maya Costume of the 1960s in Highland Guatemala.* Los Angeles, CA: UCLA Fowler Museum of Cultural History, 1992

Ames, Frank. *The Kashmir Shawl and Its Indo-European Influence.* Suffolk, U.K.: Antique Collectors' Club, 1986

Ames, Kenneth L., ed. *Victorian Furniture: Essays from a Victorian Society Autumn Symposium.* Philadelphia, PA: Victorian Society in America, 1983

Anawalt, Patricia Rieff. *The Worldwide History of Dress.* London and New York: Thames & Hudson, 2007

Ancient Peruvian Textiles: The Fifi White Collection. Overland Park, KS: Johnson County Community College Gallery of Art, 2005

Andersson, Muff, ed. *The Journey to Freedom Narratives.* Pretoria, S. Africa: UNISA Press, 2007

Anglo, Sydney. *Spectacle, Pageantry and Early Tudor Policy.* Oxford: Clarendon Press, 1969

Arment, David, and Marisa Fick-Jordaan. *Wired: Contemporary Zulu Telephone Wire Baskets.* Santa Fe, NM: Museum of New Mexico Press, 2005

Armijos, Samuel J. *Fabric Architecture: Resources for Shade, Signage, and Shelter.* New York: W.W. Norton, 2008

Ashley, Clifford W. *The Ashley Book of Knots.* London and Boston, MA: Faber & Faber, 1944

Atasoy, Nurhan, et al. *Ipek: The Crescent and the Rose: Imperial Ottoman Silks and Velvets.* Julian Raby and Alison Effeny, eds. London: Azimuth Editions, 2001

Atkins, Jacqueline M., ed. *Wearing Propaganda: Textiles on the Home Front in Japan, Britain and the United States, 1931–1945.* New Haven, CT and London: Yale University Press for Bard Graduate Center, 2005

Auther, Elissa. *String Felt Thread: The Hierarchy of Art and Craft in American Art.* Minneapolis, MN: University of Minnesota Press, 2009

Axelrod, Alan, ed. *The Colonial Revival in America.* New York: W.W. Norton, 1985

Bailey, Garrick, and Daniel C. Swan. *Art of the Osage.* St. Louis, MO: Saint Louis Art Museum with University of Washington Press, 2004

Banerjee, Mukulika, and Daniel Miller. *The Sari.* Oxford: Berg, 2003

Barber, Elizabeth Wayland. *Women's Work: The First 20,000 Years: Women, Cloth and Society in Early Times.* New York: W.W. Norton, 1994

Barnes, Ruth, ed. *Textiles in Indian Ocean Societies.* London and New York: Routledge Curzon, 2005

Bausum, Dolores. *Threading Time: A Cultural History of Threadwork.* Fort Worth, TX: TCU Press, 2001

Becker, Cynthia J. *Arts, Gender and Changing Constructions of Amazigh (Berber) Identity: The Ait Khabbash of Southeastern Morocco, 1930–1999.* Ph.D. diss. University of Wisconsin-Madison, 2000

Beer, Robert. *The Encyclopedia of Tibetan Symbols and Motifs.* Boston, MA: Shambhala Press, 1999

Berdan, Frances, and Patricia Rieff Anawalt, eds. *The Codex Mendoza.* Berkeley, CA: University of California Press, 1992

Bergman, Deborah. *The Knitting Goddess: Finding the Heart and Soul of Knitting through Instruction, Projects, and Stories.* New York: Hyperion, 2000

Berlo, Janet Catherine, and Ruth B. Phillips. *Native North American Art.* Oxford: Oxford University Press, 1998

Bespangled, Painted and Embroidered: Decorated Masonic Aprons in America, 1790–1850. Lexington, MA: Scottish Rite Masonic Museum of Our National Heritage, 1980

Bess, Nancy Moore, and Bibi Wein. *Bamboo in Japan.* Tokyo: Kodansha International, 2001

Biebuyck, Daniel P., and Nelly Van den Abbeele. *The Power of Headdresses: A Cross-Cultural Study of Forms and Functions.* Brussels: Tendi S.A., 1984

Blum, Herman. *The Loom Has a Brain.* Philadelphia and Littleton, NH: Courier Printing, 1966

Bolton, Ethel Stanwood, and Eva Johnston Coe. *American Samplers.* Boston, MA: National Society of the Colonial Dames of America, 1921

Bonar, Eulalie H., ed. *Woven by the Grandmothers: 19th-Century Navajo Textiles from the National Museum of the American Indian.* Washington, D.C.: Smithsonian Institution Press, 1996

Born, W.W. "Purple in Classical Antiquity," *Ciba Review*, 4 (Dec. 1937): 111–17

Bottomley, I., and A.P. Hopson. *Arms and Armor of the Samurai: The History of Weaponry in Ancient Japan.* New York: Crescent Books, 1988

Braddock, Sarah E., and Marie O'Mahony. *Techno Textiles: Revolutionary Fabrics for Fashion and Design.* London and New York: Thames & Hudson, 1998

Bray, Francesca, *Technology and Gender: Fabrics of Power in Late Imperial China.* Berkeley and Los Angeles, CA: University of California Press, 1997

Brown, David H. *Santería Enthroned: Art, Ritual, and Innovation in an Afro-Cuban Religion.* Chicago, IL: University of Chicago Press, 2003

Budge, E.A. Wallis. *The Gods of the Egyptians, or, Studies in Egyptian Mythology.* 2 vols. London: Methuen, 1904

Busby, Sharon. *Spruce Root Basketry of the Haida and Tlingit.* Seattle, WA: Marquand Books/ University of Washington Press, 2003

Bush, Nancy. *Folk Socks.* Loveland, CO: Interweave Press, 1994

Campbell, Thomas P. *Tapestry in the Baroque: Threads of Splendor.* New York: Yale University Press for The Metropolitan Museum of Art, 2007

Capellanus, Andreas. *The Art of Courtly Love.* Trans. and ed. John Jay Parry. New York: Frederick Ungar, 1941.

Cheesman, Patricia Naenna. *Lao-Tai Textiles: The Textiles of Xam Nuea and Muang Phuan.* Chiang Mai, Thailand: Studio Naenna, 2004

Chong, Ping. *Pojagi.* Alexandria, VA: Alexander Street Press, 2003

Colchester, Chloë. *The New Textiles: Trends and Traditions.* London and New York: Thames & Hudson, 1993

Colchester, Chloë. *Textiles Today: A Global Survey of Trends and Traditions.* London: Thames & Hudson, 2007

Collins, Jane L. *Threads: Gender, Labor, and Power in the Global Apparel Industry.* Chicago, IL: University of Chicago Press, 2003

Cooke, Ariel Zeitlin, and Marsha MacDowell, eds. *Weavings of War: Fabrics of Memory.* East Lansing, MI: Michigan State University Museum in collaboration with City Lore, Inc. and the Vermont Folklife Center, 2005

Cordwell, Justine M., and Ronald A. Schwarz, eds. *The Fabrics of Culture: The Anthropology of Clothing and Adornment.* New York and the Hague: Mouton, 1979

Crockett, Candace. *Card Weaving,* New York: Watson-Guptill, 1974

de' Marinis, Fabrizio, ed. *Velvet: History, Techniques, Fashions.* New York: Idea Books, 1994

Dell, Elizabeth, and Sandra Dudley, eds. *Textiles from Burma*. London: Philip Wilson, 2003

Denamur, Isabelle. *Moroccan Textile Embroidery*. London: Thames & Hudson, 2003

Dowry: Eastern European Painted Furniture, Textiles and Related Folk Art (video). San Diego, CA: Mingei International Museum, 1999

Drewal, Henry John, and John Mason. *Beads, Body, and Soul: Art and Light in the Yoruba Universe*. Los Angeles, CA: UCLA Fowler Museum of Cultural History, 1998

Dunnigan, Timothy, and Amy Catlin. *Hmong Art: Tradition and Change*. Sheboygan, WI: John Michael Kohler Arts Center, 1986

Eicher, Joanne B., et al., ed. (Djurdja Bartlett, vol. ed). *Encyclopedia of World Dress*. Vol. 9: East Europe, Russia, and the Caucasus, Oxford and New York: Berg, 2010

Elliott, William. *Tying Rocks to Clouds: Meetings and Conversations with Wise and Spiritual People*. Wheaton, IL: Theosophical Pub. House/Quest Books, 1995

Engelbrecht, Beate, and Bernhard Gardi, eds. *Man Does Not Go Naked: Textilien und Handwerk aus afrikanischen und anderen Ländern*. Basel: Ethnologisches Seminar der Universität und Museum für Völkerkunde, 1989

Feltwell, John. *The Story of Silk*. New York: St. Martin's Press, 1990

Ferrero, Pat. *Hearts and Hands: The Influence of Women and Quilts on American Society* (documentary film), 1987

Ferrero, Pat, Elaine Hedges, and Julie Silber. *Hearts and Hands: The Influence of Women and Quilts on American Society*. San Francisco, CA: Quilt Digest Press, 1987

Fletcher, Ifan Kyrle. *Splendid Occasions in English History, 1520–1947*. London: Cassell, 1951

Forshee, Jill. *Between the Folds: Stories of Cloth, Lives, and Travels from Sumba*. Honolulu, HI: University of Hawaii Press, 2001

Forshee, Jill. *Culture and Customs of Indonesia*. Westport, CT: Greenwood Press, 2006

Foster, Helen Bradley. *New Raiments of Self: African American Clothing in the Antebellum South*. Oxford and New York: Berg, 1997

Foster, Helen Bradley, and Donald Clay Johnson, eds. *Wedding Dress across Cultures*. London and New York, Berg, 2003

Fraser-Lu, Sylvia. *Handwoven Textiles of South-East Asia*. Singapore and New York: Oxford University Press, 1988

Friedlander, Shems. *The Whirling Dervishes*. Albany, NY: State University of New York Press, 1992

Friedman, Philip. *Roads to Extinction: Essays on the Holocaust*. New York: Jewish Publication Society of America, 1980

Gáborján, Alice. *Hungarian Peasant Costumes*. Budapest: Corvina Press, 1969

Gale, Colin, and Jasbir Kaur, *Fashion and Textiles: An Overview*. Oxford and New York: Berg, 2004

Gale, Colin, and Jasbir Kaur, *The Textile Book*. Oxford and New York: Berg Press, 2002

Gehret, Ellen J. *Rural Pennsylvania Clothing*. York, PA: Liberty Cap Books, 1976

Gillow, John. *African Textiles: Colour and Creativity across a Continent*. London: Thames & Hudson, 2003

Gillow, John. *Traditional Indonesian Textiles*. London: Thames & Hudson, 1992

Gillow, John, and Nicholas Barnard. *Traditional Indian Textiles*. London and New York: Thames & Hudson, 1991

Gittinger, Mattiebelle. *Master Dyers to the World: Technique and Trade in Early Indian Dyed Cotton Textiles*. Washington, D.C.: The Textile Museum, 1982

Gittinger, Mattiebelle. *Textiles for This World and Beyond*. Washington, D.C.: The Textile Museum; London: Scala Publishers, 2005

Glassie, Henry. *Turkish Traditional Art Today*. Bloomington and Indianapolis, IN: Indiana University Press, 1993

Goggin, Maureen Daly, and Beth Fowkes Tobin, eds. *Women and the Material Culture of Needlework and Textiles, 1750–1950*. London: Ashgate, 2009

Gordon, Beverly. *American Indian Art: The Collecting Experience*. Madison, WI: University of Wisconsin Press for Elvehjem Museum of Art, 1988

Gordon, Beverly. *Bazaars and Fair Ladies: The History of the American Fundraising Fair*. Knoxville, TN: University of Tennessee Press, 1998

Gordon, Beverly. *Domestic American Textiles: A Bibliographic Sourcebook*. Pittsburgh, PA: Center for the History of American Needlework, 1978

Gordon, Beverly. *Feltmaking: Traditions, Techniques and Contemporary Explorations*. New York: Watson-Guptill, 1980

Gordon, Beverly. *The Final Steps: Traditional Methods and Contemporary Applications for Finishing Cloth by Hand*. Loveland, CO: Interweave Press, 1982

Gordon, Beverly. "'One of the Most Valuable Fabrics': The Seemingly Limitless Promise of Crepe Paper, 1890–1935," *Ars Textrina*, 31 (1999): 107–44

Gordon, Beverly. *The Saturated World: Aesthetic Meaning, Intimate Objects, Women's Lives, 1890–1940*. Knoxville, TN: University of Tennessee Press, 2006

Gordon, Beverly. *Shaker Textile Arts*. Hanover, NH: University Press of New England, 1980

Gordon, Beverly. "Showing the Colors: America," in Jacqueline Atkins, ed. *Wearing Propaganda: Textiles on the Home Front in America, Great Britain, and Japan, 1931–1945*, New York and New Haven: Bard Graduate Center with Yale University Press, 2005

Gordon, Beverly. "Spinning Wheels, Samplers, and the Modern Priscilla: The Images and Paradoxes of Colonial Revival Needlework," *Winterthur Portfolio*, 33 nos. 2/3 (Summer/Autumn 1998): 163–94

Gordon, Beverly. "Textiles and Clothing in the Civil War: A Portrait for Contemporary Understanding," *Clothing and Textiles Research Journal*, 5, no. 3 (Spring 1987): 41–47

Gordon, Beverly. "Victorian Fancy Goods: Another Reappraisal of Shaker Material Culture," *Winterthur Portfolio*, 25, nos. 2/3 (1990): 111–29

Gordon, Beverly. "Victorian Fancywork in the American Home: Fantasy and Accommodation," in Marilyn Motz and Pat Browne, eds. *Making the American Home: Middle Class Women and Domestic Material Culture, 1840–1940*. Bowling Green, KY: Bowling Green State University Popular Press, 1988: 48–68

Gordon, Beverly. "Woman's Domestic Body: The Conceptual Conflation of Women and Interiors in the Industrial Age," *Winterthur Portfolio*, 31, no. 4 (Winter 1996): 281–302

Gordon, Beverly, and Mary Ann Fitzgerald. *Identity in Cloth: Continuity and Survival in Guatemalan Textiles*. Madison, WI: Helen Louise Allen Textile Collection, University of Wisconsin, 1993

Gordon, Stewart, ed. *Robes of Honour: Khil'at in Pre-Colonial and Colonial India*. New Delhi: Oxford University Press, 2003

Gordon, Stewart. "Suitable Luxury," *Saudi Aramco World*, 59, no. 5, September–October 2008: 10–17

Graumont, Raoul, and John Hensel. *Encyclopedia of Knots and Fancy Rope Work*. Ithaca, NY: Cornell Maritime Press, 1952 (4th edn)

Greenfield, Amy Butler. *A Perfect Red: Empire, Espionage, and the Quest for the Color of Desire*. New York: HarperCollins, 2005

Gregory, Jonathan. "Communities of Comfort: Quilts to Comfort the Families of America's Fallen in the Afghanistan and Iraq Wars." M.A. thesis, University of Nebraska-Lincoln, 2007

Grumbach, Didier, Pamela A. Parmal, and Susan Ward, *Fashion Show: Paris Style*. Boston, MA: Museum of Fine Arts, 2006

Gschwandtner, Sabrina. *Knit Knit: Profiles and Projects from Knitting's New Wave*. New York: Stewart, Tabori & Chang, 2007

Guest, Edgar. *When Day is Done*. Chicago, IL: Reilly and Lee, 1921

Gustafson, Helen, and Jonathan Chester. *Hanky Panky: An Intimate History of the Handkerchief*. Berkeley, CA: Ten Speed Press, 2002

Guy, David. *The Red Thread of Passion: Spirituality and the Paradox of Sex.* Boston, MA: Shambhala, 1999

Habermas, Gary, and Kenneth Stevenson. *The Shroud and the Controversy: Science, Skepticism, and the Search for Authenticity.* Nashville, TN: Thomas Nelson, 1990

Hansen, Karen. *Salaula: The World of Secondhand Clothing and Zambia.* Chicago, IL: University of Chicago Press, 2000

Hartley, Florence. *The Ladies' Hand Book of Fancy and Ornamental Work.* Philadelphia, PA: J.W. Bradley, 1861

Hastreiter, Kristine Louise. *Kasuri: Japan's Ikat Tradition: Textiles from the Helen Allen Collection.* Madison, WI: University of Wisconsin-Madison, 1990

Hauser-Schäublin, Brigitta, Marie-Louise Nabholz-Kartaschoff, and Urs Ramseyer. *Balinese Textiles.* London: British Museum Press, 1991

Hawthorne, Nathaniel. *The Scarlet Letter.* New York: New American Library Signet Classics, 1964 (first published 1850)

Henes, Donna. *Dressing our Wounds in Warm Clothes: Ward's Island Energy Trance Mission.* Los Angeles, CA: Astro Artz, 1982

Hickman, Patricia L. "Turkish Oya." M.S. thesis, University of California-Berkeley, 1977

Hitchcock, Michael. *Indonesian Textiles.* London, British Museum Press, 1991

Hochberg, Bette. *Spin, Span, Spun: Fact and Folklore for Spinners and Weavers.* Santa Cruz, CA: Bette and Bernard Hochberg, 1979

Hoffman, Andrea L. "'The Pride of the Block:' The Evolving Design of Baby Carriages and Changing Ideals of American Motherhood, 1900–1950." M.S. thesis. University of Wisconsin-Madison, 2008

Holloway, Julia Bolton, Joan Bechtold, and Constance S. Wright, eds. *Equally in God's Image: Women and the Middle Ages.* New York and Berne: Peter Lang, 1990. Now available online at www.umilta.net/equally.html

Home Sewn: Three Centuries of Stitching History, exhibition at New York Historical Society, Nov. 18, 2003–Apr. 18, 2004

Howard-Malverde, Rosaleen, ed. *Creating Context in Andean Cultures* (Oxford Studies in Anthropological Linguistics, 6). New York and Oxford: Oxford University Press, 1997

Humphrey, Carol. *Friends. A Common Thread: Samplers with a Quaker Influence.* Witney, Oxon, U.K.: Witney Antiques, 2008

Issenman, Betty Kobayashi. *Sinews of Survival: The Living Legacy of Inuit Clothing.* Vancouver: University of British Columbia Press, 1997

Jackson, F. Nevill, *et al. A History of Handmade Lace.* London: L.U. Gill and New York: C. Scribner's Sons, 1900

Jefferies, Janis, ed. *Reinventing Textiles: Gender and Identity.* 2 vols. Brighton, U.K.: Telos Art Publishing, 2002

Judith, Anodea. *Chakras: Eastern Body, Western Mind: Psychology and the Chakra System as a Path to the Self.* Berkeley, CA: Celestial Arts, 1997

Kanomi, Takako. *People of Myth: Textiles and Crafts of the Golden Triangle.* Tokyo: Shikosha Publications, 1991

Kapoun, Robert W., and Charles J. Lohrmann. *Language of the Robe: American Indian Trade Blankets.* Salt Lake City, UT: Peregrine Smith Books, 1992

Kapp, Elinor. *Rigmaroles & Ragamuffins: Unpicking Words We Derive from Textiles.* Evesham, U.K.: Word4Word, 2007

Karasz, Mariska. *Adventures in Stitches: A New Art of Embroidery.* New York: Funk & Wagnalls, 1949

Kaufman, Ruth. *New American Tapestry.* New York: Chapman-Reinhold, 1968

Klindienst, Patricia. "The Voice of the Shuttle is Ours," *The Stanford Literature Review*, 1 (1984): 25–53

Koonz, Claudia. *Mothers in the Fatherland: Women, the Family, and Nazi Politics.* New York: St. Martin's Press, 1987

Kopp, Joel, and Kate Kopp. *American Hooked and Sewn Rugs: Folk Art Underfoot.* New York: Dutton, 1975

Korolnik-Andersch, Annette, and Marcel Korolnik. *The Color of Henna: Painted Textiles from Southern Morocco [Die Farbe Henna: Bemalte Textilien aus Süd-Marokko].* Stuttgart: Arnoldsch, 2002

Kotz, Suzanne. *Dallas Museum of Art: A Guide to the Collection.* Dallas, TX: Dallas Museum of Art, 1997

Kreamer, Christine Mullen, and Sarah Fee, eds. *Objects as Envoys: Cloth, Imagery, and Diplomacy in Madagascar.* Washington, D.C.: Smithsonian Institution Press and National Museum of Art in conjunction with University of Washington Press, 2002

Kure, Mitsuo. *Samurai: Arms, Armor, Costume.* Edison, NJ: Chartwell Books, 2007

Kuryluk, Ewa. *Veronica and Her Cloth: History, Symbolism and Structure of a 'True' Image.* Oxford, U.K.: Blackwell, 1991

Landreau, Anthony, ed. *Yörük: The Nomadic Weaving Tradition of the Middle East.* Pittsburgh, PA: Carnegie Institute, 1978

Larcom, Lucy. *A New England Girlhood: Outlined from Memory.* 1889. Boston, MA: Northeastern University Press, 1986

Larsen, Jack Lenor, and Mildred Constantine. *The Art Fabric: Mainstream.* New York: Van Nostrand Reinhold, 1981

Larsen, Jack Lenor, and Mildred Constantine. *Beyond Craft: The Art Fabric.* New York: Van Nostrand Reinhold, 1972

Larsen, Jack Lenor, and Betty Freudenheim. *Interlacing: The Elemental Fabric.* New York: Kodansha, 1986

Leidenfrost, Isadora. *Unconscious Eloquence: An Exploration of Textiles of the Mother Goddess* (documentary video). Soulful Media, 2005

Lester, Julius. *Autobiography of God.* New York: St. Martin's Press, 2004

Levine, Faythe, and Cortney Heimerl. *Handmade Nation: The Rise of DIY, Art, Craft, and Design.* New York: Princeton Architectural Press, 2008

Lewis, Paul, and Elaine Lewis. *Peoples of the Golden Triangle: Six Tribes in Thailand.* London and New York: Thames & Hudson, 1984

Lindsay, Thomas Martin. *A History of the Reformation.* 2 vols. New York: Scribner's & Sons, 1906

Lipsett, Linda Otto. *Remember Me: Women and Their Friendship Quilts.* San Francisco, CA: Quilt Digest Press, 1985

Liu, Yujiao, Cairu Lan, and Bowei Lin. *Bonding via Baby Carriers: The Art and Soul of the Miao and Dong People (Qing xi bei er dai : zou jin Miao, Dong zu jing zhan di gong yi shi jie.)* Taibei Shi: Li ying fang, Minguo 90, 2001

Longfellow, Henry Wadsworth. *The Courtship of Miles Standish and Other Poems. 1858.* London: W. Kent, 1859

MacDowell, Marsha, and C. Kurt Dewhurst. *To Honor and Comfort: Native Quilting Traditions.* Santa Fe, NM: Museum of New Mexico Press in association with Michigan State University Museum, 1997

Maines, Rachel. *Asbestos and Fire: Technological Trade-offs and the Body at Risk.* New Brunswick, NJ: Rutgers University Press, 2005

Mangan, Kathleen Nugent, introduction by Liesbeth Crommelink. *Lenore Tawney.* Amsterdam: Stedelijk Museum, 1996

Martin, Rebecca. *Textiles in Daily Life in the Middle Ages.* Cleveland, OH: Cleveland Museum of Art and Indiana University Press, 1985

Maslow, Abraham. "A Theory of Human Motivation," *Psychological Review*, 50 (1943): 370–96

Materson, Ray, and Melanie Materson, *Sins and Needles: A Story of Spiritual Mending.* New York: Algonquin Books, 2002

Maxwell, Robyn J. *Sari to Sarong: Five Hundred Years of Indian and Indonesian Textile Exchange.* Canberra: National Gallery of Australia, 2003

McCarty, Cara, Matilda McQuaid, ed. *Structure and Surface: Contemporary Japanese Textiles.* New York: Museum of Modern Art, 1998

McDowell, John H., and Pravina Shukla. *Dancing the Ancestors: Carnival in South America.* Bloomington, IN: Mathers Museum of World Cultures, 2001

McQuaid, Matilda, ed. *Extreme Textiles: Designing for High Performance*. New York: Smithsonian Institution and Princeton Architectural Press, 2005

Modi, Jivanji Jamshedji. *The Marriage Ceremony of the Parsis*. Bombay: 1921

Moore, Mandy, and Leanne Praine. *Yarn Bombing: The Art of Crochet and Knit Graffiti*. Vancouver: Arsenal Pulp Press, 2009

Morris, Jean, and Eleanor Preston Whyte. *Speaking with Beads: Zulu Arts from Southern Africa*. London and New York: Thames & Hudson, 1994

Morrison, Skye, and Dorothy Caldwell. *Stitching Women's Lives: Sujuni and Khatwa from Bihar, India*. Toronto: Museum for Textiles (now Textile Museum of Canada), 1999

Mott, Marie Edourd. *The Green Scapular and Its Favors*. Emmitsburg, MD: Saint Joseph's College, 1942

Murphy, J. J. *Children's Handkerchiefs: A Two Hundred Year History*. Atglen, PA: Schiffer, 1998

Murra, John V. "Cloth and its Function in the Inka State," in Annette B. Weiner and Jane Schneider, eds. *Cloth and Human Experience*. Washington, D.C.: Smithsonian Institution Press, 1989: 275–303. (Originally published in a slightly different version as "Cloth and its Functions in the Inca State," in *American Anthropologist*, 64 (1962): 710–28.)

Musleah, Rahel. "Weaving Meaning and Memory into the Chuppas of Hope," *Jewish Woman*, Summer 2002: 22–25.

Neissen, Sandra. *Legacy in Cloth: Batak Textiles of Indonesia*. Leiden: KITLV Press, 2009

Newman, Thelma R. *Contemporary African Arts and Crafts: On-Site Working with Art Forms and Processes*. London: Allen & Unwin, 1974

"Nothing to Sneeze At: Handkerchiefs Presented by the Helen Louise Allen Textile Collection." Madison, WI: Helen Louise Allen Textile Collection, 1999

Oakes, Jill, and Rick Riewe. *Our Boots: An Inuit Women's Art*. London: Thames & Hudson, 1996

Odle, Robin. *The Art of the Great Lakes Indians*. Flint, MI: Flint Institute of the Arts, 1973

Oliver, George. *Signs and Symbols Illustrated and Explained, in a Course of 12 Lectures on Freemasonry*. New York: Masonic Publishing Co., 1891 (first published 1837)

O'Neale, Lila M. *Yurok-Karok Basket Weavers*. Berkeley, CA: University of California Press, 1932

Ornamental Toys and How to Make Them. Boston, MA: Cyrus Cooke, c. 1870

Palmer, Alexandra, and Hazel Clark, eds. *Old Clothes, New Looks: Second Hand Fashion*. Oxford and New York: Berg, 2005

Parker Roszika. *The Subversive Stitch: Embroidery and the Making of the Feminine*. London: Women's Press, 1984

Pastoureau, Michel. *The Devil's Cloth: A History of Stripes and Striped Fabric*. New York: Columbia University Press, 2001

Penenberg, Adam L., and Marc Barry. *Spooked: Espionage in Corporate America*. Cambridge, MA: Perseus Publishing, 2001

Peri, Paolo. *The Handkerchief (The Twentieth-Century Histories of Fashion)*. Modena, Italy: Zanfi Editori, 1992

Petroski, Catherine. *A Bride's Passage: Susan Hathorn's Year under Sail*. Boston, MA: Northeastern University Press, 1997

Phillips, Ruth Bliss, David W. Penny, and David Wooley. *On the Border: Native American Weaving Traditions of the Great Lakes and Prairie* (exhibition catalogue), Moorhead, MN: Plains Art Museum, 1990

Picton, John with Rayda Becker. *The Art of African Textiles: Technology, Tradition and Lurex*. London: Lund Humphries, Barbican Art Gallery, 1995

Piotrovsky, Mikhail B. *Earthly Beauty, Heavenly Art: Art of Islam*. Amsterdam: Lund Humphries, 1999

Plant, Sadie. *Zeros and Ones: Digital Women and The New Technoculture*. New York: Doubleday, 1997

Plath, Iona. *The Decorative Arts of Sweden*. New York: Charles Scribner's Sons, 1948

Polk, Patrick Arthur. *Haitian Vodou Flags*. Jackson, MS: University Press of Mississippi, 1997

Quilter, Jeffrey, and Gary Urton, eds. *Narrative Threads: Accounting and Recounting in Andean Khipu*. Austin, TX: University of Texas Press, 2002

Quinn, Bradley. *Techno Fashion*. Oxford and New York: Berg, 2002

Reilly, Valerie. *The Paisley Pattern: The Official Illustrated History*. Salt Lake City, UT: Peregrine Smith Books, 1987

Reina, Ruben, and Kenneth Kensinger, eds. *The Gift of Birds: Featherwork of Native South American Peoples*. Philadelphia, PA: University of Pennsylvania Museum, 1991

Renne, Elisha. *Cloth That Does Not Die: The Meaning of Cloth in Bùnú Social Life*. Seattle, WA: University of Washington Press, 1995

Rice, David Talbot, Basil Gray, ed. *The Illustrations to the 'World History' of Rashīd al-Dīn*. Edinburgh: Edinburgh University Press, 1976

Ring, Betty. *Girlhood Embroidery: American Samplers and Pictorial Needlework, 1650–1850*. 2 vols. New York: Alfred Knopf, 1993

Roach-Higgins, Mary Ellen, Joanne B. Eicher and Kim K. P. Johnson, eds. *Dress and Identity*. New York: Fairchild, 1995

Ross, Doran H., and Agbenyega Adedze. *Wrapped in Pride: Ghanaian Kente and African American Identity*. Los Angeles: UCLA Fowler Museum of Cultural History, 1998

Rossbach, Ed. *The Art of Paisley*. New York: Van Nostrand Reinhold, 1980

Rossbach, Ed. *Baskets as Textile Art*. New York: Van Nostrand Reinhold, 1973

Rossbach, Ed. *The New Basketry*. New York: Van Nostrand Reinhold, 1976

Rovine, Victoria. *Bogolan: Shaping Culture through Cloth in Contemporary Mali*. Washington, D.C.: Smithsonian Institution Press, 2001

Russell, Douglas A. *Costume History and Style*. Englewood Cliffs, NJ: Prentice-Hall, 1983

Salomon, Frank. *The Cord Keepers: Khipus and Cultural Life in a Peruvian Village*. Durham, NC: Duke University Press, 2004

Salvador, Mari Lyn. *The Art of Being Kuna: Layers of Meaning among the Kuna of Panama*. Los Angeles, CA: UCLA Fowler Museum of Cultural History, 1997

Sandberg, Gosta. *The Red Dyes: Cochineal, Madder, and Murex Purple: A World Tour of Textile Techniques*. Ashville, NC: Lark Books, 1997

Sanders, Peter. *In the Shade of the Tree: A Photographic Odyssey through the Muslim World*. Chicago, IL: Starlatch, 2002

Scarce, Jennifer M. *Domestic Culture in the Middle East: An Exploration of the Household Interior*. Edinburgh: National Museums of Scotland, 1996

Schaefer, Stacy B. *To Think with a Good Heart: Wixárika Women, Weavers, and Shamans*. Salt Lake City, UT: University of Utah Press, 2002

Scheid, John, and Jesper Svenbro. *The Craft of Zeus: Myths of Weaving and Fabric* (Revealing Antiquity 9). Trans. Carol Volk. Cambridge, MA: Harvard University Press, 1996

Schmahmann, Brenda, ed. *Material Matters: Appliqués by the Weya Women of Zimbabwe and Needlework by South African Collectives*. Johannesburg: Witwatersrand University Press, 2000

Scott, Philippa. "Millennia of Murex," *Saudi Aramco World* (Jul./Aug. 2006): 30–37

Scott, Stephen. *Why Do They Dress That Way?* Intercourse, PA: Good Books, 1986

Segelberg, Eric. *Masbuta: Studies in the Rituals of the Mandean Baptism*. Uppsala, Sweden: Almquist and Wiksells, 1958

Seng, Yvonne Bishop, "Two Middle Eastern Wedding Costumes as Vehicles of Traditional Culture." M.S. thesis, University of Wisconsin-Madison, 1982

Silverman, R., ed. *Ethiopia: Traditions of Creativity*. Michigan State University Museum and Seattle, WA: University of Washington Press, 1999

Smolin, Lee. *Three Roads to Quantum Gravity*. New York: Basic Books, 2001

Squier, E. George. *Peru: Incidents of Travel and Exploration in the Land of the Incas.* New York: Harper & Brothers, 1877

Stallybrass, Peter. "Worn Worlds: Clothes, Mourning and the Life of Things," *Yale Review*, 81.2 (Apr. 1993): 35–50

Stories to Tell: Recent Acquisitions from the Helen Louise Allen Textile Collection. Madison, WI: University of Wisconsin-Madison, 1996

Strasser, Susan. *Never Done: A History of American Housework.* New York: Pantheon Books, 1982

Swan, Susan Burrows. *Plain & Fancy: American Women and their Needlework, 1700–1850.* New York: Holt, Rinehart & Winston, 1977

Taimina, Daina. *Crocheting Adventures with Hyperbolic Planes.* Wellesley, MA: A K Peters, 2009

Takeda, Sharon Sadako, and Luke Roberts. *Japanese Fishermen's Coats from Awaji Island.* Los Angeles, CA: UCLA Fowler Museum of Cultural History, 2001

Tanavoli, Parviz. *Bread and Salt: Iranian Tribal Spreads and Salt Bags.* Trans. Shirin Samii. Tehran: Ketab Sara Co., 1991

Taylor, John. *The Needles Excellency: A New Booke wherin are diuers Admirable Workes wrought with the Needle.* London: James Boler, 1631

Textile Society of America (TSA) Symposia (www.textilesociety.org):
Textiles as Primary Sources. Minneapolis, MN, 1988
Textiles in Trade. Washington, D.C., 1990
Contact, Crossover, Continuity. Los Angeles, CA, September, 1994
Creating Textiles: Makers, Methods, Markets. New York, September, 1998
Approaching Textiles: Varying Viewpoints. Santa Fe, NM, September, 2000
Silk Roads, Other Roads, Northampton, MA, September, 2002
Appropriation, Acculturation, Transformation. Oakland, CA, October, 2004
Textile Narratives and Conversations. Toronto, October, 2006
Textiles as Cultural Expressions. Honolulu, HI, September, 2008

Thomas, Michel, Christine Mainguy, and Sophie Pommier. *Textile Art.* Trans. Andrâe Marling. New York: Rizzoli, 1985

Torimaru, Tomoko, and Sadae Torimaru. *One Needle, One Thread: Miao (Hmong) Embroidery and Fabric Piecework from Guizhou, China.* Honolulu, HI: University of Hawaii Art Gallery, 2008

Urton, Gary. *Signs of the Inka Khipu: Binary Coding in the Andean Knotted-String Records.* Austin, TX: University of Texas Press, 2003

Vainker, Shelagh. *Chinese Silk: A Cultural History.* London: British Museum Press, 2004

Vincent, Margaret. *The Ladies' Work Table: Domestic Needlework in Nineteenth-Century America.* Allentown, PA: Allentown Art Museum, 1989 (exhibition catalogue)

Vollmer, John. *Five Colours of the Universe: Symbolism in Clothes and Fabrics of the Ch'ing Dynasty (1644–1911).* Edmonton, Alberta: Edmonton Art Gallery, 1980

Vollmer, John. *Ruling from the Dragon Throne: Costume of the Qing Dynasty (1644–1911).* Berkeley, CA: Ten Speed Press, 2002

Von Luck, Hans, and Stephen Ambrose. *Panzer Commander: The Memoirs of Colonel Hans Von Luck.* New York: Bantam Dell, 1991

Watt, James C. Y., and Anne E. Wardwell. *When Silk Was Gold: Central Asian and Chinese Textiles.* New York: Metropolitan Museum of Art, 1997

Watts, Alan W. *The Joyous Cosmology: Adventures in the Chemistry of Consciousness.* New York: Vintage Books, 1962

Watts, Isaac. *Divine and Moral Songs For Children.* New York: Hurd and Houghton, 1866

Weigle, Marta. *Spiders and Spinsters: Women and Mythology.* Albuquerque, NM: University of New Mexico Press, 1982.

Weiner, Annette B., and Jane Schneider, eds. *Cloth and Human Experience.* Washington, D.C.: Smithsonian Institution Press, 1989

Weir, Shelagh. *Palestinian Embroidery: A Village Arab Craft.* London: British Museum Press, 1970

Weiss, Hillary. *The American Bandanna: Culture on Cloth from George Washington to Elvis.* San Francisco, CA: Chronicle Books, 1990

Weissman, Judith, and Wendy Lavitt. *Labors of Love.* New York: Random House, 1994

Welters, Linda, ed. *Folk Dress in Europe and Anatolia: Beliefs about Protection and Fertility.* Oxford and New York: Berg, 1999

White, E.B. *Charlotte's Web.* New York: Harper Collins, 1952

Whiteford, Andrew Hunter. *North American Indian Arts.* New York: Golden Press, 1970

Whitfield, Roderick, and Anne Farrer. *Caves of the Thousand Buddhas: Chinese Art from the Silk Route.* New York: George Braziller and London: British Museum Press, 1990

Whiting, Gertrude. *Old-Time Tools and Toys of Needlework.* New York: Dover, 1971; reprinted from *Whiting, Tools and Toys of Stitchery,* 1928

Williams, Patricia. *Persistence of Image: Search for a Common Origin of Selected Textile Motifs.* Ph.D. diss., University of Leeds, 2001

Winston, Kimberly. *Fabric of Faith: A Guide to the Prayer Quilt Ministry.* Harrisburg, PA and New York: Morehouse Publishing, 2006

Wu, Yipin, ed. *Life Styles of China's Ethnic Minorities.* Hong Kong: Peace Books, 1991

Yafa, Stephen. *Big Cotton: How a Humble Fiber Created Fortunes, Wrecked Civilizations, and Put America on the Map.* New York: Viking, 2005

Zimmerman, Jean. *Made from Scratch: Reclaiming the Pleasures of the American Hearth.* New York: Free Press, 2003

Zinn, Melissa Chase Maley. "The Values and Meanings of Çeyiz (Trousseau) Textiles for Contemporary Urban Turkish Women." M.S. thesis, University of Wisconsin-Madison, 2001

Znamenski, Andrei, ed. *Shamanism: Critical Concepts in Sociology.* New York: Routledge, 2004

FURTHER READING AND RESOURCES

We are very fortunate today in having a wealth of accessible information about textiles; in addition to countless websites about specific topics, there are journals, organizations, and many books devoted to the subject. I have compiled a list of resources I believe may be helpful to anyone wanting to learn more. Extensive as it is, the list of books is by no means comprehensive. I have tried to include both "classic" and newly published works that provide information about textiles of the past and present.

Journals and Magazines

Ars Textrina (U.K.) Journal of the University of Leeds International Textiles Archive. Annual.
Dress (U.S.): The Annual Journal of the Costume Society of America. www.costumesocietyamerica.com/dress.htm
Fabric Architecture (US) Official publication of the Industrial Fabrics Association International. Bi-monthly. fabricarchitecturemag.com
Fashion Theory: The Journal of Dress, Body and Culture (U.K.) Quarterly. www.bergpublishers.com/BergJournals/FashionTheory
Fiberarts [Magazine] (U.S.) Five issues per year.
Ornament: The Art and Craft of Personal Adornment (U.S.) The oldest international magazine covering all aspects of jewelry and beads, wearable art and costume. Five issues per year. www.ornamentmagazine.com
Piecework (U.S.) Bi-monthly magazine that celebrates and expresses historic and ethnic fabric-related handwork. www.interweave.com/needle/piecework_magazine
Selvedge (U.K.) Bi-monthly magazine featuring writing and photography on textiles. www.selvedge.org
Surface Design Journal (U.S.) Quarterly magazine on innovative artists and emerging issues in surface design. www.surfacedesign.org/publications
Textile: The Journal of Cloth & Culture (U.K.) Publishes academic research into textile studies, and appears three times a year. www.bergpublishers.com/?tabid=518
Textile Fibre Forum Magazine (Australia) Quarterly journal of the Australian Forum for Textile Arts. www.tafta.org.au/
The Textile Forum Magazine (Germany: English edition published from Frankfurt) Quarterly journal of the European Textile Network. www.textileforum.com/
Textile History (U.K.) Bi-annual journal of the Pasold Research Fund. www.pasold.co.uk/index.php/pasold-publications/textile-history

Organizations

American Textile History Museum, Lowell, MA www.athm.org/
The Costume Society (U.K.) www.costumesociety.org.uk/
Costume Society of America www.costumesocietyamerica.com
European Textile Network resources www.etn-net.org
Gallery promoting Laotian textiles www.fibre2fabric.org/index.html
International Textile and Apparel Association www.itaaonline.org
Medieval Dress and Textile Society (U.K.) www.medats.org.uk/
Ratti Center for the Study of Textiles, Metropolitan Museum of Art www.metmuseum.org/works_of_art/antonio_ratti_textile_center
Stichting Egress Foundation (includes Bibliographica Textilia Historiae) www.egressfoundation.net
Surface Design Association (U.S., international) www.surfacedesign.org
The Textile Museum, Washington, D.C. www.textilemuseum.org
Textile Society (U.K.) www.textilesociety.org/uk
Textile Society of America www.textilesociety.org
Thai Textile Society www.thaitextilesociety.org/
Tribal Textiles (focus on Asia) www.tribaltextiles.info

Books
Historical and Ethnographic Studies

Aptheker, Bettina. *Tapestries of Life: Women's Work, Women's Consciousness, and the Meaning of Daily Experience.* Amherst, MA: University of Massachusetts Press, 1989
Atkins, Jacqueline M. *Shared Threads: Quilting Together—Past and Present.* New York: Viking Studio Books in assoc. with the Museum of American Folk Art, 1994
Baines, Patricia. *Spinning Wheels: Spinners and Spinning.* London: Batsford, 1977
Barnes, Ruth and Mary Hunt Kahlenberg, eds. *The Mary Hunt Kahlenberg Collection: Five Centuries of Indonesian Textiles.* Prestel USA, 2010
Bath, Virginia Churchill. *Lace.* New York: Penguin Books, 1974
Becker, Cynthia J. *Amazigh Arts in Morocco: Women Shaping Berber Identity.* Austin, TX: University of Texas Press, 2006
Bell, Katherine. *Quilting for Peace: Make the World a Better Place One Stitch at a Time.* New York: Stewart, Tabori & Chang, 2009
Benberry, Cuesta. *Always There: The African-American Presence in American Quilts.* Louisville, KY: Kentucky Quilt Project, 1992

Berenson, Kathryn. *Marseille: The Cradle of White Corded Quilting.* Lincoln, NE: International Quilt Study Center and Museum, 2010
Berlo, Janet Catherine, Patricia Cox Crews, Carolyn Ducey, Jonathan Holstein, and Michael James, eds. *Wild by Design: Two Hundred Years of Innovation and Artistry in American Quilts.* Lincoln, NE: International Quilt Study Centre at University of Nebraska in assoc. with University of Washington Press, 2003
Bhandari, Vandana. *Costumes, Textiles & Jewellery of India.* London: Mercury Books, 2005
Bourque, Bruce and Laureen LaBar. *Uncommon Threads: Wabanaki Textiles, Clothing and Costume.* Augusta, ME: Maine State Museum in association with University of Washington Press, Seattle and London, 2009
Bredif, Josette. *Toiles de Jouy: Classic Printed Textiles from France, 1760–1843.* London: Thames & Hudson, 1989
Brown, Susan, Andrew Dent, Christine Mortens, and Matilda McQuaid, eds. *Fashioning Felt.* New York: Cooper-Hewitt, National Design Museum, 2009
Burnham, Harold B., and Dorothy K. Burnham. *Keep Me Warm One Night: Early Handweaving in Eastern Canada.* Toronto: University of Toronto Press in cooperation with the Royal Ontario Museum, 1972
Chung, Young Yang. *The Art of Oriental Embroidery: History, Aesthetics, and Techniques.* New York: Charles Scribner's Sons, 1979
Chung, Young Yang. *Silken Threads: A History of Embroidery in China, Korea, Japan, and Vietnam.* New York: Harry N. Abrams, 2005
Clarke, Duncan. *The Art of African Textiles.* San Diego, CA: Thunder Bay Press, 1997
Cole, Thomas. *Dream Weavers: Textile Art from the Tibetan Plateau.* Singapore: Times Editions, 2004
Connors, Mary F. *Lao Textiles and Traditions.* Kuala Lumpur and New York: Oxford University Press, 1996
Conway, Susan. *Thai Textiles.* London: British Museum Press, 1992
Cordry, Donald Bush, and Dorothy Cordry. *Mexican Indian Costumes.* Austin, TX: University of Texas Press, 1968
Crabtree, Caroline and Christine Shaw. *Quilting, Patchwork & Appliqué: A World Guide.* London and New York: Thames & Hudson, 2007
Crill, Rosemary. *Chintz: Indian Textiles for the West.* London: V&A Publishing, 2008
Crill, Rosemary. *Textiles from India: The Global Trade.* Calcutta and New York: Seagull Books, 2006
Dalby, Liza. *Kimono: Fashioning Culture.* Seattle, WA: University of Washington Press, 2001

De Moor, Antoine. *3500 Years of Textile Art*. Belgium: Lannoo Publishers, 2009

d'Harcourt, Raoul. *Textiles of Ancient Peru and their Techniques*. Trans. Sadie Brown. Seattle, WA and London: University of Washington Press, 1975 (reprint of revised 1962 edn; orig. edn Paris: 1935)

Denny, Walter B. *Oriental Rugs*. New York: Cooper-Hewitt, National Design Museum, 1979

Dockstader, Frederick J. *Weaving Arts of the North American Indian*. New York: Crowell, 1978

Dransart, Penny, and Helen Wolfe. *Textiles from the Andes*. London: British Museum Press, 2009

Elliott, Inger McCabe. *Batik: Fabled Cloth of Java*. Periplus Editions, 2004

Elson, Vickie C. *Dowries from Kutch*. Los Angeles, CA: Museum of Cultural History, Frederick S. Wight Art Gallery, University of California, 1979

English, Walter. *The Textile Industry: An Account of the Early Inventions of Spinning, Weaving, and Knitting Machines*. London: Longmans, 1969

Essinger, James. *Jacquard's Web: How a Hand-Loom Led to the Birth of the Information Age*. Oxford and New York: Oxford University Press, 2004

Femenias, Blenda, ed. *Andean Aesthetics: Textiles of Peru and Bolivia*. Madison, WI: Elvehjem Museum of Art and University of Wisconsin, 1987

Fisher, Nora, ed. *Mud, Mirror, and Thread: Folk Traditions of Rural India*. Ahmedabad: Grantha Corp. and Santa Fe, NM: Museum of New Mexico Press, 1993

Fitz Gibbon, Kate, and Andrew Hale. *Ikat: Silks of Central Asia: The Guido Goldman Collection*. London: Laurence King, 1997

Garrett, Valery. *Chinese Dress: From the Qing Dynasty to the Present*. North Clarendon, VT and Tokyo: Tuttle Publishing, 2008

Geijer, Agnes. *A History of Textile Art*. London: Pasold Research Fund in assoc. with Sotheby Parke Bernet, 1979

Gervers, Veronika, ed. *Studies in Textile History: In Memory of Harold B. Burnham*. Toronto: Royal Ontario Museum, 1977

Gilfoy, Peggy Stoltz. *Patterns of Life: West African Strip-Weaving Traditions*. Washington, D.C.: Smithsonian Institution Press for the National Museum of African Art, 1987

Gillow, John. *Printed and Dyed Textiles from Africa*. Seattle, WA: University of Washington Press, 2001

Gillow, John and Bryan Sentance. *World Textiles: A Visual Guide to Traditional Techniques*. London: Thames & Hudson, 1999

Gittinger, Mattiebelle. *Splendid Symbols: Textiles and Tradition in Indonesia*. Washington, D.C.: The Textile Museum, 1979

Gittinger, Mattiebelle. *To Speak with Cloth: Studies in Indonesian Textiles*. Los Angeles, CA: University of California Museum of Cultural History, 1989

Gittinger, Mattiebelle, and H. Leedom Lefferts, Jr. *Textiles and the Tai Experience in Southeast Asia*. Washington, D.C.: The Textile Museum, 1992

Globus, Dorothy Twining. *Weaving Tradition: Carol Cassidy and the Woven Silks of Laos* (exhibition catalogue). San Francisco, CA: Museum of Craft and Folk Art, 2004

Gott, Suzanne and Kristyne Loughran, eds. *Contemporary African Fashion*. Bloomington, IN: Indiana University Press, 2010

Green, Gill. *Pictorial Cambodian Textiles: Traditional Celebratory Hangings*. Bangkok: River Books Press, 2008

Green, Gillian. *Traditional Textiles of Cambodia: Cultural Threads and Material Heritage*. Chicago: Buppha Press, 2003

Guy, John. *Woven Cargoes: Indian Textiles in the East*. London and New York: Thames & Hudson, 1998

Hacker, Katherine F., and Krista Jensen Turnbull. *Courtyard, Bazaar, Temple: Traditions of Textile Expression in India*. Seattle, WA: Bellevue Art Museum in assoc. with University of Washington Press, Costume and Textile Study Center, 1982

Hamilton, Roy W., ed. *Gift of the Cotton Maiden*. Los Angeles, CA: UCLA Fowler Museum, 1994

Hann, M.A., and G.M. Thomson. *Unity in Diversity: The Textiles of Indonesia*. Leeds: University of Leeds Gallery, 1993

Harris, Jennifer, ed. *5000 Years of Textiles*. London: British Museum Press in assoc. with the Whitworth Art Gallery and the Victoria and Albert Museum, 2004 (new edn). Published in the U.S. under the title *Textiles: 5000 Years—An International History and Illustrated Survey*. New York: Harry N. Abrams, 1993

Harvey, Janet. *Traditional Textiles of Central Asia*. London: Thames & Hudson, 1997

Hilden, Joy Tota. *Bedouin Weaving of Saudi Arabia and Its Neighbours*. Oakville, CT: David Brown Books, 2010

Ho, Tong Hwa, and Sheila Hoey Middleton. *Traditional Korean Wrapping Cloths: Pojagi*. Seoul: Museum of Korean Embroidery, 1990

Hull, Alastair, and José Luczyc-Wyhowska. *Kilim: The Complete Guide. History, Pattern, Technique, Identification*. London: Thames & Hudson, 2000

Irwin, John and Katharine Brett. *The Origins of Chintz*. London: Victoria and Albert Museum, Royal Ontario Museum, 1970

Jackson, Anna. *Japanese Country Textiles*. New York: Weatherhill, 1997

Jackson, Beverley. *Splendid Slippers: A Thousand Years of an Erotic Tradition*. Berkeley, CA: Ten Speed Press, 1997

Jenkins, David, ed. *The Cambridge History of Western Textiles*. Cambridge and New York: Cambridge University Press, 2002

Johnson, Donald Clay. *Agile Hands and Creative Minds: A Bibliography of Textile Traditions in Afghanistan, Bangladesh, Bhutan, India, Nepal, Pakistan, and Sri Lanka*. Bangkok: Orchid Press, 2000

Josephson, Nancy. *Spirits in Sequins: Vodou Flags of Haiti*. Atglen, PA: Schiffer Books, 2007

Kalter, Johannes. *The Arts and Crafts of Turkestan*. Trans. Michael Heron. London and New York: Thames & Hudson, 1984

Kent, Kate Peck. *Prehistoric Textiles of the Southwest*. Albuquerque, NM: School of American Research, 1983

Kerlogue, Fiona, and Fulvio Zanettini. *Batik: Design, Style & History*. London and New York: Thames & Hudson, 2004

King, J.C.H., Birgit Pauksztat, and Robert Storrie, eds. *Arctic Clothing*. Montreal: McGill-Queen's University Press, 2005

Koslin, Désirée G., and Janet E. Snyder, eds. *Encountering Medieval Textiles and Dress: Objects, Texts, Images*. New York: Palgrave Macmillan, 2002

Krody, Sumru, ed. *Colors of the Oasis: Central Asian Ikats*. Washington, D.C.: The Textile Museum, 2010

Kunz, Grace I., and Myrna B. Garner. *Going Global: The Textile and Apparel Industry*. New York: Fairchild Publications, 2006

Kusimba, Chapurukha M., J. Claire Odland, and Bennet Bronson, eds. *Unwrapping the Textile Traditions of Madagascar*. Los Angeles, CA: UCLA Fowler Museum of Cultural History, 2004

Larsen, Jack Lenor. *The Dyer's Art: Ikat, Batik, Plangi*. New York: Van Nostrand Reinhold, 1976

Legrand, Catherine. *Textiles: A World Tour. Discovering Traditional Fabrics and Patterns*. London: Thames & Hudson, 2008

Leonard, Anne, and John Terrell. *Patterns of Paradise: The Styles and Significance of Bark Cloth around the World*. Chicago, IL: Field Museum of Natural History, 1980

Lucero, Helen R., and Suzanne Baizerman. *Chimayo Weaving*. Albuquerque, NM: University of New Mexico Press, 1999

Lynton, Linda, and Sanjay K. Singh. *The Sari: Styles, Patterns, History, Techniques*. London: Thames & Hudson, 1995

Macdonald, Anne L. *No Idle Hands: The Social History of American Knitting*. New York: Ballantine Books, 1988

Marchese, Ronald T. *Fabric of Life: Cultural Transformations in Turkish Society*. Binghamton, NY: Global Academic Publishing, 2005

Mascelloni, Enrico. *War Rugs: The Nightmare of Modernism*. Milan: Skira, 2009

Maxwell, Robyn J. *Textiles of Southeast Asia: Tradition, Trade, and Transformation.* Oxford, Melbourne, and New York: Australian National Gallery and Oxford University Press, 1990

McMorris, Penny. *Crazy Quilts.* New York: E.P. Dutton, 1984

Meller, Susan. *Russian Textiles: Printed Cloth for the Bazaars of Asia.* New York: Abrams, 2007

Meller, Susan, and Joost Elffers. *Textile Designs: Two Hundred Years of European and American Patterns for Printed Fabrics Organized by Motif, Style, Color, Layout, and Period.* New York: Harry N. Abrams, 1991

Meurant, Georges. *Shoowa Design: African Textiles from the Kingdom of Kuba.* London and New York: Thames & Hudson, 1986

Milgram, B. Lynne, and Penny Van Esterik. *The Transformative Power of Cloth in Southeast Asia.* Toronto: Museum for Textiles; Canadian Asian Studies Association, 1994

Monnas, Lisa. *Merchants, Princes, and Painters: Silk Fabrics in Italian and Northern Paintings, 1300–1550.* New Haven, CT: Yale University Press, 2009

Montgomery, Florence M. *Printed Textiles: English and American Cottons and Linens, 1700–1850.* New York: Viking Press, 1970

Montgomery, Florence M. *Textiles in America, 1650–1870: A Dictionary Based on Original Documents.* New York: Norton, 1984

Mullins, Willow. *Felt* (Textiles that Changed the World). Oxford and New York: Berg, 2009

Munsterberg, Hugo. *The Japanese Kimono* (Images of Asia). New York: Oxford University Press, 1996

Newark, Tim. *Camouflage.* London: Thames & Hudson in assoc. with the Imperial War Museum, 2009

Noma, Seiroku. *Japanese Costumes & Textile Arts* (The Heibonsha Survey of Japanese Art, vol. 16). Tokyo: Heibonsha and New York: Weatherhill, 1974

Paine, Sheila. *The Afghan Amulet: Travels from the Hindu Kush.* London and New York: Tauris Parke, 2006

Paine, Sheila. *Embroidered Textiles: A World Guide to Traditional Patterns.* London: Thames & Hudson, 2008

Paine, Sheila. *Embroidery from Afghanistan.* Seattle, WA: University of Washington Press, 2007

Paine, Sheila. *Embroidery from India and Pakistan.* Seattle, WA: University of Washington Press, 2001

Parry, Linda. *Textiles of the Arts & Crafts Movement.* London and New York: Thames & Hudson, 2005

Paydar, Niloo Imami and Ivo Grammet, eds. *The Fabric of Moroccan Life.* Indianapolis, IN: Indianapolis Museum of Art, 2002

Perani, Judith, and Norma H. Wolff. *Cloth, Dress and Art Patronage in Africa.* Oxford and New York: Berg, 1999

Phipps, Elena. "Cochineal Red: The Art History of a Color," *Metropolitan Museum of Art Bulletin,* Winter 2010

Rathbun, William Jay, ed. *Beyond the Tanabata Bridge: Traditional Japanese Textiles.* New York and London: Thames & Hudson in assoc. with Seattle Art Museum, 1994

Rehman, Sherry and Naheed Jafri. *The Kashmiri Shawl, from Jamavar to Paisley.* Ahmedabad: Mapin Publishing, 2006

Reyes, Lynda Angelica N. *The Textiles of Southern Philippines: The Textile Traditions of the Bagobo, Mandaya and Bilaan from their Beginnings to the 1900s.* Quezon City: University of the Philippines Press, 1992

Riello, Giorgio, and Prasannan Parthasarathi, eds. *The Spinning World: A Global History of Cotton Textiles, 1200–1850.* Oxford and New York: Oxford University Press, 2009

Rivers, Victoria Z. *The Shining Cloth: Dress and Adornment that Glitter.* London and New York: Thames & Hudson, 1999

Rodgers, Susan, Anne Summerfield, and John Summerfield. *Gold Cloths of Sumatra: Indonesia's Songkets from Ceremony to Commodity.* Leiden: KITLV Press; Worcester: Iris and B. Gerald Cantor Art Gallery, 2007

Rowe, Ann Pollard, ed. *Weaving and Dyeing in Highland Ecuador.* Austin, TX: University of Texas Press, 2007

Rowe, Ann Pollard, and John Cohen. *Hidden Threads of Peru: Q'ero Textiles.* Washington, D.C.: Merrell in assoc. with the Textile Museum, 2002

Rutherford, Judith, and Jackie Menzies. *Celestial Silks: Chinese Religious & Court Textiles.* Sydney: Art Gallery of New South Wales, 2004

Sayer, Chloë. *Textiles from Mexico.* Seattle, WA: University of Washington Press, 2002

Schevill, Margot Blum, Janet Catherine Berlo, and Edward B. Dwyer, eds. *Textile Traditions of Mesoamerica and the Andes: An Anthology.* Austin, TX: University of Texas Press, 1996

Schmahmann, Brenda. *Mapula: Embroidery and Empowerment in the Winterveld.* Johannesburg and New York: David Krut Publishing, 2006

Schoeser, Mary. *Silk.* New Haven, CT: Yale University Press, 2007

Schoeser, Mary. *World Textiles: A Concise History.* London and New York: Thames & Hudson, 2003

Schorsch, Anita. *The Art of the Weaver.* New York: Universe Books, 1978

Sentance, Bryan. *Basketry: A World Guide to Traditional Techniques.* London and New York: Thames & Hudson, 2007

Sentance, Bryan, and Polly Sentance. *Craft Traditions of the World: Locally Made, Globally Inspiring.* London and New York: Thames & Hudson, 2009

Shah, Shila, and Tulsi Vatsal, eds. *Peonies and Pagodas : Embroidered Parsi Textiles: Tapi Collection.* Garden Silk Mills, 2010

Singer, Margo, and Mary Spyrou. *Textile Arts: Multicultural Traditions.* London: A&C Black, 2000

Skinner, Tina. *Nomadic Embroideries: India's Tribal Textile Art.* Atglen, PA: Schiffer, 2008

Smith, Ruth. *Miao Embroidery from South West China: Textiles from the Gina Corrigan Collection.* Bognor Regis: Occidor, 2005

Snowden, James. *Folk Dress of Europe.* New York: Mayflower Books, 1979

Sommer, John L. *The Kyrgyz and their Reed Screens.* Fremont, CA: John L. Sommer, 1996

Stalp, Marybeth C. *Quilting: The Fabric of Everyday Life.* Oxford and New York: Berg, 2007

Stone-Miller, Rebecca. *To Weave for the Sun: Andean Textiles in the Museum of Fine Arts.* Boston, MA: Museum of Fine Arts, 1992

Tanavoli, Parviz. *Riding in Splendour: Horse and Camel Trappings from Tribal Iran.* Tehran: Farhangsara Yassavoli, 1998

Tarlo, Emma. *Clothing Matters: Dress and Identity in India.* Chicago, IL: University of Chicago Press, 1996

Thompson, Angela. *Textiles of Central and South America.* Ramsbury, U.K.: Crowood Press, 2006

Thompson, Angela. *Textiles of South-East Asia.* Ramsbury, U.K.: Crowood Press, 2008

Thornton, Peter. *Baroque and Rococo Silks.* London: Faber & Faber, 1965

Tyabji, Laila, ed. *Threads and Voices: Behind the Indian Textile Tradition.* Mumbai: Marg Publications, 2007

Van Gelder, Lydia. *Ikat.* New York: Watson-Guptill, 1980

Varadarajan, Lotika. *Ajrakh and Related Techniques: Traditions of Textile Printing in Kutch.* Ahmedabad: New Order Book Co., 1983

Waldvogel, Merikay. *Soft Covers for Hard Times: Quiltmaking and the Great Depression.* Nashville, TN: Rutledge Hill Press, 1990

Waller, Diane. *Textiles From the Balkans.* London: British Museum Press, 2009

Warren, Geoffrey. *A Stitch in Time: Victorian and Edwardian Needlecraft.* New York: Taplinger, 1976

Willink, Roseann Sandoval and Paul G. Zolbrod, eds. *Weaving a World: Textiles and the Navajo Way of Seeing.* Santa Fe, NM: Museum of New Mexico Press, 1996

Wilson, Kax. *A History of Textiles.* Boulder, CO: Westview Press, 1979

Yoshida, Shin-ichiro and Dai Williams. *Riches from Rags: Saki-ori and Other Recycling Traditions in Japanese Rural Clothing*. San Francisco, CA: San Francisco Craft and Folk Art Museum, 1994

Twentieth and Twenty-First Century Textiles, Fiber Art, and "Craftivism"

Anand, S.C., ed. *Medical and Healthcare Textiles*. Cambridge: Woodhead Publishing in assoc. with the Textile Institute; Boca Raton: CRC Press, 2010

Arnett, Paul, Joanne Cubbs, and Eugene W. Metcalf. *Gee's Bend: The Architecture of the Quilt*. Atlanta, GA: Tinwood Books, 2006

Bachman, Ingrid, and Ruth Scheuing, eds. *Material Matters: The Art and Culture of Contemporary Textiles*. Toronto: YYZ Books, 1998

Berti, B.J. *Threaded Together: The Pink Ribbon Quilt Project*. New York: Crafter's Choice Book Club, 2002

Chicago, Judy. *Embroidering our Heritage: The Dinner Party Needlework*. Garden City, NY: Anchor Books, 1980

Christiansen, Betty. *Knitting for Peace: Make the World a Better Place One Stitch at a Time*. New York: Stewart, Tabori & Chang, 2006

Colchester, Chloë. *Textiles Today: A Global Survey of Trends and Techniques*. London and New York: Thames & Hudson, 2007

Cole, Drusilla. *Textiles Now*. London: Laurence King, 2008

Constantine, Mildred and Jack Lenor Larsen. *Wall Hangings*. New York: Museum of Modern Art, 1969

Constantine, Mildred and Laurel Reuter. *Whole Cloth*. New York: Monacelli Press, 1997

Cooper-Hewitt, National Design Museum. *Fashioning Felt*. New York, 2009

Fiberarts Design Book (occasional publication; seven vols to date). Asheville, NC: Lark Press, 1980–2004

Gluckman, Dale Carolyn, ed. *Kimono as Art: The Landscapes of Itchiku Kubota*. London: Thames & Hudson, 2008

Greer, Betsey. "Taking Back the Knit: Creative Communities via Needlecraft." M.A. thesis, Goldsmith College, University of London, 2004

Hillestad, Robert. *Robert Hillestad: A Textiles Journey*. Lincoln, NE: Robert Hillestad Textiles Gallery and University of Nebraska Press, 2009

Inglot, Joanna. *The Figurative Sculpture of Magdalena Abakanowicz: Bodies, Environments and Myths*. Berkeley, CA: University of California Press, 2004

Koumis, Matthew, *et al. Art Textiles of the World*. (9 vols covering Australia, Canada, Great Britain, Japan, Korea, the Netherlands, Scandinavia, and the U.S.) Brighton, U.K.: Telos Art Publishing, first published 1996

Larsen, Jack Lenor. *A Weaver's Memoir*. New York: Abrams, 1998

Leventon, Melissa. *Artwear: Fashion and Anti-Fashion*. London and New York: Thames & Hudson, 2005

Levi-Strauss, Monique. *Sheila Hicks*. New York: Van Nostrand Reinhold, 1974

McFadden, David Revere. *Radical Lace and Subversive Knitting*. New York: Museum of Arts and Design, 2007

McMorris, Penny, and Michael Kile. *The Art Quilt*. San Francisco, CA: Quilt Digest Press, 1986

Millar, Lesley, ed. *21:21 The Textile Vision of Reiko Sudo and Nuno*. Canterbury: University College for the Creative Arts, 2005

Phillips, Mary Walker. *Creative Knitting: A New Art Form*. New York: Van Nostrand Reinhold, 1971

Poli, Doretta Davanzo. *Twentieth-Century Fabrics: European and American Designers and Manufacturers*. Milan: Skira, 2007

Quinn, Bradley. *Textile Designers at the Cutting Edge*. London: Laurence King, 2009

Rowe, Ann Pollard, and Rebecca A.T. Stevens. *Ed Rossbach: 40 Years of Exploration and Innovation in Fiber Art*. Asheville, NC: Lark Books, 1990

Ruskin, Cindy. *The Quilt: Stories from the NAMES Project*. New York: Pocket Books, 1988

Shaw, Robert. *The Art Quilt*. New York: Hugh Lauter Levin Associates, 1997

Troy, Virginia Gardner. *Anni Albers and Ancient American Textiles: From Bauhaus to Black Mountain*. Aldershot, U.K. and Burlington, VT: Ashgate, 2002

Troy, Virginia Gardner. *The Modernist Textiles: European and American 1890–1940*. Aldershot, U.K.: Lund Humphries, 2006

Turney, Joanne. *The Culture of Knitting*. Oxford and New York: Berg, 2009

Wada, Yoshiko Iwamoto. *Memory on Cloth: Shibori Now*. New York: Kodansha International, 2002

Theoretical Issues and Meanings of Textiles

Adamson, Glenn. *Thinking through Craft*. Oxford and New York: Berg, 2007

Burman, Barbara, ed. *The Culture of Sewing: Gender, Consumption and Home Dressmaking*. Oxford and New York: Berg, 1999

El Guindi, Fadwa. *Veil: Modesty, Privacy and Resistance*. Oxford and New York: Berg, 2003

Greenfield, Patricia M. *Weaving Generations Together: Evolving Creativity in the Maya of Chiapas*. Santa Fe, NM: School of American Research Press, 2004

Hemmings, Jessica. *Yvonne Vera: The Voice of Cloth*. Heidelberg: Kalliope, 2008

Murphy, Bernadette M. *Zen and the Art of Knitting: Exploring the Links between Knitting, Spirituality, and Creativity*. Avon, MA: Adams Media, 2002

Parker, Rozsika and Griselda Pollock. *Old Mistresses: Women, Art, and Ideology*. New York: Pantheon Books, 1981

Contemporary Technological Developments and Global Issues

Clarke, Sarah E. Braddock, and Marie O'Mahony, eds. *Techno Textiles 2: Revolutionary Fabrics for Fashion and Design*. London: Thames & Hudson, 2006

Handley, Susannah. *Nylon: The Story of a Fashion Revolution: A Celebration of Design from Art Silk to Nylon and Thinking Fibres*. Baltimore, MD: Johns Hopkins University Press, 1999

Juracek, Judy A. *Soft Surfaces: Visual Research for Artists, Architects and Designers*. New York: W.W. Norton; London: Thames & Hudson, 2000

Livingston, Joan, and John Ploof, eds. *The Object of Labor: Art, Cloth, and Cultural Production*. Cambridge, MA: MIT Press and Chicago, IL: School of the Art Institute of Chicago Press, 2007

O'Mahony, Marie, and Sarah E. Braddock. *SportsTech: Revolutionary Fabrics, Fashion and Design*. London and New York: Thames & Hudson, 2002

Quinn, Bradley. *Textile Futures: Fashion, Design and Technology*. Oxford and New York: Berg, 2010

Tarlo, Emma. *Visibly Muslim: Fashion, Politics, Faith*. Oxford and New York: Berg, 2010

SOURCES OF QUOTATIONS

p. 30, The World Hangs by a Thread: Debra Frasier, "Oral Prose Piece: 'The World Hangs by a Thread,'" *Surface Design Journal*, Summer 1985, 6–7; **p. 39**, A Great Weaving: Wade Davis, *One River: Explorations and Discoveries in the Amazon Rain Forest*. New York: Simon & Schuster, 1966, 52–53; **p. 40**, A Thread in the Hands of Fate: Opening lyric of "Eyes and No Eyes: or the Art of Seeing," a one-act musical entertainment with libretto by W.S. Gilbert (sung by Clochette), staged in 1875; **p. 61**, A First Encounter with Gutskin: Patricia Hickman, *Innerskins/Outerskins: Gut and Fishskin*. San Francisco, CA: Museum of Craft and Folk Art, 1987, 4; **p. 63**, Sewn Skin Clothing in the Arctic: Jill Oakes and Rick Riewe, *Our Boots: An Inuit Women's Art*. London and New York: Thames & Hudson, 1996, 109; **p. 66**, An American's Experience with Sericulture in Thailand, 1992: Eve Waterfall and Kristin McGuire, "Working/ Adventuring Around the World—Part XIX: Silk—Made in Thailand," *North [Westchester, N.Y.] County News*, Mar. 25, 1992, V4; **p. 67**, Cochineal in Pre-Columbian Mexico: Amy Butler Greenfield, *A Perfect Red: Empire, Espionage, and the Quest for the Color of Desire*. New York: Harper Collins, 2005, 38–40; **p. 92**, Sewing Sailors: Journal of Henry Davis, 1862, and journal of Robert Weir of the *Clara Belle*, 1856, both cited in Margaret S. Creighton, *Dogwatch and Liberty Days: Seafaring Life in the 19th Century*. Salem, MA: The Peabody Essex Museum, 1982, p. 56; **p. 97**, Uses for the Scout Neckerchief: Commodore W.E. Longfellow, "Scouting With a Neckerchief," *The Boy Scout Service Library*, Series B, No. 6, Boy Scouts of America, 1927; **p. 99**, The Output of British Industrial Tape Makers: Julie Bunting, "Bygone Industries of the Peak: Tapes and Narrow Fabrics," in *The Peak [District, Derbyshire] Advertiser*, Feb. 22, 1999, 9; **p. 106**, "The Threads that Bind": Kerrie Flanagan, "The Threads That Bind: Sometimes We All Need the Comfort of a Favorite 'Blankie,'" www.beliefnet.com/story/43/story_4314_1.html; **p. 111**, No Ordinary Blanket: Natalie Walker Whitlock, "No Ordinary Blanket," www.beliefnet.com/story/47/ story_4713_2.html; **p. 113**, Sewing as Psychic Survival: Yvonne Vera, "The Prison of Colonial Space: Narratives of Resistance," cited in Jessica Hemmings, "Speaking When No One Else Can: Textiles and Censorship," presentation at TSA Symposium, "Textile Narratives and Conversations," Toronto, Canada, October 2006, cited in Symposium Proceedings, 203; **p. 117**, A Baby's Layette: Compiled by the author from "A Lady," *The Workwoman's Guide*. London: Simpkin, Marshall, 1838; **p. 118**, To Work with Love: Kahlil Gibran, *The Prophet*. London, Melbourne, Toronto: Heinemann, 1926, 24; **p. 134**, Waulking on the Isle of Skye: Thomas Pennant, *A Tour in Scotland*, 1772, 284–85; **p. 146**, Some Charity Textile Projects: The "Sewing Charity" website (www.dotdigital.com/ sewingcharity/); **p. 161**, Robes of Honor: Stewart Gordon, "Suitable Luxury," *Saudi Aramco World*, Sept./Oct. 2008, 12; **p. 186**, The Prayse of the Needle: John Taylor, *The Needle's Excellency: A new Booke wherin are diuers Admirable Workes wrought with the Needle*. London: James Baler, 1631; **p. 194**, The Cropper's Battle Song: Beverly Gordon, *The Final Steps: Traditional Methods and Contemporary Applications for Finishing Cloth by Hand*. Loveland, CO: Interweave Press, 1982, 13; **p. 210**, "We are healed…": Marcel Proust, *Á la Recherche du temps perdu (In Search of Lost Time)*, vol. 6 (The Sweet Cheat Gone), ch. 1; **p. 217**, Didactic Sampler Verses: compiled by the author; **p. 250**, The Calming Effect of Lace-making: Gertrude Whiting, *Old-time Tools and Toys of Needlework*. New York: Dover, 1971 (reprinted from *Tools and Toys of Stitchery*, 1928), 201–202; **p. 261**, A Sufi's Description of Setting the Space for the Koran: Shaykh Muhammad Hisham Kabbani (of the Naqshbandi-Haqqani Sufi Order), "The Angels of Koran," *Angels Unveiled: A Sufi Perspective*, Chicago, IL: Kazi Publications, 1996, cited on www.naqshbandi.org/library/angels/angels3.htm; **p. 266**, Madonna of the Protecting Mantle: Herbert Haug, "The Image of Mary," in Caroline Ebertshauser, Herbert Hoag et al., *Mary: Art, Culture and Religion through the Ages*, New York: Crossroad Publications, 1997, 7; **p. 270**, The Green Scapular: R. Marie Griffith, "Material Devotion—Pentecostal Prayer Cloths," interviewed by James Hudnut-Beumler and Daniel Sack, Material History of American Religion Project, www.materialreligion.org/journal/handkerchief.html

SOURCES OF ILLUSTRATIONS

a above; *b* below; *c* centre; *l* left; *r* right

African Studies Program, University of Wisconsin-Madison: 18*l* (photo John Hutchison, 1985-03), 26 (photo Jeanne Tabachnick, 3610jt62), 53*br* (4707as04), 59 (photo Dennis Cordell, 0610as), 77*ar* (photo Sharon Hutchinson, 4210sh16), 80*bl* (photo Jeanne Tabachnick, 3010jt18), 83*a* (photo Jeanne Tabachnick, 3610jt16), 124 (photo William Mintener, 1514as02), 135*b* (photo William Brown, 2422as03), 159*r* (photo Ivan Dihoff, 3017as09), 231*l* (photo Betty Wass, 4813bw31), 249*r* (photo Jan Vansina, 5210jv15), 255*a* (photo Herb Lewis, 1117hl42), 255*br* (photo Harold Scheub, hsc0150), 264 (photo Herb Lewis, 1117hl73); AKG Images: 7 (photo Andre Held), 29 (orig. in Staatliche Museen, Kassel), 37 (orig. in Musée d'Orsay, Paris), 162 (orig. in the Louvre, Paris); Allentown Art Museum, Allentown, PA: 2 (M1978.026.374), 169*l* (1996.003.000), 235*br* (M1978.026.374); The American Textile History Museum, Lowell, MA: 154; Pat Anderson (www.patanderson.net): 31*b*; Lynne Anderson-Inman: 217; Jennifer Angus: 127*cl*, 248*b*; Robert Apholz: 27*br*, 67*b*, 99*a*, 152; J. Atkins: 223*a*; James Austin (courtesy of Thames & Hudson): 49*a*, 73, 178, 224*al*; B.A.G. Corp.®: 85*r*; Cynthia Becker: 49*b*; Larry Beede: 137*ar*; Bridgeman Art Library BAL_268453 (from Edinburgh University Library, Scotland Ms Or 20 f.121r): 161; Susan C. Burghes (courtesy of Jennifer Tenney Myers, collec. Susan Wildemuth): 113; Chicago History Museum (courtesy of Beverly Gordon): 219*a*; Colonial Williamsburg: 169*r* (1990-10, A-B. Gift of Cora Ginsburg); Martha Cooper (courtesy of Ariel Zeitlin Cooke): 211; Gerald Cubitt: 28*ar*; Taylor Dabney (courtesy of Sonya Clark): 240; Dallas Museum of Art, Texas: 131 (1978.3.MCD), 225*a* (T41299.7); Sian Davis (courtesy of Thames & Hudson): 24, 48*a*; Walter B. Denny: 193; Denver International Airport: 78*r*; Henry John Drewal: 108*r*, 272; Elliot Brown Gallery: 238; Julian Ellis, Ellis Developments Company: 87*l*, 87*ar*, 87*br*; Rae Erdahl: 40; Field Museum of Natural History, Chicago: 61 (CSA13300), 85*l* (CSA9525); Bruno Furnari: 36*b*; GandhiServe: 195 (photo Vitahalbhai Jhaveri); Luis García (via WikiMedia GNU photo license): 68; Henry Glassie: 21, 51*b*; Peter Glogg (via visipix): 122*l*; Marian Goldsmith: 66*br*; Beverly Gordon: 8*r*, 10*a*, 10*b*, 20*l*, 22, 51*ar* (used with permission from the Bodleian library, University of Oxford Folio 61F), 79*r*, 95, 115, 120*a*, 120*b*, 121, 123, 134, 135*a*, 140*l*, 143, 151*a*, 194, 252*b*, 271; Gore-Tex®: 75 inset; Gregg Museum of Art and Design, N.C. State University, Raleigh: 226*a* (1986.10.21); Jonathan Gregory: 145*a*; Tom Grotta (courtesy of Browngrotta Arts Gallery): 253; James Gunn: 30*r*; Tim Hamill, Hamill Gallery of Tribal Art, Boston, MA: 106*r*, 107, 166*r*; Karen Hansen: 198; Hargrett Library, University of Georgia: 110*ar*, 172*a*, 172*b*; Mary Hark: 156, 221; Helen Louise Allen Textile Collection, University of Wisconsin-Madison: 1 (LNE-784), 8*al* (WLE-2086), 20*r* (W-3154), 25*a* (QPUS.003), 27*bl* (1992.9.1), 30*bl* (WLCH-2889), 44 (EAI-1423), 48*cl* (E.A.E.1743), 48*b* (1996.16.3), 50 (F79), 60 (2000.18.3), 62*bl* (DCUS-108), 65 (LKPO98), 70*al* (1999.8.6), 70*ar* (WFCH-2889), 70*c* (PDPO-1027), 70*b* (W3285), 74*bl* (KHAS-2), 82*c* (LKPO-98), 82*b* (2001.1.17), 83*b* (1984.01.001), 97 (1998.9.8), 103 (EAUS 845), 106*l* (2001.6.1), 117*l* (2001.05.01), 120*a* (QSUS-4), 125*r* (1998.13.1), 127*a* (WFCA-3055), 151*b* (WLA 1412), 160 (2003.2.13), 163 (WLE-3251), 166*l* (1995.2.1), 176*al* (LNE-784), 176*bl* (WLE-3249), 176*cr* (1989.8.1), 176*br* (1991.31.52), 182*r* (2003.2.11), 187 (EAT-1636), 189*r* (EAE-1056), 189*bl* (QTE 146), 208 (P-555), 213*al* (1999.14.5), 214 (2007.1.7), 215*b* (LNT 845), 219*b* (1994.6.1), 220*al* (1992.5.608), 220*ar* (1992.5.509), 220*r* (1992.5.358), 222 (2006.9.9), 224*ar* (2006.11.2), 230*bl* (1997.2.1), 230*c* (2003.03.001), 230*br* (FCUS-63), 234*ar* and 234*br* (1989.9.7), 236 (LKOUS 653), 239*r* (1991.36.1), 250 (LNE-784), 275*l* (LCA-99); Terry Helwig: (www.threadproject.com): 279; Pat Hickman: 215*a*; E. Hockstein (courtesy of UNHCR): 76; Herbert Hoover Presidential Library and Museum, West Branch, Iowa: 179; Alistair Hull (courtesy of Thames & Hudson): 84*r*; International Quilt Study Center and Museum, Lincoln, NE: 9*b* (1997.007.0360); Istock photo: 79*l*, 126, 128, 137*br*; Jnyus (via Wikimedia GNU Free Documentation license): 138*r*; Susi Johnston: 46, 139*ar*, 227*r*, 228, 235*a*, 257, 267, 276*a*; Carolyn Kallenborn: 11*br*, 35*al*, 66*ar*, 69, 81*l*, 242; Jeeun Kim: 241; Cathryn Lahm (courtesy of Jennifer Marsh): 147; Leiden University Library, the Netherlands (courtesy of Susi Johnston): 229*b*; Isadora Leidenfrost: 260, 261; Erich Lessing (courtesy of Art Resource, New York): 130 (ART65320); Paul W. Locke: 96; Logan Museum of Anthropology, Beloit College, Beloit, WI: 226*b* (LMA2471); José Luczyc-Wyhowska (courtesy of Thames & Hudson): 11*bl*; Courtesy of Lumigram: 72*l*; Rachel Maines (courtesy of Beverly Gordon): 232*r*;

McCord Museum, Montreal: 4 (Gift of R. G. Oliver ME942.28), 62*a* (Gift of R. G. Oliver ME942.28); Meriter Hospital, Madison, WI: 145*bl*; Metropolitan Museum of Art, New York: 32 (Gift of John D. Rockefeller, Ur 37.80.4), 98 (Marquand Collection, Gift of Henry G. Marquand, 1890, 91.26), 157 (Fletcher Fund 59.135.8), 164 (14.40.634), 216 (Fletcher Fund 27.162.1); Michigan State University Museum, East Lansing, MI: 64*al* (photo Doug Elbinger), 125*l* (photo Pearl Yee Wong, acc. 1999:28.1); Gwenneth Miller, UNISA: 213*bl*; Jeff Miller (©UW-Madison University Communications): 129*b*; Larry Miller: 273*a*; Julian Mock (courtesy of Alyce Santoro): 207; Jason Moore: 35*ar*; Dudley Moss (courtesy of Thames & Hudson): 266*r*; Museum of Fine Arts, Boston: 41*a* (Maria Antoinette Evans Fund 26.54; 54 11.2891), 54 (11.2891); Museum of International Folk Art, Santa Fe, NM: 43*b* (Gift of Magdalene P. Singer); Virendra Nagrale (courtesy of Gita Sundaresh): 108*l*; Names Project Foundation: 213*r*; NASA: 75, 89; Photo courtesy of the National Gallery of Art, Washington, D.C.: 177; John Nollendorfs (courtesy of Robert Hillestad): 141; Marcus Obal (Wikimedia GNU Free Documentation License): 139*b*; Lars Olaussen: 230*ar*; Margarete Ordon: 70*b*, 100, 176*bl*, 176*cr*, 189*bl*; Sheila Paine (courtesy of Thames & Hudson): 105*r*; David G. Paul: 91; Steve Pezenik: 25*b*; Prayer Shawl Ministry (with permission by Janet Bristow & Victoria A. Cole-Galo, Co-Founders): 112; Public domain: 43*al*, 67*a*; Public domain via Visipix: 77*al*, 88*r*, 116 (original painting in Belvedere, Österreichische Galerie, Austria), 118, 149, 159*l*; Public domain via WikiMedia: 81*r* (photo Elias Friedman), 99*b*; Sarah Quinton (courtesy of Janet Morton): 243; Jon Eric Riis: 239*l*; Franklin D. Roosevelt Library, Hyde Park, New York: 11*a* (74-20(1435)); Rough Rock Community College Press (from Ethelou Yazzie, ed., *Navajo History*, Navajo Community College Press, 1971): 39*r*; Ken Rowe (courtesy of Jan Hopkins): 237; Seuty Sabur: 183; St. Louis Art Museum: 158 (1528:1983), 224*b* (Gift of Mrs. Ralph F. Bixby, 97:1978), 225*b* (285:1949); Frank Salomon: 203*l*, 203*r*; Saudi Aramco World/PADIA: 28*al* (photo Stephenie Hollyman), 30*al* (photo Brynn Bruijn), 74*al* (photo Kevin Bubriski), 77*bl* (Nik Wheeler), 77*br* (photo Dorothy Miller), 78*l* (photo S. M. Amin), 86*a* (photo George Baramki Azar), 127*bl*, 129*a* (photo Nik Wheeler), 137*al* (photo Khalil Abou El-Nasr), 185*l* (photo S.M. Amin), 227*l* (photo Ilene Perlman), 231*r* (photo Khalil Abou El-Nasr), 265*r* (photo S.M. Amin); Scala Archives: 174 (original in the National Gallery, London) NG01138; School of Human Ecology, University of Wisconsin-Madison: 244*a*, 244*b*; Daniel Schwen: 82*a* (released to Wikimedia Commons/ CC-BY-SA-2.5); Marie-Aude Serra: 80*c*; Photo courtesy of Diane Sheehan 230*al*; Stan Sherer: 122*r*; Sinopix photo: 173; Smithsonian Institution National Museum of American Art, Washington, D.C., courtesy of Art Resources: 234*al* (ART373677); Heather Sonntag: 52, 84*l*, 127*cr*; Jim Sturm: 102*a*; Syngenta: 86*b*; Daina Taimina: 17; Target Gallery, London: 223*b*; Terris Nguyen Temple: 258; Tigertail Associates, Tigertail Museum: 23; United States Holocaust Memorial Museum, Washington, D.C.: 180*a*, 180*b*, 181; United States Library of Congress: 14 (photo Edward S. Curtis, LC-USZ62-111291), 19 (LC-DIG-jpd-00091), 27*al* (photo Mishkin, N.Y., LC-USZ62-55586), 36*a* (LC-DIG-jpd-01962), 38 (LC-USZC4-2998), 39*l* (LC-USZC62-102897), 45 LC-USZ62-124810), 72*r* (Keystone View Co. stereoscope, LC-USZ62-73495), 80*ar* (photo Griffith and Griffith, LC-USZ62-112654), 80*br* (LC-USZ62-93573), 90 (photo William M. Rittase for US Office War Information, LC-USE6- D-005831), 94 (LC-USZ62-730), 101*a* (photo Detroit Publishing Co., LC-D4-18240), 109 (photo Rose and Hopkins, Denver, Colorado, LC-USZ62-111571), 138*l* (Strobridge & Co. Lithographers, POS - TH - 1893.N51, no. 1), 144 (LC-USZ62-106363), 182*l* (photo Edward S. Curtis, LC-USZ62-101175), 186 (Turkestan album), 188 (LC-DIG-ppmsca-08978), 189*al* (LC-USZC2-1976), 190 (National Child Labor Committee Collection, LC-USZ62-108765), 192 (LC-USZC4-10400), 247 (Matson Photo Service, LC-DIG-matpc-23097), 249*l* (photo Underwood & Underwood, LC-USZ62-98906), 252*a* (LC-USZ62-33219), 256 (photo Fritz W. Guerin, LC-USZ62-74347), 259 (LC-DIG-jpd-02949), 263 (LC-M34- 10254), 265*l* (LC-DIG-matpc-04658), 273*bl* (LC-USZ62-107671), 273*br* (LC-USZ62-125610); University of Massachusetts-Lowell Baseball Research Center: 137*bl*, 137*bc*; University of Rhode Island, Historic Textile and Costume Collection (Bainbridge Collection, photos by Susan J. Jerome): 28*bl* (URI 2003.12.236), 74*r* (URI 2003.12.236); University of Wisconsin Archives: 139*al*; Lori Ushman: 9*a*, 12, 13, 20*r*, 31*a*, 33, 35*b*, 43*ar*, 48*cr*, 53*al*, 62*bl*, 62*br*, 64*r*, 64*bl*, 101*b*, 102*b*, 103, 117*l*, 119, 127*br*, 133 (image courtesy of Wisconsin Union Galleries), 145*br*, 165, 185*r*, 187, 208, 212, 215, 229*a*, 230*br*, 232*l*, 233*a*, 233*b*, 235*bl*, 269 (collection Patricia Williams), 275*r*, 276*b*; Tineke van Geel: 274; Steven Vedro: 117*r*; Vlisco

Corporation (courtesy of Frans Von Rood): 47, 201; Bryan Walton: 27*ar*, 51*al*, 66*bl*, 255*bl*; Welleschik (courtesy of WikiMedia, GNU license): 266*l*; Made Wijaya: 254, 268 (courtesy of Susi Johnson); Patricia Williams: 34, 105*l*, 136, 248*a*; Wisconsin Historical Society: 28*br* (photo Alex Kreuger, image ID 9820), 53*ar* (photo Charles Van Schaick, image ID 11994), 93 (photo Andrea Hoffman, WHS 1972.2.11, Image ID 64498), 140*r* (photo Annie Sievers Schildhauer, PH 2775, WHi-33716); Wisconsin Veterans Museum: 88*l* (V1999.28.9), 104 (V1998.1.639), 110*b* (V2006.1.1., V2006.1.14, V2006.1.7), 209 (V2008.76.1); Witney Antiques, Witney, Oxon, U.K.: 218; Wyoming State Museum: 41*r* (1977.70.16); Yongming Zhou: 18*r*

ACKNOWLEDGMENTS

This project is the culmination of many years of development and so many people have assisted in its realization that it would be impossible to acknowledge them all. I have interacted with hundreds of students over the years who have led me to new areas of inquiry, for example, and with a great number of fellow craftspeople and textile scholars who have influenced my thinking. Thanks to every one of them.

I am pleased to recognize those who directly helped the book become a reality, however, and hope they know how extremely grateful I am for their contribution. I thank Victoria Rivers who put me in touch with Thames & Hudson, and managing director Jamie Camplin for believing in the project and nursing it along the way. Amanda Vinnicombe, Carolyn Jones and Ilona de Nemethy Sanigar have been equally helpful in their close editorial reading of the manuscript. Steven Vedro has been a supportive presence, reader, and "rights wrangler," and the book would not have been the same without him. Lori Ushman allowed me to share many of the textiles that I love through her wonderful photographs. The staff of the Helen Louise Allen Textile Collection at the University of Wisconsin-Madison were extremely cooperative in providing me with images and information, despite the demands of a difficult move of the collection. Diana Zlatanowski, Maya Lea, and Maggie Ordon deserve special acknowledgment. Many other university colleagues have also contributed: kudos to Frank Salomon, Carolyn Kallenborn, Jenny Angus, Mary Hark, Diane Sheehan, Jody Clowes, Henry Drewal, Yongming Zhou, and Jonie Bonfield. I am indebted too to the University of Wisconsin-Madison Graduate School for its research support and its African Studies Program for its storehouse of photographs. Students Mary Monahan and Molly Greenfield were also very helpful at different stages of the project.

I was the recipient of writing residencies at two remarkable institutions, the Anderson Center of Interdisciplinary Studies in Red Wing, Minnesota, and the Writer's Colony at Dairy Hollow in Eureka Springs, Arkansas. (I will always associate certain chapters with their supportive environments.) Thanks too to Jon Prown and the Chipstone Foundation for a subvention to help cover some of the photography costs.

The photographs came from many different institutions and individuals, and I am grateful to them all for their cooperation. Saudi Aramco World and its Public Affairs Digital Image Archive (PADIA) provided wonderful images that relate to the Muslim world. I also particularly want to thank Susi Johnston and Made Wijaya, who kept sending alternative images from Indonesia; Patricia Williams, Bryan Walton, Mary Jo Schiavoni and James Sturm, Heather Sonntag, Janine LeBlanc, Pravina Shukla and Henry Glassie, Andrea Hoffman, Gita Sundaresh, Bill Brewster, Jacqueline Atkins, Marjorie Senechal, Walter Denny, Ariel Zeitlin Cooke, Diane Fagan Affleck, Sally Evans, Clare Sheridan, Marsha MacDowell, Witney Antiques, and the many artists who contributed images of their work. Linda Welters deserves special mention for her help in finding images and her long encouragement about pursuing this project. I also had help from some excellent manuscript readers. Thanks to Danielle Devereaux-Weber, Celeste Robins, Judith Thompson, and Rhea Vedro.

INDEX

BALDWIN PUBLIC LIBRARY

3 1115 00620 2013

WITHDRAWN